PHONOLOGY

12 S·817

MODERN LINGUISTICS SERIES

Series Editors

Professor Noël Burton-Roberts
University of Newcastle upon Tyne

Dr Andrew Spencer
University of Essex

Each textbook in the **Modern Linguistics** series is designed to provide a carefully graded introduction to a topic in contemporary linguistics and allied disciplines, presented in a manner that is accessible and attractive to readers with no previous experience of the topic, but leading them to some understanding of current issues. The texts are designed to engage the active participation of the reader, favouring a problem-solving approach and including liberal and varied exercise material.

Noël Burton-Roberts founded the **Modern Linguistics** series and acted as Series Editor for the first three volumes in the series. Andrew Spencer has since joined Noël Burton-Roberts as joint Series Editor.

Titles published in the series

Phonology   Philip Carr
Linguistics and Second Language Acquisition   Vivian Cook
Morphology   Francis Katamba

Further titles in preparation

Phonology

Philip Carr

MACMILLAN

First published 1993 by
THE MACMILLAN PRESS LTD
Houndmills, Basingstoke, Hampshire RG21 2XS
and London
Companies and representatives
throughout the world

ISBN 0–333–51907–8 hardcover
ISBN 0–333–51908–6 paperback

A catalogue record for this book is available
from the British Library.

Printed in Great Britain by
Mackays of Chatham PLC
Chatham, Kent

Reprinted 1994

The Scrabble tiles on the cover design are reproduced by
kind permission of J. W. Spear and Son PLC, Enfield
EN3 7TB, England.

Contents

For Rab, Tam and Sheila

Preface

To the Student

This book is a beginners' introduction to phonology, and concentrates mostly on what is known as generative phonology. It assumes that the reader has taken a course in elementary articulatory phonetics, but it assumes no knowledge whatsoever of phonology. A revision chapter on phonetic terminology and a chart of the symbols which constitute the International Phonetic Alphabet are included for reference, or for those who need to brush up on the subject. It is hoped that the present textbook will allow students to move on to more advanced textbooks, such as Kenstowicz and Kisseberth (1979), and also to the source literature on the subject. The reader should also consult Hyman (1975) for further details and issues in standard generative phonology, Lass (1984a) for a broader view of phonology (beyond generative work), and Anderson (1985) for a historical perspective on twentieth century phonology. Syntheses and surveys of current theoretical work, such as Goldsmith (1990) and Durand (1990), as well as the literature itself, should also be approachable after reading Chapters 8–11.

The book begins with exercises within and at the end of chapters, many of which should prove easy for students who take naturally to linguistic analysis, and tractable for those who do not. After the first few chapters, there are fewer, and these are at the end of chapters. (Some sample answers are given at the end of the book.) For most students, it would be rather pointless to attempt reading the early chapters without simultaneously doing the exercises; the exercises in the later chapters are intended to help students to think about the theories discussed by focussing their attention on particular analyses. It is important for students to retain all their exercise work, since earlier exercises may be referred back to, or reworked, at a later stage.

The following abbreviations are used in exercises and examples: 'pl.' (plural), 'sg.' (singular), 1PS, 2PS, 3PS (1st, 2nd and 3rd person singular); nom. (nominative), acc. (accusative), gen. (genitive), masc. (masculine), fem. (feminine).

To the Teacher

This book is an attempt at a solution to a problem. The problem is this: how to introduce generative phonology, without trivialising the subject, within the confines of a ten-week course, to students who major in subjects other than linguistics, and thus may not take their study of the subject any further. The problem is less acute when those other subjects require similar sorts of thinking, but when the majority of students have, for several years, spent the bulk of their time following courses requiring quite different sorts of thinking, difficulties arise. In England (much less so in the US and in the continental system, which also survives in Scotland), these difficulties are in large part a consequence of the fact that many such students have been educated in the English 'narrow specialism' tradition, which has tended to bolster the 'two cultures' arts/science divide. These students often tend to view themselves as 'arts types' rather than 'science types'; for many of them, the mere sight of diagrams in a book can prove anathema. The subject therefore needs to be introduced in as gentle a way as possible, with much exemplification, and exercises which do not throw the student in at the deep end. Thereafter, more complex problems can be investigated, and the student can then find a way into the subject. The problem is a challenging one, and in attempting to resolve it, one can go some way towards undermining the rather limiting 'two cultures' division, which fails so clearly to accommodate the discipline of linguistics. While there are excellent textbook introductions to standard generative phonology, such as Kenstowicz and Kisseberth (1979), and impressive surveys of current theory, such as Goldsmith (1990), they are simply too detailed to be used on such a course, given the time available and the sorts of student in attendance.

The book aims to introduce standard generative phonology in a relatively simple way in Chapters 1–6, and then, in Chapters 7–11, to introduce the student to more recent work in phonological theory. Since the text thus falls into two parts, it is possible to teach just the first six or seven chapters if time is short; the last chapters may then be used as an introduction to a more advanced course, for which a textbook on current work, and the literature itself, may be used. No attempt is made to present alternative, non-generative, approaches to phonology: new students have enough trouble trying to get the hang of one framework without having to cope with several; other approaches can be tackled once the generative approach is familiar. This is not to say that a non-critical attitude to generative work is fostered; analyses are often shown to be revisable, competing generative theories are discussed, and the interplay of data and theory is stressed.

It is best if students have seminars/tutorials in which to discuss the exercises in each chapter before proceeding to the next, but the exercises should be tractable even if this is not possible; some sample answers are given at the end of the book.

Acknowledgements

I am grateful to Mike Davenport, Gerry Docherty and Ken Lodge for reading and commenting on several draft chapters. The following people kindly helped with the languages indicated: Inès Brulard (French), Mike Pincombe (Hungarian), Charles Prescott (Russian), Menekşe Suphi (Turkish) and Sylvana Warth (Russian and Polish). My thanks to all of them. I am grateful to Noël Burton-Roberts for persuading me to stop complaining about not having the right textbook for the course, and to have a go at writing it myself. He was also of great assistance as Series Editor: I am indebted to him for his detailed comments and discussion on many chapters. I thank two sets of second-year students at Newcastle for acting as guinea-pigs; in particular, I am grateful to John Bell and Charles Prescott for their intelligent responses. Many thanks to Rowena Bryson, who committed a large chunk of text to disk with characteristic grace and good humour.

One forever owes a debt to one's teachers. I thank those who taught me phonetics and phonology in the Linguistics Department at Edinburgh University: Ron Asher, Gill Brown, Karen Currie, Jody Higgs, Sandy Hutcheson, Alan Kemp, Roger Lass, John Laver and Betsy Uldall. John Anderson and Heinz Giegerich of the English Language Department at Edinburgh taught me Dependency and Metrical Phonology, respectively: I hope they will forgive me for any misrepresentation of those subjects which may appear in this book. I also hope that Ron Asher and Gill Brown will forgive me for any liberties which I may (inadvertently) have taken with their works, on Tamil and Lumasaaba, respectively. My greatest debt is to Roger Lass, who I was fortunate to have as a teacher and supervisor just prior to his departure from Edinburgh. I thank him for presenting phonology in such a fresh and stimulating way, and for continuing to do so.

At several stages during the writing of this textbook, Inès Brulard has put up with my incursions upon her personal computer, desk space and library card, for which she deserves praise, gratitude and a bottle of Château Monbousquet 1982.

Revision of Phonetics

Consonants

Consonants are normally specified for three descriptive parameters: voicing state, place of articulation and manner of articulation.

Voicing state. While we may reasonably describe most consonants as either **voiced** (with vocal cord vibration) or **voiceless** (without vocal cord vibration), we may also indicate full or partial devoicing by placing the diacritic [̦] beneath the symbol for the appropriate voiced segment, as in [d̦], a devoiced alveolar stop. There are other states of the glottis besides voicing and voicelessness, but we will not pursue them here.

Place of articulation distinctions are as follows. (See the diagram of the organs of speech on p. 12.) Where the articulators are the lips, the sound in question is **bilabial**. Where the active articulator is the lower lip and the passive articulators are the upper teeth, the sound is **labiodental**. **Dental** sounds are articulated with the tip of the tongue and the upper teeth. **Alveolar** sounds are articulated with the tip/blade of the tongue and the alveolar ridge. **Post-alveolar** sounds are retracted somewhat from this position; an example is the post-alveolar approximant [ɹ] found in many accents of English. **Palato-alveolar** sounds are articulated with the blade of the tongue as the active articulator and the palato-alveolar region as the passive articulator. In **palatal** sounds, the active articulator is the front of the tongue and the passive articulator is the hard palate. The back of the tongue and the soft palate are, respectively, the active and passive articulators in **velar** sounds, whereas in **uvular** sounds, the articulators are the back of the tongue and the uvula. The walls of the pharynx are the articulators in **pharyngeal** sounds, and the vocal cords themselves are the articulators in **glottal** sounds.

Manner of articulation is specified according to degree of stricture (the degree to which the articulators impede the flow of air). The three principal degrees of stricture are as follows:

1. Complete closure, where the articulators seal off the flow of air completely; these sounds are called **stops**, or **plosives**.
2. Close approximation, where the articulators come very close to one another without actually sealing off the escape of air, such that turbulence, and thus audible friction, are produced; these sounds are called **fricatives**.
3. Open approximation, where the articulators are not sufficiently close to induce turbulence and audible friction; such sounds are called **approximants**. They are normally defined as being voiced.

1

We may use these parameters to distinguish speech sounds as follows:

Bilabial

[p] is a voiceless bilabial stop.

[b] is a voiced bilabial stop.

[ɸ] is a voiceless bilabial fricative: it can be heard in Japanese in, for instance, the word *Fuji* [ɸɯ̟ji].

[β] is a voiced bilabial fricative: it occurs in Tamil, as in the word for 'twenty' [ɪɾuβaðɯ].

[β̞] is a voiced bilabial approximant: it can be heard in Spanish in, for example, [ɐβ̞ɛɾ] ('to have'). The symbol used here is the same as for the fricative, but with the subscript diacritic meaning 'frictionless' added. (In this respect we deviate from the International Phonetic Alphabet, in which this diacritic means 'less rounded'.)

Labiodental

[f] is a voiceless labiodental fricative.

[v] is its voiced counterpart.

[ʋ] is a voiced labiodental approximant; you can practise this by altering a [v] such that the lower lip does not actually come into contact with the teeth. It occurs in Tamil.

Dental

It is not easy to hear the difference between, on the one hand, the dental stops [t̪] and [d̪] and, on the other hand, the alveolar stops [t] and [d], but in many languages it is the dental rather than the alveolar stops which occur: in Tamil, Spanish and Polish, for instance.

[θ] is a voiceless dental fricative which occurs in English, as in *thing*.

[ð] is the voiced equivalent. It too occurs in English, although, in words like *that*, there is often little or no friction, in which case the diacritic meaning 'frictionless' may be placed beneath the symbol for the fricative, thus [ð̞]. This therefore denotes a voiced dental approximant, of the sort found in the Spanish word *hablado* [ɐβ̞lɐð̞o].

Alveolar

In addition to the stops [t] and [d], there are the alveolar fricatives [s] and [z].

Among the approximants and fricatives, there is a distinction between **central** and **lateral** sounds: in central sounds, the airflow escapes along a central groove in the active articulator, while in lateral sounds, there is closure at this central point, with the airflow escaping along the sides of the active articulator. Thus, the voiced lateral alveolar approximant [l] has closure at the centre of the alveolar ridge and lateral escape of airflow, while in the voiced central approximant [ɹ], there is closure between the sides of the tongue and the gums, with central escape of airflow. This sound, found in many accents of English, is also somewhat retracted (just how much varies considerably among accents) and is therefore said to be post-alveolar.

The fricatives we identify here should be assumed to be central unless otherwise specified. Lateral fricatives do occur, though: the voiceless alveolar lateral fricative [ɬ] occurs in Welsh, and its voiced equivalent, [ɮ], in Zulu.

There are further manner of articulation distinctions which can often be identified among alveolar sounds. The alveolar **trill** involves a stricture of **intermittent closure**: with a constant muscular pressure on the tongue, intermittent closure is brought about by means of an interaction between the stop closure and the air pressure building up behind that closure. This is an instance of the Bernoulli Effect which underlies vocal cord vibration: as the closure is released, the air pressure drops and the muscular tension closes the articulators again, at which point the air pressure builds up and separates the articulators. In trills, this sequence occurs several times, rather rapidly.

In **taps**, the blade of the tongue closes only momentarily against the passive articulator: we may think of taps as stops of very short duration. The voiced alveolar tap is denoted by the symbol [ɾ], and its voiceless counterpart by the same symbol with the devoicing diacritic, thus [ɾ̥].

Around the alveolar ridge, we must distinguish **retroflex** sounds from non-retroflex sounds: in retroflex sounds, the underside of the blade of the tongue acts as the active articulator against the alveolar ridge. Thus, the voiceless and voiced retroflex stops, represented as [ʈ] and [ɖ], involve complete closure, while the fricatives [ʂ] and [ʐ] involve close approximation. The retroflex [ʂ] is found in Spanish. The retroflex tap [ɽ] is like an alveolar tap, but with the underside of the tongue blade forming a momentary stricture of complete closure with the alveolar ridge. The retroflex lateral approximant [ɭ] involves closure between the underside of the blade and the alveolar ridge, but open approximation between the sides of the tongue and the gums, allowing lateral escape of airflow. Many of these retroflex sounds can be found in the Dravidian and Indo-European languages of the Indian subcontinent; you will often hear them among people with an Indian or Bangladeshi background. The term 'retroflex' is usually listed alongside the other place of articulation terms, although it identifies place of articulation by means of the active rather than the passive articulator.

Palato-alveolar
This term is not terribly precise, covering as it does an area which is part of

the continuum from the alveolar ridge to the hard palate. The voiced and voiceless fricatives [ʃ] and [ʒ], which occur in English, as in the words *ship* and *vision*, are usually said to be palato-alveolar.

So too are the **affricates** [č] and [ǰ] which occur in the English words *church* and *judge*. Affricates are characterised by a stricture of complete closure followed by a release phase in which there is close approximation between the articulators, and thus audible friction is produced. We may consider affricates as slowly released stops, where it is the absence of instantaneous release which results in a transitional phase of close approximation. Affricates can be produced at most places of articulation: [t͡s] and [d͡z], for instance, are alveolar affricates, with the superscript diacritic indicating that the two symbols should be taken to denote a unitary sound. Similarly, [k͡x] and [q͡χ] are, respectively, voiceless velar and uvular affricates. Precisely what is meant by 'unitary sound' is a phonological matter which we will not pursue here. The closure phase and release phase in affricates need not be strictly **homorganic** (occurring at the same place of articulation); thus, in [p͡f], the closure phase is bilabial while the release phase is labiodental.

You may well encounter, in any further reading you may do, the symbols [t͡ʃ] and [d͡ʒ] for [č] and [ǰ], as well as [š] and [ž] for [ʃ] and [ʒ]. In this book, we will use [č], [ǰ], [ʃ] and [ʒ] in almost all cases. But in the case of Polish, we will be a little inconsistent. The reason for this is as follows. In Polish, there is an important distinction, among fricatives and affricates, between alveolar, post-alveolar and what are called pre-palatal sounds. The post-alveolars are articulated with retraction of the tongue body while the pre-palatals are articulated fairly close to the palatal region, but further forward than strictly palatal sounds. That is, the continuum from the alveolar ridge to the hard palate is divided up into three, rather than two, places of articulation. We may distinguish, among the fricatives, between voiced and voiceless alveolar, post-alveolar and pre-palatal fricatives, and we will use the following symbols for these:

[s] and [z], as is standard, for the alveolars.

[š] and [ž] for the post-alveolars.

[ś] and [ź] for the pre-palatals.

For the affricates, we will use:

[t͡s] and [d͡z], as above, for the alveolars.

[č] and [ǰ] for the post-alveolars.

[ć] and [ʝ] for the pre-palatals.

While this choice of symbols is unproblematical for the alveolars and pre-palatals, it does mean that we will be using, in the case of Polish, the symbols [č] and [ǰ], [š] and [ž], to denote sounds which are not palato-alveolar. This should not cause problems.

Palatal

The voiceless palatal stop [c] occurs in some of the exercises in this book; it is articulated high up in the oral cavity, with the front of the tongue against the hard palate. The stop in the English word *keep* is fairly close to [c], but [c] is articulated even further forward than that. Its voiced equivalent is [ɟ], which also occurs in the exercises in this book. The fronted stop which occurs in *keep* is usually transcribed using the 'fronted' (or 'advanced') diacritic, thus [k̟].

[ç] is a voiceless palatal fricative which occurs in German, as in the word *Milch*, and in Scots, as in *driech*. Many English speakers produce something close to this in their pronunciation of *huge* in casual speech.

[ʝ] is its voiced equivalent.

[j] is a voiced palatal approximant which occurs in the English word *year*.

[ʎ] is a voiced palatal lateral; it occurs in many accents of Spanish, as in *calle* ('street').

Velar

[k] is a voiceless velar stop which occurs in many languages, including English.

[g] is its voiced equivalent.

[x] is a voiceless velar fricative. It occurs in Scots in, for instance, *loch*, and in German, as in *Buch*. If you compare this with the palatal fricative [ç], you will notice that the palatal sound has a noticeably higher pitch.

[ɣ] is its voiced equivalent; you will encounter it in the Eskimo data in Chapter 1.

[ɰ] is a voiced velar approximant; it occurs in Spanish, as in *bodega*.

Uvular

[q] is a voiceless uvular stop; you can practise it by making a [k] and retracting it, so that it is articulated against the uvula. It occurs in the Eskimo data in this book. If you compare it with [k] and [c], you will hear the pitch increase as you progress from [q] to [k] to [c].

[G] is its voiced equivalent.

[χ] is a voiceless uvular fricative. It occurs in Arabic, and in French where the voiced uvular fricative [ʁ] is devoiced.

[ʁ] is a voiced uvular approximant which occurs in French. As with [ð] and [ɣ], the symbol for the fricative is used, with the 'frictionless' diacritic added.

Pharyngeal

In pharyngeal sounds, it is the walls of the pharynx which act as the articulators. Since these cannot readily form a stricture of complete closure, it is normal to identify only two pharyngeal sounds: [ħ], the voiceless pharyngeal fricative which occurs in Arabic, and [ʕ], the voiced pharyngeal fricative, which also occurs in Arabic.

Glottal

The glottal stop [ʔ] involves closure, followed by release, of the vocal cords.

The glottal fricative [h] involves close approximation between the vocal cords.

Consonants involving more than one articulation

The approximant [w], which occurs in English, has a stricture of open approximation between the lips, and also between the back of the tongue and the velum. It is therefore usually referred to as a labial-velar approximant. The question arises whether one of these articulations should be considered primary with respect to the other. We will take the view that the two are of equal articulatory status in English.

The lateral approximant [l] involves, as we have seen, an alveolar articulation, but this is often accompanied, in accents of English, by a **secondary articulation** of either **palatalisation** or **velarisation**.

Where an alveolar lateral is palatalised, the front of the tongue forms a secondary stricture of open approximation with the hard palate, thus producing a more high-pitched sound. There is often some palatalisation of laterals for speakers of English where the lateral occurs before a high front vowel. In some accents of English (Tyneside, and Highland Scots accents, for instance), most occurrences of laterals are palatalised. The palatalised lateral is often referred to as 'clear l'. The 'palatalised' diacritic is added to the lateral symbol to indicate palatalisation, thus [lʲ].

In velarised laterals, the back of the tongue forms a secondary articulation of open approximation with the velum. For many speakers of English, laterals are velarised when they occur syllable-finally. There are accents, such as Lowland Scots, where laterals are almost always velarised. To transcribe velarisation, a diacritic is added which runs through the centre of the appropriate symbol, thus [ɫ]. The velarised lateral is often referred to as 'dark l'.

Palatalised and velarised laterals do not function to distinguish one meaning from another in English, but palatalisation does have this function in many Slavic languages, as you will see in the exercises on Polish. In that language, it occurs, not with lateral approximants, but with bilabial stops, labiodental fricatives and the dental nasal stop.

Pharyngealisation, in which the root of the tongue is retracted towards the pharynx wall, is a common secondary articulation in Arabic, and distinguishes, for instance, pharyngealised alveolar stops from their non-pharyngealised counterparts. To represent this, the same diacritic as for velarisation is overwritten on the appropriate symbol, thus [ḍ].

Aspiration

In most accents of English, when voiceless stops are followed by voiced segments such as vowels or approximants, there is often a delay between the release phase of the stop and the onset of voicing for the following segment. When this happens, there is an audible release of air from the stop closure which is referred to as **aspiration**. Aspiration is therefore definable as voice onset delay; it is transcribed with a superscript diacritic following the symbol for the voiceless stop, thus [pʰ]. It does not always occur with voiceless stops in English, and we will see that its occurrence is, in many cases, predictable. While the distinction between voiceless aspirated and voiceless unaspirated stops does not serve to distinguish one meaning from another in English, it does have this function in some languages, including Tai, as you will see in Chapter 1.

Nasal Stops and Nasalisation

Nasal stops involve lowering of the velum, accompanied by complete closure within the oral cavity, allowing continual escape of airflow through the nasal cavity; where the sound is voiced, this results in the characteristic resonance which the nasal cavity induces. Nasal stops occur at most places of articulation, as follows:

[m] is a voiced bilabial nasal stop, as in English *map*.

[ɱ] is labiodental, as in English *amphetamines* and *inform*.

[n̪] is dental, as in English *untheatrical*.

[n] is alveolar, as in English *nun*.

[ɳ] is retroflex, as in Tamil [puːɳɖʊ] ('garlic').

[ɲ] is palatal, as in Tamil [ɪɲʝɪ] ('ginger').

[ŋ] is velar, as in English *sing*.

[ɴ] is uvular.

Where these occur devoiced, the devoicing diacritic is added, thus [n̥].

Where velic opening is not accompanied by a stricture of complete closure in the oral cavity, the resulting sound is said to be **nasalised**. Thus, the fricative [v], if nasalised, would be [ṽ], with the diacritic for nasalisation added. Nasalisation in vowels is much more common than in affricates, fricatives and approximants; examples are [ɔ̃] and [ɑ̃], in French.

Vowels

All vowels are articulated with a stricture of open approximation. While voiceless vowels do occur, and are transcribed using the 'devoiced' diacritic, vowels are normally voiced. We may distinguish vowels in terms of:

1. The height of the tongue body in the oral cavity.
2. The position of the body of the tongue along the front/back dimension of the oral cavity.
3. The presence or absence of lip rounding.

Two extreme vowel heights may be distinguished: **close**, where the tongue body is as near the hard or soft palate as it can be without causing audible friction, and **open**, where the jaw is lowered and the tongue body is as far as possible from the roof of the mouth. Between these extremes, we may pick out two intermediate heights: **half-close** and **half-open**, where the four heights are equidistant: the tongue moves the same distance at each stage of the transition from [i] through [e], then [ɛ], to [a] (see diagram on p. 11). This division allows us an arbitrary but useful division of the **vowel space** (the available space within the oral cavity for the production of vowels).

   We can combine this division with the back/front dimension of the vowel space to identify certain peripheral points around the extreme edge of the vowel space. Those points are referred to as the **primary cardinal vowels**. We may depict them in an idealised representation of the vowel space, as in the diagram on p.11.

Cardinal vowel no. 1 is [i]; it is produced with the lips spread and the tongue as far forward and as high as it can go without creating friction. It is therefore close, front and unrounded.

Cardinal vowel no. 5 is [ɑ]; it is produced without any lip rounding and with the tongue as far back and as low as it can go without producing friction. It is open, back and unrounded.

   These two cardinal vowels are the principal points around which our vowel space diagram is organised.

Cardinal vowel no. 2 is [e]; it is articulated with spread lips, with the tongue at the half-close height and as far forward as it can go. It is half-close, front and unrounded.

Cardinal vowel no. 3 is [ɛ]; it is articulated as for [e], but with a half-open tongue height. It is therefore front, half-open and unrounded.

Cardinal vowel no. 4 is [a]; it is unrounded and as open and front as is possible.

Cardinal vowel no. 6 is [ɔ]; it is rounded, half-open and as far back as is possible.

Cardinal vowel no. 7 is [o]; it is half-open, fully back and rounded.

Cardinal vowel no. 8 is [u]; it is fully back, close and rounded.

In addition to these, a series of **secondary cardinal vowels** can be identified. The first eight of these (nos 9–16) are identical to the primary cardinal vowels except that they have the opposite values on the rounded/unrounded parameter. They are also represented in the vowel chart on p. 11. Of these symbols, you will often encounter [y], [ø], [œ] and [ɯ] (nos 9, 10, 11 and 16) in this book. While the vowels which occur in human languages are not often as peripheral in the vowel space as the cardinal vowels, these cardinal vowels act as points of reference, in terms of which other vowel qualities can be identified. Thus, in French, there are three front, rounded vowels which are similar to, but not quite as peripheral as, [y], [ø] and [œ].

We may use a set of diacritics in conjunction with the symbols for the cardinal vowels to pinpoint fairly precisely where a given vowel is articulated. Thus, the diacritic ⊥ is used to indicate a position raised with respect to a cardinal position, and ⊤ to indicate relative lowering. The representation [e̞] therefore denotes a front, unrounded vowel which is somewhat more close than [e], and [ɛ̝] represents a front, unrounded vowel somewhat lower than [ɛ]. Similarly, the superscript diacritic [¨] indicates a vowel articulation somewhat more centralised than is denoted by the cardinal vowel symbol: [ë] denotes a centralised, half-close, front unrounded vowel, for instance.

We will adopt the practice of not using these diacritics unless the precise details of the vowel in question are of relevance to the problem under discussion. This means, for instance, that we will use [y], [ø] and [œ] for the front, rounded vowels of French, even though the actual values are not quite those of cardinal vowels 9, 10 and 11. Similarly, we will often use [ɯ] to represent a vowel which is fairly close, fairly back and unrounded, but not quite cardinal vowel 16. This commits us to a certain degree of phonetic inaccuracy, but one has to assess the degree of phonetic accuracy needed for a given purpose, and for the purposes of an introductory book of this nature, the absence of phonetic detail is, arguably, justified.

Other vowel symbols we will use are:

[ʉ] which is central, close and rounded; something fairly close to this occurs in Lowland Scots, as in *book*.

[ɨ] which is central, close and unrounded, and often 'counts' as a back vowel in phonological systems.

[ə] referred to as 'schwa', which is central on both the vertical and horizontal axes, and is unrounded. Both the term and the symbol are used rather loosely at times by phonologists to cover vowels in a fairly large area in the centre of the vowel space.

[ɐ] which is open, central and unrounded.

In Received Pronunciation (RP), there is a systematic distinction between the long, back, open, unrounded vowel [ɑ:] (see below on length) and the short, front, open, unrounded vowel usually represented as [æ]. This symbol indicates a vowel quality somewhat higher than [a] (cardinal vowel no. 4). The distinction between a front and a back low vowel is absent in many languages and accents; for example, the words *ant* and *aunt*, which are distinct for an RP speaker, are homophones in Lowland Scots. Many writers use the symbol [a] where the frontness/backness of a low vowel is either not known or irrelevant to the task in hand; we will often use [ɐ] where a low vowel is known to be central, and [a] vs [ɑ] for front and back low vowels.

The symbol [ɪ] is used, in transcriptions of words in English and other languages, to denote an unrounded vowel which is less front and less close than [i], as in the word *bit*.

The vowel [ʊ] is back and rounded, but less back than [u], and less high.

The diacritic [:] denotes length, in both consonants and vowels. It is important to bear in mind that length is a *relative* property: [ɑ:] in RP is long with respect to other RP vowels such as [æ]. The same is true of the many long and short consonants you will encounter in this book.

This covers most of the phonetic symbols and terms you will encounter in this book (we will define one or two more, where appropriate), but it by no means provides an exhaustive account of all possible human speech sounds. For a description of those, and for greater detail on the sounds described here, you should consult a reliable phonetics textbook, such as Ladefoged (1982). For a complete list of the symbols which comprise the International Phonetic Alphabet, see the diagram on p. 11.

The International Phonetic Alphabet

CONSONANTS

	Bilabial	Labio-dental	Dental	Alveolar	Post-alveolar	Retroflex	Palatal	Velar	Uvular	Pharyngeal	Glottal
Plosive	p b			t d		ʈ ɖ	c ɟ	k ɡ	q ɢ		ʔ
Nasal	m	ɱ		n		ɳ	ɲ	ŋ	ɴ		
Trill	ʙ			r					ʀ		
Tap or Flap				ɾ		ɽ					
Fricative	ɸ β	f v	θ ð	s z	ʃ ʒ	ʂ ʐ	ç ʝ	x ɣ	χ ʁ	ħ ʕ	h ɦ
Lateral fricative				ɬ ɮ							
Approximant		ʋ		ɹ		ɻ	j	ɰ			
Lateral approximant				l		ɭ	ʎ	ʟ			
Ejective stop	p'			t'		ʈ'	c'	k'	q'		
Impulsive	ɓ ɓ			ɗ ɗ			ʄ ʄ	ɠ ɠ	ʛ ʛ		

Where symbols appear in pairs, the one to the right represents a voiced consonant. Shaded areas denote articulations judged impossible.

DIACRITICS

̥	Voiceless	n̥ d̥	̬	More rounded	ɔ̹	ʷ	Labialised	tʷ dʷ	̃	Nasalised	ẽ
̬	Voiced	s̬ t̬	̜	Less rounded	ɔ̜	ʲ	Palatalized	tʲ dʲ	ⁿ	Nasal release	dⁿ
ʰ	Voiced	tʰ dʰ	̟	Advanced	u̟	ˠ	Velarized	tˠ dˠ	ˡ	Lateral release	dˡ
̤	Breathy voiced	b̤ a̤	̠	Retracted	i̠	ˤ	Pharyngealized	tˤ dˤ	̚	No audible release	d̚
̰	Creaky voiced	b̰ a̰	̈	Centralized	ë	̴	Velarized or Pharyngealized	ɫ			
̼	Linguolabial	t̼ d̼	̽	Mid centralized	ě	̝	Raised	e̝ ɹ̝ (ɹ̝ = voiced alveolar fricative)			
̪	Dental	t̪ d̪	̘	Advanced Tongue root	e̘	̞	Lowered	e̞ β̞ (β̞ = voiced bilabial approximant)			
̺	Apical	t̺ d̺	̙	Retracted Tongue root	e̙	̩	Syllabic	l̩			
̻	Laminal	t̻ d̻	˞	Rhoticity	ɚ	̯	Non-syllabic	e̯			

VOWELS

	Front		Central		Back	
Close	i y		ɨ ʉ		ɯ u	
Close-mid		e ø		ɘ ɵ		ɤ o
Open-mid		ɛ œ		ɜ ɞ		ʌ ɔ
Open			a ɶ		ɑ ɒ	

Where symbols appear in pairs, the one to the right represents the rounded vowel.

OTHER SYMBOLS

ʍ	Voiceless labial-velar fricative	ɕ ʑ	Alveolo-palatal fricatives
w	Voiced labial-velar approximant	ɺ	Alveolar lateral flap
ɥ	Voiced labial-palatal approximant	ɧ	Simultaneous ʃ and x
ʜ	Voiceless epiglottal fricative		
ʢ	Voiced epiglottal plosive	Affricates and double articulations can be represented by two symbols joined by a tie bar if necessary.	
ʡ	Voiced epiglottal fricative		

ʘ	Bilabial click
ǀ	Dental click
ǃ	(Post)alveolar click
ǂ	Palatoalveolar click
ǁ	Alveolar lateral click

ɘ Additional mid central vowel

k͡p t͡s

SUPRASEGMENTALS

ˈ	Primary stress	
ˌ	Secondary stress	ˌfoʊnəˈtɪʃən
ː	Long	eː
ˑ	Half-long	eˑ
̆	Extra-short	ĕ
.	Syllable break	ɹi.ækt
|	Minor (foot) group	
‖	Major (intonation) group	
‿	Linking (absence of a break)	

LEVEL TONES

˝ or ̋	Extra-high
́	High
̄	Mid
̀	Low
̏	Extra-low
ꜜ	Downstep
ꜛ	Upstep

CONTOUR TONES

̌ or ̌	rise
̂	fall
᷄	high rise
᷅	low rise
᷈	rise fall
↗	Global rise
↘	Global fall

Reproduced courtesy of the International Phonetic Association

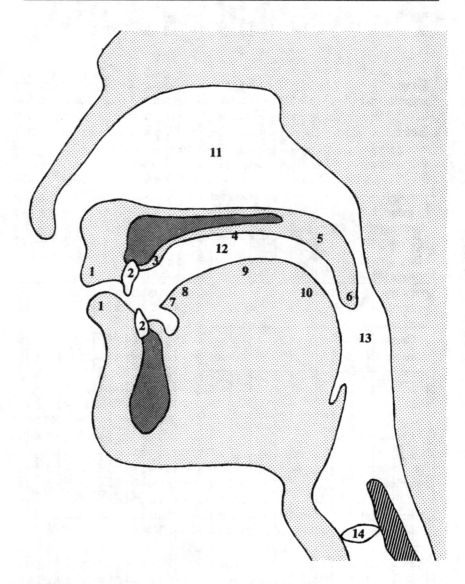

The Organs of Speech

1. Lips
2. Teeth
3. Alveolar ridge
4. Hard palate
5. Soft palate (velum)
6. Uvula
7. Tip of the tongue
8. Blade of the tongue
9. Front of the tongue
10. Back of the tongue
11. Nasal cavity
12. Oral cavity
13. Pharynx
14. Larynx

1 The Phonemic Principle

Imagine how a speaker of RP might try to convey the ways in which his speech, that of a Frenchman and that of a Spaniard sound different. We have all heard French and Spanish being spoken, and we have some kind of impression in our minds of what they sound like; we can often tell which is being spoken, even if we do not understand a word of what is being said. With our ordinary, everyday language, we can convey general impressions, in a vague sort of way; we may say that French is 'more nasal', 'more musical', 'softer' or 'more forceful' than RP, but these are not at all precise or informative expressions, and because of this, it is difficult to say whether they might be true or false. With the language of phonetics, however, we can say with considerable precision and certainty that French has, among other things, the front rounded vowels [y], [ø] and [œ], the nasalised vowels [ɛ̃], [œ̃], [ɔ̃] and [ɑ̃], and the voiced uvular fricative [ʁ], whereas RP does not. The importance of this is that, through knowing phonetics, we gain a kind of knowledge about human language, or at least a foothold on such knowledge, which we would otherwise lack.

Consider how we might put this phonetic knowledge of French and RP to use: we could investigate the acquisition of a French accent by an RP speaker, by examining the ways in which each of these French sounds is pronounced, thus pinpointing the extent to which the learner has mastered them. We would then be able to say with some precision how good someone's French accent was. But what exactly does it mean to say that someone has acquired a good French accent? One answer to this question goes like this: it means learning to pronounce those speech sounds that are present in the foreign language but absent in one's native accent, like the front rounded vowels, the uvular fricative and the nasalised vowels of French.

If this is all there is to it, then the language of phonetics will suffice in stating what it is that we have acquired in acquiring a convincing French accent. It is certainly true that, unless we learn how to pronounce these sounds, we do not stand a chance of sounding like a native when speaking French, but there's more to the acquisition of a foreign accent than just that. The purpose of this chapter is to convince you that this is so, and to introduce you to some of the terms in the language of **phonology**. We will require this to express what there is to be learned, in foreign language acquisition, over and above the pronunciation of foreign speech sounds. The importance of this extends beyond consideration of foreign language learning; if we can say what it is that constitutes having a French, a Spanish or an RP accent, we will have characterised what it is that a Frenchman, a Spaniard or an RP speaker acquires in acquiring his native accent. That is, we will have characterised a part of what it is to know those languages.

13

1.1 The Language of Phonology

Let us consider the limitations of phonetic terminology by looking at some French, Spanish and English words in phonetic transcription (the English words are given in two accents: RP and Lowland Scots).

(1)

French		Spanish		RP	Lowland Scots	
1. [ʁiɛ̃]	rien 'nothing'	[roxo]	rojo 'red'	[ɹoʊd]	[ɹod]	road
2. [ʁatɔ̃]	raton 'rat'	[real]	real 'royal'	[ɹæm]	[ɹɐm]	ram
3. [muʁiʁ]	mourir 'to die'	[foro]	forro 'lining'	[hʌɹi]	[hʌɹe]	hurry
4. [maʁi]	mari 'husband'	[foro]	foro 'forum'	[mæɹi]	[mɐɹe]	marry
5. [pʁɛ̃s]	prince 'prince'	[praðo]	prado 'meadow'	[pɹuːf]	[pɾʉf]	proof
6. [tʁɛ̃]	train 'train'	[t̪rat̪ar]	tratar 'to treat'	[tɹɪk]	[tɾɪk]	trick
7. [kʁie]	crier 'to shout'	[kreθɛr]	crecer 'to grow'	[kɹiːp]	[kɾip]	creep
8. [fʁɛne]	freiner 'to brake'	[frut̪as]	frutas 'fruits'	[fɹiː]	[fɹi]	free
9. [bʁi]	brie 'brie'	[braβo]	bravo 'brave'	[bɹɪŋ]	[brɪŋ]	bring
10. [dʁol]	drôle 'funny'	[d̪roɣa]	droga 'drug'	[dɹɪp]	[drɪp]	drip
11. [gʁɑ̃]	grand 'large'	[grit̪as]	gritas 'cries'	[gɹɪp]	[grɪp]	grip
12. [yʁle]	hurler 'to shout'	[pɛrla]	perla 'pearl'	[snɑːl]	[snɐɹl]	snarl
13. [buʁs]	bourse 'purse'	[mwɛrt̪o]	muerto 'dead'	[hɑːt]	[hɐɹt]	heart
14. [fɛʁ]	faire 'to do'	[d̪ar]	dar 'to give'	[fiə]	[fiːɹ]	fear
15. [mɛʁ]	mère 'mother'	[aθɛr]	hacer 'to make'	[hɛə]	[heːɹ]	hair

In this table of data, you are given the written form of words, a phonetic transcription of those words and, where they are not English, an indication of their meaning. Henceforth, only the meaning of non-English words will be given, and not the written form. In looking at these data, you may need to consult the phonetics revision chapter.

One interesting phonetic observation we can make about the French data is that, in addition to the voiced uvular fricative, there is a *voiceless uvular fricative* [χ] and a voiced uvular *approximant* [ʁ]. Our RP speaker therefore has to master three kinds of uvular sound in acquiring French, and so do the Lowland Scots and Spanish speakers. There is something more to be learned about these sounds in French, though. Let us consider *where they occur* within a word. The voiceless fricative occurs only after voiceless sounds (as in 5–8); the approximant occurs only before consonants and at the ends of words (as in 12–15); the voiced fricative occurs at the beginning of words (1 and 2), between vowels (3 and 4) and after voiced consonants (9–11). It is clear that where these sounds occur is not an *arbitrary* matter, but is *systematic*.

In the language of phonology, we express this systematic relationship between these sounds by saying that they occur in different **environments** (different slots), and we describe the set of environments in which a sound occurs as its **distribution**. Thus, the distribution of the voiced uvular approximant in French is before consonants and at the end of a word. Notice that the distribution of the three types of uvular sound is mutually exclusive: where we find one type, we never find either of the others. This kind of mutually exclusive distribution is called **complementary distribution**. It is this kind of distribution we find when we look at the following three sounds in Lowland Scots: the voiced post-alveolar approximant [ɹ], the voiced alveolar tap [ɾ], and the voiceless alveolar tap [ɾ̥]. The voiced tap occurs only between a voiced consonant and a vowel (as in 9–11), the voiceless tap only between a voiceless stop and a vowel (5–7) and the approximant elsewhere – at the beginnings and ends of words (1 and 2, 14 and 15), before consonants (12 and 13), after fricatives (8) and between vowels (3 and 4).

Compare this situation with the distribution of the voiced alveolar tap [ɾ] and the voiced alveolar trill in Spanish. There, we find that the tap may occur at the beginnings and ends of words, between vowels, and before and after consonants. The trill may also occur (as in 4) between vowels, and the distribution of the two sounds is therefore overlapping: there is at least one environment in which they may both occur. We refer to this pattern of distribution as **parallel distribution**. (We mean by this, not that the two sounds necessarily have identical distribution, but that their distributions overlap, partially or wholly.)

Parallel distribution has an interesting consequence: if two sounds can occur in the same slot, then it is possible for two words to differ *only* with respect to those two sounds. Thus, the words pronounced [foɾo] and [foro] in Spanish differ only with respect to the sounds between the vowels; we refer to such a pair of words as a **minimal pair**. Some other examples in Spanish are [peɾo] ('but') and [pero] ('dog'), [koɾal] ('corral') and [koɾal] ('coral'). The difference between the two sounds therefore has an important linguistic function: it serves to signal distinct words, and thus distinct meanings. We refer to this function by saying that the phonetic distinction is **contrastive**. Clearly, this is of enormous importance in human communication; by means of small phonetic differences, we are able to signal different words and hence different meanings. We want to say that the two sounds in question function as distinct linguistic units, and the term we shall use for those units is **phoneme**: the voiced alveolar stop and the voiced alveolar trill in Spanish represent distinct phonemes; the distinction between them is **phonemic** (i.e. contrastive).

Let us return to the French uvulars: [ʁ], [χ̞], [ʁ̞]. Notice that, because the members of this set of sounds never occur in the same slot, they could not *in principle* function contrastively; that is, the difference between them *cannot* be *phonemic*. While the *phonetic* (physical) difference is real enough, it is not, and cannot be, a *phonemic* (linguistic) distinction. For a French speaker, these three sounds are all somehow *different versions of the same thing*: if [ʁ] is substituted for [ʁ̞] in the word *bourse* (13), for instance, we produce what is, not a different word, but a slightly odd pronunciation of the same word: [buʁs]. The same can be said for the alveolar tap and the alveolar approximant in Lowland Scots. In uttering [hɐɹt] and then [hɐrt], we utter the same word twice; all that has changed is the *physical form* of that *abstract* word. In contrast to this, if we substitute [r] for [ɾ] in the Spanish word [foɾo], we utter a different word.

The question is how we express this; we know that the three French uvulars are phonetically distinct, and yet, for the French speaker, they are in some real sense 'the same thing'. If we were to say both that they are different sounds *and* that they are the same sound, that would be simply to utter a contradiction. We need a term to express the sense in which phonetically distinct sounds all count as instances of the same thing, and the term 'phoneme' will do this. We say that there are three phonetically distinct sounds, but that they are **realisations** of, or versions of, the same phoneme, the same linguistic unit. In order to make this claim, we will require, not just that the sounds [ʁ], [χ̞] and [ʁ̞] be in complementary distribution, but that they also be **phonetically similar**, which is indeed the case here: they are all uvulars. The structural slot will determine which version occurs, and we refer to these contextually determined realisations as **allophones** of the phoneme. The distinction between the three uvulars in French is therefore **allophonic**, not phonemic.

We have now introduced rather a lot of phonological terminology in one go. Let us concentrate on the notions *phonemic distinction* and *allophonic distinction*: a phonetic distinction between two or more sounds is phonemic if the two sounds occur in parallel distribution and function contrastively, and allophonic if they occur in complementary distribution and are phonetically similar.

A. *Farsi* (the principal language spoken in Iran; data from O'Connor 1973 and Windfuhr 1979)

Examine the following data from Farsi. It too contains voiced alveolar trills (transcribed as [r]) and voiced alveolar taps (transcribed as [ɾ]), as in Spanish. We saw there that the distinction between the two is phonemic, rather than allophonic. Is this the case for Farsi?

1.	[rah]	'road'	2.	[ruz]	'day'
3.	[bazgi:ɾ]	'towel'	4.	[omɾ]	'life'
5.	[ziɾa]	'because'	6.	[siɾini]	'pastry'
7.	[ran]	'paint'	8.	[barg]	'leaf'
9.	[farsi]	'Persian'	10.	[biɾan]	'pale'

You may well have found this question easy to answer. If you had difficulty in answering it, you will need to establish what the distribution of the two sounds is. To do that, you will need to have an idea of what can count as an environment. We have seen examples of environments in our discussion of French and Spanish: the beginnings and ends of words, between vowels, after consonants and before consonants. The relevant environments can be of these very broad sorts (which will suffice for the Farsi data), or they may need to be more particular, as we will see later. Once you have the answer, consider the status of the voiceless alveolar trill [ɾ̥] in Farsi. What is its distribution with respect to the other two sounds: parallel or complementary? Once you have this answer, you will be in a position to say whether these three sounds are realisations of only one, or of more than one, phoneme in Farsi.

Let us consider some environments which are narrower than these. We saw that in Lowland Scots, the voiceless alveolar tap occurs, not after *any* consonant, but after voiceless stops in particular. In order to manipulate phonetic data of the sort given in the problems in this book, you will need to think in terms of classes and subclasses of sounds; the stops are a subclass of the class of consonants, for instance, and the voiceless stops are in turn a subclass of the stops. In the following two exercises, you will need to be a little more specific than in the Farsi problem in stating the relevant environments.

B. *Siamese Tai* (the Tai spoken in Bangkok; data from Harris 1975, Harris and Noss 1972)

1.	[lɔ:]	'handsome'	2.	[len]	'to play'
3.	[lɯ: m]	'to forget'	4.	[lak]	'to steal'
5.	[lɛ:n]	'late meal'	6.	[lu:p]	'to stroke'
7.	[lʲin]	'monkey'	8.	[lʲi:k]	'to avoid'
9.	[pla:u]	'empty'	10.	[plɯai]	'naked'
11.	[pʰlɔ:i]	'precious stone'	12.	[klam]	'dark red'
13.	[klɔ:n]	'drum'	14.	[kʰl̥ɔ:n]	'canal'
15.	[kʰl̥ai]	'dirt'	16.	[pʰl̥ʲik]	'to turn over'

Phonetic notes
1. The superscript [ʰ] denotes aspiration.
2. The diacritic [:] after a vowel denotes length.

There are four kinds of lateral in this data:

[lʲ], which is palatalised.
[l̥], which is devoiced.
[l̥ʲ], which is both palatalised and devoiced.
[l], which is neither palatalised nor devoiced.

Answer the following questions:

(a) Which context does devoicing of the lateral occur in?
(b) Which context does palatalisation occur in?
(c) Which context will therefore guarantee both devoicing and palatalisation of laterals in Tai?

Now try the following exercise, concentrating again on specific environments.

C. *Polish* (data from Rubach 1984, Gussman 1980, Majewicz 1986)

1.	[ruf]	'a ditch'	2.	[pɛrtɛ]	'a party'
3.	[vʲetʃ]	'a wind'	4.	[sʲerkɛ]	'sulphur'
5.	[kɾfʲi]	'bloody'	6.	[sʲostrɛ]	'a sister'
7.	[bɛr]	'a bar'	8.	[gurɛ]	'a mountain'
9.	[kur]	'a cockerel'	10.	[xur]	'a choir'
11.	[kurɛ]	'a hen'	12.	[kɾtɛn]	'larynx'

The distinction between voiced and voiceless alveolar trills is allophonic; which *two* contexts does the voiceless allophone occur in? (The diacritic [ʲ] in 3–6 above indicates palatalisation; you may ignore it for the purposes here.)

We have now seen several cases where the distinction between a voiced sound and its voiceless counterpart is allophonic. Looking back over the Polish data in C, can you see any cases of *phonemic* voicing (cases where the distinction between a voiced sound and its voiceless counterpart is contrastive)? Now look at the following data from Polish.

D. *Polish* (data from Gussman 1980, Majewicz 1986, Gussman 1980)

1.	[pɔmpɐ]	'a pump'	2.	[nɛnɔd͡zɛ]	'on the leg'
3.	[ʈʂɛfʲić]	'guess right'	4.	[dɐmɐ]	'a lady'
5.	[kurɐ]	'a hen'	6.	[śɛść]	'six'
7.	[fɐzɐ]	'a phase'	8.	[sɐk]	'a travelling bag'
9.	[kur]	'a cock'	10.	[kɔzɐ]	'a goat'
11.	[šɐl]	'a scarf'	12.	[pɔrt]	'harbour'
13.	[xur]	'a choir'	14.	[źɛć]	'breathe'
15.	[tɐk]	'yes'	16.	[ʈʂɛvʲić]	'digest'
17.	[nɛnɔt͡sɛ]	'for nights'	18.	[sɔk]	'juice'
19.	[śɛć]	'sow'	20.	[ǰɛmu]	'of jam'
21.	[ćɛń]	'a shadow'	22.	[ʈɔrʈ]	'layer cake'
23.	[bɔmbɐ]	'a bomb'	24.	[ʈɐmɐ]	'a dam'
25.	[gurɐ]	'a mountain'	26.	[vɐzɐ]	'a vase'
27.	[žɐl]	'a sorrow'	28.	[kɔsɐ]	'a scythe'
29.	[čɛmu]	'why'	30.	[ǰɛń]	'a day'

Phonetic note
For the symbols [š], [ž], [č], [ǰ] and [ś], [ź], [ć], [ǰ] see phonetics revision chapter.

(a) The voiced/voiceless distinction is contrastive. Pair the sounds which exhibit this contrast.

(b) What phonetic classes do these sounds fall into?

Phonemic distinctions among consonants can be based on all three of the categories by which we classified consonants in the phonetics revision chapter: voicing, place of articulation and manner of articulation. We have now established that voicing is phonemic among a large class of Polish consonants. This is an extremely common state of affairs in human languages. Try listing voiced vs voiceless minimal pairs in English; what classes of sounds exhibit this voiced/voiceless contrast?

Let us now consider place of articulation distinctions.

E. Polish (data from Majewicz 1986)

1.	[pɔrʈ]	'harbour'	2.	[tɔrʈ]	'layer cake'
3.	[kɔrʈ]	'(tennis) court'	4.	[rɛfɐ]	'a reef'
5.	[rɛsɐ]	'a race'	6.	[šɔk]	'shock'
7.	[sɔk]	'juice'	8.	[fɔk]	'a foresail'
9.	[zãb]	'a tooth'	10.	[źãb]	'a chill'

What places of articulation function as the basis for phonemic distinctions in Polish consonants?

In Spanish, we noted (see p. 16) a phonemic distinction based on *manner of articulation*: voiced alveolar taps and trills are contrastive. A more common phonemic distinction involving manner of articulation is the stop vs fricative vs affricate difference, as you can see from the following Polish data:

(2) *Polish stops, fricatives and affricates*

1.	[ʈɛk]	'yes'	2.	[sɛk]	'a travelling bag'
3.	[kur]	'a cock'	4.	[xur]	'a choir'
5.	[śɛrkɐ]	'sulphur'	6.	[ćɛrkɐ]	'a sloe'
7.	[śɛść]	'six'	8.	[čɛść]	'hello!'

We have now established that voicing, place of articulation and manner of articulation are phonemic among Polish consonants. This is true in most languages, including Spanish, as you can see from the following data:

F. Spanish

1.	[pɛθ]	'fish'	2.	[bɛθ]	'time'
3.	[ţia]	'aunt'	4.	[d̪ia]	'day'
5.	[kaţa]	'tasting'	6.	[gaţa]	'she–wolf'
7.	[paţa]	'foot'	8.	[papa]	'pope'
9.	[ţoɾo]	'bull'	10.	[koɾo]	'chorus'
11.	[θima]	'peak'	12.	[sima]	'abyss'

| 13. | [fjesta] | 'fiesta' | 14. | [sjesta] | 'siesta' |
| 15. | [oxo] | 'eye' | 16. | [oso] | 'bear' |

(a) For which category of sounds is voicing phonemic?
(b) What places of articulation are relevant for phonemic distinctions among (i) stops and (ii) fricatives?

1.2 Phonemic Rules

Let us return to our question of what it is to have acquired a native-sounding accent in a foreign language. We can see that, in the case of Spanish, this means knowing (though not necessarily consciously) that [r] and [ɾ] are realisations of distinct phonemes. Consider the task facing a Farsi speaker learning Spanish: in his language, the phonemic distinction does not exist; the two sounds seem pretty much the same *because* they are allophones of the same phoneme. For the Farsi speaker, the difficulty does not reside in learning to pronounce new, foreign sounds (the two sounds are perfectly common in Farsi). What the Farsi speaker must do is to learn to *perceive* them differently, as contrastive units. Now this fact alone shows that the first answer we considered to our question must be wrong: the learner of a foreign language has to acquire, not just the ability to pronounce new sounds, but a kind of perceptual strategy. In this case, we may say that the Farsi speaker ends up with two different perceptual strategies for perceiving alveolar trills and taps: one (the native language strategy) in which they count as the same thing (are allophones of the same phoneme) and another in which they count as quite distinct things (are realisations of separate phonemes). Let us adopt a means of representing these two states of affairs: we will use slanted brackets to indicate phonemes, and the usual square brackets to represent physical sounds, thus:

(3)

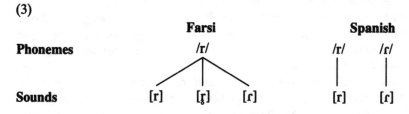

Representing phonemes and their realisations in this way allows us to express the sense in which the two languages differ with respect to these two sounds: at the phonemic, rather than at the phonetic, level. We can expand on this by showing in which contexts the Farsi allophones occur, thus:

(4)

$$/r/ \rightarrow \begin{Bmatrix} [\mathrm{r}] & / & V\_\_V \\ [\mathrm{r̥}] & / & \_\_\# \end{Bmatrix}$$

The formalism is interpreted in this way: on the left of the arrow, we have the representation for the phoneme /r/ in Farsi; the arrow means 'is realised as'; the slash (/) means 'in the environment of', or 'in the context of'. The horizontal bars indicate structural slots, with information preceding and/or following them. In this case, on the uppermost line, the bar shows a vowel (V) preceding and following the segment; on the second line, a word boundary (#) follows the segment (i.e. the phoneme occurs at the end of a word). Thus, the right-hand side indicates the devoiced and tapped allophones and the contexts in which they occur. The curly brackets (or **brace notation**) indicate a choice between the realisations enclosed within the brackets: we must choose *one* of the realisations enclosed within the brackets, but we may not choose more than one. The entire statement expresses a general **rule** about the occurrence of the allophones, which in prose would be: 'the phoneme /r/ is realised as a voiced alveolar tap between vowels, a voiceless alveolar trill word-finally, and a voiced alveolar trill elsewhere'. That is, we are assuming here that the representation /r/ indicates that the phoneme is 'fundamentally' a voiced trill, and that it emerges as a voiceless trill or a voiced tap only in the word-final and intervocalic environments, respectively. The [r] is the 'default' realisation of the phoneme, and this is encoded in the representation we give for the phoneme: /r/. There are several important issues which bear on this matter of the interpretation of phonological rules; we will return to them in Chapters 6 and 7.

The principal point to bear in mind about such a rule is that it expresses a **generalisation** about the language: not only do these three sounds occur in this language, but there is a systematic, predictable, relationship between them, just as there is with the uvulars in French. Their occurrence is **rule-governed**. What our foreign learners have to acquire, over and above pronunciation of sounds, describable in the language of phonetics, are *generalisations*, expressible as *rules*. This fact is of immense importance to our understanding of human language; in recognising the status of phonemes and the rules governing their realisations, we have gained something – an insight into the way speech sounds function in human language. Native speakers, we want to say, have acquired these generalisations unconsciously, and they perceive speech sounds in terms of them. They constitute a kind of unconscious knowledge. This fundamental phonemic insight into what it is to know a language allows us to state significant generalisations about the organisation of that knowledge. As we will see in later chapters, this linguistic knowledge is structured to quite a remarkable extent.

To recapitulate: in answer to the question of what it is to acquire a foreign accent (or, for that matter, a different accent of one's native language), we have said that it is mistaken to assume that this is simply a matter of learning to produce new sounds. Rather, the speaker must acquire the phonological rules of the foreign language. Let us briefly consider what might be taken to be an alternative answer to the question. We might say that acquiring a foreign accent means learning to produce the sounds of the language, and learning to utter them in the right places. But this answer amounts to conceding that one must acquire the rules, since 'producing the sounds in the right places' results from having acquired the rules, which govern where the sounds should occur.

Let us look now at another case of rule-governedness.

(5) *Spanish*

1.	[baŋko]	'bank'	2.	[boðeɣa]	'bodega'
3.	[ambos]	'both'	4.	[sɛmblaɾ]	'to seem'
5.	[deβɛɾ]	'to have to'	6.	[aβɛɾ]	'to have'
7.	[daɾ]	'to give'	8.	[dias]	'days'
9.	[dando]	'giving'	10.	[banda]	'ribbon'
11.	[naða]	'nothing'	12.	[ablaðo]	'spoken'
13.	[ganar]	'to gain'	14.	[gata]	'she-wolf'
15.	[lɛŋgwa]	'language'	16.	[saŋgria]	'sangria'
17.	[aɣwa]	'water'	18.	[muɣa]	'boundary'

We have already seen that [b], [d] and [g] function contrastively with [p], [t] and [k] in this language. Looking at the distribution of [b] and [β], we see that [b] may occur at the beginning of a word (1, 2 and 10), after a nasal (3 and 4) and before a consonant (12). The approximant [β] does not occur in any of these environments, but does occur between vowels (5 and 6), where [b] never occurs. The two are in complementary distribution. They are also phonetically similar: both are voiced and bilabial, differing only as to manner of articulation. We are justified in saying therefore that they are members of the same phoneme, the occurrence of one allophone rather than the other being predictable from context. Using our rule formalism, we may express this as:

(6)

/b/ → [β] / V__V

We are assuming here that the [b] realisation is the default one, and that this stop phoneme is realised as an approximant intervocalically. That

seems to make sense phonetically; the stop **assimilates** in degree of stricture to the surrounding vowels by becoming more vowel-like (i.e. by
becoming an approximant). This reduction in degree of stricture is known
as **lenition**, or weakening; its converse is known as **fortition**, or strengthening. Given that the phonetic relationship between [b] and [β] is the same as
that between the dentals [d̪] and [ð], and the velars [g] and [ɣ], it is
interesting to ask whether the same *phonological* relationship holds for the
velars and the dentals. This is indeed the case, as you can tell by looking
over the data. We may write another two phonemic rules, parallel to our
first one:

(7)

/d̪/ → [ð] / V__V

/g/ → [ɣ] / V__V

This expectation of phonological symmetry across parallel classes of
sounds (referred to as system congruity or **pattern congruity**) is not always
fulfilled, but it is worth adopting as a general guiding principle in establishing a phonemic analysis. Notice that this kind of system symmetry held for
voiced and voiceless stops in Spanish and Polish: just as [p] contrasts with
[b], so does [t̪] with [d̪] and [k] with [g]. In order to make use of this notion,
you will need to be able to notice the phonetic parallelism between sets of
sounds such as the three pairs of stops and approximants in the Spanish
data. This means being able to manipulate independently the different
factors of place, manner and voicing which we adopted in the phonetics
revision chapter. Try using the notion of system congruity with the following data from Tamil (a Dravidian language spoken in Southern India and
Sri Lanka).

G. *Tamil* (data from Asher 1982)

1.	[pʊli]	'tiger'	2.	[t̪an̠:i]	'water'
3.	[kasɪ]	'political party'	4.	[pa:mbɯ]	'snake'
5.	[paɳɖɯ]	'ball'	6.	[ʋa:ŋgɯ]	'buy'
7.	[ɪɾʊβaðɯ]	'twenty'	8.	[ka:ðɯ]	'ear'
9.	[maɣẽ]	'son'	10.	[t̪ɪɳ:ɯ]	'can'
11.	[ʋaɳɖɯ]	'cart'	12.	[kuɽʊ]	'give'
13.	[čaɳɖɪɾẽ]	'moon'	14.	[n̠eɲɟɯ]	'heart'
15.	[pasɪ]	'hunger'	16.	[čeɳɖɾẽ]	'I went'
17.	[ka:ɽɯ]	'forest'	18.	[taβam]	'penance'

19.	[kaɤam]	'crow'	20.	[tɑŋgai]	'younger'
21.	[ɪɲjɪ]	'ginger'	22.	[puːɳɖʊ]	'garlic'

Phonetic notes
1. [t] and [ɖ] are voiceless and voiced retroflex stops.
2. [ʋ] is a voiced labiodental approximant.
3. [ɯ] is a high, central-back, unrounded vowel.
4. [ɾ] is a voiced retroflex tap.
5. The diacritic [ː] after a symbol denotes length.

(a) State the distribution of the bilabials [p], [b] and [β].
(b) Write a phonemic rule, of the sort we used for Farsi and Spanish, which expresses a general rule about the bilabials.
(c) Then examine the dentals [t̪], [d̪] and [ð], and the velars [k], [g] and [ɤ]. Write rules for these too.
(d) Do [t] and [ɖ] occur where you would expect them to?
(e) What is the intervocalic allophone for this phoneme? What would you have expected it to be?
(f) Now look at [č] and [ǰ]. Do they occur where you would expect them to? Can you suggest an analysis for [s] which would make it conform to our expectations of pattern congruity?

In writing these phonemic rules, you may have been struck by the following question: what symbol should one enter in the slanted brackets, to denote the phoneme in question? What phonetic significance, if any, does this symbol have? One way of responding to this question is to suggest that, since phonemes are not sounds as such, but something rather more abstract (the units in a linguistic system), then the symbol in the brackets is largely empty of phonetic meaning. We might therefore use numerical symbols to indicate which of the finite stock of phonemes in a language we are referring to. In this view, the phonetic symbols are largely a convenience which help us to remember some of the shared phonetic properties of the allophones of phonemes.

This would be a rather bizarre response, given that one of our criteria for allocating allophones to phonemes is phonetic similarity. In insisting that [β] be classed with [b] in Spanish we are suggesting that the phoneme is fundamentally bilabial and voiced, its allophones varying only with regard to manner of articulation. Otherwise, we could perfectly well group [b] with [ð] and [d̪] with [β].

Consider too the relationship between the allophone and the context to which it is tied. In many cases, we have specified the determining environments for all but one of the allophones of a phoneme, suggesting that it is in some sense 'basic', the others being deviations from it in those particular contexts. We said that the intervocalic context in which the Spanish approximants occur may reasonably be suggested as the phonetic *cause* for the change in manner of articulation: since vowels are characterised by a stricture of open approximation, what is fundamentally a stop consonant, with complete closure, assimilates to the surrounding vowels.

The same may be said of devoiced allophones. In Polish, the devoiced allophone [ɹ] of the phoneme /r/ occurs in a voiceless context (between voiceless consonants or word-finally after a voiceless consonant). In Tai, the devoiced allophones of /l/ occur after aspirated voiceless stops, and the palatalised allophones before the high front vowel /i/, which is articulated close to the hard palate. In this case, there is a clear basis for saying that the phoneme is fundamentally voiced and non-palatalised, with devoicing and palatalisation occurring as kinds of assimilations to adjacent sounds. This is implicit in the use of the representation /l/, rather than /l̥/ or /lʲ/, as the symbol for the phoneme.

We will therefore adopt the view that there is indeed phonetic significance in the choice of symbol we adopt for the representation of phonemes. We shall see in later chapters that the matter is not always as simple as these examples suggest, and that it raises fundamental questions about the nature of phonological units. For the moment, however, in devising phonological analyses, it should help if you look for phonetic connections between the phonetic properties of allophones and the context in which those allophones occur. Try this with the following exercise.

H. Lumasaaba (a Bantu language spoken in Uganda; data from Brown 1972)

1.	[katemu]	'a small snake'	2.	[kucina]	'to dance'
3.	[kunila]	'to wince'	4.	[iŋka:fu]	'a cow'
5.	[kubululuka]	'to fly'	6.	[cinaga]	'a pipe'
7.	[cisiɟe]	'an eyebrow'	8.	[lusece]	'a straw'
9.	[iɲcese]	'a sheep'	10.	[kacese]	'a small sheep'
11.	[mugunda]	'a farm'	12.	[iŋɟega]	'I mix'
13.	[umuɟelema]	'a wife'	14.	[li:ɟi]	'an egg'

Phonetic note
[ɟ] is a voiced palatal stop.

The velar and palatal stops [k] and [c] are allophones of the phoneme /k/.

(a) State the environment in which [c] occurs.
(b) Write a phonemic rule which expresses this.

(c) What is the phonetic link between this allophone and its environment?
(d) What other pair of stops would you expect, on the principle of system symmetry, to exhibit the same regularity? Do they?

Thus far, we have been considering allophonic and phonemic distinctions among consonants only. As with consonants, vowels exhibit phonemic and allophonic distinctions based on their descriptive parameters: height, backness/frontness and roundedness. Phonemic height distinctions can be seen in the following data from Siamese Tai:

(8) *Siamese Tai* (data from Harris 1975, Harris and Noss 1972)

1.	[dom]	'to smell'	2.	[dam]	'to swim'
3.	[pet]	'duck'	4.	[pɛ:t]	'eight'
5.	[pʰi:]	'fat'	6.	[pʰɛ:]	'raft'
7.	[tok]	'to drop'	8.	[tɔ:k]	'bamboo strip'

Phonemic back/front and rounded/unrounded distinctions in vowels can be seen in the following data from French:

(9) *French*

1.	[vo]	'veal'	2.	[vø]	'wishes'
3.	[vu]	'you' (plural)	4.	[vy]	'seen'
5.	[li]	'bed'	6.	[ly]	'read'
7.	[ble]	'wheat'	8.	[blø]	'blue'

Vowel length may be phonemic, as you can see from the following data from Limbu (a Tibeto-Burman language spoken in Nepal):

(10) *Limbu* (data from Weidert and Subba 1985)

1.	[sapma]	'to write'	2.	[sa:pma]	'to flatter'
3.	[am:a]	'to warm up'	4.	[a:m:a]	'to be rough'
5.	[ikma]	'to twist'	6.	[i:kma]	'to be in surplus'
7.	[inma]	'to buy'	8.	[i:nma]	'to sow'
9.	[supma]	'to close'	10.	[su:pma]	'to finish something'
11.	[sukma]	'to be able'	12.	[su:kma]	'to buzz'

All of these distinctions between vowels may also be *allophonic*. Let us look at an example involving vowel height. In Greenlandic Eskimo, there are five phonetic vowels: [i], [e], [a], [o], [u]. There are, however, only three vowel phonemes: /i/, /a/ and /u/. The phoneme /i/ has the allophones [i] and [e], and the phoneme /u/ has allophones [u] and [o].

1. Greenlandic Eskimo (data from Swadesh 1944)

By examining the following data, can you say what environment the [e] and [o] allophones occur in?

1.	[pisuk]	'to go'	2.	[teʁianiaq]	'a fox'
3.	[saβik]	'knife'	4.	[inuk]	'person'
5.	[ajoqeʁsoʁti]	'teacher'	6.	[oʁsoq]	'blubber'
7.	[nuɣβik]	'single-pointed dart'	8.	[noʁlut]	'ligature'
9.	[tikeq]	'index finger'	10.	[uβiɣlaɣneq]	'widow'

Phonetic notes
1. [ʁ] is a voiced uvular fricative.
2. [q] is a voiceless uvular stop.

Recalling our earlier point about the phonetic link which may exist between an allophone and its determining environment, can you suggest why it should be that these allophones occur in that particular environment?

We have now made considerable headway in expressing generalisations about the organisation and function of speech sounds in human languages using our criteria of, on the one hand, parallel distribution and contrast, and, on the other hand, complementary distribution and phonetic similarity. We may refer to these criteria jointly as **the phonemic principle**: in satisfying either the first or the second of these two sets, we can decide the phonemic status of a given set of speech sounds. There is one kind of case, however, where we may satisfy the criterion of parallel distribution without establishing that the distinction is contrastive. For some speakers of Lowland Scots, for instance, [ɹ] and [r] occur, not in complementary distribution, but in parallel distribution: [ɹ] or [r] may occur in most environments. But with these cases in this accent, the substitution of one sound for another does not result in a change of meaning: the two sounds thus fail the twin criteria for being phonemically distinct, and are said to be in **free variation**.

There are also cases of *phonemic* free variation, where two sounds which are phonemically distinct may be substituted one for the other in particular words without a change of meaning. Thus, while the distinction between the vowels [iː] and [ɛ] is phonemic in many English accents, the substitution of one for the other in *economics* does not result in a change of meaning. Such cases are of marginal interest for us, however, as they are idiosyncratic facts about particular words.

1.3 Phonological Representations

An interesting consequence of the way we have been speaking of phonemes, as opposed to speech sounds, is that, for any given word, we will be able to represent it in terms of the phonemes of which it is composed. Thus, in the case of Tamil (see p. 24), we may say that, while [ɪɾʊβaðɯ] represents the way in which the word for 'twenty' is uttered, /ɪɾʊpat̪u/ represents the phonemes which combine to give the phonological form of the word. That is, the phonemic rules we have devised will *mediate* between the phonological and phonetic **representations** of a word. In other words, the rules fill in *predictable* information about the way in which the phonemes of a word are realised. We may say that, while it is an arbitrary, accidental, fact that the word for 'twenty' in Tamil has this series of phonemes, not all of the properties of their phonetic realisations are accidental: given a /p/ between vowels, for instance, it is bound to be [β], and given a /t̪/ between vowels, it is bound to be [ð]. And these are only some of the predictable properties of the phonetic representation of this word. The phonological representation therefore reflects, one might say, the form of the word stripped of all of its predictable, rule-governed phonetic properties.

Let us take an example from English. The distinction between [m] and [n] is contrastive, as we can see from minimal pairs such as *male/nail*, *mitt/knit*, *can/cam*, *Jimmy/Ginny* and so on. Thus, the phonemes /m/ and /n/ have the realisations [m] and [n] respectively. But consider the words *input* and *inset*. You will probably be happy to agree that these should be represented phonologically as /ɪnpʊt/ and /ɪnsɛt/. The nasal in *input* is, however, uttered as an [m]: try it and you will see that one needs to use conscious effort *not* to utter it this way. This is because the /n/ assimilates in place of articulation to the following stop. What this means is that we must allow that the phoneme /n/ has an [m] allophone. Phonetically, this [m] is identical to the [m] in *male*.

What is interesting is that we nevertheless have no difficulty in decoding these occurrences of [m] as realisations of /n/, not /m/, and this is because there is a *generalisation* governing the occurrence of these bilabial realisations of /n/ which is expressible in the following rule:

(11)

$$/n/ \rightarrow [m] \; / \; \_\_ \; \begin{Bmatrix} p \\ b \end{Bmatrix}$$

Again, the curly brackets (or brace notation) around the /p/ and /b/ indicate a choice between the elements within the brackets; that is, /n/ → [m] before *either* a /p/ *or* a /b/.

Can you see how subtle a trick of perception this is? We decode the [m] in *input* so readily as an /n/ that normally we simply do not even *notice* that it is physically an [m]; it must be pointed out to us! The point is that a given physical sound may be interpreted in more than one way (may have more than one linguistic function), and it is through being in possession of the rules of our phonology that we can impose these different interpretations with such ease. You might therefore want to think about the distinction between the phonological and the phonetic representation of words in this way: the phonetic representation shows the sounds we utter, but the phonological one shows the more abstract shape of the words we perceive. Phonological units, we may say, are units of perception. And phonological rules express the generalisations which allow us to decode phonetic signals in terms of those units.

1.4 Concluding Remarks

The main thrust of this chapter has been this: that speakers, in acquiring their native language phonologies, unconsciously acquire generalisations, which the phonologist seeks to express explicitly in the form of rules. Those generalisations concern, not just speech sounds, but the linguistic units (phonemes) by which those sounds are organised and given a linguistic function. While the language of phonetics will express the nature of the speech sounds themselves, we need a phonological language to express the speaker's unconsciously acquired phonological generalisations. The speaker's unconscious phonological knowledge is highly structured and remarkably systematic, as I hope you will soon be persuaded. Our task from now on will therefore be to seek to make our statements about that store of unconscious knowledge as general and as systematic as possible.

EXERCISES

1. Malayalam (a Dravidian language closely related to Tamil)
    Examine the following data and list the vowel phonemes. Is vowel length phonemic or allophonic?

1.	[koʈ:a]	'basket'	2.	[kiʈ: i]	'got'
3.	[ap:am]	'bread'	4.	[at:am]	'end'
5.	[keʈ:u]	'burnt out'	6.	[kaʈi]	'biting'
7.	[palam]	'a weight'	8.	[keʈ:i]	'tied'
9.	[ke:ʈ:u]	'heard'	10.	[ka:ʈi]	'sour gruel'
11.	[pa:la]	'a tree'	12.	[ciri]	'smile'
13.	[koʈ:i]	'drummed'	14.	[kuʈi]	'drinking'
15.	[ci:ri]	'shrieked'	16.	[wi:ʈə]	'house'
17.	[ku:ʈi]	'increased'	18.	[ko:ʈ:a]	'castle'
19.	[kaʈ:i]	'thickness'	20.	[a:ɳə]	'man'
21.	[wen:a]	'butter'	22.	[kuʈ:i]	'child'

2. Japanese (data from Hinds 1986).

In the following data from Japanese, the voiceless fricatives [s] and [ʃ] are allophones of the /s/ phoneme; [j] and [z] are allophones of the /z/ phoneme. In which environment do the palato-alveolar allophones occur?

1.	[ʃiawase]	'happiness'	2.	[sate]	'well'
3.	[sɯp:ai]	'sour'	4.	[oji:san]	'grandfather'
5.	[somkei]	'respect'	6.	[zɯzɯʃi:]	'forward'
7.	[onaji]	'same'	8.	[sensei]	'teacher'
9.	[zaʃ:i]	'magazine'	10.	[zenzen]	'absolutely'
11.	[jit:o]	'straight'	12.	[zo:]	'elephant'

3. Tamil (data from Asher 1982)

The vowels [ɯ] and [ʊ] are allophones of the phoneme /ʊ/ in Tamil. Examine the following data and determine what context the [ɯ] allophone occurs in.

1.	[ʊp:ʊ]	'salt'	2.	[ʊmi]	'husk'
3.	[mʊrɔ̃]	'winnowing fair'	4.	[pʊz̪ʊ]	'worm'
5.	[pɑ:z̪ɯ]	'waste'	6.	[t̪erɯ]	'street'
7.	[u:rʊ]	'village'	8.	[aðɯ]	'it'
9.	[pu:ʈ:ʊ]	'lock'	10.	[t̪o:lʊ]	'leather'
11.	[ʈo:lʊ]	'shoulder'	12.	[ne:ʈ:ɯ]	'yesterday'
13.	[mi:ɳɯ]	'fish'	14.	[neɲjɯ]	'heart'

Hint: The answer to this one is a little less obvious. To answer it, you will need to look beyond the segments which are immediately adjacent to the vowels in question. You will also need to identify a class which is a little more specific than the general classes 'consonant' and 'vowel'.

4. Korean (data from Pyun 1987)
   Examine the following data and draw up a table of the consonant phonemes of Korean (including lateral and nasal phonemes).

1.	[tal]	'moon'		2.	[kɛda]	'fold'
3.	[pul]	'fire'		4.	[kʰɛda]	'dig'
5.	[sada]	'buy'		6.	[kam]	'persimmon'
7.	[panɨl]	'needle'		8.	[kan]	'liver'
9.	[k*ɛda]	'wake'		10.	[pʰul]	'grass'
11.	[t*al]	'daughter'		12.	[čada]	'sleep'
13.	[tʰal]	'mask'		14.	[p*ul]	'horn'
15.	[tol]	'birthday'		16.	[kaŋ]	'river'
17.	[hanɨl]	'sky'		18.	[čʰada]	'kick'
19.	[ton]	'money'		20.	[s*ada]	'wrap'
21.	[č*ada]	'be salty'				

Phonetic notes
The diacritic [*] indicates an articulation with glottal tension.

Further Reading

For a more detailed introduction to the phonemic principle, which introduces some of the problems we will discuss in Chapter 4, see Lass (1984a), Chapter 1. We have adopted a 'perceptual' (or 'psychological') view of the phoneme; for a clear discussion of this, and two other ways of interpreting the phoneme, see Hyman (1975), Chapter 3. For source material on phonemic analysis, see the papers in Joos (1958); Twaddell's contribution to that volume, first published in 1935, gives a good survey of the issues involved in interpreting the 'phoneme' notion. Anderson (1985), Chapters 2–4 and 9–12, gives a well-informed account of the history of the phoneme concept. For further exercises on phonemic analysis, see Pike (1947).

2 Alternations

2.1 The Internal Structure of Words

In Chapter 1, we were able to show the sequence of phonemes which combine to make up the phonological form of a word. Thus, the phonological form of the Tamil word for 'twenty' is, we proposed (see p. 29), /ɪrʊpaṭʊ/. We referred to this as the *phonological* representation of the word, and [ɪrʊβaðɯ] as the *phonetic* representation. The rules we devised were said to *mediate* between these representations, so that we *derive* the phonetic representation from the phonological representation. In arriving at such rules and representations, we took *the word* as our domain: we considered environments at the beginnings and ends of words, and within words. We made no attempt to define what we meant by 'word', and we will not do so now; we will assume that it is perfectly clear what is meant by that term. But to understand the way phonological rules work within words, we need to consider the internal structure of words a little more carefully. The linguistic term for the study of such structure is **morphology**, and from now on, we shall be considering the morphological structure of words as well as their phonological form.

Recall the discussion of the words *inset* and *input* (see p. 29): you were asked to assume that the phonological representation of these should be /ɪnsɛt/ and /ɪnpʊt/, respectively, and this seemed right, at least as far as our discussion of the nasals was concerned. We took the nasal in both words to be phonologically an /n/, which is realised phonetically as an [m] in *input*, but as an [n] in *inset*. This analysis implies that there is a prefix /ɪn/ within both words, and this seems right too. That is, we want to say that both words are **morphologically complex**: they consist of more than one morphological element. We refer to such elements as **morphemes**. We may say that, while a word is a linguistic unit which signals a meaning, morphemes are units *within* the word which signal identifiable meanings. You will probably agree that the prefix in the words *inset* and *input* signals one kind of meaning, while the rest of the word (let us call it the **root** or **stem**) signals another. Since we are assuming that this awareness constitutes part of the speaker's knowledge of the language, we can reflect this kind of morphological structure within our phonological representation, thus /ɪn + sɛt/ and /ɪn + pʊt/, where the '+' symbol indicates a **morpheme boundary**.

That is, the word *input* has two morphemes: one a **prefix** and the other a root, which have the phonological forms /ɪn/ and /pʊt/, respectively. Now this analysis commits us to allowing that the morpheme with the phonological form /ɪn/ has two different phonetic forms: [ɪn] and [ɪm]. Let us call these phonetic forms **morphs**. Following our practice in describing the contextually governed phonetic realisations of phonemes as allophones, we shall refer to the contextually governed realisations of morphemes as **allomorphs**. Thus, we say that this morpheme, with the phonological form /ɪn/, has (at least) the two allomorphs [ɪn] and [ɪm]. And, just as we said that phonemes, as units in a linguistic system, are distinct from phonetic segments (sometimes called phones) which act as their realisations, so we distinguish between morphemes, as units of meaning in a linguistic system with a specific phonological form, and morphs, the sequences of phonetic segments which act as their realisations. That is, the linguistic objects we call morphemes are a kind of *connection* (or union) of a phonological form with a meaning. And that phonological form may be realised phonetically in more than one way (it may have more than one phonetic manifestation).

Let us take an example from English. There is a morpheme whose meaning we might represent informally as 'plural'; it has, let us say, the phonological form /ɪz/, and this phonological form is realised as the morphs (the phonetic forms) [ɪz], [s] and [z] (as in *horses*, *cats*, and *dogs*). Since the occurrence of one morph rather than another is rule-governed (it depends on the stem-final segment of the noun stem to which the 'plural' suffix is added), the morphs are allomorphs of the 'plural' morpheme. In much of the analysis we will be carrying out in the chapters that follow, we will try to come up with hypotheses about the phonological form of morphemes. In doing this, we will proceed by referring to a morpheme by means of expressions like 'plural', 'dog', 'past', etc., and expressing the phonological form of morphemes in slanted brackets. Morphs, which are phonetic objects, will be enclosed in phonetic (square) brackets.

To further exemplify this new set of terms, let us examine a case in Lumasaaba which is similar to our English example. In this language, [b], [ɓ], [d], [l], [ɟ] and [j] function contrastively. That is, Lumasaaba has the phonemes /b/, /ɓ/, /d/, /l/, /ɟ/ and /j/. In the following data, all the words are morphologically complex; like our two examples from English, they are composed of prefixes followed by a root.

(1)

1. (a)	[cibati]	'a knife'	(b)	[zimbati]	'knives'
2. (a)	[kaɓua]	'a small dog'	(b)	[zimbua]	'dogs'
3. (a)	[ludaha]	'a wing'	(b)	[zindaha]	'wings'
4. (a)	[luli]	'a root'	(b)	[zindi]	'roots'
5. (a)	[luɟeɟele]	'a chain'	(b)	[ziɲɟeɟele]	'chains'
6. (a)	[luɟo:jo]	'a bud'	(b)	[ziɲɟo:jo]	'buds'
7. (a)	[kagunija]	'a small bag'	(b)	[ziŋgunija]	'bags'

In Lumasaaba, as in many Bantu languages, there are many different *classes* of noun (nouns denoting animals might constitute a different class from nouns denoting household objects, for instance). The basis of this classification need not detain us here, but we do need to note that it is a prefix in the word which indicates the class of the noun. It is evident that the nouns on the right-hand side are plural forms of the indefinite singular nouns on the left. Thus, for each word on the left-hand side, there is a morph which expresses what might be called the dictionary (or **lexical**) meaning of the word, and another morph (a prefix) which signals the class of the noun and the meanings 'indefinite' and 'singular'. Thus, in 1(a), [ci] indicates 'indefinite' and 'singular', while [bati] means 'knife'. In the case of [ka] in 2 and 7, the prefix morph signals the meaning 'small' as well as 'indefinite' and singular'. On the right-hand side, the meaning 'plural' is signalled by a prefix [zi], followed by another prefix (whose meaning is not important for our purposes); in these cases, this morph takes the form of a nasal stop.

By contrasting each word on the left with its plural form on the right, we can see which parts constitute the roots and which parts the prefixes. Thus, the left-hand column shows the following prefixes: [ci], [ka] and [lu]. (We might recall, in passing, that the phonological form of [ci] is /ki/: cf p. 26.) The right-hand column shows the plural prefix [zi] in each case, followed by a class prefix taking the form [m], [n], [ɲ] or [ŋ].

Let us consider very briefly the second of the morphs in the plural forms of the words; each is a nasal, and like the prefix we have just considered in English, this varies in its place of articulation, depending on the place of articulation of the following stop: bilabial [m] occurs before bilabial [b], alveolar [n] before alveolar [d], palatal [ɲ] before palatal [ɟ], and velar [ŋ] before velar [g]. Let us assume that the phonological form of each of these morphemes is /n/; the following rule will express the predictability of their phonetic form:

(2)

$$/n/ \rightarrow \begin{Bmatrix} [m] & / & \_\_b \\ [ɲ] & / & \_\_ɟ \\ [ŋ] & / & \_\_g \end{Bmatrix}$$

Having decided on the phonological form of these morphemes, we can begin to come up with phonological representations of the plural words, with morpheme boundaries marked. The words meaning 'knives', 'wings', 'chains' and 'bags' will be, respectively, /zi + n + bati/, /zi + n + daha/, /zi + n + ɟeɟele/ and /zi + n + gunija/. But what of the representations for the words meaning 'dogs', 'roots' and 'buds'? The problem here is that the roots come in more than one phonetic form. These are, for 'dog', [bua] and

[ß ua], for 'root', [di] and [li], and for 'bud', [ɟoːjo] and [joːjo]. The question
then arises what the phonological form of these roots is.

2.2 Testing Hypotheses about Rules and Representations

Let us begin by noting that there are striking phonetic similarities between
the two forms in each case: only the initial segment differentiates the two,
and even then, the two segments share, in each case, the same voicing state
and place of articulation. Thus, [b] and [ß] differ only in that the first is a
stop and the second is an approximant. The same is true of [d] and [l], and
[ɟ] and [j]. Let us adopt an assumption of *regularity*; that is, let us assume
that in cases like these, the variation is predictable, and that it is our task to
determine exactly what it is that governs the occurrence of one rather than
the other segment. What we will then need to do in this case is to decide
what it is that governs the occurrence of a stop in one form and an
approximant in the other.

There are two obvious ways of approaching this. We could suggest that
these morphemes have stops in their phonological representations, and
that something in the phonetic context causes them to be realised as
approximants. Under this hypothesis, the morphemes have the representations /bua/, /di/ and /ɟoːjo/. Alternatively, we could suggest the converse:
that they have approximants in their phonological representations, and
that something in the immediate context causes these to be realised as
stops. That would mean having the representations /ß ua/, /li/ and /joːjo/.
Let us consider these alternatives in turn.

Under the first hypothesis, we need to find a phonetic context which
would act as the governing factor. Clearly, this must be something about
the prefix, since that is what varies between the singular and plural forms.
A reasonable suggestion would be to say that voiced stops are realised as
approximants between vowels. This was what we saw to be the case in
Spanish (see p. 23). We would suggest therefore that, with the addition of a
prefix which ends in a vowel, the stop in the phonological representation
occurs between vowels, and thus is realised as an approximant. This would
mean having three rules of the form:

(3)

/b/ → [ß] / V (+) __V
/d/ → [l] / V (+) __V
/ɟ/ → [j] / V (+) __V

The morpheme boundary sign '+' here occurs in the **round brackets**, which
indicate **optionality**. The expression '(+)' therefore shows that such a

boundary *may* occur after the first vowel. That is, the first vowel may belong to another morph, which is the case with the first vowel in all of the (a) forms. While we will enclose all other optional elements in round brackets in the chapters that follow, we will follow the convention, with respect to the morpheme boundary marker '+', that if it is not given in a rule, the rule may apply to sequences of segments which may or may not contain a morpheme boundary (we will explain why in Chapter 6). Thus, the above rules may be written as /b/ → [β] / V__V, where the expression V__V will cover the environments V__V, V + __V, and V __ + V. A rule which contains a '+' will require a morpheme boundary to be present.

So far, so good: the analysis is perfectly plausible, and it certainly works for our three cases. What we must do, however, is to *test* the hypothesis; that is, to try to show that it is false, by looking for disconfirming evidence. It is clear that this analysis is disconfirmed by the data here. With /ki + bati/, the prefixing of /ki/ to the stem /bati/ does not produce [ciβati], as our analysis predicts. Nor do the stops in /daha/, /ɟeɟele/ or /gunija/ change to approximants when a prefix ending in a vowel is added. So we either abandon the hypothesis or modify it. We could modify it to suggest that phonological voiced stops are realised as approximants *only* when a morpheme boundary follows the first vowel, but that will not solve our problem: the stops in /ludaha/, /ɟeɟele/ and /gunija/ all occur after a morpheme boundary. So we will abandon the hypothesis.

Let us then pursue the second hypothesis. Here, we suggest the representations /βua/, /li/ and /jo:jo/. Looking for a conditioning phonetic context, we can suggest that the occurrence of a nasal stop before the approximant will change it to a stop. Recall that nasal stops have a stricture of complete closure within the oral cavity, and thus it is reasonable to see this process as one of assimilation in manner of articulation. This analysis will require the three rules:

(4)

/β/ → [b] / m__
/l/ → [d] / n__
/j/ → [ɟ] / ɲ__

Now, when we come to test this hypothesis, there is nothing in the available data which will disconfirm it. The point, however, is that we can say exactly what *would* count as counter-evidence: the existence in the language of words which invariably have a stem-initial approximant, regardless of whether it is preceded by a prefix ending in a vowel or one ending in a nasal. For our analysis insists that such approximants must *always* be realised as stops after nasals.

In the absence of any such disconfirming evidence, we will take it that the second hypothesis is right, and thus we will represent these three plural forms as /zi + n + ß ati/, /zi + n + li/ and /zi + n + jo:jo/. Notice that there is a kind of *mutual dependency* between the nasal prefix and the stem-initial segment: the place of articulation of the nasal prefix depends on the place of articulation of the stem-initial segment, which in turn depends for its manner of articulation on the nasal.

2.3 Morphophonological Alternations

The point in going over this data in such depth is to convey the exact details of the *method* by which we analyse such phenomena. We have now looked at two cases of variation in Lumasaaba nouns and one of variation in the phonetic form of an English prefix. They all serve to illustrate a very common feature of the organisation of human languages: when the phonological forms of two or more morphemes are combined to form a word, this may result in changes in the phonetic realisation of the phonemes which compose those forms. This phenomenon of contextually determined variation in the realisation of morphemes is referred to as **morphophonological alternation**. Where we find that morphemes vary in their phonetic realisations in this way, we refer to the allomorphs as **alternants**. The expression 'morphophonological' is used since this phenomenon is a matter of phonological processes being set off as a consequence of the building up of words from morphemes. The concept of 'alternation' is of considerable importance in phonology; it will be central to many of the issues we shall be examining in the chapters that follow. The following exercise is designed to help you to understand the notion by applying the method we have just adopted.

A. *Hungarian* (data from Vago 1980a)

1.	[kalap]	'hat'	[kalabban]
2.	[rab]	'prisoner'	[rabban]
3.	[kuṭ]	'well'	[kuḍban]
4.	[kaḍ]	'tub'	[kaḍban]
5.	[zak]	'sack'	[zagban]
6.	[meleg]	'warm'	[melegben]
7.	[res]	'part'	[rezben]
8.	[viz]	'water'	[vizben]
9.	[lakaʃ]	'apartment'	[lakaʒban]
10.	[varaʒ]	'magic'	[varaʒban]

Morphological notes

The words in the right-hand column all have a suffix morpheme meaning 'in'. There are two allomorphs for this morpheme: [ben] and [bɑn]. You may ignore this fact for the purposes of this exercise.

(a) In some of the nouns, the root morpheme has two allomorphs. What are these, and what property of which segment in the root alternates?
(b) There are two obvious possibilities for the phonological representation of such morphemes. What are these?
(c) Write the rule which must accompany each representation in order to yield the phonetic representations.
(d) You now have two general hypotheses about the nature of these alternations. Test them against the entire body of data. Which is falsified?

2.4 Choosing between Analyses

A different kind of choice faces us in other cases. In the case given in the previous section, we simply chose the analysis which was not falsified by the data. There are other cases, however, where all of the hypotheses under consideration will be compatible with the data. In cases like these, we may find one analysis more simple than another, for instance, or more plausible phonetically. Take the following example of Polish nouns:

(5) *Polish nouns* (data from Rubach 1984)

	Nominative		**Diminutive**	**Augmentative**
1.	[kɐpeluš]	'hat'	[kɐpeluśik]	[kɐpeluśisko]
2.	[ɐrkuš]	'sheet'	[ɐrkuśik]	[ɐrkuśisko]
3.	[kontuš]	'nobleman's overcoat'	[kontuśik]	[kontuśisko]
4.	[groš]	'monetary unit'	[grośik]	[grośivo]

The distinction between alveolar, post-alveolar and pre-palatal places of articulation is *phonemic* in Polish fricatives and affricates; thus, Polish has /š/ and /ś/. By contrasting the nominative forms with the others, we can see that each root has two alternants: [kapeluś] and [kapeluš], for instance. There are therefore two principal ways of representing the root phonologically; in this instance, /kapeluś/ and /kapeluš/. Taking the first of these, we will need to formulate a rule which changes /ś/ to [š] in the appropriate environment. The only obvious environment is at the end of a word. The rule would therefore look like this:

(6)

/š/ → [š] / ___#

Taking the second hypothesis, we can suggest that /š/ becomes [ś] before a high front vowel, thus:

(7)

/š/ → [ś] / ___i

Looking over the data, we see that neither hypothesis is disconfirmed. The first one says that (voiceless) pre-palatal fricatives are realised as post-alveolar fricatives word-finally; the second says that (voiceless) post-alveolar fricatives are realised as pre-palatals before a high front vowel. Now, since the vowel [i] is articulated in the palatal area, it seems perfectly plausible to suggest that a post-alveolar sound should assimilate partially to a following palatal sound, becoming pre-palatal. The second rule thus has a high degree of phonetic plausibility. The same cannot be said for the first rule: there is no clear phonetic sense in which a word boundary should induce a pre-palatal to move forward to the post-alveolar place of articulation. We will therefore opt for the second analysis, on the grounds of phonetic plausibility. Try using this criterion in the following exercise.

B. *Polish* (data partly from Rubach 1984)

	Nominative singular		Locative singular
1.	[pɐs]	'belt'	[pɐśe]
2.	[rɐz]	'time'	[rɐźe]
3.	[brɛt̪]	'brother'	[brɛće]
4.	[cud̪]	'miracle'	[cuje]
5.	[d͡zvon̪]	'bell'	[d͡zvońe]

Phonetic notes

For a description of [ś], [ź], [ć], [j] and [ń], see p. 4 on pre-palatals.

The phonological form of the locative singular morpheme is /ie/; under certain conditions, a rule applies to it which deletes the /i/. For our purposes here, you should assume an /ie/ form for this suffix.

(a) State two possible phonological forms for each of the noun roots.
(b) Write the rules which will have to accompany each phonological representation to give the phonetic representations.
(c) Say which analysis is preferable, and why.
(d) There is a generalisation to be made about the set of rules you have decided on. What is it?

2.5 Deletion and Insertion

The rules we have written thus far all involve changing some segment to another, but not all rules have that function. It was just mentioned, in passing, that the /i/ in the suffix /ie/ in Polish gets elided (is not uttered) in certain cases. This phenomenon of **elision** of segments is a very common one, and we express it by writing rules in which the segment in question is deleted. In our Polish case, the rule would look like this:

/i/ → 0 / ___e

Here, the symbol '0' means 'zero', and we interpret the rule thus: /i/ is deleted when immediately followed by /e/. The converse process of elision is **epenthesis**, in which a segment is inserted in a specific environment. This process would be represented by a rule of the form:

0 → [i] / ___e

We will see that both of these rule formats will be useful in our analyses. Try using the rule format for deletion in the following exercise.

C. English (RP)
In the data on p. 14, the realisations of the /r/ phoneme in Lowland Scots can be given, somewhat informally, by the following rule:

/r/ → $\left\{ \begin{array}{l} [\underset{\circ}{r}] \ / \ \text{voiceless stops} \underline{\quad} \\ [r] \ / \ \text{voiced consonants} \underline{\quad} \end{array} \right\}$

The realisations of the /r/ phoneme in RP, given in the adjoining column in that data, are [ɹ], [ɻ] and 0 in 12–15. That is, there is deletion in 12–15 (compare them with the Lowland Scots forms in 12–15). Write a rule which gives the realisations and their governing contexts.

If the data on p. 14 seems insufficient to you, the following transcriptions of English words as uttered in an RP accent should help:

1. (a) [bɑ:]   (bar)   (b) [bɑ:ɹɪŋ]   (barring)
2. (a) [pʰʊə]   (poor)   (b) [pʰʊəɹə]   (poorer)
3.   [pʰɔ:d]   (poured)   4. [fɜ:tɪv]   (furtive)
5.   [bɜ:gə]   (burger)   6. [pʰɑ:zɪŋ]   (parsing)

2.6 The Ordering of Rules

We have proceeded thus far by segmenting words into their component morphs and then proposing and testing hypotheses about the phonological representations for the morphemes in question, and the rules we would need to accompany them. We have referred to this combination of representation and rule as an analysis. What needs to be stressed now is that the notion of hypothesising and testing which we use to arrive at an analysis is all-important. So much so that, in many cases, we cannot set about the segmentation of words into their component morphs without *presupposing an analysis*. This is a perfectly reasonable thing to do, as we will see shortly, but it is crucial that we *notice* when we have done this, and what it is we have presupposed. We must also notice what *follows* from the claims we make with our rules and representations. Engaging in phonological analysis is thus very much a matter of being aware of what one is claiming, and what one is committed to. We can see this in the analysis of the following nouns in Xhosa (a Bantu language spoken in Southern Africa).

(8) *Xhosa nouns* (data from Boyce 1834)

Nominative		**Partitive**	
1. [udaka]	'mud'	2. [kudaka]	
3. [ubuso]	'face'	4. [kubuso]	
5. [ukutja]	'food'	6. [kukutja]	
7. [ihashe]	'horse'	8. [kwihashe]	
9. [iŋkosi]	'chief'	10. [kwiŋkosi]	
11. [izitja]	'basket'	12. [kwizitja]	
13. [abantu]	'people'	14. [kubantu]	
15. [amadoda]	'men'	16. [kumadoda]	

The nouns in the left-hand column consist of two morphemes: the first vowel is a class prefix and the following part is the root. Thus 1 can be analysed as [u + daka], 3 as [u + buso], and so on (the '+' is used informally here to show an analysis into morphs of a phonetic representation). The words in the right-hand column consist of a partitive prefix, followed by the class prefix (except for 2, 4, 6, 14 and 16 where it is elided), followed by the root. The 'partitive' morpheme expresses the meaning 'some of'. Let us make the assumption that it has the two allomorphs [ku] and [kw]. Thus, 2 can be analysed as [ku + daka], 8 as [kw + i + hashe], and so on. If this is so, there are two ways of representing this morpheme phonologically: /ku/ and /kw/. With /ku/, we will need a rule like this:

(9)

/u/ → [w] / __i

With /kw/, we will need the following rule:

(10)

/w/ → [u] / __C

(We shall use the symbol 'C' to mean 'any consonant'.)

The rule which has /u/ being realised as [w] is the more phonetically plausible of the two. To ascertain that this is so, you might try uttering sequences of [u] and [i] fairly quickly, and listening to what happens: in making the transition from [u] to [i], it is easy to utter the [u] as a [w], especially if the two are uttered as a single syllable with [i] as the most salient element. In other words, [w] and [u] are almost identical in articulatory terms, but often differ in the role they play in syllable structure: [w] may occur as a kind of non-syllabic version of [u].

Adopting this analysis, we still need to account for the elision of the class prefix /a/ in 14 and 16, and the class prefix /u/ in 2, 4 and 6. For 14 and 16, we could write a rule which would delete the /a/ when it is preceded by a vowel, thus:

(11)

/a/ → 0 / V__

(We will use the symbol 'V' to mean 'any vowel'.) And for 2, 4 and 6, we could then write another deletion rule which deletes /u/ when it is preceded by a vowel:

(12)

/u/ → 0 / V__

But let us assume that there is a more general rule at work here, which states that any vowel is deleted when preceded by another vowel:

(13)

$$V \rightarrow \emptyset \ / \ V\_\_$$

(We will see that the order of application of this rule and our rule for the [w] and [u] allophones of /u/ is crucial.)

In generalising the left-hand side of the rule to include any vowel, we express a more general claim about the phonology of this language. Another way of expressing this generalisation is to say that the second of two adjacent vowels is elided. From this generalisation, it will follow that class prefixes are elided when the preceding prefix ends in a vowel. Let us assume that, in checking this generalisation out against further data from Xhosa, we find that it is not falsified. When we succeed in getting a particular phenomenon to follow from a generalisation in this way, we may claim to have given an *explanation* of the phenomenon.

Explanation is thus very much a matter of showing how particular states of affairs follow from general principles. It will be our goal throughout this book to try to show how the particular (*the data*) follows from the general (*the rules*). Our aim, you will recall, is to build up a picture of the generalisations in terms of which phonetic data are decoded.

Notice that, in allowing for this analysis, we allow that the class prefix morphemes, such as /a/ in 13 and 15, and /u/ in 1, 3 and 5, each have two allomorphs, thus:

(14)

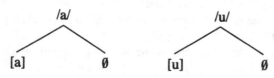

That is, we allow for **zero morphs**, where $\emptyset$ counts as a 'zero realisation' of the morpheme. Here, we have alternations between [a] and $\emptyset$ and between [u] and $\emptyset$. We say that [a] alternates with $\emptyset$ and [u] with $\emptyset$. The symbol '~' is used to express the meaning 'alternates with', as follows: [a]~$\emptyset$, and [u]~$\emptyset$.

This analysis (let us call it Analysis A) seems perfectly feasible. We arrived at it in this way: the representation /ku/ was preferred over /kw/, on the grounds of the phonetic plausibility of the rules needed for /ku/. And the rules which went with /ku/ expressed a simple generalisation.

But having decided on /ku/ as the phonological form of the prefix, there is a question that might still be raised. We have been working with the assumption that we analyse the words in 2, 4 and 6 as [ku + daka], [ku + buso] and [ku + kutja], with the vowel in the class prefix deleted.

We might equally have analysed those forms as [k + u + daka], [k + u + buso] and [k + u + kutja], where the /u/ of the /ku/ prefix has been deleted.

This would mean allowing for *three* allomorphs of the partitive morpheme: [k], [kw] and [ku]. Let us call this Analysis B. The question raised is this: is the [u] in 2, 4 and 6 the realisation of the /u/ in /ku/? Or is it the realisation of the /u/ in the class prefix /u/? Under Analysis B, we would have the following rule deleting the /u/ of /ku/ in 2, 4 and 6:

(15)

/u/ → 0 / ___u

There is a clear advantage in adopting Analysis A. If Analysis B is correct for 2, 4 and 6, then there is a problem with 14 and 16: there, the class prefix /a/, in [a + bantu] and [a + madoda], has undeniably been deleted. Analysis B would require us to write a rule deleting the class prefix in 14 and 16. This would mean that Analysis B is less simple than Analysis A, and less general: in A, we say simply that the /u/ of /ku/ becomes [w] before /i/, and that the class prefix vowels delete following the vowel of /ku/.

Under B, we have to say that the /u/ of /ku/ deletes *only* before /u/, becomes [w] before [i], and is retained before [a]. Under this analysis, [a] is the *sole* class prefix to be deleted. Clearly, this is more complex and less general than Analysis A. Where we are faced with a choice of this sort, we will prefer the more simple and general analysis.

The simple generalisation about vowel deletion contained in Analysis A is appealing: it shows why the class prefix vowels are elided when the prefix /ku/ is attached. Note that this generalisation depends crucially on the notion that [w] does not count as a vowel, so that, in the case of 8, 10 and 12, we may say that the class prefix does not delete because it is not preceded by a vowel, but by [w].

It is also important to note that this more simple analysis *commits* us to the claim that the rule /u/ → [w] applies *before* the rule deleting the class prefix vowel. If 8, 10 and 12 have the phonological form /ku + i + hase/, as we are claiming, then they are subject to the generalisation which states that the second of two adjacent vowels is elided. That is, they are subject to our rule (let us call it Rule 1):

(16) *Rule 1*

V → 0 / V___

If the rule /u/ → [w] / ___ i (call it Rule 2) applies before Rule 1, it will prevent Rule 1 from applying where the class prefix is /u/ (because in those cases, /u/ → [w], which is not a V). This notion of **rule ordering** will prove to be of considerable importance to us. It is a notion which arises as a consequence of the way we have been speaking of phonology and phonetics: once we acknowledge that there is a systematic distinction to be made between phonological representation and phonetic representation, and that phonological rules mediate between the two, the possibility of the ordering of rules arises. In our Xhosa case, we may view the mapping process in this way:

(17)

Phonological representation (/ /)

↓

Rule 2

↓

Rule 1

↓

Phonetic representation ([ ])

The idea is that we derive the phonetic representation from the phonological representation by applying the rules. Consequently, we refer to the process as a **derivation**. This notion of derivations in phonology is of great importance; we will return to it in more depth in due course.

Note the way in which we proceeded with this problem. We needed a preliminary segmentation of phonetic representations into their component morphs, in order to get started on proposing and testing hypotheses. We did this, analysing forms like [kubuso] as [ku + buso], and then proceeding from there. But this preliminary segmentation *presupposed* an analysis in which the class prefix /u/ is elided. It is clear therefore that we do not always start absolutely from scratch, but often incorporate hypotheses into our most fundamental starting point. This means that hypothetical notions will determine, to a certain extent, what the 'facts' are that we are seeking to account for.

This relationship between hypothesis and fact is of particular interest; it rather undermines the everyday notion that facts and theories are two entirely different sorts of thing. Its importance therefore extends well beyond the domain of linguistics. An awareness of it will almost certainly help you to tackle phonological problems. The following exercise requires this kind of awareness.

D. Japanese /t/ allophones (data from Hinds 1986)
The phoneme /t/ in Japanese has at least the three allophones [t], [t͡s], and [č]. From the following words, say what different environments the [č] and [t͡s] allophones occur in.

1.	[taʦɯ]	'stand'	2.	[teʦɯ]	'iron'
3.	[toɾɯ]	'take'	4.	[čiba]	'Chiba'
5.	[ʦɯči]	'dirt'	6.	[jaɾimiči]	'gravel road'

(a) What is the phonological form of the word for 'dirt'?

(b) Write the phonemic rule for the realisation of the allophones of /t/.

Now look at the Japanese verb forms below and answer the questions.

E. *Japanese verbs* (data from Hinds 1986)

	Stem	Gloss	Past	Conditional	Provisional
1.	[maʦɯ]	'wait'	[matta]	[mattaɾa]	[mateba]
2.	[ʦɯkɯɾɯ]	'build'	[ʦɯkɯtta]	[ʦɯkɯttaɾa]	[ʦɯkɯreba]
3.	[jomɯ]	'read'	[jonda]	[jondaɾa]	[jomeba]
4.	[jobɯ]	'call'	[jonda]	[jondaɾa]	[jobeba]
5.	[ʃinɯ]	'die'	[ʃinda]	[ʃindaɾa]	[ʃineba]

Morphological notes

1. The 'conditional' morpheme has the form /ɾa/; conditional forms are created by adding this as a suffix to the 'past' form.
2. Where affixes are added to a form which consists of a root plus one or more affixes, we refer to the resulting form as a **stem**; the term is not crucial in this exercise. The forms in the first column can be analysed as consisting of a root followed by the vowel /ɯ/.

(a) Which morph signals the 'provisional' morpheme? What are the two allomorphs of the 'past' morpheme?

(b) The root morpheme 'wait' has two alternants. What are they? What does your rule for the realisations of /t/ in Exercise D above suggest for their phonological form?

(c) The root morpheme 'build' also has two alternants. What are they? There are two good candidates for the phonological representations for this morpheme. What are they? For each, write the rule needed to accompany it. Say why both analyses are phonetically plausible. One of the analyses is falsified by the data. Which one?

(d) The root morphemes 'read' and 'call' each have two alternants. What are they? For the two alternative phonological forms of each morpheme, write the appropriate phonemic rule which will yield the alternants. One analysis is clearly preferable to the other. Which one, and for what reasons?

2.7 Concluding Remarks

In adopting the notion that phonemic representations are mapped on to phonetic representations by means of a set of phonological rules, we have been able to express significant generalisations about the way morphophonological alternations work. We have also committed ourselves, in depicting phonological organisation in this way, to the idea that phonological rules may apply in a stated order. This has allowed us to make considerable headway in our principal task of expressing significant generalisations. In the next chapter, we will try to extend the means available to us for this task.

EXERCISES

1. *Lac Simon* (an Algonquin language spoken in North America; data from Kaye 1981)

1.(a)	[te:ʃɨbɨwa:gɨn]	'chair'	(b)	[nɨde:ʃɨbɨwa:gɨn]	'my chair'
2.(a)	[či:ma:n]	'canoe'	(b)	[oiǰ:ma:n]	'his canoe'
3.(a)	[pi:goʃka:]	'it breaks'	(b)	[ki:bi:goʃka:]	'it broke'
4.(a)	[ʃo:ʃkose:]	'it slides'	(b)	[niʒo:ʃkose:]	'I slide'

Morphological notes
Assume that each of these forms counts as a word in this language. Assume too that the prefix [nɨ]/[ni] in 1(b) and 4(b) signals first person singular, that [o] in 2(b) means 'his', and that [ki:] in 3(b) signals 'past' tense. You should also assume that there is no morph meaning 'it' in 3(a), 3(b) and 4(a).

(i) Comparing the (a) forms with the (b) forms, it is clear that each of the morphemes meaning 'chair', 'canoe', 'break' and 'slide' has two allomorphs. What are these? Which phonetic property of which segment changes from one alternant to the other?

(ii) What are the two rather obvious hypotheses concerning this alternation?

(iii) For each of the two analyses, write the phonemic representations for the morphemes, and, for each one, the phonemic rule which will mediate between these and the phonetic representations.

(iv) How do the two analyses fare, in terms of simplicity and phonetic plausibility? Is there any evidence against either analysis? How do the following data bear on your response?

1.(a)   [kɨn]   'bone'   (b)   [nɨkɨn]   'my bone'
2.(a)   [ʃogona:]   'nose'   (b)   [kɨʃogona:] 'your nose'
3.(a)   [towɨk]   'ear'   (b)   [nɨtowɨk]   'my ear'
4.(a)   [kon]   'liver'   (b)   [okon]   'his liver'
5.(a)   [ka:t]   'leg'   (b)   [nɨka:t]   'my leg'

2. *Maori*

The following (much discussed) data from Maori exemplify active and passive verb forms, and derived gerundives (data from Hale 1973 and Sanders 1990):

	Active	Passive	Gerundive	Gloss
1.	[afi]	[afitia]	[afitaŋa]	'embrace'
2.	[hopu]	[hopukia]	[hopukaŋa]	'catch'
3.	[mau]	[mauria]	[mauraŋa]	'carry'
4.	[inu]	[inumia]	[inumaŋa]	'drink'
5.	[tohu]	[tohuŋia]	[tohuŋa]	'point out'
6.	[kimi]	[kimihia]	[kimihaŋa]	'seek'
7.	[patu]	[patua]	[patuŋa]	'kill/strike'
8.	[kite]	[kitea]	[kiteŋa]	'see/find'

We ignore active/passive pairs like [aroha]/[arohaina] and [tahu]/[tahuna], which result from the application of a rule which switches round sequences of morpheme-final non-labial nasals and front vowels when the nasal is preceded by a vowel that differs from the high vowel in backness.

One analysis of the data, widely referred to, following Hale (1973), as the 'conjugation analysis', claims that there are at least seven passive suffixes (/-tia/, /-kia/, etc.; more accurately, there are twelve: we show only seven here) and six gerundive suffixes (/-taŋa/, /-kaŋa/, etc.). Under this analysis, we would say that verbs fall into classes in Maori, such that the speaker must know the class of the verb in order to know which passive (or gerundive) suffix it takes. This analysis claims that Maori verbs are rather like verbs in French, in which one has to know which of three conjugational classes a verb belongs to in order to determine which inflections it takes.

(i)   It is known that, in Maori, words cannot end in a consonant. In the light of this fact, can you suggest an alternative analysis (let us call it, again following Hale (1973), the 'phonological analysis'), which postulates a single phonemic representation for the passive suffix, and a single phonemic representation for the gerundive suffix? Ignore the gerundive form of 'point out', which is accounted for by a rule which we will not examine here.

(ii) Your analysis will have included a rule which will mediate between the phonemic and phonetic representations of the verb roots. You will need another rule to yield all the alternants of the suffix morphemes. What does that rule do?

(iii) Which analysis do you prefer, and why?

3. *Korean* (data from Pyun 1987)

In this chapter, we considered cases where a morpheme has two (or more) alternants, and we assumed that one of these corresponded to the phonemic representation. A further logical possibility exists: that the phonemic representation of a morpheme may not correspond to *any* of its alternants. This exercise requires you to consider that possibility (the implications of which we will consider in Chapters 6 and 7).

Examine the alternations in the root-final consonants of the following Korean words:

1. (a) [pap˥] 'cooked rice'
   (b) [pap˥k*wa] 'cooked rice and'
   (c) [pabi] 'cooked rice' (subjective)

2. (a) [jəp˥] 'side'
   (b) [jəp˥č*ari] 'next seat'
   (c) [jəpʰə] 'to the side'

3. (a) [tat˥t*a] 'closes'
   (b) [tadara] 'close it!'

4. (a) [pat˥] 'field'
   (b) [pat˥s*ai] 'between fields'
   (c) [patʰe] 'in the field'

5. (a) [čʰɛk˥] 'book'
   (b) [čʰɛk˥t*o] 'book also'
   (c) [čʰɛk˥p*an] 'bookshop'
   (d) [čʰɛgi] 'book' (subjective)

6. (a) [puək˥] 'kitchen'
   (b) [puək˥k˥wa] 'kitchen and'
   (c) [puəkʰe] 'in the kitchen'

Phonetic notes

1. The diacritic [˥] denotes an unreleased stop.
2. The diacritic [*] denotes an articulation with glottal tension; this is not relevant for this exercise.

Bearing in mind that the aspirated vs unaspirated distinction is phonemic among Korean stops and affricates, suggest competing analyses (representations and rules) for the roots. Say which is to be preferred and why. Note that there are no voiced stops in the Korean phonemic system.

Further Reading

There is a great deal of literature on the subject of morphophonological alternations, but much of it cannot profitably be approached by the new student at this stage. Lass (1984a), Chapter 4, covers the issues in more detail.

For more exercises on alternations, see the end of chapter exercises in Kenstowicz and Kisseberth (1979), Chapter 3, and the Section 2 exercises in Halle and Clements (1983).

3 Features, Classes and Systems

3.1 Expressing Generalisations

In examining the voiced stops and approximants in Spanish, we saw (see p. 24) that the distinction between them is allophonic, and accordingly, we wrote three rules which expressed the contexts in which the allophones of the bilabial, dental and velar phonemes occurred:

(1)

/b/ → [β] / V__V
/d̪/ → [ð] / V__V
/g/ → [ɣ] / V__V

Our claim was that a native speaker of Spanish perceives [b] and [β] as instances of the same thing, and likewise [d̪] and [ð], and [g] and [ɣ]. We said in Chapter 1 that the rules we write should express the generalisations the speaker has unconsciously acquired. Expressing our claim in terms of three rules therefore amounts to claiming that the speaker has acquired three different generalisations concerning, respectively, the bilabials, the dentals and the velars. Do you agree that there is something unsatisfactory about this? We can make a single, more general, statement about these stops and approximants in Spanish: in this language, voiced stops are realised as approximants intervocalically, regardless of their place of articulation.

We can see that our set of three phoneme-based rules implicitly *suggests* this in three ways: firstly, the environments on the right-hand sides of the rules are identical. That is, each rule redundantly repeats the same environmental information for each phoneme. Secondly, each rule has a voiced stop symbol on the left-hand side. Thirdly, on the right-hand side of each rule, there is an approximant. Thus, although the notion that stops are realised as approximants intervocalically is *implicit* in our set of three rules, it is not expressed *explicitly*. We have said that rules express generalisations; since there is really only a single generalisation to be made here, then we need a single rule which will express it.

Here we come upon a major limitation of the phonemic notation we have been using: what we want to say is that place of articulation plays no part in the generalisation. We want our rule to express a generalisation about two *classes* of sounds, the voiced stops and approximants, rather

53

than three individual phonemes. With the notation we have been using, this is impossible: symbols like /b/ are unitary; that is, they have no internal structure: they represent, not component properties of sounds, but combinations of articulatory properties (here, bilabiality, voicing and complete closure). In order to make statements about *classes* of sounds, we need to be able to decompose segments into their *component properties*. The purpose of this chapter is to achieve this by adopting a set of phonetic *features* denoting the articulatory components which together constitute the production of speech sounds (in some cases, the features will denote acoustic properties of speech sounds). These are, we will assume, the features upon which both contrastive and allophonic distinctions in languages may be made.

We have said that symbols like /b/ act as representations of phonological units, and symbols like [b] as representations of phonetic units. The rules we have devised make reference to such representations; more exactly, we said that they map one kind of representation on to another (they show us how the phonemic units are realised phonetically). What we require, in order to express generalisations like the one concerning Spanish voiced stops and approximants, is a different *sort* of representation, expressed in terms of features. If we then write our rules in terms of these features, they will map our feature-based phonological representations onto feature-based phonetic ones, just as our phoneme-based rules mapped phonemic representations onto phonetic representations. Note that, in seeking a new, feature-based form for our rules and representations, we are not abandoning the important notions of contrast and allophonic variation which are so central to the phonemic insight; rather, we are seeking to retain those notions while expressing generalisations which the phonemic notation did not allow us to express.

3.2 Features (i)

In setting about our task, we will first of all need to distinguish the two broadest categories of segments: consonants and vowels. The term 'consonant' may convey two sorts of notion. Firstly, we may speak of consonants as being typically non-syllabic: there are probably no human languages which do not have vowels functioning as the **nucleus** of the syllable, in combination with consonants as non-syllabic segments (segments which do not constitute the nucleus of a syllable). Thus, in the monosyllabic English word *beat*, it is the vowel which is the nucleus of the syllable; the stop consonants are non-syllabic. Secondly, we describe consonants in terms of our three degrees of stricture, and only one of these (open approximation) applies to vowels. Most consonants are therefore characterised as having a more radical stricture than vowels. This means that approximants are consonants in terms of their function in syllables in many languages, but are like vowels in their stricture: in the English word *yes*, the approximant is like a vowel which is non-syllabic (thus the term 'semi-vowel'). Our features will have to express this.

Let us adopt a feature **[syllabic]** ([syll] for short) and give it a value, either '+' or '−', such that a [+syll] segment functions as a syllabic nucleus, whereas a [−syll] segment does not. All vowels will therefore be [+syll], and consonants will normally be [−syll]. Where we encounter syllabic consonants, as in a great many people's pronunciation of the English word *button* ([bʌtn̩]), we will either write phonological rules which change [−syll] consonants to [+syll] under specific conditions (as in this case, where a vowel has been elided), or mark them as [+syll] in phonological representations (in languages which have words with consonants which are invariably syllabic).

We will use the feature **[consonantal]** ([cons] for short) to characterise the degree of stricture shared by all consonants except approximants. Segments which are [+cons] are defined as having a radical constriction in the oral cavity, where 'radical' means any stricture from close approximation to complete closure. Thus, all vowels will be [−cons], and all consonants except for approximants will be [+cons].

This means that all approximants are [−cons, −syll]. Thus, in Spanish, the approximants [β], [ð] and [ɣ], which are allophones of the voiced stop phonemes /b/, /d/ and /g/, are [−cons], which helps to reflect the assimilation process: voiced stops in Spanish become vowel-like ([−cons]) between vowels. However, they are still functioning as consonants, as far as their function in the syllable is concerned (they are not syllabic nuclei), and the designation [−syll] expresses this. The attraction of this designation is that it expresses our notion that approximants are 'semi-vowels', i.e. non-syllabic vowels.

An important assumption we will be making is that any segment in any language, once it reaches the level of phonetic representation, will be represented with a '+' or '−' value for each and every feature (later in this chapter, we will propose features in phonological representations which are not marked for values). The idea is that we can identify an exhaustive set of features which will act as a kind of universal stock of properties upon which human language phonologies are built. However, in this book, we will not be identifying all of the features necessary for this task, and in any case, we will soon express some reservations about the wisdom of marking each segment in a language with a value for each and every feature described here.

We will need to distinguish voiced and voiceless segments; let us use the feature **[voice]** for the former distinction, with [+voice] denoting voiced sounds and [−voice] denoting voiceless sounds. For this feature, we will assume a definition of voicing which states that voiced segments are characterised by a regular vibration of the vocal cords; for our purposes, this will be a satisfactory definition.

In examining subclasses of consonants, we will need to distinguish **obstruents** (the class of oral stops, affricates and fricatives) from **sonorants**. This latter class is usually taken to subsume the nasal stops and the 'liquids', /r/ and /l/. While there is good reason for identifying such a class, it is problematical. Firstly, the range of segment types we might represent phonologically as /r/ is very varied, and may, in a given language, consist solely of obstruents. Secondly, laterals are a problem. They are like stops in that they often involve closure, but unlike stops in that this closure is not complete: it allows lateral escape of airflow. We return to this matter shortly. For this distinction between obstruents and sonorants, we will adopt the feature **[obstruent]**, with obstruents being [+obs] and sonorants being [−obs]. Let us assume that the feature can be adequately defined in terms of the acoustic properties of obstruents (the details of the definition concern the properties of the wave forms of the acoustic energy generated in producing obstruents). We might alternatively have defined and adopted the feature [sonorant], thus classifying the obstruents as [−son]. The choice is arbitrary; you will encounter the feature [son] in supplementary reading you may do, but it should not cause you any difficulty.

Among the class of obstruents, we want to distinguish stops from fricatives; we will say that fricatives differ from stops in that the airflow through the central ('mid-sagittal') area of the oral cavity is not totally blocked at any point during their production. We will use the feature **[continuant]** to represent this: segments produced with this kind of airflow are [+cont]. In stops, the opposite is true: there is a sustained blockage in this area. Thus, oral and nasal stops are [−cont], while vowels, fricatives and approximants are [+cont]. Our definitions of [+cons] and [+cont] are such that if a segment is [−cons], i.e. does not have a radical constriction in the oral cavity, then it follows that it will be [+cont], with the airflow through the central area not totally blocked at any point. That is, the designation [−cons] *implies* [+cont]. We will return to this notion of implicational relations between feature specifications later.

If we are to assume that approximants are [−cons] and thus [+cont], how do we characterise *lateral* approximants? In our Lumasaaba case (see p. 37), we saw that {/ɓ/, /l/, /j/} functioned as a class of segments which are realised as the non-continuants {[b], [d], [ɟ]} after nasal stops. Since nasal stops are [−cont], it seems most plausible to say that it is this property to which the following approximant assimilates: the [+cont] segments in this class become [−cont] after a nasal stop. Now, we have said that approximants are [−cons, −syll], and that [−cons] segments will, by definition, be [+cont]. So, in the Lumasaaba case, a class of [−cons, −syll] (and thus [+cont]) segments become [+cons, +obs, −cont] after nasal stops. This commits us to saying that, in this case at least, lateral approximants are [+cont], just like other approximants. According to our definition, however, they are [−cont]. Lateral approximants are odd in that they involve both closure in the central region and absence of closure at the sides of the tongue; we will have to allow that, because of this, they may function as [−cont] segments (as they seem to in Lowland Scots: see Chapter 4).

Note too that affricates could be viewed as being [−cont] if the closure phase is 'sustained' but [+cont] if not; it depends very much on what is meant by 'sustained' in our definition. Let us assume that affricates are [−cont]. This would accord with the idea (see p. 4) that they are, phonetically, slowly released stops. If this is so, then stops and affricates may be distinguished by a feature **[delayed release]**, where affricates are [+del rel] and stops (and all other segments) are [−del rel].

We can now sum up, on the basis of the features we have introduced thus far, our characterisation of some of the main classes of consonants:

(2)

	Stops	**Affricates**	**Fricatives**	**Approximants**
cons	+	+	+	−
syll	−	−	−	−
obs	+	+	+	−
cont	−	−	+	+
del rel	−	+	−	−

Among the affricates and fricatives, we can distinguish those which are characterised by the presence of high frequency noise; we will use the feature **[strident]** here, taking [+stri] sounds to have high frequency noise, and [−stri] to lack it. Like our feature [obs], this has an acoustic definition (whose details are somewhat problematical). The feature will distinguish fricatives and affricates as follows:

(3)

	Bilabial	Labiodental	Dental	Alveolar	Palato–alveolar	Palatal	Velar	Uvular
	ɸ, β	f, v	θ, ð	s, z, t͡s, d͡z	ʃ, ʒ, č, ǰ	ç, ʝ	x, ɣ	χ, ʁ
stri	−	+	−	+	+	−	−	+

What of taps and trills, of the sort we considered in Farsi, Lowland Scots and Spanish? Trills present us with something of a problem: their articulation does involve a stricture of complete closure, and airflow is thus blocked, which suggests a [−cont] specification, but the blockage involved is intermittent (see p. 3). Let us assume that they are not obstruents, but sonorants ([−obs]), and that they are [+cont].

Taps are also somewhat problematical with respect to the feature [cons], and thus [obs] and [cont]: the blockage involved is very brief in duration. We will assume that taps are [−obs, −cont]. Thus, in Spanish, the trill [r] will be distinguished from [ɾ] in that the former is [+cont] and the latter is [−cont]. We will assume that what distinguishes [ɾ] from [d], as in Lowland Scots, where these are phonemically distinct, is the feature [obs]: the voiced alveolar tap [ɾ] is [−obs, −cont] whereas the voiced alveolar stop [d] is [+obs, −cont]. This characterisation of voiced taps seems to undermine our notion (cf p. 3) that they are like 'short' stops, since it denies that they are obstruents at all, but it does bring out the manner of articulation property ([−cont]) shared by stops and taps. Further support for this characterisation of voiced taps comes from intervocalic realisations of the /t/ allophone in some American and Scottish accents of English, where /t/ is realised as a voiced alveolar tap in words like *matter*. We can say that, in these cases, the voiceless stop assimilates to the surrounding vowels in becoming [+voice], and [−obs], while retaining its non-continuant, i.e. [−cont], property.

But what about the voiced post-alveolar approximant [ɹ] which is so common in English accents, and occurs alongside the tap [ɾ] in Lowland Scots? If approximants are [−cons, −syll], then this approximant will differ from the alveolar tap, trill and stop with respect to those feature specifications. We can summarise our distinctions between voiced alveolar taps, approximants, trills and stops thus:

(4)

	[ɾ]	[ɹ]	[r]	[d]
cons	+	−	+	+
syll	−	−	−	−
obs	−	−	−	+
cont	−	+	+	−

There is one further property, of voiceless obstruents, notably stops, which we need to characterise: aspiration. We will adopt the feature **[aspirated]**, defining aspiration as *voice onset delay* (see p. 7), with [+asp] segments being characterised as possessing this property, and [−asp] as not possessing it. We ought to mention in passing that, while it would be true to say of voiced obstruents that they are [−asp], that is because, with this definition of aspiration, they could not *in principle* be [+asp].

What of the sonorants? This class of segments contains vowels, approximants (both lateral and central), nasals, and taps and trills, as we have seen. We may distinguish between the laterals and all the others by using the representation **[+lateral]**, where this denotes lateral escape of airflow; all non-lateral segments are of course [−lateral]. We will also use **[+nasal]**, where this denotes velic opening, to pick out the nasal stops and any other nasalised segments, with all other non-nasal segments being [−nasal]. Note that the difference between [l] and [ɹ] in our characterisation, is that the lateral approximant [l] is [−cons, −syll, +lat], whereas [ɹ] is [−cons, −syll, −lat]; that is, they are both approximants, but differ only as to whether the airflow escapes laterally or not. This minimal distinction is appealing; the two sounds create a similar acoustic effect, and are frequently substituted one for the other in historical change. In those languages which lack one of the two sounds, e.g. [ɹ], it is often the segment [l], rather than any other in the language, which is substituted.

We will treat the approximant [w] just as we treated the approximants /ʁ/, /l/ and /j/ earlier: as [−cons, −syll]. We may say that [w] and [j] often function like non-syllabic versions of the vowels [u] and [i]. They will therefore have the same feature specification as [u] and [i], except that the latter are [−cons, +syll] and the semi-vowels are [−cons, −syll].

3.3 General Remarks

A few general comments are in order before we proceed further. Firstly, note that we are not adopting features of the sort [+stop] or [+fricative]. That is because, in adopting such features, we would defeat the object of the exercise: the two classes 'stop' and 'fricative' simultaneously *belong* to the class of obstruents and *are distinguished* by their manner of articulation. Fricatives and stops are subclasses of obstruents, and our adopted features express this. A feature like [+stop] would conflate these component properties of obstruency and non-continuancy, just as the representation /b/ conflates voicing, place and manner of articulation. But it is precisely this which we are seeking to avoid!

Secondly, it is clear that, to pick out the class of stops, we will need the combined designation [+cons, +obs, −cont, −del rel], and for the class of fricatives, [+cons, +obs, +cont, −del rel]. That is, it will require only two features, [+cons] and [+obs], to denote the set of obstruents, but *four* features to denote either of its subsets. Thus, the more general the set, the fewer the number of features we will require to isolate it.

Thirdly, although it is true that each segment in a language will be given a value for every feature by the time it reaches the level of phonetic representation, there will be a certain amount of redundancy in such representations. Fricatives, for instance, will have the designation [−del rel] in phonetic representation. But fricatives could not ever be [+del rel] *in principle*: there is no closure involved in producing fricatives, and thus no possibility of the release phase found in stops; there can therefore be no possibility of delayed release of closure. Our problem here is similar to that with the specification [−asp]: voiced obstruents cannot in principle be

[+asp]. We will therefore shortly propose a set of statements which are located in the grammar of each language, which express such relationships between feature values, and consequently avoid marking those features for values in underlying representations.

3.4 Features (ii)

The features given thus far denote, among other things, voicing state and manner of articulation, but we will need to distinguish segments with respect to place of articulation. For place of articulation distinctions, it is clear that we need to be able to pick out the entire range of places described in the phonetics revision chapter, any classes among those segment types, and the different points in the vowel space.

Let us distinguish between two general classes of segment on the basis of their place of articulation: those articulated in front of the palato-alveolar region and those articulated in or behind it. We will use the feature **[anterior]** here, defining the former class as [+ant] and the latter as [−ant]. Thus, pharyngeals, uvulars, velars, palatals and palato-alveolars are all [−ant], and bilabials, labiodentals, dentals and alveolars are all [+ant]. The use of this feature will become clear in due course.

Let us then isolate what we will call the 'neutral' position of the tongue: we will define this as the position of the tongue in the vowel [ə], where the front lies slightly higher than the blade, which slopes down towards the bottom of the mouth, just behind the lower gum. We may distinguish segments articulated with the blade of the tongue raised above its neutral position from those where this does not happen. In the phonetics revision chapter we defined place of articulation mostly according to the passive articulator; this feature concerns the active, rather than the passive articulator, but clearly it is nonetheless to do with place rather than manner. We will say that segments articulated in this way are **[+coronal]**, and this class will subsume the dentals, alveolars, retroflexes and palato-alveolars. The [−cor] segments are the bilabials, labiodentals, palatals, velars, uvulars and pharyngeals.

Before we introduce further feature definitions, let us see how such features operate in the phonology of a language we have already looked at. In Polish, we saw (see p. 40) that the dental and alveolar phonemes /s/, /z/, /t̪/, /d̪/ and /n̪/ are realised as the pre-palatals [ś], [ź], [ć], [j] and [ń] in alternations between nominative singular and locative singular forms of nouns. No segment outside of this class undergoes this alternation. That is, the bilabials, post-alveolars and velars are not involved. If we characterise these classes of Polish consonant with respect to our features [cor] and [ant], their values are as follows:

(5)

	Bilabial	Dental	Alveolar	Post-alveolar	Pre-palatal	Velar
ant	+	+	+	−	−	−
cor	−	+	+	+	+	−

It is clear that only dentals and alveolars are [+ant, +cor], and it is that class of segments alone which undergoes this alternation with the pre-palatals. The designation [+ant, +cor] will pick out exactly the class of segments affected by the rule.

We now continue with our feature definitions. Recall the point made in Chapter 1 (see p. 25) concerning the sorts of phonetic link we often find between allophones and their contexts. We saw, for instance, that in Lumasaaba the palatal stops [c] and [ɟ] are allophones of, respectively, the phonemes /k/ and /g/, in the context of a following /i/ or /e/. We can make articulatory sense of this: what is fundamentally a velar segment, articulated high up and at the back of the oral cavity, gets fronted, i.e. assimilates to, a following vowel which is articulated in the palatal region. If our feature system can reflect this, that would be a major gain. One of the aims of requiring of our features that they all hold for each and every segment, and thus for both consonants and vowels, is to express this kind of connection; we will see that in the case of the Spanish approximants, we are able to reflect the phonetic connection between the approximants and their inter-vocalic environment. We will also see that we can reflect the allophone/environment connection in the case of the Lumasaaba palatal stops too.

The connection is that high front vowels and palatals have two shared articulatory properties: they are both articulated high up in the oral cavity, with the front of the tongue. We will designate these properties as [+high] and [−back]. Segments which are [+high] are produced with the body of the tongue raised above what we have called the neutral tongue position. The feature [+back] defines segments which are articulated with the body of the tongue retracted from this neutral position; [−back] segments do not possess this property. Thus, palatals are [+high] and [−back], as are high front vowels. A similar connection exists between velars and high back vowels: both are [+high, +back].

Just as we used the feature specification [+high] to pick out segments articulated with the body of the tongue raised above the neutral position, so we will use [+low] to characterise those articulated with the body of the tongue lowered from the neutral position. All low vowels will thus be represented as [+low]. Note that, while velars are [+high], and thus [−low], uvulars are [−high] and [−low]. The uvular stop [q], for instance, is articulated with the body of the tongue lower than it is in [k].

What about pharyngeal consonants, which involve a retraction of the tongue root which pulls down the body of the tongue from the neutral position? Pharyngeals are arguably [+low], and consequently [−high], but it is quite possible that we need another feature to characterise the properties of retracted tongue root and constriction of the pharynx, in order to characterise properly pharyngeals and pharyngealisation in consonants and vowels; we will not pursue this, however.

We must distinguish rounded vowels from unrounded vowels. Let us adopt the feature **[round]** for such distinctions: vowels with lip rounding are [+round], and those without are [−round]. Thus, in French, for instance, the [−round] front vowels [i], [e] and [ε] will be distinguished from their [+round] counterparts [y], [ø] and [œ] by their values for this feature. Pairs of front, unrounded and back, rounded vowels will also be differentiated phonetically by means of this feature, but in many cases, the feature specification [+back] will imply [+round]; we will return to this kind of implication later.

How are we to characterise central vowels, such as [ɨ], [ʉ], [ə] and [ɐ]? With the definition of 'neutral tongue position' (the position for [ə]) which we have adopted, we can say that front vowels are articulated with the tongue body forward of the neutral position, and are thus [+front]. We may say that central vowels are articulated with the tongue body neither advanced nor retracted from the neutral position: they are [−front, −back]. As well as allowing us to pick out the central vowels, as opposed to either the front or the back vowels, this would allow us to specify the central vowels with the back vowels as a class, by means of the specification [−front], and with the front vowels as a class, by means of the specification [−back]. However, it is remarkable how few phonological analyses seem to require reference to the feature [front], and we will in practice often omit reference to it.

What about mid vowels like [e], [o], [ɔ] and [ε]? Let us assume that these will be characterised as being [−high, −low]. The trouble with this characterisation of mid vowels, however, is that languages often have four distinct vowel heights. In Lowland Scots, for instance, the following are all phonemically distinct: [i], [e], [ε], [ɐ], [ɔ], [o], [ʉ]. We might depict them as a system, in the form of a diagram which covers points in the vowel space as follows:

(6)

i		ʉ
e		o
ε		ɔ
	ɐ	

Lowland Scots is similar to French in this respect, except that French has a series of front rounded vowels in addition to the front unrounded ones, thus:

(7)

y   i   u

ø   e   o

œ   ɛ   ɔ

We must seek another feature which distinguishes high-mid and low-mid vowels. Let us reconsider the vowel space: while we have represented it as a trapezium (see p. 11), we acknowledge that this is a rather idealised representation. A less idealised one would look like this:

(8)

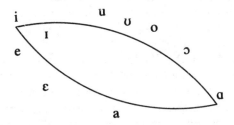

Now, imagine the effect on vowel articulations if the *root of the tongue* were to be pushed forward: it could result in raising and/or fronting a given vowel articulation. This can be demonstrated if we consider the many vowel systems which subdivide into two subsystems, according to this parameter. In Akan, a Kwa language spoken in Ghana, these two subsystems are:

(9)

i   u   ɪ   ʊ

e   o   ɛ   ɔ

                      ɑ

There are many alternations in the language which involve pairs of vowels taken from these sets. Thus, the word for 'nest' is [ebuo], and consists of a root [bu], with a vowel from the first set, and with affixes [e] and [o], also from the first set. The word for 'stone', on the other hand, is [ɛbʊɔ], where the root [bʊ] has the vowel [ʊ], which is from the second set, and the form of the affixes changes: [ɛ] instead of [e], [ɔ] instead of [o]. Clearly, the affix vowels display the alternations [e] ~ [ɛ], and [o] ~ [ɔ]. And what determines the shape of the affix vowel is the shape of the root vowel: if the root vowel is from the first set, so are the affix vowels, and vice versa.

Each vowel in the first set corresponds to an 'opposite number' in the second set; the difference is that the vowels in the first set are articulated with the tongue root advanced. We will adopt a feature [+**Advanced Tongue Root**] ([+ATR] for short) to designate this property. Thus, we can say that if the root in an Akan word has a [+ATR] vowel, so will its affixes, and if the root vowel is [−ATR], then its affixes will be [−ATR] (it is a little more complex than this, but we will pursue those complexities in Chapter 10).

Let us then distinguish our high-mid and low-mid vowels in terms of this feature: [e] and [o] in Lowland Scots, or French, will be [+ATR], and [ɛ] and [ɔ] are [−ATR].[1]

To sum up our characterisation of vowels, here is a table giving the feature specifications for many of the vowels you are likely to come across, using just the features we have been discussing for vowels:[2]

(10)

	i	ɪ	e	ɛ	a	ɑ	ɔ	o	ʊ	u	ɯ	y	ø	œ	ɐ	ə	ɨ	ʉ
high	+	+	−	−	−	−	−	−	+	+	+	+	−	−	−	−	+	+
low	−	−	−	−	+	+	−	−	−	−	−	−	−	−	+	−	−	−
ATR	+	−	+	−	+	−	−	+	−	+	+	+	+	−	−	−	+	+
back	−	−	−	−	−	+	+	+	+	+	+	−	−	−	−	−	−	−
front	+	+	+	+	+	−	−	−	−	−	−	+	+	+	−	−	−	−
round	−	−	−	−	−	−	+	+	+	+	−	+	+	+	−	−	−	+

In addition to these features, we saw that, in Tai, vowel length is phonemic; it is allophonic in Lowland Scots, as we will see. Both phonemic and allophonic vowel length are very common. Let us use the feature [**long**] to characterise this difference; long consonants or vowels will be [+long], while their short counterparts will be [−long]. This approach to consonant and vowel length is inadequate, for reasons we will return to later, and will have to be reconsidered. For the moment, it will suffice.

Two segments we have not characterised so far are the glottal stop [ʔ] and the glottal fricative [h]. There is a sense in which the glottal fricative [h] is 'not a full consonant'. The same could be said for the glottal stop [ʔ]. This is because they are articulated *in the glottis*: [h] involves close approximation between the vocal cords, while [ʔ] involves complete closure then release of the vocal cords. Now, the distinctions we have been making between segments concern place and manner of articulation in the oral cavity, but neither of these segments is articulated there! They are 'not full consonants' in the sense that they have no values for any of the oral cavity features.

Furthermore, the one feature we have introduced which does not concern the oral cavity is [voice], but even this feature is irrelevant to the characterisation of [h] and [ʔ], since we cannot 'overlay' vocal cord vibration on glottal sounds: [+voice] and [−voice] are states of the glottis, but so are [h] and [ʔ]! As a solution to this problem, let us use the feature specifications [+cons, +cont] for [h], and [+cons, −cont] for [ʔ], to express the sense in which these are, respectively, a fricative and a stop, and then mark both segments with the value '−' for every other feature. We see here even more clearly the drawbacks of insisting that every feature be marked for a value; what we are doing here is using '−' to mean 'not relevant', or 'valueless' and that is not what '−' means in a two-valued system. Nor do these specifications accord with our definitions of the features [cons] and [cont]; they are defined for constriction in the oral cavity. However, they will suffice as an *ad hoc* solution until we address the issue in more depth at a later stage.

To sum up, here are the feature specifications for obstruents and sonorants (which are repeated on pp. 305–6 for ease of reference):

(11) *Obstruents*

```
         p t̪ t c k q b d̪ d ɟ g G  t͡s d͡z č ǰ ɸ f θ s ʃ ś ç x χ β v ð z ʒ ź j ɣ ʁ
cons     + + + + + + + + + + + +   + + + + + + + + + + + + + + + + + + + + + +
syll     − − − − − − − − − − − −   − − − − − − − − − − − − − − − − − − − − − −
voice    − − − − − − + + + + + +   − + − + − − − − − − − − − + + + + + + + + +
obs      + + + + + + + + + + + +   + + + + + + + + + + + + + + + + + + + + + +
cont     − − − − − − − − − − − −   − − − − + + + + + + + + + + + + + + + + + +
del rel  − − − − − − − − − − − −   + + + + − − − − − − − − − − − − − − − − − −
asp      − − − − − − − − − − − −   − − − − − − − − − − − − − − − − − − − − − −
lat      − − − − − − − − − − − −   − − − − − − − − − − − − − − − − − − − − − −
nas      − − − − − − − − − − − −   − − − − − − − − − − − − − − − − − − − − − −
ant      + + − − − − + + − − − −   + + − − + + + + − − − − − + + + + − − − − −
cor      − + + − − − − + + − − −   + + + + − − + + + + − − − − + + + + − − − −
high     − − − + + − − − − + + −   − − − − − − − − − + + + − − − − − − + + + −
low      − − − − − − − − − − − −   − − − − − − − − − − − − − − − − − − − − − −
back     − − − − + + − − − − + +   − − − − − − − − − − + + − − − − − − − − + +
round    − − − − − − − − − − − −   − − − − − − − − − − − − − − − − − − − − − −
stri     − − − − − − − − − − − −   + + + + − + − + + + − − + − + − + + + − − +
```

(12) *Sonorants*

	m	n	ɳ	ɲ	ŋ	N	ß	w	ʋ	ð̞	ɹ	j	ɣ	ɰ	l	ɭ	ʎ	r	R	ɾ	ɽ
cons	+	+	+	+	+	+	−	−	−	−	−	−	−	−	−	−	−	+	+	+	+
syll	−	−	−	−	−	−	−	−	−	−	−	−	−	−	−	−	−	−	−	−	−
voice	+	+	+	+	+	+	+	+	+	+	+	+	+	+	+	+	+	+	+	+	+
obs	−	−	−	−	−	−	−	−	−	−	−	−	−	−	−	−	−	−	−	−	−
cont	−	−	−	−	−	−	+	+	+	+	+	+	+	+	+	+	+	+	+	−	−
del rel	−	−	−	−	−	−	−	−	−	−	−	−	−	−	−	−	−	−	−	−	−
asp	−	−	−	−	−	−	−	−	−	−	−	−	−	−	−	−	−	−	−	−	−
lat	−	−	−	−	−	−	−	−	−	−	−	−	−	−	+	+	+	−	−	−	−
nas	+	+	+	+	+	+	−	−	−	−	−	−	−	−	−	−	−	−	−	−	−
ant	+	+	−	−	−	−	+	+	+	+	+	−	−	−	+	−	−	+	−	+	−
cor	−	+	+	−	−	−	−	−	−	+	+	−	−	−	+	+	−	+	−	+	+
high	−	−	−	+	+	−	−	+	−	−	−	+	+	−	−	−	+	−	−	−	−
low	−	−	−	−	−	−	−	−	−	−	−	−	−	−	−	−	−	−	−	−	−
back	−	−	−	−	+	+	−	+	−	−	−	−	+	+	−	−	−	−	−	−	−
round	−	−	−	−	−	−	−	+	−	−	+	−	−	−	−	−	−	−	−	−	−

Now let us look at how our features function in rules and representations.

3.5 Features in Representations

With our phonemic representations, we could have depicted the vowel phoneme system of Greenlandic Eskimo (see p. 28) like this:

(13a)

/i/   /u/

/a/

In this kind of depiction, as in our display of French and Lowland Scots vowels, we arrange the phonemes in a layout which accords roughly with the vowel space notion, with front vowels to the left, back vowels to the right, and height depicted on the vertical axis. Now, we know that the phonetic vowel system of this language is:

(13b)

[i]   [u]

[e]   [o]

[a]

And we know that our rules (see p. 28) successfully mapped the /i/ and /u/

phonemes onto their *allophonic* realisations in (13b). What we want is to write a rule which will map the *feature specifications* of /i/ and /u/ onto the *feature specifications* of [e] and [o] in the appropriate contexts.

To do this, we must consider the consonants. We could have represented the consonant phoneme system in terms of place of articulation, manner of articulation and voicing, as follows:

(14)

	Bilabial	Alveolar	Palatal	Velar	Uvular
Stops	p	t		k	q
Fricatives	β	s		ɣ	ʁ
Nasals	m	n	ɲ	ŋ	
Approximants		l	j		

With our feature-based representations, we will assume that, for each phonological segment in every language, we can give it a unique set of feature specifications, of the sort we have just seen in the tables at the end of the last section. For the phonemically distinct vowels in Greenlandic Eskimo, these will be (irrelevant features have been omitted):

(15)

	i	a	u
high	+	−	+
low	−	+	−
back	−	−	+
round	−	−	−

For the consonants, these will be:

(16)

	p	t	k	q	β	ɣ	ʁ	s	m	n	ɲ	ŋ	l	j
cons	+	+	+	+	+	+	+	+	+	+	+	+	−	−
syll	−	−	−	−	−	−	−	−	−	−	−	−	−	−
obs	+	+	+	+	+	+	+	+	−	−	−	−	−	−
cont	−	−	−	−	+	+	+	+	−	−	−	−	+	+
voice	−	−	−	−	+	+	+	−	+	+	+	+	+	+
nas	−	−	−	−	−	−	−	−	+	+	+	+	−	−
lat	−	−	−	−	−	−	−	−	−	−	−	−	−	+
cor	−	+	−	−	−	−	−	+	−	+	+	−	+	−
ant	+	+	−	−	+	−	−	+	+	+	−	−	−	−
high	−	−	+	−	−	+	−	−	−	−	+	+	−	+
low	−	−	−	−	−	−	−	−	−	−	−	−	−	−
back	−	−	+	+	−	+	+	−	−	−	−	+	−	−

Your phonemic analysis of the Eskimo data on p. 28 should have suggested, for the word [tikeq] ('index finger'), the representation /tikiq/, with a phonemic rule of the form:

(17)

$$/i/ \rightarrow [e] \ / \ \underline{\quad} \ \left\{ \begin{matrix} q \\ ʁ \end{matrix} \right\}$$

The word meaning 'blubber', which has the phonetic form [oʁsoq], will have the phonemic representation /uʁsuq/, and the following rule will mediate between the representations:

(18)

$$/u/ \rightarrow [o] \ / \ \underline{\quad} \ \left\{ \begin{matrix} q \\ ʁ \end{matrix} \right\}$$

Let us consider the feature-based representations for these words. They are:

(19)

	t	i	k	i	q	u	ʁ	s	u	q
cons	−	−	+	−	+	−	+	+	−	+
syll	−	+	−	+	−	+	−	−	+	−
obs	+	−	+	−	+	−	+	+	−	+
cont	−	+	−	+	−	+	+	+	+	−
voice	−	+	−	+	−	+	+	−	+	−
cor	+	−	−	−	−	−	−	+	−	−
ant	+	−	−	−	−	−	−	+	−	−
high	−	+	+	+	−	+	−	−	+	−
low	−	−	−	−	−	−	−	−	−	−
back	−	−	+	−	+	+	+	−	+	+
ATR	−	+	−	+	−	+	−	−	+	−
round	−	−	−	−	−	+	−	−	+	−

We want to map these representations onto the phonetic representations for these words: those phonetic representations will be the same as the phonological ones in all respects but the following: the second vowel in [tikeq] is an [e], which is a mid vowel, and the [o] vowels of [oʁsoq] are mid vowels. Since we define the mid vowels as [−high, −low], which distinguishes them phonetically from the high vowels [i] and [u], and the low vowel [a], we can see that it is the feature [high] which must change its

value if we are to make the mapping from these phonological representations onto the appropriate phonetic ones.

3.6 Features in Rules

Let us try writing the rule which will do this. It will have to pick out just the
class of vowels {/i/, /u/}. This class, as you will agree, is the class of high
vowels in this language. Do you agree that we designate these alone by
means of the feature specifications [+syll] and [+high]? By inspecting the
matrix of feature specifications for the consonants and vowels of
Greenlandic Eskimo, we see that only those two segments in this language
have that particular combination of features. That will then constitute the
left-hand side of our rule:

(20a)

$$
\begin{bmatrix} +\text{syll} \\ +\text{high} \end{bmatrix} \rightarrow
$$

We have said that the feature [high] must change. Thus, that will constitute
the next part of the rule:

(20b)

$$
\begin{bmatrix} +\text{syll} \\ +\text{high} \end{bmatrix} \rightarrow [-\text{high}] \ / \ \underline{\quad}
$$

We now need to pick out the class {q, ʁ}, that is the class of uvulars in this
language. If you inspect the feature specifications for the consonants of this
language, you will agree that these are [+cons, +back, −high]: that
combination of features picks out solely that class in this language. The
rule is therefore:

(20c)

$$
\begin{bmatrix} +\text{syll} \\ +\text{high} \end{bmatrix} \rightarrow [-\text{high}] \ / \ \underline{\quad} \begin{bmatrix} +\text{cons} \\ -\text{high} \\ +\text{back} \end{bmatrix}
$$

This rule will yield representations exactly like those above in all respects
but one: the value for the feature [high] will change from '+' to '−' for the

second vowel of /tikiq/ and both vowels of /uʁsuq/, and those phonetic representations will mean exactly what [tikeq] and [oʁsoq] mean. Note that the rule will not alter the value for the feature [high] in the first vowel in /tikiq/. That is because it is not followed by a segment which has the appropriate feature combination (i.e. it is not followed by a uvular).

The new rule is attractive for two reasons. Firstly, it expresses the *generalisation* not expressed by the two separate phonemic rules: that high vowels are lowered before uvulars. That is, there is a single rule at work here, not two, as our phonemic analysis wrongly suggests. Secondly, we can see that there is a clear phonetic motivation for this. The uvulars are articulated with the body of the tongue lower than it is for the velars, and this is parallel to the difference between the high vowels and the mid vowels. Our feature-based analysis is therefore attractive because it brings out this phonetic motivation.

Let us now see how we can rewrite our three phonemic rules (see pp. 23–4) for Spanish voiced stops and approximants as a single rule expressing a single generalisation. First, we need a matrix showing the feature specifications for the non-syllabic phonological segments of that language:

(21)

	p	ṭ	k	f	θ	s	x	č	b	ḍ	g	r	ɾ	l	m	n	ɲ
cons	+	+	+	+	+	+	+	+	+	+	+	+	+	−	+	+	+
syll	−	−	−	−	−	−	−	−	−	−	−	−	−	−	−	−	−
obs	+	+	+	+	+	+	+	+	+	+	+	−	−	−	−	−	−
cont	−	−	−	+	+	+	+	−	−	−	−	+	−	+	−	−	−
del rel	−	−	−	−	−	−	−	+	−	−	−	−	−	−	−	−	−
stri	−	−	−	+	−	+	−	+	−	−	−	−	−	−	−	−	−
voice	−	−	−	−	−	−	−	−	+	+	+	+	+	+	+	+	+
cor	−	+	−	−	+	+	−	+	−	+	−	+	+	+	−	+	−
ant	+	+	−	+	+	+	−	−	+	+	−	+	+	+	+	+	−
high	−	−	+	−	−	−	+	+	−	−	+	−	−	−	−	−	+

We know that the phonemes /b/, /ḍ/ and /g/ have the allophones [b] and [ß], [ḍ] and [ð̞], [g] and [ɣ], respectively. Compare their phonetic specifications:

(22)

	ß	ð̧	ɣ	b	ḑ	g
cons	−	−	−	+	+	+
syll	−	−	−	−	−	−
obs	−	−	−	+	+	+
cont	+	+	+	−	−	−
del rel	−	−	−	−	−	−
stri	−	−	−	−	−	−
voice	+	+	+	+	+	+
cor	−	+	−	−	+	−
ant	+	+	−	+	+	−
high	−	−	+	−	−	+

The two sets, as you can see, differ systematically in their values for the features [cons], [obs] and [cont]. To write the rule, we need, for the left-hand side, to pick out just the set of voiced stops. We can designate this set thus: [+cons, +obs, −cont, −del rel, +voice], but note that since the obstruents are a proper subset of the consonants, then [+obs] *implies* [+cons]; we may therefore omit the [+cons] designation from the rule. Note too that there is only one affricate in this language (the palato-alveolar [č]), and that it is voiceless; thus, the only [+del rel] segment is voiceless, and any [+obs, +voice] segment will be [−del rel]. That is, for this language, [+obs, +voice] *implies* [−del rel], and so we may omit [−del rel] from our rule too. Thus, instead of having the three representations /b/, /ḑ/ and /g/ on the left-hand sides of three rules, we will simply have:

(23a)

$$\begin{bmatrix} +\text{obs} \\ +\text{voice} \end{bmatrix} \rightarrow$$

Now, we have argued that it is the feature specification [+cons] which changes to [−cons] when the voiced stops appear between vowels. We will therefore state the feature which changes on the right-hand side of the rule. Since the class of vowels is distinguished by means of the designation [−cons], we may write the entire rule (let us call it Weakening) as:

(23b)

$$\begin{bmatrix} +\text{obs} \\ +\text{voice} \end{bmatrix} \rightarrow [-\text{cons}] \ / \ [-\text{cons}]\_\_\_[-\text{cons}]$$

We need not state [−obs] as a feature which changes its value, on the right-hand side of the rule, since, as we have seen, [−cons] *implies* [−obs].

Nor need we state [+cont] on the right-hand side of the rule, since [−cons] implies [+cont]. All other features remain stable for their values. This rule expresses the generalisation that voiced stops are realised as approximants between vowels. We know that the rule has a clear phonetic basis (cf p. 24), and our rule expresses this: it is the [−cons], and thus the [+cont] and [−obs], property of vowels to which the voiced stops assimilate.

Let us look at one more case where the use of features may help us to express an important generalisation. In Chapter 1 (p. 29), we argued that the nasal stop in the word *input* assimilates to the following /p/ and becomes [m]. It will also assimilate to a following stop which is velar, so that *incoming* has the phonetic form [ɪŋkʌmɪŋ]. The phonemic rule, which we can call Nasal Assimilation, would be:

(24)

$$/n/ \longrightarrow \left\{ \begin{array}{l} [m] \ / \underline{\quad\quad} \left\{ \begin{array}{l} p \\ b \end{array} \right\} \\ \\ [ŋ] \ / \underline{\quad\quad} \left\{ \begin{array}{l} k \\ g \end{array} \right\} \end{array} \right\}$$

What is wrong with this rule is that it does not express the relationship between (a) the stops within the brackets (they are at the same place of articulation) or (b) the place of articulation of the allophones and the place of articulation of the following stop. That is, it does not express the assimilatory nature of the process, which can be expressed by means of the generalisation: alveolar nasal stops assimilate in place of articulation to a following oral stop.

Let us see how the nasals are distinguished for place of articulation in their feature specifications:

(25)

	m	n	ŋ
ant	+	+	−
cor	−	+	−

On the left-hand side of the rule, we can pick out the alveolar nasal thus:

(26)

$$\begin{bmatrix} +\text{nas} \\ +\text{ant} \\ +\text{cor} \end{bmatrix}$$

For the right-hand side, we want to distinguish the bilabial and velar stops.

If we look at the following table of English stops, we can see how this will be done:

(27)

	p	b	t	d	k	g
ant	+	+	+	+	−	−
cor	−	−	+	+	−	−

The bilabials are [+ant, −cor], whereas the velars are [−ant, −cor]. The rule will therefore look like this:

(28)

$$
\begin{bmatrix} +\text{nas} \\ +\text{ant} \\ +\text{cor} \end{bmatrix} \longrightarrow
\left\{
\begin{array}{l}
\begin{bmatrix} +\text{ant} \\ -\text{cor} \end{bmatrix} \quad / \underline{\hspace{1cm}} \quad \begin{bmatrix} +\text{obs} \\ -\text{cont} \\ +\text{ant} \\ -\text{cor} \end{bmatrix} \\[2em]
\begin{bmatrix} -\text{ant} \\ -\text{cor} \end{bmatrix} \quad / \underline{\hspace{1cm}} \quad \begin{bmatrix} +\text{obs} \\ -\text{cont} \\ -\text{ant} \\ -\text{cor} \end{bmatrix}
\end{array}
\right\}
$$

Formulated in this way, the rule expresses the sense in which {p, b, m} and {k, g, ŋ} are classes with respect to place of articulation. It does not quite express the generalisation that the values for [ant] and [cor] in the nasal will be whatever their values are in the following stop, but we will rectify that in a later chapter.

In the following exercise, try applying the feature-based approach to your phonemic rules which front velar stops in Lumasaaba (see p. 26).

A. Lumasaaba
The phonemic rules you wrote for the realisations of the phonemes /k/ and /g/ in Lumasaaba were probably as follows:

(29)

$$
/k/ \rightarrow [c] \ / \ \underline{\hspace{0.5cm}} \left\{ \begin{array}{c} i \\ e \end{array} \right\}
$$

$$
/g/ \rightarrow [ɟ] \ / \ \underline{\hspace{0.5cm}} \left\{ \begin{array}{c} i \\ e \end{array} \right\}
$$

Clearly, there is a single generalisation to be expressed here: velar stops get fronted and become palatals before non-low front vowels. The generalisation does not make reference to voicing, but with our phonemic rules and representations, we cannot express it. Your task is to express this generalisation in the form of a rule written in distinctive features.

Firstly, here are the phonemic vowels of Lumasaaba:

(30)

	i	e	a	o	u
high	+	−	−	−	+
low	−	−	+	−	−
back	−	−	−	+	+
round	−	−	−	+	+

The consonant system is:

(31)

	p	t	k	f	s	z	b	d	g	ß	l	j	m	n	ɲ
cons	+	+	+	+	+	+	+	+	+	−	−	−	+	+	+
syll	−	−	−	−	−	−	−	−	−	−	−	−	−	−	−
obs	+	+	+	+	+	+	+	+	+	−	−	−	−	−	−
cont	−	−	−	+	+	+	−	−	−	+	+	+	−	−	−
voice	−	−	−	−	−	+	+	+	+	+	+	+	+	+	+
cor	−	+	−	−	+	+	−	+	−	−	+	+	−	+	−
ant	+	+	−	+	+	+	+	+	−	+	+	−	+	+	−
high	−	−	+	−	−	−	−	−	+	−	−	+	−	−	+
low	−	−	−	−	−	−	−	−	−	−	−	−	−	−	−
back	−	−	+	−	−	−	−	−	+	−	−	−	−	−	−

(a) We can see from this what the feature specifications for the velars /k/ and /g/ are. What will the feature specifications for the allophones [c] and [ɟ] be?

(b) To write the left-hand side of the rule, you will need to pick out just the class of velar stops, with as few features as possible. Try that.

(c) Decide which feature of the velar stops changes its value when they are realised as palatal stops and write this on the right-hand side of the rule.

(d) Now for the environment. Decide which combination of feature specifications will pick out just the class {/i/, /e/} and write that after the environment bar.

You now have the required rule. Check that it expresses the generalisation.

(e) Draw up the feature matrix for the phonological form of the word /kakese/ ('a small sheep'), which has the phonetic form [kacese]. Show how the rule works, explaining why the rule does not change the first /k/ to [c], but does change the second to [c].

(f) In what way does the rule reflect the phonetic motivation of the fronting process?

B. French

We saw in Chapter 1 that the /ʁ/ phoneme is realised as a voiced uvular approximant word-finally or before another consonant, as a voiceless uvular fricative after voiceless sounds, and as a voiced uvular fricative elsewhere.

(a) Given the following feature matrix for French consonants, write the rule, in features, which expresses this generalisation. Assume that the phonological specification of the segment corresponds to the 'elsewhere' form.

(32)

	p	t	k	b	d	g	f	s	ʃ	v	z	ʒ	l	ʁ	m	n	ɲ	j	w	ɥ
cons	+	+	+	+	+	+	+	+	+	+	+	+	+	+	+	+	+	−	−	−
syll	−	−	−	−	−	−	−	−	−	−	−	−	−	−	−	−	−	−	−	−
obs	+	+	+	+	+	+	+	+	+	+	+	+	−	+	−	−	−	−	−	−
cont	−	−	−	−	−	−	+	+	+	+	+	+	+	+	−	−	−	+	+	+
voice	−	−	−	+	+	+	−	−	−	+	+	+	+	+	+	+	+	+	+	+
ant	+	+	−	+	+	−	+	+	−	+	+	−	+	−	+	+	−	−	−	−
cor	−	+	−	−	+	−	−	+	+	−	+	+	+	−	−	+	−	−	−	−
high	−	−	+	−	−	+	−	−	−	−	−	−	−	−	−	−	+	+	+	+
low	−	−	−	−	−	−	−	−	−	−	−	−	−	−	−	−	−	−	−	−
back	−	−	+	−	−	+	−	−	−	−	−	−	−	+	−	−	−	−	+	−
round	−	−	−	−	−	−	−	−	−	−	−	−	−	−	−	−	−	−	+	+
nas	−	−	−	−	−	−	−	−	−	−	−	−	−	−	+	+	+	−	−	−
lat	−	−	−	−	−	−	−	−	−	−	−	−	+	−	−	−	−	−	−	−

Notes

You will, of course, have to work out the feature specifications for the voiced uvular approximant [ʁ] and the voiceless uvular fricative [χ].

The approximant [ɥ] will be new to you; just as [j] and [w] are like non-syllabic versions of [i] and [u], this segment is like a non-syllabic version of the high front, rounded vowel [y]; it appears in words like *huitre* ('oyster').

(b) There is something that seems odd, in terms of phonetic motivation, about the link between the approximant allophone and one of the environments. Can you say what this is?

3.7 Implicational Relationships

At several points in this chapter, we have appealed to the idea of one feature specification implying another. Let us distinguish two types of **implicational relationship**: the **universal** and the **language-specific**. Universal implications come about by virtue of the definitions we have given for the features. Thus, [+obs] will always imply [+cons]: obstruents are a subclass of the class of consonants. We may express this relationship in the form of a **feature co-occurrence restriction** (FCR),[3] as in the following (the arrow is interpreted as 'implies'):

(33)

[+obs] → [+cons]

Similarly, with the tongue height features [high] and [low], it will always be the case that [+high] implies [−low], and [+low] implies [−high]: the body of the tongue cannot simultaneously be raised and lowered from the neutral position, thus:

(34a)   (34b)

[+high] → [−low]   [+low] → [−high]

Language-specific implicational relationships depend on the system in a given language. We saw that, in Spanish, the fricatives in the system are all voiceless. Since the feature specification [+obs, +cont] picks out the fricatives, it follows that, in this language, [+obs, +cont] implies [−voice]: if a segment is a fricative in Spanish, it is voiceless. Thus, the grammar of Spanish contains an FCR of the form:

(35)

[+obs, +cont] → [−voice]

We shall see many more such relationships, and in due course we will consider them in more detail. In adopting such FCRs, we will take it that phonological representations in a language are left unspecified for values on such features, and this will considerably reduce the amount of redundant information present in the sorts of large feature matrix we have been presenting.

There is another sort of implication which involves what are referred to as 'unmarked' states of affairs. For instance, sonorants are almost always voiced in human languages; we may say that they are voiced 'in the unmarked case', and leave them unspecified for a value in underlying representations. We may express the implicational relationship between the two feature specifications [−obs] and [+voice] in a **default rule**:

(36)

[−obs] → [+voice]

By 'default specification', we mean a specification which applies unless there is some overt statement to the contrary. While it is true that sonorants are voiced in the unmarked case, there are other cases where the notion 'marked' proves problematical.[4] For instance, among the Lowland Scots vowels as given on p. 62, it is clear that if a vowel is [+round], it is [+back]: there are, we claimed, no front, rounded vowels in the system. It is very common to find that front vowels are unrounded and back vowels rounded; we may therefore propose that back vowels are rounded, and front vowels are unrounded, in the unmarked case (i.e. back, unrounded and front, rounded vowels are marked), as stated in the following default rule:

(37)

[−cons, −back] → [−round]

One of the difficulties with this notion of 'markedness' is that there are often many 'marked' cases in languages, which have been stable over long periods. The implicational relationship stated in (37) is not true of French, for instance: both front and back vowels may be [+round] in French (and indeed in many languages). Furthermore, the vowel we have represented as /u/ in Lowland Scots is very much fronted in certain accents. We will return to the idea of default rules in Chapter 8.

We have now introduced all of the features we will be using; we have assumed that there is a universal set of features which each language may draw on, although we have omitted several from the set, which characterise segments we will not be considering.

EXERCISES

1. Polish

In Exercise C in Chapter 1 (see p.18), you formulated a phonemic rule which devoiced /r/, let us say, when preceded by a voiceless consonant and followed by either a word boundary or another voiceless consonant:

$$/r/ \rightarrow [\r{r}] \ / \ \text{voiceless consonant} \ \underline{\hphantom{xx}} \ \left\{ \begin{array}{c} \# \\ \text{voiceless} \\ \text{consonant} \end{array} \right\}$$

Given the feature specifications for Polish consonants listed below, write the rule in features.

	p	b	t̪	d̪	k	g	t͡s	d͡z	č	ǰ	ć	ɉ	f	v	s	z	š	ž	ś	ź	x	m	n	ń	r	l	ł	w	j
cons	+	+	+	+	+	+	+	+	+	+	+	+	+	+	+	+	+	+	+	+	+	+	+	+	+	+	+	–	–
syll	–	–	–	–	–	–	–	–	–	–	–	–	–	–	–	–	–	–	–	–	–	–	–	–	–	–	–	–	–
obs	+	+	+	+	+	+	+	+	+	+	+	+	+	+	+	+	+	+	+	+	+	–	–	–	–	–	–	–	–
cont	–	–	–	–	–	–	–	–	–	–	–	–	+	+	+	+	+	+	+	+	+	–	–	–	+	+	+	+	+
del rel	–	–	–	–	–	–	+	+	+	+	+	+	–	–	–	–	–	–	–	–	–	–	–	–	–	–	–	–	–
stri	–	–	–	–	–	–	+	+	+	+	+	+	–	–	+	+	+	+	–	–	–	–	–	–	–	–	–	–	–
voice	–	+	–	+	–	+	–	+	–	+	–	+	–	+	–	+	–	+	–	+	–	+	+	+	+	+	+	+	+
ant	+	+	+	+	–	–	+	+	–	–	–	–	+	+	+	+	–	–	–	–	–	+	+	–	+	+	+	–	–
cor	–	–	+	+	–	–	+	+	+	+	+	+	–	–	+	+	+	+	+	+	–	–	+	+	+	+	+	–	+
back	+	+	+	+	+	+	+	+	+	+	–	–	+	+	+	+	+	+	–	–	+	+	+	–	+	+	+	+	–
high	–	–	–	–	+	+	–	–	–	–	+	+	–	–	–	–	–	–	+	+	+	–	–	+	–	–	–	+	+
low	–	–	–	–	–	–	–	–	–	–	–	–	–	–	–	–	–	–	–	–	–	–	–	–	–	–	–	–	–
lat	–	–	–	–	–	–	–	–	–	–	–	–	–	–	–	–	–	–	–	–	–	–	–	–	–	+	+	–	–
nas	–	–	–	–	–	–	–	–	–	–	–	–	–	–	–	–	–	–	–	–	–	+	+	+	–	–	–	–	–

Phonetic note

For reasons we will pursue later, all [+ant] segments in Polish are characterised as [+back], i.e. with the body of the tongue retracted. This is not relevant for this exercise.

An interlude concerning method

Your rule will need to pick out, with as few features as possible, just the segment /r/. How does one go about this task of arriving at a set of features which pick out just the segment(s) which undergo a rule? As a first step, you should think in universal terms. Classes and subclasses of segments can be thought of as follows: is the set of segments a class of consonants, or of vowels? If it is clearly a class of non-syllabic consonants, it will be [−syll]; if vowels, [+syll].

Let us say the class in question is [−syll]. That class can in turn be broken down into the two classes of obstruents ([+obs]), on the one hand, and sonorant consonants (which are [−obs]), on the other hand; these are usually taken to include the nasal stops and the 'liquids' /r/ and /l/.

Let us then say the class in question is a class of obstruents. We can then ask: is it a class of fricatives or not? If so, then [+cont]; if not, [−cont]. If it were [−cont], we need to ask whether it is a class of just stops or of stops and affricates. For the former, it will be designated with [−del rel]. Similarly, if the class is a class of sonorants, we will have to ask whether it is a class of nasal stops or not; the feature [nas] would work here, and in some cases, the feature [cont], since all nasal stops are [−cont]. We can represent this set of classes and subclasses like this:

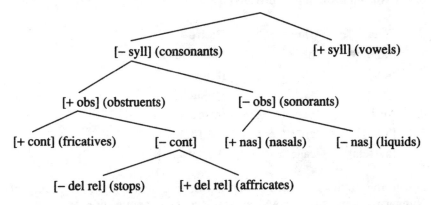

Let us say we've arrived at [−syll, +obs, −cont, −del rel] (stops) as the left-hand side for the rule. Since [+obs] implies [+cons], we can omit [+cons], on a universal basis.

That is the first step, and it gives you a universal feature characterisation of the class, or single segment, you are interested in. But there are no human languages which have all possible human language segments in their phonological inventory. So the next step is language-specific. That is where you look at the feature matrix for the language in question. If your rule applies to stops, but there are no affricates in the language, the feature [del rel] can be omitted from the rule. If there were no fricatives in the language (an unlikely event, but possible), then [−cont] could also be omitted from the rule, giving you [+obs] alone.

When you are dealing with a single segment, rather than a class containing more than one member, as in this Polish case, you would expect to have to use more features than you would for larger classes. But this need not be the case (in English, the lateral approximant alone can be picked out using just the feature [+lat], for instance). And in that kind of case, there will often be more than one means of picking out the relevant segment; this fact simply follows from the way phonological systems are organised. You may well be influenced in your choice by a desire to bring out the phonetic motivation of the rule.

2. *Hungarian* (data from Vago 1980a)

For the Hungarian exercises on p. 38, you needed six phonemic rules which showed that each of the voiceless obstruent phonemes, /p/, /t/, /k/, /f/, /s/ and /ʃ/, is voiced when followed by the voiced stop /b/. The phonemes /tʲ/, /t͡s/ and /č/ also undergo that process. In addition to /b/, the phonemes /d/, /g/, /gʲ/, /z/, /ʒ/, /d͡z/ and /ǰ/ also set off this voicing assimilation process. By looking at the following data, in which voicing assimilation does not take place, can you suggest a generalisation about which segments are involved in the voicing assimilation process?

	Stem	Gloss	Dative
1.	[kɑlɑp]	'hat'	[kɑlɑpnɑk]
2.	[kut]	'well'	[kutnɑk]
3.	[ʒɑk]	'sack'	[ʒɑknɑk]
4.	[res]	'part'	[resnek]
5.	[lakɑʃ]	'apartment'	[lakʃnɑk]
6.	[ketret͡s]	'cage'	[ketret͡snek]

Given the following feature matrix for the non-syllabic segments of Hungarian, write the rule which expresses the generalisation.

	p	t	k	b	d	g	tʲ	gʲ	f	s	ʃ	v	z	ʒ	t͡s	d͡z	č	ǰ	m	n	ɲ	l	r	w
cons	+	+	+	+	+	+	+	+	+	+	+	+	+	+	+	+	+	+	+	+	+	−	−	−
syll	−	−	−	−	−	−	−	−	−	−	−	−	−	−	−	−	−	−	−	−	−	−	−	−
obs	+	+	+	+	+	+	+	+	+	+	+	−	+	+	+	+	+	+	−	−	−	−	−	−
cont	−	−	−	−	−	−	−	−	+	+	+	+	+	+	+	−	−	−	−	−	−	−	+	+
del rel	−	−	−	−	−	−	−	−	−	−	−	−	−	−	+	+	+	+	−	−	−	−	−	−
voice	−	−	−	+	+	+	−	+	−	−	−	+	+	+	−	+	−	+	+	+	+	+	+	+
stri	−	−	−	−	−	−	−	−	−	+	+	−	+	+	+	+	+	+	−	−	−	−	−	−
ant	+	+	−	+	+	−	−	−	+	+	−	+	+	−	+	+	−	−	+	+	−	+	+	+
cor	−	+	−	−	+	−	+	−	−	+	+	−	+	+	+	+	+	+	−	+	−	+	+	−
high	−	−	+	−	−	+	+	+	−	−	−	−	−	−	−	−	−	−	−	−	+	−	−	+
low	−	−	−	−	−	−	−	−	−	−	−	−	−	−	−	−	−	−	−	−	−	−	−	−
back	−	−	+	−	−	+	−	+	−	−	−	−	−	−	−	−	−	−	−	−	−	−	−	+
nas	−	−	−	−	−	−	−	−	−	−	−	−	−	−	−	−	−	−	+	+	+	−	−	−
lat	−	−	−	−	−	−	−	−	−	−	−	−	−	−	−	−	−	−	−	−	−	+	−	−

Note

For reasons we will not pursue here, /v/ in Hungarian is characterised as [−obs], and /f/ and /v/ are characterised as [−stri]. The segments [tʲ] and [gʲ] are palatalised stops.

3. *Standard French and Brussels French* (data from Baetens-Beardsmore 1971)

(a) The Standard French vowel system is: /i, y, u, e, ø, o, ε, œ, ɔ, ɐ, ə/. Draw up a feature matrix which will distinguish the vowels, using [high], [low], [ATR], [back] and [round]. Treat /ɐ/ as [+back].

(b) The Brussels French vowel system (spoken by Flemish/French bilinguals) is: /ɪ, ʏ, ʊ, ε,œ, ɔ, ɑ, ə/. Draw up a feature matrix for this system, using the same features. Note that the vowel [ʏ] is a rounded [ɪ].

(c) A simple generalisation, referring to only one feature, can be about the difference between the two systems. What is it?

Notes

1. We ought to mention a problem in passing, although we will return to it later. It concerns the meaning of the specification [−ATR]. We want it to mean only that the tongue root is not advanced, and not that it is retracted. And yet it is undeniable that the term 'retracted' implies 'non-advanced'. There *are* segments which involve a retraction of the tongue root, such as pharyngealised consonants and vowels, of the sort found in Arabic, and we need a feature which will characterise them, but that feature may well have to be independent of the feature [ATR]. For the moment, we will continue to use the feature [ATR], with '+' and '−' values, to deal with vowels distinguished for that property, but we will eventually give a more satisfactory representation for such pairs of vowels.

2. You may well encounter the feature [tense] in further reading. We have avoided reference to that feature here because of difficulties in defining it. It is, however, widely used, to characterise long and short pairs of vowels, pairs like /iː/ and /ɪ/, and high vs low mid vowels, such as /e/ vs /ε/. It is perhaps simplest, for our purposes, if the reader equates [ATR] with [tense] (although such an equation is mistaken). See Lass (1976b) for criticism, and Wood (1975) for phonetic correlates of the feature.

3. The term is taken from Gazdar *et al.* (1985: 28). We do not adopt their term 'feature specification default' for our default rules, as they differ somewhat from those proposed by Gazdar *et al.* For more on defaults and redundancy, see Chapter 8.

4. Lass (1975) provides some trenchant critical remarks on the notion 'markedness'.

Further Reading

It is probably unwise for most students to begin examining alternative theories of distinctive features before getting the hang of the one presented here. Hyman (1975) provides a good overview of three such theories, none of which corresponds exactly to the one adopted here, which owes much to that given in Lass (1984a), Chapter 5. Hyman (1975) covers acoustically defined features, which we have avoided discussing here. Both Hyman and Lass deal with segment types which we have not covered in this book.

4 Problems with the Phonemic Principle

We saw in the last chapter that the phonemic rules and representations of Chapters 1 and 2 prevented us from expressing certain significant generalisations; the principal motive for adopting feature-based analyses was to allow our rules to express those generalisations. There are other ways in which generalising power is lost in the phonemic type of analysis we used in Chapters 1 and 2; let us see what those are, and how they can be overcome.

4.1 Contrast and Neutralisation

4.1.1 Spanish and Lumasaaba

The rules we wrote in Chapter 1 all concerned allophonic variation. For instance, we looked at a set of phonemic rules in Spanish, whereby the voiced stops /b/, /d̪/ and /g/ are realised as the approximants [β], [ð̪] and [ɣ] between vowels. In Chapter 2, we considered morphophonological alternations, and we wrote similar sorts of rule to account for those alternations. Thus, in Lumasaaba, the voiced stops [b], [d] and [ɟ] alternate with the approximants [β], [l] and [j]: morpheme-initial voiced approximants are realised as stops when preceded by a nasal. But it might be argued that there are two different *sorts* of rule involved in the analyses we proposed in those two chapters.

Take the status of the approximants in Spanish: [β], [ð̪] and [ɣ] are allophones of /b/, /d̪/ and /g/. Thus, [b] can never be contrastive with [β]. Compare that situation with the one we found in Lumasaaba (p. 34): there, the bilabials [b] and [β] are contrastive, as are [d] and [l], [ɟ] and [j]. That is, Lumasaaba, unlike Spanish, has the approximant phoneme /β/, as well as the voiced stop phoneme /b/. Now, since /b/ is realised as [b] in Lumasaaba, and /β/ is realised as [β] or [b], what we are dealing with here is a kind of *overlapping*: a given occurrence of [b] may be a realisation of /b/ *or* of /β/. What this means is that, in Lumasaaba, we will never encounter the approximants [β], [l], and [j] after nasal stops. There are contexts in which either may occur (between vowels, for instance), and because of this parallel distribution, they may function contrastively. But that contrast is said to be **neutralised** (or suspended) immediately following a nasal stop. We say that this context is a *neutralising* context. We may also refer to the kind of rule which induces this sort of neutralisation as a **neutralisation rule**. This notion of neutralisation is important, and we will return to it in Chapters 6 and 8. Its importance for those chapters, and for this one, concerns the status of the phonemic principle; let us see how.

In Lumasaaba, the operation of the rule means that, in the word [zimbua] ('dogs'), the [b] is a realisation of /ß/ (the underlying representation for 'dog' is /ß ua/), whereas in [zimbati] ('knives'), the [b] is a realisation of /b/ (the underlying representation for 'knife' is /bati/). Clearly, this does not cause problems for speakers of Lumasaaba: just as speakers of English readily interpret the [m] in *input* as a realisation of /n/, and the [m] in *man* as a realisation of /m/, so speakers of Lumasaaba interpret [b] in two different ways. In both cases, it is the combination of the underlying representations and the rule system which allows this to happen.

There is an important sense in which the rule for the realisations of Lumasaaba /ß/ is different from the rule for Spanish /b/. In Lumasaaba, the two realisations are contrastive in other contexts, and thus phonemically distinct in the language, whereas in Spanish they are not. That is, the Spanish rule is not a neutralising rule. This is an important fact when it comes to considering the phonemic principle. To maintain that principle, we *must* distinguish between neutralising rules and rules, like the Spanish one, which yield only allophonically distinct segments. According to the phonemic principle, once we have established that two (or more) sounds are in parallel distribution and contrastive, we must represent them as realisations of different phonemes. Because, in Lumasaaba, [b] and [ß] satisfy these criteria, they are clearly realisations of /b/ and /ß/, respectively. From the phonemic point of view therefore the rule which mediates between alternants like [bua] and [ß ua] is a rule which mediates between /b/ and /ß/.

Phonemic theory refers to the latter sort of rule as a **morphophonemic (MP) rule**, and the former as a strictly **phonological (P) rule**. The MP rule yields the representations /b/ and /ß/, whereas the P rule yields the representations [b] and [ß]. This means allowing for a level of representation above the level of the phoneme, referred to as the *morphophonemic* level of representation. Phonemic theory adopts a **morphophonemic representation** which represents the properties of bilabiality and voicing which the /b/ and /ß/ phonemes in Lumasaaba share. Let us use the representation /B/ for this. The MP rules map this level on to the phonemic level, with P rules mapping the phonemic level on to the phonetic, like this:

(1)

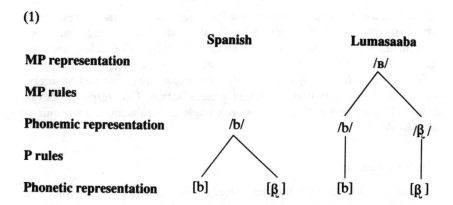

	Spanish	Lumasaaba
MP representation		/ʙ/
MP rules		
Phonemic representation	/b/	/b/ / β̞ /
P rules		
Phonetic representation	[b] [β̞]	[b] [β̞]

The idea is that, in Lumasaaba, the MP rule maps the uppermost level of analysis on to the phonemic level, whereas the P rule maps the phonemic level on to the allophonic level. Thus, in the Spanish word [ɐβ ɛr], which has the phonological representation /ɐbɐr/, there is no question of any morphophonological alternation taking place, whereas in the Lumasaaba sort of case, there is.

It is clear that there is a distinction to be made between neutralising rules and non-neutralising rules, and in phonemic theory, that distinction *must* be made: the theory, based on the criteria of parallel distribution and contrast, requires it. But let us consider whether such a distinction results in a gain or a loss of generalising power. The rule for the realisation of Spanish voiced stops is purely phonological in cases like /ɐbɐr/. But consider a word like /boḍegɐ/ which is realised, we said, as [boðeɣɐ]. There is no doubt that our single rule (see p. 71) will cause each of the voiced stops /ḍ/ and /g/ in the phonological representation to be realised as approximants, since they occur between vowels. Now, this phonetic representation for the word is correct in a phrase like *unas bodegas* ('some bodegas'), but not in a phrase like *la bodega* ('the bodega'), which is realised phonetically as [lɐβ oðeɣɐ], with the /b/ of /boḍegɐ/ realised as a [β̞].

It is easy enough to see why the /b/ should be realised as an approximant in this case: even across the boundary between the definite article *la* and the noun, the intervocalic environment will set off the phonological process. Now, this means that the word /boḍegɐ/ has two *alternants*: [β̞ oðeɣɐ] and [boðeɣɐ]. That is, the [b] ~ [β̞] variation in this case is a matter of morphorphonemic alternation. Now, if we insist on distinguishing between neutralising MP rules and non-neutralising P rules, we are committed to saying that the realisation of the /b/ in this occurrence of /boḍegɐ/ is distinct in kind from the realisation of the /d/ and the /g/, and that there are *two* rules at work in the realisation of the voiced stops in this word!

But it is clear that the realisations of *all three* of these voiced stops are subsumed under the *same* generalisation: that voiced stops are realised as approximants between vowels. Clearly, if we insist on distinguishing systematically between MP rules and strictly phonological P rules, with two distinct levels of representation above the phonetic level, our analysis of this case will suffer badly in terms of generalising power: we will be unable to subsume the facts under a single generalisation. Our response can be summed up by saying that to express a single generalisation, we require a single rule.

4.1.2 Russian

Russian provides us with another, very famous, example of the limitations of the phonemic principle, first pointed out and discussed by Halle (1959). In this language, the obstruents [t͡s], [d͡z], [č], [ǰ], [x] and [ɣ] occur, but the distinction between these voiced and voiceless pairs is purely allophonic; phonologically, they are voiceless, but have voiced allophones when they occur adjacent to another voiced obstruent. That is, they undergo a Voicing Assimilation rule. However, voicing is contrastive among all other obstruents, such as [p], [b], [t], [d], [s], [z], [ʃ], [ʒ], [k] and [g]. That is, Russian has the phonemes /p/, /b/, /t/, /d/, /s/, /z/, /ʃ/, /ʒ/, /k/ and /g/, and also the phonemes /t͡s/, /č/ and /x/, but not /d͡z/, /ǰ/ and /ɣ/. What we see here is that our expectations of system symmetry (see p. 24) are not fulfilled: we would expect, given the phonemic voicing for the former class of segments, that voicing would be phonemic for all stops, affricates and fricatives at *each* place of articulation. But our expectations are not met: the obstruent system is asymmetrical with respect to the voiced/voiceless distinction. We can sum up the phonemic and allophonic voicing picture as in (2a) and (2b), respectively:

(2a) *Phonemic Voicing*

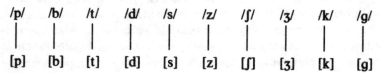

(2b) *Allophonic Voicing*

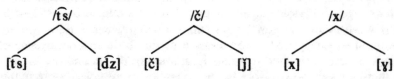

The following alternations show what happens when there are two adjacent obstruents in a word:

(3)

1. (a) [mokli] 'was he getting wet?' 1. (b) [mogbɨ] 'were he getting wet'
2. (a) [ʒečli] 'should one burn?' 2. (b) [ʒeĭbɨ] 'were one to burn'

In 1(a) and (b), the words have the suffixes [li] and [bɨ], respectively; since [bɨ] begins with a voiced obstruent, the root-final voiceless obstruent in 1(b) is voiced by the voicing assimilation process. Since [li] does not begin with a voiced obstruent, the root-final voiceless obstruent is not voiced. Now, since [k] and [g] are phonemically distinct, we must, within phonemic theory, say that the rule which yields the alternation in the root is an MP rule: it yields the phonemes /k/ and /g/. We therefore represent the root with an MP representation like this:

(4)

MP representation	/moK + li/	/moK + bɨ/
MP rules		
Phonemic representation	/mokli/	/mogbɨ/
Phonemic rules		
Phonetic representation	[mokli]	[mogbɨ]

Compare this with 2(a) and (b): there, the voicing assimilation process yields the allophones of /č/. In phonemic theory, we represent this as:

(5)

Phonemic representation	/ʒeč + li/	/ʒeč + bɨ/
Phonemic rules		
Phonetic representation	[ʒečli]	[ʒeĭbɨ]

This commits us to claiming that there are *two* voicing asimilation rules in Russian: one, a neutralising MP rule which maps the MP level on to the phonemic level, thus yielding phonemically distinct segments, and another, a non-neutralising P rule, which maps the phonemic level on to the phonetic, thus yielding segments which are only allophonically distinct. But this analysis is wrong, surely. There is a *single* generalisation here: voiceless obstruents are voiced when followed by a voiced obstruent, regardless of their place or manner of articulation. As far as voicing assimilation goes, there is nothing special about /ts/, /č/ and /x/; they are subsumed under a single rule of Voicing Assimilation, which we could write as:

(6)

$$\begin{bmatrix} +\text{obs} \\ -\text{voice} \end{bmatrix} \rightarrow [+\text{voice}] \ / \ \underline{\quad\quad} \begin{bmatrix} +\text{obs} \\ +\text{voice} \end{bmatrix}$$

This rule is both simple and phonetically motivated; it expresses the single generalisation to be captured (we will see in due course that it is even more general than this). Note too that, with the use of features, we can express this single generalisation, whereas, with the unitary phonemes of phonemic theory, we are unable to do so. This is important for the notion of neutralisation. The rule, when it has a neutralising effect, will neutralise the distinction between voiced and voiceless obstruents. The phonological property of voicing is contrastive for a *subset* of the class of Russian obstruents. Our phonemic rules cannot reflect the fact that *particular* phonological properties may be contrastive for *particular* sets of segments in a language, since they are expressed in terms of unitary segments which are *clusters* of properties. This fact proves important when we come to consider the notion 'minimal pair' in more depth.

4.2 Contrast and the Minimal Pair

The classic case of contrast, which is central to the phonemic principle, is the *minimal pair* phenomenon: if two words differ as to only one sound, then the distinction between the two sounds must be phonemic. Let us examine two case studies of the application of the 'minimal pair' criterion: French nasalised vowels, and vowel length in Lowland Scots.

4.2.1 French Nasalised Vowels

Recall our phonetic observations (see p. 13) about the French nasalised vowels: we said that there are four of them: [ɛ̃], [œ̃], [ɔ̃] and [ɑ̃]. The following data contain a variety of nasalised and non-nasalised vowels:

(7)

[vi]	'life'	[vɛ̃]	'wine'	(3ə) [vɛ]	'(I) go'
[vɑ̃]	'wind'	[vø]	'wishes'	[vo]	'veal'
[vɔ̃]	'(they) go'	[vy]	'saw'	[vu]	'you' (plural)

According to the phonemic principle, these data reveal that the nasalised vowels are phonemically distinct from the non-nasalised vowels. As we contrast each word with each of the others, the /v/ remains constant but the vowel changes. Thus, for instance, if we substitute the sound [i] for the sound [ɛ̃], this signals a contrast in meaning. So, French has a vowel phoneme /i/ and a vowel phoneme /ɛ̃/. Indeed, each word here forms a minimal pair with each of the others. But another way of thinking about the notion of contrast is to ask: are there any pairs in which the vowels differ *solely* with respect to nasalisation? Inspection of the data reveals only [ɛ] vs [ɛ̃] as exhibiting this kind of contrast. So, with this second notion of contrast, there is only one minimal pair in the data. Now, *that* notion of contrast is distinct from the sort appealed to by the phonemic principle: it involves contrast for a *particular* phonological property (nasalisation) within a *particular* class of sounds (vowels). We have seen that, without adopting distinctive features, that notion cannot be expressed.

Consideration of particular phonological properties, rather than unitary phonemes, shows that the notion of minimal pairs *conceals* a distinction which is allophonic. Take the two forms of the adjective for 'good': [bɔ̃] in the masculine (*bon*), and [bɔn] in the feminine (*bonne*). Let us note that the feminine form can sometimes be heard as [bɔnə]. From this, we will assume that the two forms differ in that the feminine form has a feminine suffix consisting of a schwa vowel in its phonological representation, while the masculine does not. That is, the masculine has the phonolgical form /bɔn/, while the feminine has the form /bɔn + ə/.

Let us formulate a rule for nasalisation of vowels: a vowel is nasalised if it is followed by a nasal stop which is in turn followed by a word boundary or a consonant:

(8) *Nasalisation*

$$[+syll] \rightarrow [+nas] / \underline{\quad}[+nasal]\begin{Bmatrix} [+cons] \\ \# \end{Bmatrix}$$

If you apply this rule to /bɔn/ and /bɔn + ə/, you will see that we need further rules. One of these deletes a nasal stop when it is preceded by a nasalised vowel:

(9) *Nasal Deletion*

$$\begin{bmatrix} +cons \\ +nas \end{bmatrix} \rightarrow \emptyset / \begin{bmatrix} +syll \\ +nas \end{bmatrix}\underline{\quad}$$

Since, in most cases, word-final schwa is deleted, we will write, informally, a second rule, for word-final schwa deletion:

(10) *Word-Final Schwa Deletion*

$$/ə/ \rightarrow \emptyset / \underline{\quad}\#$$

Adopting our notion (see p. 45) that phonological rules may apply in a stated order, to yield a phonological derivation, we may say that the rules operate like this:

(11)

Phonological representation	#bɔn#	#bɔn + ə#
Nasalisation	bɔ̃n	———
Nasal Deletion	bɔ̃	———
Word–final schwa Deletion	—	bɔn
Phonetic representation	[bɔ̃]	[bɔn]

What justification is there for these rules (apart from the fact that they seem right for this pair of words)? Well, each of them is very general. Take the Nasalisation rule: there are many alternations in French involving nasalised vowels, and non-nasalised vowels followed by a nasal consonant (as shown in Casagrande 1984):

(12)

[in]		[ɛ̃]		[yn/ym]		[œ̃]
copine	'pal'	copain		aucune	'any'	aucun
divine	'divine'	divin		parfumer	'perfume'	parfum

[ɔn]		[ɔ̃]		[ɛn]		[ɛ̃]
bonne	'good'	bon		pleine	'full'	plein
patronne	'patron'	patron		sereine	'serene'	serein

[œn]		[œ̃]
jeuner	'to fast'	à jeun 'fasting'

[ɐn]		[ɑ̃]
volcanique	'volcanic'	volcan 'volcano'

As you can see, the alternations are between masculine and feminine forms of nouns and adjectives, as well as between verb forms and the adjectives derived from them, and derived noun/adjective and noun/verb pairs. The following sums up the alternations:

(13)

[i] ~ [ɛ̃]	[y] ~ [œ̃]	[ɐ] ~ [ɑ̃]
[ɛ] ~ [ɛ̃]	[œ] ~ [œ̃]	[ɔ] ~ [ɔ̃]

That is, there is a neutralisation of the contrast between /i/ and /ɛ/, /y/ and /œ/ when they are nasalised; the underlying height contrast between these is neutralised in specific contexts (the nasalisation contexts). To see how the neutralisation process can be expressed in a rule, consider the tongue height specifications of the nasalised vowels by looking at the following specifications for the French oral vowels:

(14)

	i	y	e	ø	ɛ	œ	ɐ	ɔ	o	u
high	+	+	−	−	−	−	−	−	−	+
low	−	−	−	−	−	−	+	−	−	−
ATR	+	+	+	+	−	−	−	−	+	+
back	−	−	−	−	−	−	−	+	+	+
round	−	+	−	+	−	+	−	+	+	+
nasal	−	−	−	−	−	−	−	−	−	−

The generalisation about the height of nasalised vowels becomes clear: the four nasalised vowels are all [−high, −ATR]. We can write a rule (let us call it Nasal Vowel Lowering) which expresses this:

(15) *Nasal Vowel Lowering*

$$\begin{bmatrix} +\text{syll} \\ +\text{nas} \end{bmatrix} \rightarrow \begin{bmatrix} -\text{high} \\ -\text{ATR} \end{bmatrix}$$

Our four nasalised vowels will have the specifications:

(16)

	[ɛ̃]	[œ̃]	[ɔ̃]	[ɑ̃]
high	−	−	−	−
low	−	−	−	+
ATR	−	−	−	−
back	−	−	+	+
round	−	+	+	−
nas	+	+	+	+

Thus, when /i/ and /y/ are nasalised, their specifications change to [−high, −ATR, +nas]; that is, they are realised as [ɛ̃] and [œ̃]. When the [−high, −ATR] vowels /ɛ/, /ɔ/ and /ɐ/ are nasalised, their specifications change to [+nas]. Apart from the change in the value for [back] which occurs when [ɐ] is nasalised, the rule expresses the generalisation under which all of these changes are subsumed. This will produce derivations like the following, for *copine* and *copain*:

(17)

	#kopin + ə#	#kopin#
Nasalisation	—————	kopĩn
Nasal Vowel Lowering	—————	kopɛ̃n
Nasal Deletion	—————	kopɛ̃
Word–Final Schwa Deletion	kopin	——
Phonetic representation	[kopin]	[kopɛ̃]

We can see that the same rules we formulated earlier apply here, where the relevant context is present, as does the rule which lowers vowels when they become nasalised. What has emerged is that, with the twin ideas of *derivation* and *rule ordering* we adopted towards the end of Chapter 2, we will be able to capture generalisations which would be missed if we stuck rigidly to the phonemic principle. In this case, we want to say that, although it is true that there are minimal pairs involving nasal and oral vowels in French, this is a case of apparent, or *superficial* contrast: the contrast exists at the phonetic level, at what we call the 'surface' level. But at the more abstract *underlying* level, there is no contrast at all between oral and nasalised vowels: there are no nasalised vowels in French at the underlying, phonological level. And this underlying level reflects part of the phonological knowledge of native speakers of French. We predict that, if a speaker of French is given a made-up feminine adjective or noun ending in [in], let us say [gʁin], and asked for the masculine, they will utter a word which ends in [ɛ̃], in this case [gʁɛ̃]. There is an important point to be made here, concerning the way in which underlying segments are decoded. Our analysis allows that, where the rules of Nasalisation and Nasal Deletion have applied, the speaker can 'tell' that there is a nasal stop in the underlying representation of a morpheme because of the nasalisation on the vowel. That is, phonological properties may be transmitted from one segment to an adjacent one, and those properties help us to decode speech. In this case, although the nasal stop segment has been deleted, a 'trace' of it has been left on the preceding segment.

We must acknowledge that, to get a clear picture of the way phonological knowledge is organised, it is necessary to override the purely surface level criteria of the phonemic principle. The necessity for this more abstract approach to phonological analysis can be seen in the following case from Lowland Scots.

4.2.2 Vowel Length in Lowland Scots

As a preliminary to the data, here are the feature matrices for the (monophthong) vowels and the consonants of Lowland Scots:

(18) *Lowland Scots vowels*

	i	ɪ	e	ɛ	æ	ɔ	ʌ	o	u
high	+	+	−	−	−	−	−	−	+
low	−	−	−	−	+	−	−	−	−
ATR	+	−	+	−	−	−	−	+	+
back	−	−	−	−	−	+	+	+	+
round	−	−	−	−	−	+	−	+	+
long	−	−	−	−	−	−	−	−	−

(19) *Lowland Scots consonants*

	p	t	k	b	d	g	č	ǰ	ʍ	f	θ	s	ʃ	x	v	ð	z	ʒ	l	w	j	m	n	ɹ
cons	+	+	+	+	+	+	+	+	+	+	+	+	+	+	+	+	+	+	+	−	−	−	+	+
syll	−	−	−	−	−	−	−	−	−	−	−	−	−	−	−	−	−	−	−	−	−	−	−	−
obs	+	+	+	+	+	+	+	+	+	+	+	+	+	+	+	+	+	+	−	−	−	−	−	−
cont	−	−	−	−	−	−	−	−	+	+	+	+	+	+	+	+	+	+	−	+	+	−	−	+
asp	−	−	−	−	−	−	−	−	−	−	−	−	−	−	−	−	−	−	−	−	−	−	−	−
voice	−	−	−	+	+	+	−	+	−	−	−	−	−	−	+	+	+	+	+	+	+	+	+	+
del rel	−	−	−	−	−	−	+	+	−	−	−	−	−	−	−	−	−	−	−	−	−	−	−	−
stri	−	−	−	−	−	−	+	+	−	+	−	+	+	−	+	−	+	+	−	−	−	−	−	−
ant	+	+	−	+	+	−	−	−	−	+	+	+	+	−	−	+	+	+	−	+	+	−	+	+
cor	−	+	−	−	+	−	+	+	−	−	+	+	+	−	−	+	+	+	+	−	+	−	+	+
high	−	−	+	−	−	+	+	+	−	−	−	−	+	+	−	−	−	+	−	+	+	−	−	−
low	−	−	−	−	−	−	−	−	−	−	−	−	−	−	−	−	−	−	−	−	−	−	−	−
ATR	−	−	−	−	−	−	−	−	−	−	−	−	−	−	−	−	−	−	−	−	−	−	−	−
back	−	−	+	−	−	+	−	−	−	−	−	−	−	+	−	−	−	−	−	+	−	−	−	−
round	−	−	−	−	−	−	−	−	+	−	−	−	+	−	−	−	−	−	−	+	+	−	−	+
nas	−	−	−	−	−	−	−	−	−	−	−	−	−	−	−	−	−	−	−	−	−	+	+	−
lat	−	−	−	−	−	−	−	−	−	−	−	−	−	−	−	−	−	−	+	−	−	−	−	−

Now consider the following data, which show the contexts in which long vowels occur:

(20)

[i:]	heave	[hi:v]	breathe	[bɾi:ð]	breeze	[bɾi:z]
	beer	[bi:ɹ]	bee	[bi:]		
[i]	beef	[bif]	heath	[hiθ]	fleece	[flis]
	deal	[dil]	beet	[bit]		
[e:]	stave	[ste:v]	swathe	[swe:ð]	faze	[fe:z]
	fair	[fe:ɹ]	day	[de:]		
[e]	waif	[wef]	faith	[feθ]	face	[fes]
	nail	[nel]	fate	[fet]		

[ʉ:]	move	[mʉ:v]	smooth	[smʉ:ð]	lose	[lʉ:z]
	boor	[bʉ:ɹ]	blew	[blʉ:]		
[ʉ]	hoof	[hʉf]	tooth	[tʰʉθ]	loose	[lʉs]
	pool	[pʰʉl]	loot	[lʉt]		
[o:]	stove	[sto:v]	loathe	[lo:ð]	hose	[ho:z]
	bore	[bo:ɹ]	hoe	[ho:]		
[o]	loaf	[lof]	oath	[oθ]	close	[kʰlos]
	whole	[hol]	boat	[bot]		

The contexts in which the long vowels occur are: before the voiced fricatives {v, ð, z}, before [ɹ], and at the end of a word. We can therefore say that certain vowels in the system, namely {i, e, o, u}, have allophones which are long in this context. That is, vowel length is allophonic, rather than phonemic, in Lowland Scots. If we write the rule for vowel length, using features, it will be:

(21)

$$
\begin{bmatrix} +\text{syll} \\ +\text{ATR} \end{bmatrix} \longrightarrow [+\text{long}] \ / \ \underline{\hspace{2cm}} \left\{ \begin{bmatrix} -\text{syll} \\ +\text{voice} \\ +\text{cont} \end{bmatrix} \right\}
$$

What this rule states is that it is the voiced continuant consonants which set off the lengthening process. You will note that this class includes /ʒ/, /w/ and /j/, none of which are exemplified in the data. There is a reason for this. Firstly, the palato-alveolar fricative /ʒ/ has an extremely restricted distribution, never occurring word-initially or word-finally, but always medially (as in *measure*, *vision* and *azure*). Similarly, /w/ and /j/ occur only at the beginning of syllables, so they will never follow one of these vowels within the same syllable. This does, of course, suggest that we need to insist that if a voiced continuant is to lenghten a vowel, it must occur within the same syllable as that vowel. Our rule does not express this; nor have we attempted to give any account of why it should be just this class of vowels which undergoes lengthening.

It seems clear that vowel length is allophonic in Lowland Scots, and not phonemic as in Limbu (see p. 27) or Malayalam (see p. 31). But consider the following data:

(22)

| need | [nid] | vs | kneed | [ni:d] |
| road | [ɹod] | vs | rowed | [ɹo:d] |

| crude [kʰɹʉd] | vs | crewed | [kʰɹʉːd] |
| staid [sted] | vs | stayed | [steːd] |

The phonemic principle would force us to admit that these are minimal pairs: they differ *only* with respect to vowel length. And this leaves us with claiming that vowel length is *both* phonemic *and* allophonic! The trouble is that the two criteria, of complementary distribution plus phonetic similarity, on the one hand, and parallel distribution plus contrast, on the other hand, are in collision here. Now, because facts about surface level distribution are fundamental to the phonemic principle, the view that vowel length is phonemic must predominate: the long and short vowels can be shown *not* to be in complementary distribution after all, even if the first set of data suggested that they were.

It is interesting that while the [d]s in the words in the left-hand column are phonetically identical to the [d]s in the words on the right, they do not have the same linguistic function. The words in the right-hand column are all past tense forms of verbs. Now, the past tense morpheme has the allomorphs [d], [t] and [ɪd], as in the following words:

(23)

passed [pɐst]   dreamed [dɹiimd]   added [ɐdɪd]

That is, if the root-final segment in the vowel is /d/ or /t/, the [ɪd] allomorph occurs. Otherwise, if the root-final segment is voiceless, [t] will occur, and if voiced, [d] will occur. This means that for roots ending in vowels, which are voiced, the [d] allomorph will occur.

This makes it clear that the [d]s in the second column are allomorphs of the past tense morpheme, whereas the [d]s in the first are not. This kind of information, we have claimed, is a part of the speaker's knowledge of the language. We could represent these two different states of affairs like this:

(24)

/bɹʉd/ 'brood'   /bɹʉ + ɪd/ 'brewed'

Nor, when the vowel in question is root-final, it will be long, just as it would in the word *brew*, where it is both root-final and word-final. The generalisation is that these vowels are long root-finally (regardless of whether the word has any suffixes or not). We can (almost) express this by adding the morpheme boundary symbol ('+') to our rule, thus:

(25)

$$
\begin{bmatrix} +\text{syll} \\ +\text{ATR} \end{bmatrix} \longrightarrow [+\text{long}] \;/\; \underline{\hspace{2cm}} \left\{ \begin{array}{c} \begin{bmatrix} -\text{syll} \\ +\text{voice} \\ +\text{cont} \end{bmatrix} \\ \# \\ + \end{array} \right\}
$$

That is, the rule will have to have access to the morphological structure of
the word, as well as the feature specifications of segments: it accesses two
different sorts of information. (As it stands, the rule does not express the
generalisation we have made, but we will return to that problem in Chapter
8.) If we allow the phonemic principle to be overridden, then we can say
that vowel length appears to be phonemic at the surface phonetic level, but
is seen to be purely allophonic if we consider non-phonetic factors such as
the morphological structure of the word.

As an interesting aside to this analysis, consider the pair *face/faze*. Note
that we can take pairs like this to be minimal pairs, differing as to the
voicing of the fricative. The length of the vowel in *faze*, we are claiming, is
brought about by the presence of a voiced fricative immediately following
it. Interestingly, voiced obstruents are partially, and sometimes even fully,
devoiced at the ends of words. If the fricative were fully devoiced, then the
length of the vowel will help us to decode the word: if it is long, then the
final fricative is phonologically voiced. We see here how allophonic information, as in the nasalisation of French vowels, is not just redundant
'noise', but allows us to allocate sounds to their phonemes when we decode
speech. This claim will, of course, commit us to the idea that the vowel
lengthening rule operates *before* the devoicing rule. Thus, we also see how
the idea of ordering of rules reflects the way we decode speech.

In the case of the past tense forms, vowel length gives us a clue as to the
linguistic status of the [d] at the end of the word: it helps us to decode it as
an allomorph of the past tense morpheme. These are thus rather intriguing
tricks of linguistic perception. They show that perception of speech is not
strictly a matter of allocating allophones to their respective phonemes, and
then determining the morphological function of those phonemes: vital
clues to the morphological function of a speech sound often reside in
neighbouring segments, allowing us to arrive at the phonological form of
words and morphemes.

In the following exercise, you will need to appeal to this idea of the
'underlying' phonological form of morphemes and words.

A. Lumasaaba

In Chapter 1, we decided that the velar stops /k/ and /g/ are realised as the
palatal stops [c] and [ɟ], respectively, when immediately followed by either

/i/ or /e/ in Lumasaaba. That is, there are no palatal stop phonemes in the language. In Chapter 3, you were asked to express this as a single rule (let us call it Velar Fronting), which looked like this:

Velar Fronting

$$
\begin{bmatrix} +\text{obs} \\ +\text{back} \end{bmatrix} \rightarrow [-\text{back}] \ / \ \underline{\hspace{1cm}} \begin{bmatrix} +\text{syll} \\ -\text{back} \\ -\text{low} \end{bmatrix}
$$

The following data should therefore come as something of a disappointment to you:

1. (a) [cica:na:ga] 'a creak' (b) [ßiß a:na:ga] 'creaks'
2. (a) [kaki:ko] 'a piece' (b) [ßuß i:ko] 'pieces'

(a) In which two ways does this data appear to falsify the claim made in the rule? That is, in what ways do these words seem to provide counter-examples, or exceptions, to the rule?
(b) What are the roots in each word?
(c) If our rule does not have exceptions after all, what will the phonological form of the [c]s in l(a) be? What kind of vowel would there be after the second [c] in 1(a)? What kind of vowel would there be after the second [k] in 2(a)? Assume that in each word there are *two* prefixes. Can you suggest what the phonological form of these should be, for each word? Your suggestion should allow us to deny that the rule has any exceptions.
(d) If you got that right, then you will need to allow for another rule which deletes the first of two adjacent vowels. Write that rule; it is a fairly simple one (call it Elision).
(e) In what order will the two rules, Velar Fronting and Elision, have to apply?
(f) Draw up the phonological representation, including morpheme boundaries, for each of the words, and show how the rules apply to yield the surface forms.
(g) What bearing does your analysis have on the claim that generalisations often hold at the underlying, rather than the surface, level of analysis?

4.3 An Alternative to the Phonemic Principle: Generative Phonology

It looks as though we must reject the idea of a separate level of morpho-phonemic representation, with a distinct category of MP rules. We will therefore proceed with the idea that there is a *single* level of representation above the phonetic level, and a single kind of rule. We will refer to this level simply as the level of **underlying representation**. This is clearly distinct from the phonetic level of representation, which we will alternatively refer to as the **surface level** of representation. The idea is that the physical sounds we hear and can transcribe are, as it were, the tip of the iceberg: underneath lie the more abstract sorts of representation with which we perceive speech sounds, and a highly organised system of rules. We will refer to the rules, whether they yield allophonically or phonemically distinct segments, simply as phonological rules; that is, we are abandoning phonemic theory. In doing so, we have not entirely given up the notions of contrast and predictability introduced in Chapter 1; rather, we have insisted that they must apply at a more abstract level of analysis.

This view has been central to much of **Generative Phonology**, and distinguishes it from alternative views, both past and present, which insist on making the distinction we have rejected. Generative Phonology (GP) is a subdiscipline within **Generative Grammar**, an approach to linguistic theory whose aim is to characterise the unconscious knowledge which constitutes our knowing a language. This linguistic knowledge may be subdivided into morphological, syntactic, semantic and phonological knowledge. To oversimplify somewhat, morphological knowledge allows word formation to take place, syntactic knowledge allows us to distinguish well-formed sentences from one another, and to distinguish those from non-sentences, whereas semantic knowledge allows us to interpret the meaning of sentences.

It is the goal of Generative Phonology to characterise the nature of phonological knowledge, and thus to state what it is that constitutes having a native accent. This is precisely the goal we set ourselves at the outset of this book. We will therefore be concerned entirely with GP in the chapters that follow.

EXERCISES

1. Tyneside English
In Tyneside English, as in most accents of English, the aspirated voiceless stops [pʰ], [tʰ] and [kʰ] are contrastive:

(a) [pʰɛn] 'pan'   [tʰɛn] 'tan'   [kʰɛn] 'can'

[pʰ], [tʰ] and [kʰ] are realisations of /p/, /t/ and /k/, respectively.

These phonemes have unaspirated allophones after /s/:

(b) [spɪl] 'spill'   [stɪl] 'still'   [skɪl] 'skill'

A rule of Nasal Assimilation states that nasal stops are assimilated in place of articulation to a following obstruent:

(c) [ɪmpoːt] 'import' [ɪntɹuːd] 'intrude' [ɪŋkʰɹɛdɪbḷ] 'incredible'

The contrast between /p/, /t/ and /k/ is *neutralised* (see p. 83) after nasal stops and before syllabic nasals (if the preceding vowel is stressed) by a rule of Reduction under which /p/, /t/ and /k/ are realised as glottal stops:

(d) [skɛmʔi] 'scampi' [ɐnʔi] 'aunt' [hɛŋʔi] 'hanky'

(e) [hɛʔm̩] 'happen' [bʌʔn̩] 'button' [čɪʔŋ̩] 'chicken'

(i) Glottal stop is always an allophone of either /p/, /t/ or /k/: it never functions contrastively; that is, there is no /ʔ/. What phonetic information is there in the immediate context of the glottal stops in the data in (e) which gives a clue as to the phonemic status of [ʔ] in those words?

(ii) We need two additional rules, Nasal Syllabification and Schwa Elision, to account for the forms in (e). What order do they apply in?

(iii) In what order must Reduction and Nasal Assimilation apply?

(iv) State the order of all four rules.

(v) How does the idea of rule ordering reflect the way that the glottal stops and syllabic nasals in (e) are decoded?

2. Standard English

We formulated a rule of Nasal Assimilation for English in the last chapter (see p. 73): it assimilates the alveolar nasal stop to the place of articulation of a following oral stop. If we consider the distribution of the three nasal stops [m], [n] and [ŋ] in English, it is clear that the bilabial and alveolar stops can occur word-initially, as in *map* and *nut*, but the velar nasal cannot. All three occur between vowels, before stops, and word-finally:

1. (a) [jɪmi] 'Jimmy'   (b) [jɪni] 'Ginny'   (c) [sɪŋə] 'singer'

2. (a) [æmbə] 'amber'   (b) [ʌndə] 'under'   (c) [æŋgə] 'anger'

3. (a) [hæm] 'ham'   (b) [sɪn] 'sin'   (c) [sɪŋ] 'sing'

These three are in parallel distribution and are contrastive, as we can see from minimal pairs like *sin/sing* and *Jimmy/Ginny*. There must therefore be three nasal stop phonemes /m/, /n/ and /ŋ/, according to the phonemic principle. The phoneme /ŋ/ is odd, according to this analysis, in that it never occurs word-initially, but, under this analysis, that is an entirely arbitrary, accidental, fact.

Let us argue, against this, that there are only two nasal stop phonemes in Standard English (/m/ and /n/) and that all surface occurrences of [ŋ] derive from underlying /n/.

(i)   The word *anger* has the phonetic representation [æŋgə]. If Nasal Assimilation causes underlying /n/ to surface as [ŋ], what must the underlying representation of *anger* be? (Assume that it ends in /r/; this fact is not important here.)

(ii) How will this differ from the underlying representation of *singer*? That is, what is the difference in morphological structure between *anger* and *singer*?

(iii) We will need another rule, besides the rule which deletes the /r/, which will operate on *singer* to yield its phonetic representation [sɪŋə]. What does that rule do?

(iv) In which contexts will it apply? Your answer should allow you to say why it does not apply to *anger*.

(v)   In what order must the two rules, Nasal Assimilation and the new rule, apply?

(vi) In most accents of English, words can begin with /m/ or /n/ so long as the nasal is not immediately followed by another consonant. Thus, words cannot begin with the sequences /mb/ or /nd/. In the light of your analysis, can you say what relevance this fact has for the non-occurrence of [ŋ] word-initially?

(vii) For many speakers of English, the comparative forms of the adjectives *young*, *long* and *strong* have a [g] in their phonetic representation: [jʌŋgə], [lɒŋgə]] and [stɹɒŋgə]. In what way do they differ morphologically from words like *singer*, *wringer* and *stinger*?

(viii) What implications does this have for the rule you formulated in (iii)?

(ix) Some accents have a [g] both word-finally (as in *sing*) and word-internally (as in *singer*). How would our generative approach characterise the distinction between those accents and those where a [g] does not occur in such forms?

(x)   Fromkin (1971) recorded a wide range of different 'tongue slip' phenomena, among which the phrase *Springtime for Hitler* was uttered mistakenly as [spɹɪgtaimfəhɪntlə]. What bearing does this have on the analysis you have proposed?

(xi) For some speakers with /g/ deletion, morphologically simple words like *hangar* and *dinghy* occur without [g]. What implications does this have for the analysis you have formulated?

3. Spanish

Spanish has a five-vowel monophthong system as follows: /i, e, a, o, u/. This is true for many dialects of Spanish, including the standard dialect, Castillian Spanish. There is allophonic variation among the mid vowels, involving high and low mid realisations:

1.	[jose]	'I know'	2.	[sjɛmpɾe]	'always'
3.	[tɔrnar]	'to turn'	4.	[bweno]	'good' (singular)
5.	[bwenɔs]	'good' (plural)	6.	[komo]	'I eat'
7.	[komɛs]	'you eat' (2PS)	8.	[kome]	'he/she eats'
9.	[tjɛmplo]	'temple'	10.	[sɔldaɗo]	'soldier'

(i) Write a rule for the realisation of /o/ and /e/.

In Andalucian Spanish, the phonetic forms of the second and third person singular forms of verbs such as 'eat' are (respectively): [komɛ] ('you eat') and [kome] ('he/she eats'). Similarly, the plural and singular forms of adjectives such as 'good' are (respectively): [bwenɔ] and [bweno].

(ii) What would the phonemic principle force us to say about pairs like this, and about the distinction between [e] and [ɛ] and [o] and [ɔ] in Andalucian Spanish?

(iii) Can you suggest an alternative, generative, analysis which abandons the phonemic principle of surface contrast?

Further Reading

Hyman (1975), Chapter 4, covers the formalism of standard generative phonology, more of which will be introduced in the following two chapters. Schane (1973) provides a clear, simplified account of standard generative phonology; the beginning student will find it useful, but should be warned against relying exclusively on it. Having started with Schane (1973), the reader is advised to progress to Hyman (1975), Chapters 4–5, which are very clearly written. Kenstowicz and Kisseberth (1979) remains an excellent introduction to the subject and contains a wealth of worthwhile exercises.

5 The Organisation of the Grammar

In the last chapter, we considered the generative phonology (GP) approach to phonological rules and representations. We said that a generative grammar is a *model* of the native speaker's unconscious linguistic knowledge. We also claimed that this knowledge is organised such that there are distinct areas of syntactic, semantic and phonological knowledge. These hypotheses are reflected in the **modular** organisation of the generative grammar of a language: we depict these different sorts of knowledge as discrete, but interacting, **modules**, or components, within the grammar. Let us see how this is done within the model of generative grammar assumed by Noam Chomsky and Morris Halle in their 1968 book *The Sound Pattern of English* (often abbreviated to 'SPE'). This model, which was developed and applied to other languages by phonologists in the late sixties and early seventies, is usually referred to as 'the SPE model' or 'the standard model' of generative phonology.

5.1 The Lexicon

We will assume that morphemes are stored in a kind of memory bank which we will call **the lexicon**. It is from the lexicon that speakers retrieve the morphemes of the language. Recall that we defined a morpheme (see p. 34) as the *union* of a phonological form and a meaning: for each morpheme stored in the lexicon, the native speaker knows what its meaning is and has some kind of mental representation of its phonological form. These two things taken together constitute a morpheme. Take the morpheme 'song' in an RP speaker's lexicon: the speaker knows what it means (though this need not be entirely conscious knowledge) and has a mental representation of its phonological form. Now, it is an entirely *arbitrary* fact that the union of that meaning with that form constitutes a morpheme in the language: that particular phonological form has no *necessary* link with that meaning. We have argued that the Tamil morpheme which we have glossed as meaning what the word 'snake' means in English has the phonological form /pɑːnpʊ/, but its translation has the phonological form /sneik/ for RP speakers of English. Neither form is more appropriate for the meaning it signals than the other: it just so happens that the form is /sneik/ in one language and /pɑːnpʊ/ in another.

103

We get so used to the fact that a particular phonological form expresses a particular meaning in our native language that it can appear to us somehow appropriate or 'natural' that that meaning should be conveyed by *that* form. But this feeling of the 'appropriateness' of a form for its meaning is dispelled when we are confronted by (more or less) parallel meanings in foreign languages which are signalled by an entirely different phonological form, as in the Tamil word for 'snake', the French word for 'face' (/vizɐʒ/, written as *visage*) and in the many foreign words given in this book.

In the standard model of GP, the lexicon is taken to be the repository for these sorts of arbitrary fact. Similarly, the lexicon is where we would store purely idiosyncratic facts like the one we mentioned on p. 28: it so happens that the word *either* may have the form /iːðər/ or /aiðər/, but this is a fact about *that particular word*, and does not reflect any generalisation about /iː/ and /ai/ in contemporary English (though a knowledge of the history of the language would shed some light on this state of affairs).

We can contrast this kind of knowledge with the kinds of rule-governed phonological variation we have been looking at: these reflect a kind of knowledge which is entirely distinct from our knowledge of idiosyncratic and arbitrary facts about particular words. To depict this difference, the rules governing this kind of variation will be assigned to a separate module in the grammar: the **phonological component**. This is the block of all the phonological rules of the language. Thus, the phonological component of the grammar of Lumasaaba will include Velar Fronting (see p. 97), Nasal Assimilation (see p. 35) and Elision (see p. 97); for French, it will contain the rules of Nasalisation, Nasal Vowel Lowering, Nasal Consonant Deletion and Word-Final Schwa Deletion which we discussed in Chapter 4. In English, it will contain rules like Nasal Assimilation (see p. 72) and the Voiced Velar Stop Deletion rule which you will have appealed to in the exercise on Standard English at the end of Chapter 4.

Let us exemplify this distinction between lexical facts and rule-governed facts. In the Tamil word for 'snake', the phonological form of the word just *happens* to be /paːnpʊ/, where (syllable structure apart) this fact is not something which is predictable or could be said to follow from any generalisation. But given that there is such a phonological form, there are properties of the way it is uttered which most certainly *do* follow from general rules: the stop after the nasal is predictably voiced, the nasal stop is predictably bilabial, and the vowel is predictably [ɯ] rather than [ʊ]. Similarly, in Lumasaaba, the phonological form of the word for 'chains' is /zi + n + gegele/, and those underlying forms for those morphemes are simply stored in the lexicon (we will see that this is almost, but not quite, correct). But certain properties of [ziɲɟeɟele], the phonetic form of the word, are rule-governed: the place of articulation of the nasal stop (governed by Nasal Assimilation) and the place of articulation of the palatal stops (governed by Velar Fronting). We will be claiming therefore that it is the phonological component, and not the lexicon, which contains the rules which express this sort of generalisation.

To take a final example, from English: it is a fact that the nasals in the words *map* and *input* are bilabial in normal conversational pronunciation. But behind this phonetic fact lie two different phonological facts. The bilabiality of the [m] in *map* is not rule-governed: *map* just happens to begin with an /m/. Similarly, the word *input* has a prefix whose form just happens to be /in/. But the bilabiality of the [m] in *input* is not an arbitrary fact: it is rule-governed, and due to the bilabiality of the /p/ in /pʊt/, whereas the bilabiality of the /m/ in *map* is not due to anything. Now, these two states of affairs, the arbitrary and the predictable, reflect different sorts of knowledge. The [m] in *input* is decoded, via the phonological component, as the /n/ in the phonological form of the word, stored in the lexicon. But the [m] in *map* is decoded, however speedily and unconsciously, as the /m/ which is in the phonological form of the word stored in the lexicon, without the mediation of the Nasal Assimilation rule (which could not apply here). One way of expressing this distinction between lexical facts and rule-governed facts is to say that the underlying phonological form of a morpheme is like a representation of its surface forms, stripped of all predictable phonetic properties; it is the phonological rules of the language which supply these properties.

Those rules will include, not only feature-changing rules like Nasal Assimilation in English, but also rules expressing both language-specific and universal restrictions. Some language-specific restrictions take the form of restrictions on the phonological shape of morphemes in a language. For instance, in English, morphemes may not begin with nasal plus consonant clusters. Thus, while /blit/ is a possible, but not an actual, phonological representation for a morpheme in English, /msit/ is not a possible representation. Such **phonotactic** restrictions (often referred to as 'the phonotactics' of the language) are said to be expressed by means of **morpheme structure rules (MSRs)**. Other universal and language-specific restrictions concern the sorts of implicational relationships expressed by the FCRs and default rules we discussed in Chapter 3. We may conceive of the MSRs, default rules and FCRs as applying to fill in values for features on a morpheme before it is retrieved from the lexicon. In Lowland Scots, for instance, the morpheme 'know' will have the following phonological representation:

(1)

	/n	o/
cons	+	−
syll	−	+
obs	−	
cont	−	+
voice	+	
ant	+	−
cor	+	−
high	−	−
low	−	−
ATR	−	+
back	−	+
round		
nas	+	

A batch of FCRs and default rules will apply to fill in predictable values in this matrix; you may wish to try formulating them. Further phonological rules may change feature values (in this case, the Scottish Vowel Length Rule). The idea of unspecified values for features is important, since, in adopting it, we allow for segments in phonological representations which are **underspecified**, and are therefore 'less concrete' than fully specified representations. The importance of this 'abstract' view of phonological representations will become apparent in Chapter 6.

How, according to this model, are morphemes retrieved from the lexicon, how are words built up from morphemes, and how do the phonological rules come to apply to phonological forms? To answer these questions, let us say that sentences are strings of words with a highly organised structure; that is, words appear in structural slots in sentences. Generative grammarians claim that the syntactic structure of each and every sentence of a language can be generated by a set of syntactic rules. By 'generated' is meant 'explicitly represented'. We will assume that these rules form the **syntactic component** of the grammar, which reflects our rule-governed syntactic knowledge. We need not pursue the question of what form these rules take, but we will assume that the structure of each sentence generated by the rules can be represented in the form of a **phrase marker**. These are tree diagrams which explicitly represent sentence structure. For the English sentence *The song ended*, we may assume the following phrase marker:[1]

(2)

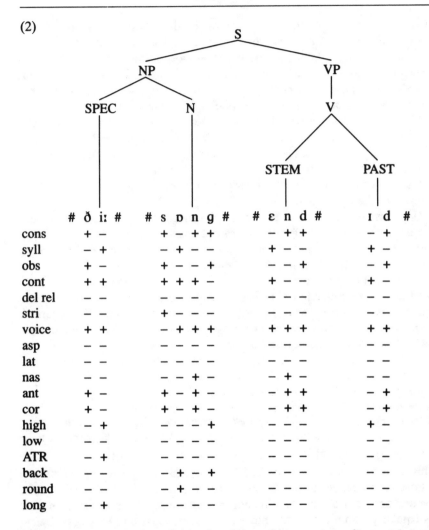

	#	ð	iː	#	#	s	ɒ	ŋ	g	#	#	ɛ	n	d	#	ɪ	d	#
cons		+	−			+	−	+	+			−	+	+		−	+	
syll		−	+			−	+	−	−			+	−	−		+	−	
obs		+	−			+	−	−	+			−	−	+		−	+	
cont		+	+			+	+	+	−			+	−	−		+	−	
del rel		−	−			−	−	−	−			−	−	−		−	−	
stri		−	−			+	−	−	−			−	−	−		−	−	
voice		+	+			−	+	+	+			+	+	+		+	+	
asp		−	−			−	−	−	−			−	−	−		−	−	
lat		−	−			−	−	−	−			−	−	−		−	−	
nas		−	−			−	−	+	−			−	+	−		−	−	
ant		+	−			+	−	+	−			−	+	+		−	+	
cor		+	−			+	−	+	−			−	+	+		−	+	
high		−	+			−	−	−	+			−	−	−		+	−	
low		−	−			−	−	−	−			−	−	−		−	−	
ATR		−	+			−	−	−	−			−	−	−		−	−	
back		−	−			−	+	−	+			−	−	−		−	−	
round		−	−			−	+	−	−			−	−	−		−	−	
long		−	+			−	−	−	−			−	−	−		−	−	

These phrase markers embody the claims that sentences have structure, and that the syntactic structure of a sentence is generated by a syntactic component in the grammar. From this, we can go on to make two observations. Firstly, words, which are formed from the morphemes stored in the lexicon, must be inserted into syntactic structures. For this to happen, the morphemes from which they are constructed must be marked, in the lexicon, for their **lexical category**. By 'lexical category', we mean, broadly speaking, categories like 'noun', 'adjective', 'verb' and 'preposition'. What this means is that only morphemes marked as nouns can be inserted under an 'N' in the diagram, only morphemes marked as verbs under 'V', and so on. In saying that morphemes are marked in the lexicon for their category, we are claiming (a) that speakers intuitively know what the lexical category of a morpheme is (if there is one) and (b) that these are arbitrary facts about those items. Take the word *song* in English: it consists only of the morpheme 'song' (unlike *songs*, which is morphologically complex, consisting of the morphemes 'song' and 'plural'). It just so happens that *song* is a noun in English, and not a verb or preposition, for instance, so that information is stored with that morpheme in the lexicon.

Secondly, when we say that a morpheme is inserted into a syntactic structure from the lexicon, we mean that what is inserted is something which has a phonological form, a meaning and a lexical category (except in cases like 'past', which are grammatical, rather than lexical, morphemes). What concerns us here is that the string of morphemes in the sentence are present in their *phonological form*.

It follows that the rules of the phonology have not yet operated to yield the phonetic representations of the morphemes. This commits us to saying that the rules of the syntax operate, taking words from the lexicon, to generate syntactic structures, and then the rules of the phonology operate to yield the phonetic representations of the words in those structures. We say that the grammar has generated a sentence when it has generated the union of its syntactic, semantic and phonetic representation. If we were to depict this view of the relationship between the lexicon, the syntax and the phonology, it would look like this:

(3)

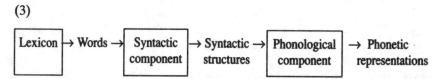

This diagram depicts a model of the way these three components are related. Let us look at the details of how this works for our word *song* in the sentence *The song ended*. The morpheme is stored in the lexicon with its category 'noun', a representation of its meaning and its phonological form. Since the word *song* is not morphologically complex, the word in this case corresponds to the morpheme; no morphological processes apply to add prefixes or suffixes to the 'song' morpheme to yield other words (like *songs* or *songsmith*). And since it is marked in the lexicon as a noun, it then is admitted into the phrase marker on p. 107, under the 'N'. Here, it is bounded by word boundaries, as in the phrase marker. Once the syntactic rules have operated, the phonological rules operate on the string of segments, boundaries included. That is, the phonological rules operate on the *output* of the syntactic component of the grammar.

It should be noted here that any phrase marker may be equivalently represented as a bracketed string of morphemes, with labels on the brackets indicating lexical categories, as in

(4)

[S [NP [DET#ði:#] DET [N#sɒng#]N]NP [VP [V#ɛnd#ɪd#]V]VP]S

As the phonological rules operate, the brackets are erased (we will look at this in a little more detail shortly). Then, once the ordered rules in the phonological component have applied, the resulting representation is the phonetic representation. Our Nasal Assimilation rule will operate to change the features on the nasal stop, and then Voiced Velar Stop Deletion will operate to delete the /g/, thus:

(5)

	[N# sɒng #]N
Nasal Assimilation	sɒŋg
Voiced Velar Stop Deletion	sɒŋ (No more rules apply, so that the output of VVSD is the phonetic representation)
Phonetic Representation	[sɒŋ]

Since a phonetic representation of a stretch of continuous speech will not contain boundary symbols or brackets, we need to ask what happens to these. Let us now do so.

5.2 The Location of Morphology

There is a distinction made, within the field of morphology, between two sorts of morphological process: **derivational morphology** and **inflectional morphology**. To exemplify this distinction, let us look again at some of the affixes (prefixes and suffixes) we have encountered. We saw that the 'feminine' morpheme in French has the phonological form /ə/. We want to say that the feminine form of nouns and adjectives in French is created by attaching the phonological form of this suffix to a noun or adjective stem. This kind of morphological process is known as inflectional morphology; it usually involves marking categories like plurality, gender and number on nouns and adjectives, and categories like tense, person and number on verbs. Inflectional morphology is usually regular. There are, of course, irregular forms in most languages: while the plural of *cat* in English is the regular form *cats*, the plural of *ox* is *oxen*. We will characterise these latter sorts of irregular form in our model by simply *listing* them in the lexicon. This means that we are treating them, just like the listed phonological forms of morphemes, as entirely arbitrary facts, and that seems right: it is just an arbitrary fact about the word *ox* that its plural form is *oxen*.

Compare the case of *copain/copine* in French with the relationship between the words *volcan* and *volcanique* (see p. 90): in the latter case, we *derive* an independent word from the noun by adding the suffix /ikə/. This kind of morphological process is a derivational one, whereas in the case of *copain/copine*, having inflected the noun, we are left with that same word (in its feminine form), rather than deriving an independent word from the noun. It is often the case that derivational morphology is less predictable than inflection. Thus, while we can safely say what the plural of a newly invented noun (say, *blick*) in English would be, we cannot be so certain, with a given noun, of what its derived forms will be. Consider, for instance, the form of the adjectives derived from the names *Marx*, *Thatcher* and *Popper*: *Marxist*, *Thatcherite*, *Popperian*. Similarly, while we derive the noun *curiosity* from the adjective *curious*, we may, but tend not to, derive the noun *spuriosity* from the adjective *spurious*.

In examining alternations in French vowels in Chapter 4, we considered evidence from pairs of words morphologically related in both ways: *copine/copain* are inflectionally related, while *volcan/volcanique* are derivationally related. This reflects the classical SPE view that phonological rules operate to relate alternants yielded by *both* sorts of morphological process. The standard model also assumes that both types of morphological process operate within the lexicon, so that all word formation takes place in the lexicon, and the phonological rules apply, after the products of word formation have been entered into sentence structure (which itself is operated on by the syntactic component, as in (3)).

You should therefore assume, when formulating phonological rules, that the morphological structure of a morphologically complex word is already given, having been constructed by the syntactic component, from the lexicon. This might be summed up by saying that, in this classical SPE model of GP, it is a matter of 'morphology first, phonology later'. Let us look at a particular case. Let us take as our example sentence *The singer ended*. The word *singer* would be formed from the morpheme *sing* (which will, of course, be marked as a verb) and the appropriate nominalising suffix morpheme (a morpheme added to verbs to yield nouns), thus.

(6)

[N#	[V s ɪ n g]V#	ə r #]N
cons	+ − + +	− +
syll	− + − −	+ −
obs	+ − − +	− −
cont	+ + − −	+ +
voice	− + + +	+ +
ant	+ − + −	− +
cor	+ − + −	− +
high	− + − +	− −
low	− − − −	− −
back	− − − +	− −
nas	− − + −	− −

The rules of Nasal Assimilation, /g/ Deletion, /r/ Realisation, another rule of /ɪd/ Assimilation (discussed below) will then be applied, thus:

(7)

	[N [V # s ɪ n g]V # ə r#]N	[V# ɛ n d # ɪ d #]V
Nasal Assimilation	s ɪ ŋ g # ər	————————
/g/ Deletion	s ɪ ŋ # ər	————————
/ɪd/ Assimilation	————————	————————
/r/ Realisation	s ɪ ŋ ə ɹ	————————
Phonetic Representation	[s ɪ ŋ ə ɹ ɛ ndɪd]	

The idea not explicitly represented in (7) is that the rules apply from the innermost brackets to the outermost. In the case of *singer*, we start with the innermost string of segments, *sing*, which itself contains no brackets. All of the cyclic rules have a chance to apply at this stage. Nasal Assimilation will assimilate the /n/ to the /g/. The rule which deletes /g/ when it follows a velar nasal stop will also apply. This rule may be said to apply (in many dialects of English) at the '#' boundary, as in *singing*, *singer*, *sing* and *sings*. This entails an assumption, which we will look at shortly, that the '#' boundary separates the members of one class of English affixes from their stems, while the members of another class are separated from their stems by the '+' boundary.

Once all the rules have been given the chance to apply, the brackets are erased, giving #sɪŋər#, and all of the rules apply again (where, by 'apply', we mean, 'have a chance to have their conditions met', regardless of whether the conditions are actually met, and a change thus effected). For instance, Nasal Assimilation applies within the innermost brackets in the case of *sing*; but in other cases it will apply later, as in morphologically complex words like *income*. This mode of application is referred to as the **cyclic principle** of rule application, or **cyclicity**.[2] The rule of /r/ Realisation does not get a chance to apply at this stage; we will see why shortly.

The same cyclic application takes place in *ended*, starting with the stem *end*. Nasal Assimilation will effect no change in the /n/ of *end*. Brackets are then erased, and the rules all get a chance to apply to *ended*. With the verb /ɛnd#ɪd/, the phonetic form of the 'past' morpheme is [ɪd]: [ɛndɪd]. This alternates with [d], as in *chewed*: [ču:d] and [t], as in *passed*: [pɑ:st]. The rule (/ɪd/ Assimilation) which governs this alternation expresses the following generalisation: where the stem-final segment is /d/ or /t/, [ɪd] occurs; otherwise, where the stem-final segment is voiceless, [t] occurs, and, where it is voiced, [d] occurs. The exact formulation of the rule, and the phonological form of the 'past' morpheme need not concern us here. In the above derivation, the conditions for /ɪd/ Assimilation (and, indeed, a host of other rules) are not met.

The rule of /r/ Realisation differs from Nasal Assimilation and Voiced Velar Stop Deletion (VVSD) in that it applies *after* all of the cyclic rules have applied. This is because it applies regardless of structure. That is, the generalisation expressed by the rule (delete the /r/ if the following segment is not a vowel) holds for morphologically simple words such as *error* and *car*, for morphologically complex words such as *hairy* and *sorely*, and across word boundaries, as in *singer ended* and *singer died*. That is, it is blind to the presence of brackets and boundaries. We can express this by saying that it applies after the erasure of all brackets (and boundaries: we will assume that these too are erased at a later stage), or **post-cyclically**.

We said that we would provide a comment on boundaries in the standard theory. Look at the following data from Russian:

(8)

	Phonological form	**Phonetic representation**	
(a)	#gorod + k + a#	[gorotka]	'little town'
(b)	#mt͡sɛnsk#bɨ#	[mt͡sɛnzgbɨ]	'if Mcensk'
(c)	#mt͡sɛnsk##bɨl#	[mt͡sɛnzgbɨl]	'it was Mcensk'

In this data, we see that a rule of Voicing Assimilation operates across a morpheme boundary, as in (a), and across a word boundary, as in (c), where this is represented by '##', the 'double word boundary' symbol (representing one boundary at the end of one word, and another at the beginning of the next). It also operates across a kind of boundary we have not yet allowed for: the *single* word boundary between /mt͡sɛnsk/ and the form /bɨ/. The idea here is that there is a type of boundary half-way between a morpheme boundary and a full ('double') word boundary. This reflects the claim that, while /k/ is clearly a suffix, and /bɨl/ is a verb, and thus a full word, the form /bɨ/ in (b) is intermediate in status between these.

The term **clitic** is often used by linguists to denote such forms. To take another example, in Spanish, the pronouns *se*, *lo* and *la* may occur before verbs, as in *Aquí se habla ingles* ('English is spoken here'). We might therefore think of them as being parallel to full words, as in *Juan habla ingles* ('Juan speaks English'), but these pronouns seem more like suffixes in expressions like *Juan estaba hablandoselo* ('Juan was talking to him about it'). It is common to say that such forms are attached or 'cliticised' to verbs; we therefore refer to these Spanish pronouns as *clitic pronouns*.

It is because of their intermediate status that we may represent clitics as being separated from the words they attach to by a boundary ('#') intermediate between the full word boundary and the morpheme boundary. While some rules are 'blocked' by morpheme or clitic boundaries, there are other rules which are not, but are blocked by the word boundary (the backness vowel harmony rule of Hungarian, for instance). This distinction between boundary types can also be used to capture certain facts about distinct sorts of affix. For instance, the suffixes of English can be divided into two classes: stem-neutral and stem-affecting. Thus, the suffix-*ity*, when affixed to stems, may shift the stress on that stem, as in *personal/ personality*. The suffix -*ness*, on the other hand, does not have this effect, as can be seen from the pair *rotten/rottenness*. Furthermore, regular inflectional suffixes appear outside of the derivational suffixes. The following singular/plural noun pairs, for example, are well-formed: *practice*, *practices*; *practical*, *practicals*; and *practicality*, *practicalities*. In each case, the regular plural suffix is added after affixation of any derivational suffixes like -*al* and -*ity*. But it is not possible for the derivational suffixes -*al* or -*ity* to occur outside of the regular plural suffix: **practicesal*, **practicesality*, **practicalsity*.

It has therefore proved useful to recognise two classes of English affix: **Class I, the stress-affecting affixes**, and **Class II, the stress-neutral affixes**. Certain phonological rules in English are sensitive to the class of these affixes. The rule of Trisyllabic Shortening (TSS), for instance, yields a range of alternations between a long or diphthong vowel and a short vowel. Examples of this are the following pairs: *divine/divinity*, *sane/sanity*, *ferocious/ferocity*, *serene/serenity* where the short member of the alternation occurs in the derived noun.

TSS operates across Class I suffixes, but not across Class II. Thus, *maiden/maidenhood* does not exhibit an [ei] ~ [æ] alternation of the sort found in *sane/sanity*. This sensitivity to the class of affixes in English was dealt with in SPE by claiming that Class I affixes are separated from their stems by a '+' boundary, whereas Class II affixes are separated from their stems by the '#' boundary we are using for clitic attachment. We can then formulate rules like TSS to incorporate the appropriate boundary. /g/ Deletion also operates only at a '#' boundary, as in /sɪng#er/, but not in /jʌng + er/ (younger).

5.3 The Phonological Component vs the Lexicon

Let us look in a little more detail at the relationship between the phonological component and the lexicon in a generative grammar. We have said that the phonological component consists of all the phonological rules of the language, specified, where necessary, as to the order in which they apply. We will assume that, in any derivation, all the rules apply, even though most, in a given word, will fail to have their conditions met, and thus fail to effect any change (in our derivation in (7) on p. 111, on Nasal Assimilation, /g/ Deletion and /r/ Deletion have no effect on the word /ɛnd#ɪd/, for instance). However, we will adopt the simplifying convention of listing, in a derivation, only the rules whose operation is relevant to the issue we are addressing. The term 'apply' is often used in a systematically ambiguous way by phonologists. We have been using the term, in our discussion of the principle of cyclic application, to mean 'gets a chance to scan a sequence of segments to see whether its conditions are met'. It is also sometimes used to mean, in addition to this, 'effects a change'. Thus, we may say that Nasal Assimilation 'fails to apply' in the English word *end*, when what we mean, more precisely, is that the rule applies but fails to effect any change. The distinction is important, but context will usually make it clear which meaning is intended.

This notion of conditions being met brings us to two terms used in generative phonology to describe the form of phonological rules. The first of these is the **structural description** of a rule. This is simply the sequence (string) of elements which act as input to the rule. Thus, a rule of the form A→B / C___D has in input string, or structural description, of the form CAD, and has as its output the string CBD. On the right-hand side of the rule are all and only the features whose values change; we call this the **structural change** of the rule.

The rules we have considered (deletion and insertion rules apart) have all had the function of changing values of features. Let us consider a rule format with a slightly different function. We saw, in Lumasaaba (see p. 35), a class prefix which had the allomorphs [m], [n], [ɲ] and [ŋ], as in the words [zimbati] ('knives'), [zindaha] ('wings'), [ziɲɉeɟle] ('buds') and [ziŋgunija] ('bags'). This particular class prefix only ever gets added to noun roots which begin with consonants, and its place of articulation is always identical to that of the following consonant: bilabial when the following consonant is bilabial, velar when it is velar, and so on.

Although we suggested (see p. 35) that the phonological form of this prefix was /n/, it is clear that there is no way of choosing between its four alternative phonological forms: whether it is /m/, /n/, /ɲ/ or /ŋ/, an appropriate, and phonetically motivated, rule can be formulated which will yield the four allomorphs. Now, this has the effect of making our choice of /n/ for the phonological representation quite arbitrary. The generalisation here would seem to be that the prefix is a nasal stop, but that its place of articulation is entirely predictable.

We have said that the phonological representations of morphemes stored in the lexicon contain the arbitrary phonetic properties of morphemes, and that the phonological rules supply all of their predictable properties. What we need to do here, then, is to have a rule which fills in the place of articulation properties of the nasal stop, and represents the phonological form of the morpheme as a nasal stop, *unspecified as to place of articulation*. Informally, we might represent this as /N/; as for the place of articulation properties, they are signalled by means of the values for the features [ant], [cor], [back] and [high]. We will, accordingly, leave those features unspecified in the phonological representation, thus:

(9)

	/N/
cons	+
syll	−
obs	−
cont	−
ant	
cor	
high	
back	
nas	+
lat	−
voice	+

This representation is interpreted as 'a nasal stop', without indication of place of articulation, and that seems right here. It is worth repeating that such a segment is *unpronounceable*, and this fact reflects the abstract nature of phonological representations. But what of the rule? It will have to fill in the values for those features, according to their values in the following consonant. To represent this, we will adopt the **Greek Letter Variable** convention, whereby a Greek letter acts as a variable for the values '+' and '−', thus:

(10)

$$[+nas] \rightarrow \begin{bmatrix} \alpha \text{ ant} \\ \beta \text{ cor} \\ \gamma \text{ high} \\ \delta \text{ back} \end{bmatrix} / \underline{\quad} \begin{bmatrix} -\text{syll} \\ \alpha \text{ ant} \\ \beta \text{ cor} \\ \gamma \text{ high} \\ \delta \text{ back} \end{bmatrix}$$

You might attempt to write out the alternative set of rules which we will require if the Greek Letter Variable notation were not available to us: such a set will complicate the grammar considerably. The variables in the above rule are interpreted as follows. Where a variable is shared between the structural change of the rule and its environment, it has the same value. Thus, if the root-initial consonant is [+ant], then the value for [ant] in the nasal will be '+' too, and if [−ant], it will be '−'. The same applies for all the other features in the rule. Where the variables on each feature are all different, as they are here, this means that they function independently of one another: from the fact that the feature [ant] has the value '+', for instance, it need not follow that the feature [cor] will have the value '+'.

The rule will apply to yield all four of the alternants, whose values are:

(11)

	m	n	ɲ	ŋ
ant	+	+	−	−
cor	−	+	−	−
high	−	−	+	+
back	−	−	−	+

The point of this notation is that it allows us to express a dependency relation (here, between the class prefix and the root-initial consonant) as a regular (rule-governed) phonological fact, rather than as an arbitrary lexical fact. Our previous analysis (see p. 35) wrongly suggested that the prefix had the form /n/, i.e. that it was an arbitrary lexical fact that the nasal stop was alveolar. What we have seen is that it is an arbitrary lexical fact that the class prefix is a nasal stop (and this information is therefore stated in the lexicon), but that the place of articulation of that nasal stop is rule-governed: it *agrees* in its place of articulation with the following consonant. It is thus expressed as a rule in the phonological component.

In the matrix of Lumasaaba consonants in Chapter 3 (see p. 74), Lumasaaba is shown as having three nasal segments: /m/, /n/ and /ɲ/. What our analysis is claiming is that, while there are indeed place of articulation contrasts between Lumasaaba nasal stops, this contrast is suspended, or neutralised (see p. 83), in the __C environment: place of articulation among nasal stops in that environment cannot be contrastive. This is similar to our case of Russian obstruents in Chapter 4 (see p. 88): before another obstruent, voicing cannot be contrastive (is neutralised) among Russian obstruents.

We have just seen Greek letter variables functioning to *fill in* values on features; they may function to *change* values too. Take our Nasal Assimilation rule for English (see p. 73): it too assimilates nasal stops to the place of articulation of a following consonant. Thus, in *impure*, the nasal is bilabial, in *intolerant* it is alveolar, in *incurable* it is velar. When it comes to deciding on the place of articulation of the nasal in this prefix, it might seem at first that it too is unspecified as to place. But when we consider its place of articulation when it is not followed by a consonant, it is alveolar, as in *inarticulate*, *inactive* and *inoperative*. We are justified therefore in representing it as /ɪn/, with the appropriate values for the features [ant], [cor], [high] and [back] on the nasal stop, and using our rule to change those values according to their values on a following bilabial or velar consonant, thus (as in (10)):

(12)

$$[+\text{nas}] \rightarrow \begin{bmatrix} \alpha \text{ ant} \\ \beta \text{ cor} \\ \gamma \text{ high} \\ \delta \text{ back} \end{bmatrix} / \underline{\quad} \begin{bmatrix} -\text{syll} \\ \alpha \text{ ant} \\ \beta \text{ cor} \\ \gamma \text{ high} \\ \delta \text{ back} \end{bmatrix}$$

The advantage of this rule over our earlier formulation (see p. 73) is, of course, that it brings out the *dependency*, for those feature values, between the nasal stop and the following consonant. Try using this notation in the following exercise.

A. Tamil

Look back at the Tamil data on p. 24–5. In particular, look at the sequences of nasal stop plus obstruent. The feature matrix for the underlying consonants in Tamil looks like this:

	p	ʈ	t	k	č	m	ṇ	ɳ	ɲ	l	ɭ	r	ʋ
obs	+	+	+	+	+	−	−	−	−	−	−	−	−
cont	−	−	−	−	−	−	−	−	−	+	+	+	+
del rel	−	−	−	−	+	−	−	−	−	−	−	−	−
voice	−	−	−	−	−	+	+	+	+	+	+	+	+
cor	−	+	+	−	+	−	+	+	+	+	+	+	−
ant	+	+	−	−	−	+	+	−	+	−	−	−	+
high	−	−	−	+	+	−	−	−	−	−	−	−	−
back	−	−	−	+	−	−	−	−	−	−	−	−	−
lat	−	−	−	−	−	−	−	−	−	+	+	−	−
nas	−	−	−	−	−	+	+	+	−	−	−	−	−

The data show five nasal stops at the surface level in Tamil: [m], [ṇ], [ɳ], [ɲ], [ŋ]. But, as the matrix shows, there are only three nasal stops underlyingly: /m/, /n/ and /ŋ/.

(a) Using the Greek Letter Variable notation, write the rule which determines the place of articulation of nasal stops when they are followed by an obstruent.

(b) Recall your phonemic rules for the Tamil obstruents /p/, /ṭ/, /t/ and /k/ on p. 25: they yielded voiced stop allophones after nasal stops. Write a rule (call it Voicing) which takes the underlying forms of the segments to be voiceless, and yields voiced stop allophones.

(c) Show what the feature matrix is, in underlying representation, for the nasal stop in the morpheme /pa:Npʋ/.

(d) In what ways does this Nasal Assimilation analysis differ from the one we adopted for the nasal in the prefix /ɪn/ in English?

(e) Do the Nasal Assimilation and Voicing rules need to be ordered with respect to one another?

There is a further interesting use to which we can put our Greek letter notation. Look at the Hungarian data below:

(13) *Hungarian* (data from Vago 1980a)

1. (a)	[hɑːz]	'house	(b)	[hɑːstoːl]	
2. (a)	[moːkuʃ]	'squirrel'	(b)	[moːkuʃtoːl]	
3. (a)	[vɑːroʃ]	'city'	(b)	[vɑːroʃtoːl]	
4. (a)	[ørøm]	'joy'	(b)	[ørømtøːl]	
5. (a)	[byːn]	'crime'	(b)	[byːntøːl]	

The forms in the right-hand column are the ablative forms of the nominatives on the left. It is clear that there is an 'ablative' morpheme (meaning 'from') which is added to noun roots to yield the ablative forms. That morpheme has the allomorphs [to:l] and [tø:l], which differ as to the value for [back] on the suffix vowel. Can you say what determines which allomorph will occur?

It seems that the vowel in the root determines which vowel will occur in the suffix: the roots in 1–3 have [+back] vowels, and therefore appear with the [to:l] allomorph, whereas the roots in 4–6 have [−back] vowels, and thus appear with the [tø:l] allomorph. That is, [+back] roots take the [+back] allomorph, and [−back] roots take the [−back] allomorph.

This kind of dependency between the phonetic properties of an affix vowel and those of a root vowel is referred to as **vowel harmony**. Here, we have *back/front* harmony: it is in its value for the feature [back] that the affix vowels depend on the root vowels. The question arises: what is the phonological representation for the vowel in this suffix? The *phonetic* forms of the long vowels of Hungarian can be represented in a system like this:

(14)

y: i: u:
ø: e: o:
             ɑ:

The distinguishing features are, let us say, as follows:

(15)

	y:	i:	u:	ø:	e:	o:	ɑ:
back	−	−	+	−	−	+	+
round	+	−	+	+	−	+	−
high	+	+	+	−	−	−	−
low	−	−	−	−	−	−	+

That is, we will assume that the features [front] and [ATR] are not relevant in the Hungarian system. Let us assume, for the moment, that this represents the system of *underlying* long vowels too. If that is so, then we can say that the vowel in the phonological representation of the 'ablative' morpheme is a long rounded mid vowel, i.e. that it is specified as [−high, −low, +round, +long]. We could plausibly suggest that its value for the feature [back] is *unspecified*. If we adopt this analysis, we could write a rule to account for the alternating feature, thus:

(15)

$$[+\text{syll}] \rightarrow [\alpha\ \text{back}]\ /\ \begin{bmatrix} +\text{syll} \\ \alpha\ \text{back} \end{bmatrix} C_0 + \underline{\quad}$$

The rule is interpreted as follows: a vowel agrees in the value for [back] with the nearest preceding root vowel. (The expression 'C_0' which we have used here is referred to as a **cover symbol** which denotes varying numbers of consonants intervening between the suffix and root vowels. We will have occasion to use this device in Chapters 6, 7 and 8. If we want to express upper and lower limits on the number of possible intervening consonants, we express them thus: C_1^3, where the subscript numeral indicates the lower limit and the superscript denotes the upper limit. In most cases, C_0, which means 'zero or more', will suffice.)

What the rule allows for is a representation of the suffix with a vowel unspecified for a value on the feature [back], as follows (we leave the other features specified for convenience):

(17)

	/t	O:	l/
cons	+	−	+
syll	−	+	−
obs	+	−	−
cont	−	+	+
ant	+	−	+
voice	−	+	+
high	−	−	−
low	−	−	−
back	−		−
long	−	+	−
lat	−	−	+
nas	−	−	−

This backness harmony affects more than just the 'ablative' morpheme in Hungarian; many other suffix morphemes, expressing a wide range of different cases (like dative and accusative), are affected. An adequate analysis of the relevant rule and underlying representations is therefore of considerable importance in the phonology of Hungarian.

Note that this kind of hypothesis as to the phonological representation for a morpheme differs from the sort we proposed in Chapters 1–4. In those chapters, where we encountered an alternation, we proposed, as the underlying representation, the phonetic properties of either one or the other of the alternants: for the alternation [bua] ~ [ß ua] in Lumasaaba, for instance, we suggested either /bua/ or /ß ua/. Here, given the alternation [to:l] ~ [tø:l], we suggest *neither*, but rather a representation which expresses all of the phonetic properties shared by the alternants. We would, of course, have to consider other possible analyses for Hungarian backness harmony; it could be that the suffix has a vowel which is specified

for its value on the feature [back]). If it is underlyingly [+back], then our
rule will be a fronting rule, as follows:

(18)

$$[+syll] \rightarrow [-back] \ / \ \begin{bmatrix} +syll \\ -back \end{bmatrix} C_0 + \underline{\hspace{1.5cm}}$$

If it is underlyingly [−back], then we will need a backing rule like this:

(19)

$$[+syll] \rightarrow [+back] \ / \ \begin{bmatrix} +syll \\ +back \end{bmatrix} C_0 + \underline{\hspace{1.5cm}}$$

All three analyses result in the neutralisation, in suffixes, of the contrast
between [o:] and [ø:]. We will not pursue here the question of which
analysis is most plausible; it is clear that, with this minimal amount of data,
we cannot resolve the matter. But it is an interesting question. What we
will ask, though, is this: where roots have more than one vowel, must they
all have the same values for the feature [back]? The answer is that roots do
not combine back vowels and front, *rounded* vowels, as you can see from
the following forms:

(20)

(a) [bekɑ] 'frog'   (b) [rɑdir] 'eraser'   (c) [tɑɲer] 'plate'

But there is an interesting question to be asked here, which might shed
some light on the matter: what sorts of affix (back or front) do these
morphemes, with back vowels and front, unrounded vowels, take? The
answer is that they take back affixes:

(21)

(a)   [rɑdir]   [rɑdirnɑk]   [rɑdirto:l]
(b)   [tɑɲe:r]   [tɑɲe:rnɑk]   [tɑɲe:rto:l]
(c)   [be:kɑ]   [be:kɑnɑk]   [be:kɑto:l]

Thus, the vowel harmony rule simply 'ignores' a front, unrounded vowel if
it intervenes between a [+back] root vowel and the suffix vowel. Where a
certain class of root vowel fails to participate in a vowel harmony process in
this way, we refer to them as **neutral vowels**; in Hungarian, these are the
class of front, unrounded vowels: { i, i:, e, e:}. We will have to amend our
vowel harmony rule to 'skip' an intervening neutral vowel, if there is one,
thus:

(22)

$$[+\text{syll}] \rightarrow [\alpha \text{ back}] \Big/ \begin{bmatrix} +\text{syll} \\ \alpha \text{ back} \end{bmatrix} C_0 \left(\begin{bmatrix} +\text{syll} \\ -\text{back} \\ -\text{round} \end{bmatrix} C_0 \right) + \underline{\quad}$$

The rule, with a front, unrounded vowel and zero or more consonants placed in parentheses, allows for optional intervening syllables containing neutral vowels. Thus, in the following forms, it is the non-neutral root vowel which governs the backness of the affix:

(23)

1. (a) [idø:]   'time'   (b) [idø:tø:l]
2. (a) [tømeg]   'crowd'   (b) [tømektø:l]

5.4 Summing Up

What is the point in trying to devise a model of the way human languages are organised? Generative linguists answer that its value lies in the fact that the structure of language reveals something about the nature of the human mind, that is, about the organisation of (at least one kind of) human knowledge. With a clearly articulated model of that organisation, and hypotheses (rules and representations) which are explicitly stated, we can make clear and testable claims about the nature of human language, and thus about human knowledge. In the model we have now presented, we are committed to a great many explicit claims, both general and specific. At the most general, we claim that linguistic knowledge is modular: there are distinct sorts of linguistic knowledge which interact with one another in specifiable ways.

The model we are considering commits us to a claim about the way such interaction takes place. One of these is a claim about the relationship between phonology and the lexicon. Arbitrary phonetic facts about morphemes, we are assuming, are simply stored in memory (in our model, the lexicon). These are distinct in kind from the significant linguistic generalisations which the speaker has acquired (which are thus represented as rules, belonging to a separate component in the grammar). It also commits us to a claim about the relationship between morphology and phonology: morphological structure, we said, is built up in the lexicon, and only later do the phonological rules of the language have access to it.

We have claimed that phonological rules have access to syntactic information, such as the lexical category of a morpheme, and that they operate cyclically, 'from the inside out'. We have also allowed that they may be crucially ordered with respect to one another. And we have begun to commit ourselves to certain claims about the relationship between phonetics and phonology. In allowing that an underlying representation of a morpheme may be distinct from all of its surface forms, we are allowing for a certain degree of *abstractness* in the underlying phonological representations stored in the lexicon. In our underspecified representation of the Lumasaaba class prefix /N/, for instance, we claimed that the stored form is a nasal stop, *without place of articulation*. Now, since it is physically impossible to utter a nasal stop without its having a place of articulation, we are allowing for underlying representations which are in principle unutterable.

Since these claims are capable of falsification, we will run the risk of being shown to be wrong on almost all of them. The consequence, and purpose, of making clear, explicit claims is that it is quite clear what would count as counter-evidence. In generative linguistics, we positively welcome this state of affairs. Not that we *want* to be wrong, but we want to be *capable of being wrong*, to be able to find out when we are wrong; otherwise we are not saying anything of substance about the nature of linguistic reality. It is only if a hypothesis *could* be wrong that we will in fact be sticking our necks out and claiming anything of substance. If we are then not shown to be wrong (and even when we *are*), then we have made some progress in understanding how human language phonologies work. Theories that never *could* be wrong in principle are uninteresting, because they are not claiming anything.

In the following chapter, we will look in a little more detail at the consequences of the claims expressed by our model, and in particular at the ideas that phonological representations may be distinct from all of their surface realisations, and that phonological rules may apply in a stipulated order.

EXERCISES

1. Hungarian voicing assimilation (data from Vago 1980a)
Here are some root/ablative pairs from Hungarian, which show, not just alternations in the suffix vowel, induced by the vowel harmony rule, but also root-final consonant alternations:

1. (a)	[kɑ:d]	'tub'	(b)	[kɑ:tto:l]
2. (a)	[vɑrɑ:ʒ]	'magic'	(b)	[vɑrɑ:ʃto:l]
3. (a)	[by:n]	'crime'	(b)	[by:ntø:l]
4. (a)	[meleg]	'warm'	(b)	[melektø:l]
5. (a)	[hɑ:z]	'house'	(b)	[hɑ:sto:l]
6. (a)	[rɑb]	'prisoner'	(b)	[rɑpto:l]
7. (a)	[fɑl]	'wall'	(b)	[fɑlto:l]
8. (a)	[sɑ:v]	'stripe'	(b)	[sɑ:fto:l]

(i)   Is this a devoicing or a voicing phenomenon?

(ii) Ignoring /v/ (which, we said on p. 81, is [−obs] in Hungarian), write the appropriate rule.

(iii) In the exercise on Hungarian in Chapter 3 (see p. 81), you formulated another rule for obstruents in this language. Look at the two rules you now have. There is a single generalisation to be made here. What is it?

(iv) Write a single rule which expresses this generalisation, using the Greek Letter Variable notation.

(v)   The form in 9(b) below is derived from the form in 9(a) by addition of a suffix beginning with /v/:

9. (a) [hɑt] 'six'   (b) [hɑtvɑn] 'sixty'

By contrasting these with the behaviour of root-final /v/, can say what precisely the problem is with /v/?

Optional additional questions

(vi) What is the justification for having /v/ as [−obs] in phonological representation?

(vii) Alter your Voicing Assimilation rule so that /v/ will undergo, but not trigger, voicing assimilation.

(viii) We will now need a further rule in the phonology of Hungarian which has /v/ as its input. What will that rule do?

2. Akan vowel harmony
We claimed, in Chapter 3 (p. 63), that the Akan vowel system can be represented as two subsystems, like this (data from Clements 1981).

[+ATR]		[−ATR]	
i	u	ɪ	ʊ
e	o	ɛ	ɔ
	ɑ		

Notes

1. [ɑ] has no [+ATR] counterpart.

2. In the root morphemes of this language (with some apparent exceptions which we will ignore here), the vowels must be all [+ATR] or all [−ATR]. Thus, for example, /fiti/, /fite/, /fito/ and /fitu/ are possible roots, as are /čırı/, čırɛ/, /čırɑ/, /čırɔ/ and /čıru/. But the following roots are not possible: /fitı/, /fitɛ/, /fitɔ/ and /fitu/.

(i) Using the features [high, low, back, round], and [ATR], draw up a feature matrix which distinguishes all nine vowels.

Now look at the following data:

1.	[o–fiti–i]	'he pierced it'	2.	[ɔ–čırɛ–ı]	'he showed it'
3.	[e–bu–o]	'nest'	4.	[ɛ–bʊ–ɔ]	'stone'

(ii) Each of these forms consists of a prefix, a root and a suffix; list the allomorphs for each prefix and suffix.

(iii) Devise an underspecified phonological representation for the prefix whose alternants are [o] and [ɔ].

(iv) Write a vowel harmony rule which will yield all of the prefix alternations, i.e. [e] ~ [ɛ] and [o] ~ [ɔ].

(v) Because of the nature of the representations and rules of standard GP, rules cannot take the form: X→Y /___ Z ___. Nor can they take the form X→Y / Z. Bearing this in mind, write a single rule, using the brace notation, which will yield the suffixes *and* prefixes.

(vi) There is something unsatisfactory about the rule, as an attempted expression of the generalisation. Can you say what it is?

Notes

1. The '#' (as opposed to '+') in *singer* and *ended* is explained on p. 113.

2. The notion of 'cyclicity' has a long and complex history in generative linguistics. The notion has had considerable appeal in syntactic theory, and in the treatment of stress assignment in English, as begun in Chomsky, Halle and Lukoff (1956) and developed in Chomsky and Halle (1968). The latter work (SPE) assumes that most of the phonological rules of a language, both segmental and stress assigning, apply cyclically, but the exemplification they give concerns stress assignment only. Anderson (1974: 141) claims that the putative cyclic application of segmental rules is less convincingly established than that of the stress assignment rules, since cyclic application is most clearly motivated where syntactic structure in general and lexical category in particular are important (which is often the case with stress assignment rules).

Many phonological rules, he points out, are not sensitive to such factors, and with those, the idea of cyclic application seems less useful. However, the idea that many segmental phonological rules are indeed cyclic gained considerable ground within the theory of lexical phonology, which we deal with in Chapter 8.

Further Reading

While Chomsky and Halle (1968) remains the classic text, and is now available in paperback, it is not easy reading for a beginning student. The reader is advised to begin with the texts on generative phonology given at the end of Chapter 4, before proceeding to Chomsky and Halle (1968), much of which is still rewarding reading, and remains relevant to current phonological theory. For a general introduction to generative linguistics, see Smith and Wilson (1979); it sets generative phonology in its context, and serves as a good, easy-to-read, introduction to the literature on generative linguistics.

6 Abstractness and Ordering

6.1 Ordering Relations and Rule Application

We have said that the phonological component is an ordered block of all of the phonological rules of the language. With this conception of the way the rules are organised, we need to look in a little more detail at the way in which rules apply, and at the *effects* of rules upon one another, that is, at *rule interaction*. Let us look again at the Russian data presented in Chapter 5:

(1)

Phonological form	Phonetic representation	
1. #gorod + k + a#	[gorotka]	'little town'
2. #mt͡sɛnsk#bɨ#	[mt͡sɛnzgbɨ]	'if Mcensk'
3. #mt͡sɛnsk##bɨl#	[mt͡sɛnzgbɨl]	'it was Mcensk'

We said that this data exemplifies a rule of Voicing Assimilation (VA). That rule expresses the generalisation that all of the obstruents in a sequence of obstruents assimilate in voicing to the final obstruent. Another rule of Word-Final Devoicing (W-FD) operates on obstruents, as in /sad/ ('garden'), which is [sat] in the nominative singular, but [sada] in the genitive singular. Other examples are nominative singular/dative singular pairs like [xlep] / [xlebu] ('bread'), [storoʃ]/[storoʒu] ('guard'), [rok]/[rogu] ('horn'), and nominative /genitive pairs like [ras]/[raza] ('time').

Let us consider the form of the two rules, the way they apply and then their ordering. The formulation of W-FD is relatively straightforward:

(2) *Word-Final Devoicing*

$$[+obs] \rightarrow [-voice] / \_\_\#$$

Note that when the rule (thus formulated) applies to a voiceless obstruent, it fails to create any change (this is referred to as 'vacuous application' of the rule). For the VA rule, the following formulation will suffice for our purposes:

(3) *Voicing Assimilation*

$$[+obs] \rightarrow [\alpha voice] / \_\_(\#(\#)) \begin{bmatrix} +obs \\ \alpha\, voice \end{bmatrix}$$

127

This means that an obstruent will assimilate in voicing to a following
obstruent, independently of whether there is an intervening morpheme
boundary, or a single or double word boundary.[1] But what of the cases,
like 2 and 3 on p. 127, where more than two obstruents are involved? Here,
we must allow that when the rule 'applies' (in the sense of 'gets the chance
to have its conditions met'), it may 'apply' (in the sense of 'have an effect')
more than once, like this:

(4)

	# mt͡sɛnsk## bɨl#	
VA	mt͡sɛnsg	bɨl
VA	mt͡sɛnzg	bɨl
Phonetic representation	[mt͡sɛnzgbɨl]	

Where we allow for a rule to have an effect more than once, we say that it
applies *iteratively*; we allow for **iterative rule application** (but we have not
supplied here any theory of the circumstances whereby a rule may or may
not apply in this way).[2]

Now let us look at the ordering of the two rules. We say that two
rules are **affecting** if they have overlapping inputs, conditions or structural changes. Since these two rules have overlapping inputs (both pick
out the class of obstruents) and overlapping structural changes (they
both change values on the feature [voice]), they are clearly affecting.
This means that the operation of one of them will have implications
for the operation of the other. What we need to ask, then, is how they
are ordered; that is, what the direction of influence is. We can see from
the morpheme /mozg/ ('brain') that W-FD precedes VA: without affixes,
the phonetic form of the morpheme is [mosk], with the following
derivation:

(5)

	# mozg#
W-FD	mozk
VA	mosk
Phonetic representation	[mosk]

Note that, by virtue of its application, W-FD creates circumstances under
which VA may effect a change: it allows VA to change the voicing state of
the underlying /z/. Where a rule A precedes and creates conditions under
which another rule B may have an effect, we say that A **feeds** B, that the
ordering is a **feeding order**. In this case, it is clear that the Voicing

Assimilation rule would have no effect on the underlying sequence /zg/, but once the Word Final Devoicing rule has applied, conditions are created under which the rule *can* induce a change.[3]

Let us look at another kind of ordering relationship. We saw on p. 39 that in Polish nouns, root-final /š/ (the voiceless post-alveolar fricative) becomes pre-palatal before a high front vowel. This rule, known as Nominal Strident Palatalisation (NSP), may be written as:

(6) *Nominal Strident Palatalisation*

$$
\begin{bmatrix} +\text{stri} \\ +\text{cont} \\ -\text{ant} \\ -\text{voice} \end{bmatrix} \rightarrow [+\text{high}] \ / \ \underline{\quad} \ + \begin{bmatrix} +\text{syll} \\ -\text{back} \\ +\text{high} \end{bmatrix}_{]N}
$$

Note that we use the representation ']N' to restrict the rule to nominal roots.

Another rule, known as First Velar Palatalisation (FVP), operates on underlying velar obstruents (/k/, /g/, /x/) to yield [č], [ǰ] and [š], respectively, where the velar is followed by a front vowel (ignore the vowel deletion in 2(b); data from Rubach 1984):

(7)

1. (a)	[kšɨk]	'a shout'	(b)	[kšičei]	'shout'
2. (a)	[mʲažaga]	'a squash'	(b)	[mʲažǰɨtś]	'to squash'
3. (a)	[strax]	'fear'	(b)	[strašɨtś]	'to fear'

It may be written as follows (note that palatalisation, in this case, does not consist in changing the value on the feature [back]):

(8) *First Velar Palatisation*

$$
\begin{bmatrix} +\text{obs} \\ -\text{cor} \\ +\text{back} \end{bmatrix} \rightarrow \begin{bmatrix} +\text{cor} \\ +\text{stri} \end{bmatrix} \ / \ \underline{\quad} \begin{bmatrix} -\text{cons} \\ -\text{back} \end{bmatrix}
$$

If the underlying form of the morpheme meaning 'building' is /gmax/, and the phonetic form of the augmentative ('big building') is [gmašisko], what order do the rules NSP and FVP apply in? Draw up a derivation for the augmentative form.

Derivations for both /gmax/ and /gmax + isko/ look like this:

(9)

	/gmax/	/gmax + ɨsko/
NSP	——	——————
FVP	——	gmašɨsko
Phonetic representation	[gmax]	[gmašɨsko]

What this ordering expresses is the fact that where post-alveolar [š] derives from /x/ via FVP, it does not undergo NSP. What is clear is that FVP and NSP are affecting: FVP can create input for NSP (it can yield [š], the input segment for NSP). That is, FVP could feed NSP. But in ordering the rules such that NSP precedes FVP, we prevent this from happening. Such an ordering is referred to as **counter-feeding order**. Note that this presupposes a restriction on the application of the two rules to the effect that, once a rule has applied, it may not subsequently reapply if its conditions are met later in the derivation.[4]

Let us now look at the interaction of two rules in Lithuanian: Degemination and Metathesis. We begin by attempting to formulate the Degemination rule, which reduces geminate (i.e. double) consonant clusters to single consonants, as in the following (data from Kenstowicz and Kisseberth 1973):

(10)

Past	Imperfect plural	1PS future	Gloss
[kase]	[kaskite]	[kasiu]	'dig'
[gere]	[gerkite]	[gersiu]	'drink'
[teko]	[tekite]	[teksiu]	'flow'

Thus, /kas + siu/ is realised as [kasiu], and /tek + kite/ as [tekite]. To formulate the rule, we would have to insist that it applies to two [+obs] segments which are adjacent to one another and are identical. This is problematic, since it means using Greek Letter Variable notation for each and every feature (other than [cons] and [syll], which need not be included), such that the two segments in question have identical feature specifications. This seems a complicated way of expressing what is a simple generalisation (we will abbreviate the representations here to save space and readdress the problem in Chapter 9). We might suggest a deletion rule:

(11)

$$
\begin{bmatrix} + \text{obs} \\ \alpha \text{ cor} \\ \beta \text{ ant} \\ . \\ . \\ . \end{bmatrix} \longrightarrow \emptyset \ / \ \begin{bmatrix} + \text{obs} \\ \alpha \text{ cor} \\ \beta \text{ ant} \\ . \\ . \\ . \end{bmatrix} \underline{\qquad}
$$

This makes an explicit claim as to which obstruent is deleted, but there is no non-arbitrary way of choosing between that formulation, which deletes the second in the sequence, and the following one, which deletes the first:

(12)

$$
\begin{bmatrix} + \text{obs} \\ \alpha \text{ ant} \\ \beta \text{ cor} \\ . \\ . \\ . \end{bmatrix} \longrightarrow \emptyset \ / \ \underline{\qquad} \begin{bmatrix} + \text{obs} \\ \alpha \text{ ant} \\ \beta \text{ cor} \\ . \\ . \\ . \end{bmatrix}
$$

There is, of course, something wrong with the idea that it is one or the other which is deleted. We may therefore suggest a slightly different rule format for Degemination which has more than one segment on its left-hand side, as follows:

(13)

$$
\begin{bmatrix} + \text{obs} \\ \alpha \text{ cor} \\ \beta \text{ ant} \\ . \\ . \\ . \end{bmatrix} \begin{bmatrix} + \text{obs} \\ \alpha \text{ cor} \\ \beta \text{ ant} \\ . \\ . \\ . \end{bmatrix} \longrightarrow \begin{bmatrix} + \text{obs} \\ \alpha \text{ cor} \\ \beta \text{ ant} \\ . \\ . \\ . \end{bmatrix}
$$

The rule of Metathesis in Lithuanian interchanges fricative + velar stop clusters, where they occur before a consonant. The morpheme /dresk/ ('to bind'), for example, has the following forms:

(14)

Past	Imperfect Plural	1PS future	Infinitive
[dreske]	[drekskite]	[dreksiu]	[dreksti]

In attempting to formulate the Metathesis rule, we also require a rule with more than one segment on the left-hand side (and, in this case, more than one on the right-hand side), as in:

(15)

$$\begin{bmatrix} +\text{obs} \\ +\text{cont} \end{bmatrix} \begin{bmatrix} +\text{obs} \\ -\text{cont} \\ +\text{back} \end{bmatrix} \longrightarrow \begin{bmatrix} +\text{obs} \\ -\text{cont} \\ +\text{back} \end{bmatrix} \begin{bmatrix} +\text{obs} \\ +\text{cont} \end{bmatrix} / \text{—} [+\text{cons}]$$

The two rules are affecting, since both concern sequences of obstruents: Degemination has an obstruent in its input and in its conditions, and metathesis has obstruents in its input and its structural change. The underlying representations for the four forms in (14) are /dresk + e/, /dresk + kite/, /dresk + siu/ and /dresk + ti/, respectively. Show the derivations for each of these.

You will have noticed that Metathesis is ordered before Degemination, with derivations as follows:

(16)

	Past	Imperfect plural	1PS future	Infinitive
	/dresk + e/	/dresk + kite/	/dresk + siu/	/dresk + ti/
Metathesis	————	drekskite	drekssiu	dreksti
Degemination	————	————	dreksiu	————
Phonetic representation	[dreske]	[drekskite]	[dreksiu]	[dreksti]

Note that, in [dreksiu], Metathesis *feeds* Degemination: it creates a geminate consonant cluster, which acts as input to the Degemination rule. In [drekskite], however, Metathesis *deprives* Degemination of input: the /k + k/ geminate cluster could act as input to Degemination, but that piece of potential input is destroyed by Metathesis. In cases like this, where a rule A precedes a rule B, and by virtue of its application deprives Rule B of input, we say that Rule A **bleeds** Rule B. A rule may bleed another in one of two ways: either by destroying potential input, as in this case, or in destroying potential conditions. In either case, we say that a rule bleeds another if it destroys a representation in which the bled rule could have effected a change.

We have now established three sorts of ordering relationship: feeding, counter-feeding and bleeding (we will look at another, counter-bleeding, presently). Try to establish the ordering relationships in the following exercise.

A. Hungarian (data from Vago 1980a)

The rules in question are: Degemination, Voicing Assimilation and Palatalisation. The Degemination rule reduces geminate consonant clusters when they are preceded or followed by another consonant; the following data show some examples:

1. (a) [sɑkk]   'chess'
   (b) [sɑkto:l]   'from chess'
   (c) [sɑkkom]   'my chess'
   (d) [sɑktɑ:blɑ]   'chess board'

Voicing Assimilation (cf p. 124) assimilates an obstruent to the voicing state of a following obstruent. Palatalisation (PAL) causes the coronal segments {/t/, /d/, /n/, /l/} to become palatal [c], [ɟ], [ɲ] and [ʎ], respectively, before a following palatal consonant. It is formulated as:

$$\begin{bmatrix} +\text{cor} \\ -\text{del rel} \end{bmatrix} \rightarrow \begin{bmatrix} -\text{ant} \\ -\text{cor} \\ +\text{high} \end{bmatrix} / \underline{\quad} \begin{bmatrix} -\text{syll} \\ -\text{cor} \\ +\text{high} \\ -\text{back} \end{bmatrix}$$

(a) The underlying representations #kyld + te:ged# ('he sends you') and #kyld + ɟ + yk# ('we send it') have the surface forms [kylte: ged] and [kylɟyk], respectively. For each one, give the derivation, with the rules ordered where necessary.

(b) What are the ordering relationships between (a) PAL and Degemination and (b) Voicing Assimilation and Degemination?

The Hungarian exercise exemplifies the most natural of ordering relationships: that of feeding. We could, of course, allow rules to apply in a random sequential order, applying wherever and whenever their conditions are met. Rules would still, under this picture of rule application, contract ordering relationships, but the ordering would emerge as a consequence of the nature of the rules themselves. This sort of ordering is referred to as **intrinsic ordering**: the order arises from the intrinsic properties of the rules; it is distinct from **extrinsic ordering**, in which an order is stipulated in the grammar, rather than arising naturally from the nature of the rules. It should be clear that we must insist on extrinsic ordering if our analysis, in many of the cases we have looked at, is to work. We will take the view therefore that extrinsic ordering is crucial, but we will consider arguments against, and problems with, such ordering in the interlude and in Chapter 7.

Clearly, with a large number of ordered phonological rules intervening between phonological and phonetic representation, the possibility arises of a large gulf opening up between the two levels of representation. Let us look at how wide this gulf can get.

6.2 Absolute Neutralisation

In Chapter 5, we considered three different versions of the rule for backness harmony in Hungarian vowels. Let us assume, without going into the evidence, that the following is the correct formulation:

(17)

$$[+\text{syll}] \rightarrow [+\text{back}] \ / \ \begin{bmatrix} +\text{syll} \\ +\text{back} \end{bmatrix} C_0 \left(\begin{bmatrix} +\text{syll} \\ -\text{back} \\ -\text{round} \end{bmatrix} C_0 \right) \underline{\quad}$$

That is, the suffix vowels are underlyingly [−back], and are realised as [+back] vowels when preceded by a [+back] root vowel. The rule 'ignores' intervening neutral vowels, which are [−back, −round].

The rule will therefore cope perfectly well with roots that have all [+back] or all [−back] vowels, and it will also cover 'mixed' roots, which have neutral vowels in them. But what of roots which have only neutral vowels in them? We would expect them always to take suffixes with [−back] vowels, since the conditions of the vowel harmony rule would not be met: they do not contain [+back] vowels. And this is indeed the case in the following data:

(18)

1. (a) [kert]   'garden'   (b) [kertnek]   (c) [kerttø: l]
2. (a) [ʃi: n]   'colour'   (b) [ʃi:nnek]   (c) [ʃi:ntø:l]
3. (a) [ʃege:ɲ]   'poor'   (b) [ʃege: ɲnek]   (c) [ʃege: ɲtø:l]

But a rather large number of all-neutral roots (more than sixty) take [+back] affixes, for example:

(19)

1. (a) [ɲi:l]   'arrow'   (b) [ɲi:lnɑk]   (c) [ɲi:lto:l]
2. (a) [fing]   'fart'   (b) [fingnɑk]   (c) [finkto:l]
3. (a) [hi:d]   'bridge'   (b) [hi:dnɑk]   (c) [hi:tto:l]

This raises the question of how these should be treated in the grammar. We could simply view all such roots as exceptional: they constitute exceptions to the vowel harmony generalisation. To reflect the fact that such roots arbitrarily take [+back] affixes, we would simply list their variants in the lexicon. Thus, for /hi:d/, we would list, as phonological representations in the lexicon, every form it has. To do so is to insist that the surface forms are not yielded by rule, but simply have to be stored in memory. This would make such cases parallel to, for instance, the irregular surface forms of the /bi:/ (*be*) morpheme in English: we must simply list irregular forms like /æm/, /ɪz/ and /wɜ:r/ in the lexicon. Let us refer to this approach to our recalcitrant Hungarian cases as the 'exception analysis'.

There is something odd about the exception analysis, though. The parallelism drawn between the Hungarian cases and the irregular English verb forms is not very convincing. The Hungarian forms are exceptional in a very odd way, surely! Firstly, the English forms are exceptional in that they fail to conform to the rules for tense, person and number inflection. But the Hungarian forms are different: they actually undergo the vowel harmony rule where we do not expect them to. Now, those are two different sorts of exceptionality; had the Hungarian forms simply failed to undergo vowel harmony when we expected them to, they could reasonably have been treated as exceptions to the rule, just as the past tense of *are* is an exception to the rule for past tense formation. But that is not what is happening. Secondly, their exceptionality is remarkably regular: it is not the case that morphemes like /hi:d/ will take *either* [+back] *or* [−back] affixes indifferently; they *invariably* take [+back] affixes. Nor do they take, say, the [+back] form of /nAk/ but the [−back] form of /tO:l/; for *every* affix (and there are a great many such affixes in Hungarian), they take the [+back] form.

These 'irregular' roots are therefore suspiciously regular in their behaviour: they invariably behave as though they had [+back] root vowels. To express this regularity, let us adopt an alternative to the exception analysis: let us postulate underlying vowels in these roots which are [+back], thus:

(20)

	/ɲ	ɨ	l/
cons	+	−	−
syll	−	+	−
high	−	+	−
low	−	−	−
back	−	+	−
round	−	−	−
long	−	+	−
nas	+	−	−
lat	−	−	+

This means that, when an affix like /nAk/ is added to the root, the vowel harmony rule will yield the [+back] form [nɑk]. What the analysis commits us to is the existence of underlying vowels which are [+high, +back, −round]. The underlying system, according to this analysis, will differ from the surface system, in that it will look like this:

(21)

Short vowels				Long vowels			
[−back]	[+back]			[−back]	[+back]		
i	y	ɨ	u	i:	y:	ɨ:	u:
e	o		ɔ	e:	o:		ɔ:
			ɑ				ɑ:

This analysis also commits us to postulating a rule which applies after vowel harmony and changes the value on the feature [back] in underlying vowels which are [+high, +back, −round], thus:

(22)

$$\begin{bmatrix} +\text{syll} \\ +\text{high} \\ +\text{back} \\ -\text{round} \end{bmatrix} \rightarrow [-\text{back}]$$

That is, although there is an underlying distinction between [+high, −back, −round] vowels (i.e. /i/ and /i:/) and vowels which are [+high, +back, −round] (i.e. /ɨ/ and /ɨ:/), this contrast manifests itself only in the vowel harmony phenomena, and is neutralised as follows:

(23)

/i/   /ɨ/   /i:/   /ɨ:/

[i]   [i:]

In all of the cases of neutralisation we have considered so far, there have been specific contexts in which an underlying contrast is neutralised; here, the underlying contrast is neutralised in *all* contexts (the neutralising rule we have just formulated is context-free: there is no slash followed by a statement of the neutralising context). That is, the underlying vowels /ɨ/ and /ɨ:/ never surface; for this reason, they are viewed by some phonologists as abstract segments. Cases like this exemplify rather a radical kind of neutralisation, which is called **absolute neutralisation**.

Note the relationship between the postulating of such abstract underlying vowels and the idea of extrinsic ordering: it is crucial in this case that the absolute neutralisation rule be extrinsically ordered to operate after the vowel harmony rule, as in the following derivations:

(24)

	/fɨng + nAk/	/ɲiːl + nAk/
Vowel Harmony	fɨngnak	ɲɨːlnak
Absolute neutralisation	fingnak	ɲiːlnak
Phonetic representation	[fingnak]	[ɲiːlnak]

Rules of absolute neutralisation may, like this one, be of the form X→Y, with no statement of a context. Alternatively, they may contain contexts, such that the stated contexts exhaust all possibilities and have the effect of neutralising a contrast in all contexts. Imagine two underlying segments A and B occurring in contexts __X , Y__ and __Z. A rule of the form:

(25)

$$A \rightarrow B \quad \left\{ \begin{array}{l} \text{—} \left\{ \begin{array}{l} X \\ Z \end{array} \right\} \\ Y\text{—} \end{array} \right\}$$

will effectively wipe out the underlying contrast. A third type of rule will simply delete the underlying segment in all contexts, thus:

(26)

X → ∅

Finally, some rules will combine these, collapsing the contrast in some specific context(s) and, say, deleting the underlying segment elsewhere. Let us look at a case of that sort.

In Polish, the following contrastive vowels occur:

(27)

i		u
	ɨ	
e		
ɛ	ɐ	ɔ

Their feature specifications are:

(28)

	i	ɨ	u	e	ɛ	ɔ	ɐ
high	+	+	+	−	−	−	−
low	−	−	−	−	−	−	+
ATR	+	+	+	+	−	−	−
back	−	+	+	−	−	+	+
round	−	−	+	−	−	+	−

There are many alternations between presence and absence of the vowel [ɛ] (i.e. between [ɛ] and ∅) as follows (data from Rubach 1984):

(29)

1. [pɔsɛł]   'envoy'   (nom. sg.)   [pɔsłɐ]   'envoy'   (gen. sg.)
2. [mɛx]   'moss'   (nom. sg.)   [mxi]   'moss'   (nom. pl.)
3. [sɛn]   'dream'   (nom. sg.)   [sni]   'dream'   (nom. pl.)

There are also non-alternating [ɛ]s:

4. [gʒɛx]   'sin'   (nom. sg.)   [gʒɛxi]   'sin'   (nom. pl.)
5. [fɔtɛl]   'armchair' (nom. sg.)   [fɔtɛlɐ] 'armchair' (gen. sg.)
6. [tlɛn]   'oxygen'   (nom. sg.)   [tlɛnu]   'oxygen'   (gen. sg.)

Furthermore, the alternating [ɛ]s also alternate with [ɨ] in some morphemes and with [i] in others as follows:

(30)

1. [zɛmɛk] 'lock'   [zɛmɨkɐjɐ] 'they lock'   [zɛmknɛ̃] 'they will lock'
2. [vićɛ́ćɐ] 'cutting' [vićinɛš] 'you cut out'   [vɨtńɛš]   'you will cut out'

Let us adopt the same strategy as we did with the 'irregular' Hungarian roots: there, we said that they behaved regularly as if they had underlyingly [+back] vowels. Here, the alternating roots behave differently from the non-alternating roots. Let us assume that the [ɛ] vowels in 1–3 are phonologically distinct from the [ɛ] vowels in 4–6. That is, let us postulate a source other than /ɛ/ for the roots in 1–3: underlying vowels which are [+high, −round], like [i] and [ɨ], but which differ from them in being [−ATR]. These underlying vowels, which we will transcribe as /ĩ/ and /ɨ̃/, are distinct from one another in that the former is [−back] and the latter is

[+back]. They are usually referred to informally as 'yers' by Polish phonologists.

In postulating them, we assume an underlying system of vowels, like this:

(31)

	i	ɨ	ǐ	ɨ̆	u	e	ɛ	ɔ	ɐ
high	+	+	+	+	+	−	−	−	−
low	−	−	−	−	−	−	−	−	+
ATR	+	+	−	−	+	+	−	−	−
back	−	+	−	+	+	−	−	+	+
round	−	−	−	−	+	−	−	+	−

The neutralising rule which collapses these with /ɛ/ in certain contexts is called Lower, and looks like this:

(32) *Lower*

$$
\begin{bmatrix} +\text{syll} \\ +\text{high} \\ -\text{ATR} \end{bmatrix} \rightarrow \begin{bmatrix} -\text{high} \\ -\text{back} \end{bmatrix} / \underline{\quad} C_0 \begin{bmatrix} +\text{syll} \\ +\text{high} \\ -\text{ATR} \end{bmatrix}
$$

That is, where an underlying yer is followed by another yer, it is realised as [ɛ]. We must also formulate a deletion rule which deletes yers,[5] but not /ɛ/:

(33) *Yer Deletion*

$$
\begin{bmatrix} +\text{syll} \\ +\text{high} \\ -\text{ATR} \end{bmatrix} \rightarrow \emptyset
$$

Now, given that this is a context-free deletion rule (there is no context stated in the rule), it is a rule of absolute neutralisation. Note too that if the rules are ordered with Yer Deletion first, Lower would always be bled. That is, Lower would be *absolutely bled*, and would never have an effect, since it would be deprived of all possible input. So they would have to be ordered such that Lower precedes, and does not bleed, Yer Deletion. This ordering relationship is known as **counter-bleeding**.

With this analysis, we take it that the roots in 1–3 on p. 138 have underlying yers, as in 1: /posɨł/. As with the morpheme 'lock' (see p. 138), this root has alternants, not just with [ɛ] and ∅, but also with [i]:

(34)

[pɔsɛɫ]	'envoy'	(nom. sg.)
[pɔsɫɐ]	'envoy'	(gen. sg.)
[pɔsiɫɐj]	'send'	(derived imperfect)

We now see that there are three surface alternants for the 'send' morpheme: [pɔsɛɫ], [pɔsɫ] and [pɔsiɫ]. Let us assume the following underlying forms for the other morphemes in (34):

(35)

'genitive singular':   /-ɐ/   'imperative of imperfective':   /-ɐj/

If we assume that the underlying form of the 'nom. sing.' masculine suffix consists of just a yer, then the underlying representation for the nominative singular (masculine) form will be /pɔsiɫ + ɨ/. We can then formulate a rule which changes the value on the feature [ATR] in yers when they are followed by the Derived Imperfective (DI), as follows:

(36) *Derived Imperfective*

$$\begin{bmatrix} +\text{syll} \\ +\text{high} \\ -\text{ATR} \end{bmatrix} \rightarrow [+\text{ATR}] \ / \ \underline{\quad} \ C_0 \ \text{ɐj}_{[\text{imperf}]}$$

This will yield the following derivations:

(37)

	# pɔsiɫ+ɨ#	# pɔsiɫ+ɐ#	# pɔsiɫ+ɐj#imperf]
Lower	pɔsɛɫɨ	———	———
DI	———	———	pɔsiɫɐj
Yer Deletion	pɔsɛɫ	pɔsɫɐ	———
Phonetic representation	[pɔsɛɫ]	[pɔsɫɐ]	[pɔsiɫɐj]

The attraction of this analysis is that it allows us to account for a set of widely occurring alternations, not just between presence and absence of [ɛ] (between [ɛ] and ∅), but also between [ɛ], ∅ and [i], and between [ɛ], ∅ and [i]. It is fundamental to the strategy of generative phonology to claim that, where a morpheme displays alternations, these are to be derived from a single underlying representation. Our analysis of these Polish morphemes is based entirely on this strategy. Like our analysis of roots in Hungarian which have neutral vowels but take [+back] affixes, it allows for an underlying representation of a morpheme which is abstract in that it is distinct from each of its surface realisations. It also demands, as in our Hungarian case, extrinsic ordering and rules of absolute neutralisation.

6.3 Conclusion and Prospect

In this chapter, we have seen some of the implications of a model of phonological organisation which allows not only for extrinsic ordering, but also for a considerable 'distance' between phonological and phonetic representation. That is, the number of rules which apply in the derivation of the phonetic representation for a morpheme from its underlying representation may be large, and because of this, the phonetically defined properties of the segments in the phonetic representation may differ radically from the characterisation of those segments at the underlying level.

While it is important, for an understanding of the development of phonological theory, that the idea of extrinsic ordering is understood, it is not crucial to understand the details of notions like partial and total ordering relationships, and counter-feeding and counter-bleeding. It is important, however, to understand that a rule-based, derivational phonology naturally gives rise to such notions.

As we have now allowed for a remarkable degree of abstractness in phonological representations, with underlying segments which do not emerge on the surface in their underlying form, and with rules of absolute neutralisation which effect this state of affairs, one might object that this is 'going too far' in some sense. But in what senses *precisely* might we be accused of going too far? That is the question we will examine in Chapter 7.

EXERCISES

1. Polish (data from Rubach 1984)
In Polish, there is a rule of Non-continuant Depalatalisation (ND), which depalatalises the pre-palatals /ć/, /j́/ and /ń/ where they occur before coronal sonorants. That is, they are realised in this context as alveolar [t], [d] and [n], respectively. Here are some examples of the alternations produced:

1. (a) [vilgoć]   'moisture'   (b) [vilgotnɨ]   'moist'
2. (a) [tseladj]   'household'   (b) [tseladdnɨ]   'of the household'
3. (a) [koń]   'horse'   (b) [konnɨ]   'horse–like'

The rule may be formulated as follows (from Rubach 1984, slightly amended):

$$
\begin{bmatrix} +\text{high} \\ +\text{cor} \\ -\text{cont} \\ -\text{lat} \end{bmatrix} \rightarrow \begin{bmatrix} -\text{high} \\ -\text{del rel} \\ +\text{ant} \end{bmatrix} \ / \ \underline{\quad} \begin{bmatrix} -\text{syll} \\ +\text{cor} \\ -\text{obs} \end{bmatrix}
$$

(i) The forms [viɳɛn] 'guilty' (masculine) and [vinnɛ] 'guilty' (feminine) are derived from the morpheme /viɳ/ ('guilt'). The underlying representations are /viɳ + ĭn + ĭ/ for the masculine and /viɳ + ĭn + ɛ/ for the feminine. Show what the derivations are.

(ii) What is the ordering relationship between ND and Yer Deletion?

2. French

A rule of Elision in French deletes a vowel if it is word-final and followed by a word which begins with a vowel. It yields the following sorts of alternation:

1. [limɐӡ]   'the image'   2. [lɐvɐʃ]   'the cow'
3. [lɐ ̈jeʁ]   'the backs'   4. [ləmutɔ̃]   'the sheep'
5. [lo]   'the water'   6. [lɐbuʃ]   'the mouth'
7. [lotœʁ]   'the author'   8. [ləvɛ̃]   'the wine'

The alternations are, of course, in the form of the masculine and feminine definite article, which have the phonological form /lə/ and /lɐ/, respectively, and the alternants [lə] [l] and [lɐ] [l]. We may formulate the rule as follows:

$[+\text{syll}] \rightarrow \emptyset \ / \ \underline{\quad}\# \#[+\text{syll}]$

Another rule, Truncation, deletes a word-final consonant where it is followed by a word beginning in a consonant, yielding the following sorts of alternation:

1.	[lezimɐʒ]	'the images'	2.	[levɐʃ]	'the cows'
3.	[lezɐʁjɛʁ]	'the backs'	4.	[lemutɔ̃]	'the sheep'
5.	[lezo]	'the waters'	6.	[lebuʃ]	'the mouths'
7.	[ptitotœʁ]	'little authors'	8.	[ptimutɔ̃]	'little sheep'

The underlying representation for the definite article (plural) is /lez/, with surface alternants [le] and [lez], and the underlying representation for the masculine form of the adjective 'little' is /pɔtit/. The rule, formulated below, operates on these to yield the surface forms:

$$[-\text{syll}] \rightarrow \emptyset \; / \; \underline{\quad}\# \; \#[-\text{syll}]$$

There is a class of nouns (all spelled with an 'h' and called 'h-aspiré' words) which begin with a vowel in their surface form but do not induce Elision, for example:

1.	[lɔɐʃ]	'the axe'	2.	[lɔibu]	'the owl'
3.	[lɔɛʁo]	'the hero'	4.	[lɔotœʁ]	'the height'

These words induce Truncation:

1.	[leɐʃ]	'the axes'	2.	[leibu]	'the owls'
3.	[leeʁo]	'the heroes'	4.	[leotœʁ]	'the heights'

An 'exception analyis' would insist that these be marked in the lexicon as irregularly failing to induce Elision and irregularly inducing Truncation.

(i) Can you suggest an analysis of the underlying representations for these nouns which would explain why it is that both 'irregularities' invariably (i.e. regularly) go together? (That is, an analysis which shows why there are no nouns which fail to induce Elision *and* Truncation or which induce both.)

(ii) What sort of absolute neutralisation rule will you need to yield the surface forms of these nouns?

(iii) How will it be ordered with respect to Elision and Truncation?

(iv) Given the extrinsic ordering of the absolute neutralisation rule after the rules of Truncation and Elision what ordering relations does it contract with those rules? You might answer this by considering what ordering relations it would contract with them if it were ordered to apply before those rules.

(v) One way of explaining these cases would be to appeal to the influence, on French speakers, of the written form of the nouns in question. How does the following data bear on that explanation?

	Written form	Phonetic Representation	Gloss
1. (a)	*l'hotel*	[lotel]	'the hotel'
(b)	*les hotels*	[lezotel]	'the hotels'
2. (a)	*l'hiver*	[livɛʁ]	'the winter'
(b)	*les hivers*	[lezivɛʁ]	'the winters'
3. (a)	*l'horreur*	[lɔʁœʁ]	'the horrors'
(b)	*les horreurs*	[lezɔʁœʁ]	'the horrors'

3. Brussels French

The French spoken in Brussels (as described in Baetens-Beardsmore 1971) differs phonologically from Standard French in a variety of ways, among which are a set of allophonic rules which do not occur in Standard French. One of these, Obstruent Devoicing, applies word-finally, as in [ãtɪp] (*Antibes*), [mɛrt]. (*merde*), [kɑmɑrk] (*Camargue*), [rezɛrf] (*réserve*), [gœs] (*gueze*), [bɛłʃ] (*Belge*). Another, Lateral Velarisation, applies after a vowel, as in [lɔtɛł] (*l'hotel*), [lɔkɒł] (*locale*). The latter word exhibits the operation of another rule, /ɑ/ Rounding, also seen in [famɪłjɒł] (*familiale*) which applies to an /ɑ/ preceding velarised /l/. A final rule of /l/ Deletion, which Brussels French shares with Standard French, applies to word-final laterals which are preceded by a consonant, as in [kɑpɑp] (*capable*).

(i) The underlying representation for *capable* is /kɑpɑblə/, and for *familiale* is /famɪlɪɑlə/. Assuming a rule of Word-Final Schwa Deletion and a rule of Glide Formation (which changes /i/ to [j] when it precedes a vowel in the same syllable), draw derivations for both words.

(ii) State what ordering relations, if any, hold between each pair of rules, and say whether the ordering is extrinsic or intrinsic.

4. Xhosa

This exercise is designed to bring out an interesting ordering relationship which we have not yet discussed. It concerns the two ordered rules in Xhosa given in Chapter 2. One of these, Elision, deletes the first of two adjacent vowels. It may be formulated as follows:

[+syll] → Ø / [+syll]___

The rule will yield, for instance, [kudaka] from /ku + u + daka/ ('some mud') and [kubantu] from /ku + a + bantu/ ('some people'). The other rule, Glide Formation, derives a non-syllabic approximant, [w], from an underlying /u/, where this precedes /i/, as in [kwihase], from /ku + i + hase/ ('some horses'). It may be formulated thus:

$$\begin{bmatrix} +\text{syll} \\ +\text{high} \\ +\text{back} \end{bmatrix} \rightarrow [-\text{syll}] \; / \; \underline{\hspace{1em}} \; \begin{bmatrix} +\text{syll} \\ +\text{high} \\ -\text{low} \\ -\text{back} \end{bmatrix}$$

(The term 'glide' identifies semi-vowels like [w], [j] and [ɥ], which are often desyllabified versions of /u/, /i/ and /y/; see Chapter 9 for examples from French and Okpe.)

(i) The order of application suggested in Chapter 2 is Glide Formation before Elision. Draw derivations for /ku + a + bantu/ and /ku + i + hase/ and say what the ordering relationship between the two rules is.

(ii) The reverse order will clearly produce the wrong results. But. what would the ordering relationship be if the rules were ordered that way?

You should have noticed that, even in the reverse order, a bleeding relationship obtains.[6] This means that, whatever the order, the relationship is simultaneously bleeding and counter-bleeding. This relationship is referred to as *mutual bleeding*; its existence demonstrates just how complex ordering relationships can get in a phonology with ordered rules. We will look at a further complication in the interlude.

Notes

1. Sonorants are 'transparent' to VA, as can be seen from the following nasal stops:

#iz#mt͡sɛnsk + a#	[ismt͡sɛnska]	'from Mcensk'
#ot#mzd + ɨ#	[odmzdɨ]	'from the bribe'
#ot#naukɨ#	[otnaukɨ]	'from science'

That is, they do not undergo VA, but they do not 'block' it either: the rule simply skips any intervening sonorants. Note that /v/ is odd: it is like a sonorant in that it does not induce, and is transparent to, VA:

#ot#vdov + ɨ#	[odvdovɨ]	'from the widow'
#ot#vtor + ogo#	[otvtorgo]	'from another'

But it is like an obstruent in that it undergoes Word-Final Devoicing: /trezv/ → [trezf] ('sober'). We will look again at /v/ in Russian in Chapter 8.

2. A distinction can be made between cases like this, where a rule applies, and applies again to the string which is its output, and other cases, where a Rule A applies and may apply again after the application of *another* Rule B. The rules of u-Umlaut (/a/→ø/___C u) and Vowel Reduction (ø→u when unstressed) in Icelandic, as discussed by Anderson (1974: 185–9), exemplify this situation:

	/fatnað+um/
u–Umlaut	fatnøðúm
Vowel Reduction	fatnuðúm
u–Umlaut	føtnuðúm
Phonetic Representation	[føtnuðúm]

(where the "'" indicates stress).

3. It is possible to distinguish between this situation, where a rule, in feeding another, *adds* to its input, and another possible situation, where a rule creates *all of the input* for another. These are referred to, respectively, as *partial* and *absolute* feeding, but we will not insist, in this book, on making that distinction.

4. This restriction on rule application is in direct contradiction to other cases where we must allow that a rule *may* reapply later in the derivation, as in note 2 above. Anderson (1974) addresses these sorts of problem for the standard model. Kenstowicz and Kisseberth (1979, Chapter 8) also address problems with rule application and interaction in the standard model. See also Kenstowicz and Kisseberth (1977: Chapters 4–6) for discussion of the issues.

5. Yer deletion phenomena are common in Slavic languages; see Halle and Vergnaud (1987: 82) for discussion of yers in Russian (with respect to the notion 'cyclicity') and Kenstowicz and Rubach (1987) for an account of yer phenomena in Slovak.

6. The observant reader will have noticed that, while Glide Formation partially bleeds Elision, Elision absolutely bleeds Glide Formation.

Further Reading

Among the detractors of standard generative phonology, Derwing (1973) and Ohala (1974) insist on 'external' evidence, from psychological and instrumental phonetic experiments, respectively. Foley (1977), on the other hand, argues that standard generative phonology is not abstract enough, and that the primitives of phonological representation must be entirely non-phonetic. Both camps insist that generative phonology cannot otherwise be considered 'scientific'. For an interesting reply to the Ohala position, see Anderson (1981), and for discussion of the issue of whether generative phonology may be said to be 'scientific', see Carr (1990: 6.3).

There is a rather large literature on rule ordering and application, and on the abstractness issue. For detailed discussion on problems of rule ordering and application, see Kenstowicz and Kisseberth (1977), Chapters 4–6, and Kenstowicz and Kisseberth (1979), Chapter 8. See also Anderson (1974), Chapters 5–9. Lass (1984a), Chapter 9, gives a critical overview of the problems and issues in the abstractness debate; his conclusions concerning generative phonology are much more critical than those adopted in this book.

Interlude. Post-SPE Phonology: Some Questions about the Standard Model

We have already begun to touch on some of the problems associated with the standard model of generative phonology. We will briefly discuss three sets of problems here, and then set out to examine those problems, and the issues arising from our discussion of them, in the chapters that follow. These three problematical areas are (a) the degree of abstractness in the underlying representations allowed by the model, (b) the extrinsic ordering which enables abstract analyses to be postulated and (c) the form of the rules and representations used in the standard model. Let us look at these in turn.

The abstractness problem, which we will examine in more detail in Chapter 7, concerns the relationship between phonetics, phonology, morphology and the notion of 'psychological reality'. We have been using features in both phonological and phonetic representations, such that, unless a phonological rule changes or fills in values on features in segments, those segments appear in phonetic representations just as they appear in phonological representations. Take the Tamil word /paːɳpu/ (snake): while the last three segments have feature values added or changed by phonological rules, the first two segments appear in the surface representation [paːmbɯ] just as they are in the phonological representation. In the case of the first segment, the rule which governs the realisation of stops (see p. 118) takes the underlying representations of stops to be [−voice]. Since the stop in this case does not occur either intervocalically or after a nasal, no feature change is induced. This means that this segment is *inherently* a voiceless bilabial stop, and that its feature specification in phonological form has phonetic significance. That is, the features we have been using have inherent, or intrinsic, **phonetic content**: they express real phonetic properties of speech sounds. Given that we make this claim of the features we use in phonological representations, we must ask what the phonetic status of the features in abstract representations might be. In Hungarian, for instance, we postulated [+back] vowels in roots which have the neutral vowels [i] and [iː] phonetically, but systematically take [+back] affixes. Our claim was that, among the high vowels of Hungarian, there is a contrast between back and front, unrounded high vowels, thus:

(1)

	i	y	ɨ	u	i:	y:	ɨ:	u:
high	+	+	+	+	+	+	+	+
low	−	−	−	−	−	−	−	−
back	−	−	+	+	−	−	+	+
round	−	+	−	+	−	+	−	+
long	−	−	−	−	+	+	+	+

Our rule of absolute neutralisation wipes out this underlying contrast as follows:

(2)

$$
\begin{bmatrix} +\text{syll} \\ +\text{high} \\ +\text{back} \\ -\text{round} \end{bmatrix} \rightarrow [-\text{back}]
$$

The rule also has the effect of neutralising the distinction between rounded and unrounded high back vowels (i.e. between /u/ and /ɨ/, and /u:/ and /ɨ:/). The following question arises: how it can be that speakers of Hungarian acquire these underlying contrasts if they have never been exposed to phonetic vowels which actually are high, back and unrounded? We may ask whether speakers really do have the abstracting capacities we have now attributed to them, and whether it is reasonable to say that they may possess underlying representations of segments which they do not actually hear. We will address that question in Chapter 7, and consider some of the responses which have been made to it.

This will raise questions about the relationship between phonology and morphology. We might ask whether the analyses we have been formulating are not rather too abstract in another sense: in some cases, they assume unique underlying representations for apparently restricted sets of alternants, where the relevant rules operate in restricted morphological contexts. For instance, in analysing alternants in English like [jʌŋ] ~ [jʌŋg] (in *young/younger* as opposed to *sing/singer*), we postulate underlying representations with a stem-final /g/, like /sɪŋ/ and /jʌŋg/, and a rule of /g/ Deletion, which is restricted so as not to apply to cases like *younger*. It might be objected that this is to underestimate the role of lexical storage in speakers of English; perhaps they just *remember* that the adjectives *strong*, *long* and *young* have [g] in their comparative forms. Perhaps we should distinguish between truly phonological rules, governed by phonetic factors, and this sort of phenomenon. The proposals for dealing with this question, which we look at in Chapter 7, will be found wanting, but the issues raised will be shown to be of fundamental importance. We will therefore proceed, in Chapter 8, to an alternative set of proposals for reorganising the standard model so as to express the distinction between rules which operate in highly restricted morphological contexts and rules which are phonetically motivated.

The abstractness problem is related to the second of our three problems, the scope for abstractness afforded by a model which permits extrinsic ordering (every case of absolute neutralisation, for instance, requires such ordering). We will look at objections to extrinsic ordering with respect to abstractness in Chapter 7. But extrinsic ordering appears to raise problems even where absolute neutralisation is not involved. This can be seen in the case of the ordering, in French, of the rules of Liaison, Nasalisation and Nasal Deletion. Let us formulate the three rules and then look at their ordering. The rule of Liaison in French is formulated by Dell (1973) so as to take a word-final consonant over into the first syllable of a following word, as in *petit ami*, which has the phonetic form [ptitɐmi] and the syllable structure [pə. ti. ta. mi] (we will justify this in more detail in Chapter 9; the '.' indicates syllable boundary). A slightly adapted form of Dell's rule is:

(3) *Liaison*

$$C\#\#V \rightarrow \#\#CV$$

The Nasalisation rule may be stated thus: a vowel is nasalised if it is immediately followed by a nasal stop which in turn is followed by a consonant or a word boundary:

(4) *Nasalisation*

$$[+\text{syll}] \rightarrow [+\text{nas}] \ / \ \underline{\hspace{1em}} \left\{ \begin{array}{c} \# \\ [+\text{cons}] \end{array} \right\}$$

Nasal Deletion deletes a nasal stop which is immediately preceded by a nasalised vowel:

(5) *Nasal Deletion*

$$\left[\begin{array}{c} +\text{cons} \\ +\text{nas} \end{array} \right] \rightarrow \emptyset \ / \ \left[\begin{array}{c} +\text{syll} \\ +\text{nas} \end{array} \right] \underline{\hspace{1em}}$$

Now to the ordering of the rules. Consider firstly the expressions *bon ami* and *bonne amie* ('good friend', masculine and feminine, respectively), which have the same phonetic representation: [bɔnami]. We know that Nasalisation (and thus Nasal Deletion) does not have its conditions met in *bonne amie* because the adjective, being in the feminine, has a schwa after the nasal consonant, rather than a C or a #: /bɔn + ə/. With *bon ami*, there is no such underlying schwa, but the nasal consonant is taken over (according to Dell), by Liaison,[1] into *ami*. This provides evidence that Liaison precedes (and bleeds) Nasalisation, as in the following:

(6)

	bɔn##ami
Liaison	bɔ##nami
Nasalisation	———
Nasal Deletion	———
Phonetic Representation	[bɔnami]

The standard model, with its extrinsically ordered block of rules, gets these facts right in a fairly simple and general manner. However, there is a set of cases which prove problematical for the ordering we have given. These are exemplified in the following:

(7)

1. (a) [ɔ̃nɐʁiv]   (*on arrive*:   'we're coming/arriving')
   (b) [ɑ̃nɐʁivɑ̃]   (*en arrivent*: 'in coming/arriving')
   (c) [mɔ̃nami]   (*mon ami*:   'my friend')

The trouble here is that, while Nasalisation has applied, Nasal Deletion has not (this data is therefore said to constitute evidence that the two are separate processes, and not a single process of nasalisation of the vowel accompanied by deletion of the consonant). That is, words like the determiners *mon*, *ton* and *son* ('my', 'your' and 'his/her/its') differ from words like *bon*, in that the former have a nasalised vowel in both alternants, whereas the latter do not: [mɔ̃n] and [mɔ̃], but [bɔ̃] and [bɔn]. (Note that the noun *son*, meaning 'sound', is like *bon* and thus forms a minimal pair with the determiner *son*; this might be taken to suggest rather strongly that not all nasalised vowels in French are derivable from underlying VN sequences.) Other words are like *on*, *en* and *mon* in this respect: *bien* and *rien*, for example. It seems that in cases involving these words, Nasalisation has applied first, and then Liaison has applied, before Nasal Deletion, to move the nasal consonant into the following word:

(8)

	mɔn##ami
Nasalisation	mɔ̃n##ami
Liaison	mɔ̃##nami
Nasal Deletion	———
Phonetic Representation	[mɔ̃nami]

We are therefore faced with evidence for the order Nasalisation →
Liaison → Nasal Deletion, *and* with evidence for the order Liaison →
Nasalisation → Nasal Deletion. This unfortunate state of affairs, referred
to as an **ordering paradox**, will potentially arise as a natural consequence
of any model which incorporates ordered rules. In this case, the matter is
complicated by the fact that it is not evident whether it is the *bon ami*
cases which are exceptional or the *mon ami* cases (or, ideally, neither).
Dell (1973) assumes that the *bon ami* cases are the exceptional ones, and
allows for their derivations to count as cases of exceptional ordering. But
to appeal to the notion of 'exceptional ordering' is merely to restate the
problem, and to allow that grammars may accommodate a class of excep-
tionally ordered derivations is severely to undermine the very idea of rule
ordering in the SPE model of phonological organisation. If we take the
mon ami cases to be exceptional, we are faced with the peculiar fact that
words with nasalisation in both allomorphs, like *mon*, are increasing in
number, at least in Parisian French, as reported in Encrevé (1988), and, in
some varieties of Wallonian French, even *bon* has a nasalised vowel in
both alternants.[2]

We may respond to cases involving ordering paradoxes in one of at least
four ways. Firstly, we may say that the rules have been misformulated, and
that this has created the problem.[3] Alternatively, and more generally, we
may say that there is something wrong with the idea of extrinsic ordering,
and seek constraints on its use. Thirdly, and more radically, we may
suggest that the whole idea of extrinsic ordering is mistaken and should be
forbidden. Lastly, we may suggest that the very idea of rules in phonology
is mistaken, and attempt to devise a model of phonological organisation
which does without rules; in such a model, the possibility of ordering of
rules does not arise.

The proposal that extrinsic ordering should be forbidden is considered
in Chapter 7, and a proposal for a phonology without rules is examined in
Chapter 11. With respect to this particular case, we will look at alternative
formulations of the rules in Chapter 9, and we will discuss ways of
constraining extrinsic ordering in Chapter 8. For the moment, we may
mention a general principle which constrains the amount of extrinsic
ordering in the phonological component, proposed by Kiparsky (1973),
and known as the **Elsewhere Condition**. It states that, where two rules
may in principle apply to the same representation, the more specific
applies first, and the more general second. That is, the more specific one
applies first, then the more general applies 'elsewhere'. Let us look at an
example.

We saw in Chapter 4 (see p. 94) that, in Lowland Scots, a class of vowels
is lengthened if they occur before voiced continuants, a morpheme boundary or a word boundary. We formulated this rule, which we will now call
the Scottish Vowel Length Rule (SVLR) as follows:

(9) *Scottish Vowel Length Rule*

$$\begin{bmatrix} +\text{syll} \\ +\text{ATR} \end{bmatrix} \longrightarrow [+\text{long}] \; / \; \underline{\quad\quad} \left\{ \begin{array}{c} \begin{bmatrix} -\text{syll} \\ +\text{voice} \\ +\text{cont} \end{bmatrix} \\ \# \\ + \end{array} \right\}$$

There is another vowel lengthening rule, not restricted to Scots or Scottish English, which lengthens vowels before any voiced consonant. Let us call it Low Level Lengthening (LLL) and formulate it as follows:

(10) *Low Level Lengthening*

$$[+\text{syll}] \to [+\text{long}] \; / \; \underline{\quad\quad} \begin{bmatrix} -\text{syll} \\ +\text{voice} \end{bmatrix}$$

It is clear that SVLR applies to a subclass ([+ATR] vowels) of the segments (all vowels) which LLL applies to, and that it applies in contexts (before voiced continuants) which are a subclass of the contexts (before voiced consonants) in which LLL applies. The Elsewhere Condition (EC) therefore insists that SVLR applies before LLL, and we will see in Chapter 8 that this prediction is borne out. The EC is a general constraint on rule application which effectively helps to curtail the extent to which extrinsic ordering has to be stated for rules. In this case, we need not extrinsically order SVLR before LLL, since their order is governed by a general principle. This is clearly an improvement on simply stipulating their order of application, since we want to insist that, where possible, particular states of affairs should follow from some generalisation. We will examine other proposals which have this effect in Chapters 7 and 8.

The third problematical area we mentioned concerns difficulties which arise from the very form of the rules and representations given in the standard model, and which therefore call for radical departures from that model. One example of this was the case of the ATR vowel harmony rule in Akan (see p. 125). It may have become clear to you that a rule of the following form was missing the point:

(11)

$$[+\text{syll}] \longrightarrow [\alpha \text{ATR}] \; / \; \left\{ \begin{array}{c} \begin{bmatrix} +\text{syll} \\ \alpha\,\text{ATR} \end{bmatrix} C_0 + \underline{\quad\quad\quad} \\ \underline{\quad\quad\quad} + C_0 \begin{bmatrix} +\text{syll} \\ \alpha\,\text{ATR} \end{bmatrix} \end{array} \right\}$$

The rule suggests that it is the first vowel in the root which governs prefix harmony, and the last which governs suffix harmony. But the generalisation would appear to be that the root itself is specified as [+ATR] or [−ATR], regardless of how many syllables it contains, and that it is *no particular vowel* which induces the vowel harmony in the affixes.[4] Our rules, operating on representations which consist of linear sequences of segments, cannot accommodate this sort of generalisation. We will investigate, in Chapters 9 and 10, ways of revising our conception of rules and representations such that these generalisations can be simply and elegantly expressed. In particular, we will ask the following questions:

1. Do the features [syllabic] and [stress] allow us adequately to express generalisations about syllabic structure and stress assignment?
2. Do segments have a more highly articulated internal structure than that expressed by an unordered bundle of features?

Our investigations in Chapters 9 and 10 will attempt to answer these questions, respectively, and will point us in the direction of increasingly major revisions of our conceptions of rules and representations; we will pursue some of the more radical consequences of those revisions in Chapter 11.

Notes

1. We will examine an alternative conception of Liaison in Chapter 9.
2. Professor G. Jucquois, personal communication.
3. We will reconsider the rules involved in Chapter 9.
4. Kiparsky (1985: 121) claims that the first vowel in the root determines prefix harmony, and the last vowel suffix harmony. This claim is falsified by his observation that mixed roots, with ATR and non-ATR vowels, are possible only when /ɑ/ intervenes, as in the root /fuɲɑnɪ/ ('to search'). See Chapter 10 for further analysis.

7 Naturalness in Generative Phonology

7.1 Underlying Representations and Extrinsic Ordering

We raised the problem of the abstractness of underlying representations in the interlude and suggested there that, in some cases (e.g. the postulated high back, unrounded vowels of Hungarian), we might question the supposed psychological reality of those representations. The objection is to underlying representations which appear not to be *directly induced* by the sounds to which the speaker is exposed. Let us examine that line of argument. One very clear expression of this objection to abstract underlying representations is given by Hooper (1976). We have argued all along that the combined rules and representations we have formulated are psychologically real, and that they allow us to characterise the knowledge which enables speakers to decode a multiplicity of different speech sounds. Hooper claims that standard generative phonology cannot sustain these claims to psychological reality for analyses involving absolute neutralisation (AN) analyses and extrinsic ordering. She accordingly imposes two general conditions on phonological analyses which, she argues, will help to guarantee their psychological plausibility. Those conditions may be stated as follows:

The True Generalisation Condition (TGC)
No phonological generalisation is a true one unless it is true at the level of surface phonetic representation.

The No Ordering Condition (NOC)
Rules may contract intrinsic ordering relations, but they may not be extrinsically ordered.

The reasoning behind the first of these conditions is as follows. Speakers have access only to the speech sounds they are exposed to on learning their languages, and cannot reasonably be expected to have mental representations which do not correspond to those speech sounds. The idea is that phonological rules and representations must be largely phonetic, or in Hooper's words, **natural**; her constrained version of generative phonology is therefore called **Natural Generative Phonology (NGP)**. In our Hungarian case, this means that speakers cannot come to possess representations of high back unrounded vowels, since they are never exposed to such sounds. This condition alone will disallow our analysis of Hungarian, and so another analysis must accordingly be sought. The only other alternative we have considered is the 'exception analysis', whereby each and every one of these 60 morphemes is stored in the lexicon, with some kind of marker indicating that they take back affixes. Central to this analysis is the idea, which Hooper stresses, that speakers are very good at storing large amounts of representations.

It is clear that the TGC also rules out our analysis of the Polish [ɛ] ~ ∅ alternations (see p. 140). There, the various phonetic forms of each and every morpheme we considered must be stored in memory; that is, all morphemes which appear with [ɛ] and ∅, with [ɛ], ∅ and [ɨ], and with [ɛ], ∅ and [i]. This amounts to claiming, of course, that there are *no alternations at all* in these cases (since alternations are, by definition, rule-governed). That is, speakers of Polish cannot have underlying yers, since they have never heard sounds with exactly those combinations of feature specifications, and they do not derive a wide variety of surface alternants from a single underlying representation. Rather, speakers are very good at storing alternative forms of morphemes, and this is what they are doing in this case.

It is not just cases of absolute neutralisation which are characterised as illegitimate by the TGC, however. It is also clear that even our less abstract rule of Velar Fronting in Lumasaaba cannot count as expressing a true phonological generalisation. The Velar Fronting rule in Lumasaaba, you will recall, looks like this:

(1)

$$
\begin{bmatrix} +\text{obs} \\ +\text{back} \end{bmatrix} \rightarrow [-\text{back}] \ / \ \underline{\quad} \begin{bmatrix} -\text{syll} \\ -\text{back} \\ -\text{low} \end{bmatrix}
$$

The generalisation expressed by this rule (see p. 97) was said to hold between the phonological and the phonetic levels of representation. We explicitly deny that the rule expresses a generalisation about permitted sequences of phonetic segments in Lumasaaba, and indeed there are phonetic sequences of velar stops followed by high front vowels, and palatal stops followed by vowels which are not high front vowels, as in [cica:na̩ga:] and [kaki:ko]. These, we say, derive from underlying representations with double prefixes, /ki + ki + a:naga/ and /ka + ka + i:ko/, on which a Vowel Deletion rule has operated. Now, the TGC requires that a true phonological generalisation expresses a generalisation which is true at the surface, and therefore this rule, by definition, does not express a true phonological generalisation. In Hooper's view, the phonological generalisations which speakers acquire hold between surface forms: they do not mediate between putative underlying representations and surface forms.

But the claim that Velar Fronting does not express a true phonological generalisation in Lumasaaba is surely mistaken: there is a vast amount of data showing that the [c]/[k] and [ɟ] /[g] distinctions are allophonic, and the only exceptions to that generalisation are themselves subject to a generalisation: they occur in morphologically complex forms where a prefix vowel has been deleted. This case alone makes it clear that the TGC is too strong: it requires us to reject highly plausible analyses such as this one.

Hooper also claims that there is a crucial distinction to be made between properly phonological rules (**P rules**), which express entirely phonetically motivated allophonic variations, and rules which are inextricably tied up with morphological factors. Rules in this latter category are referred to by Hooper as morphophonological, or **MP rules**. This distinction between rule types is very close to the distinction we discussed, and rejected, in Chapter 4, in connection with Weakening in Spanish and Halle's argument from Voicing Assimilation in Russian. And since our argument there was an argument from generality, it is clear that Hooper is committed to claiming that, in each of those cases, the single generalisation we said was so apparent is simply not a single generalisation at all. Thus, for Hooper, the Spanish rule of Weakening, which weakens voiced stops to approximants intervocalically, would be expressed in terms of two rules: a P rule which refers strictly to intervocalic environment (as in the last two stops in *la bodega*) and another which refers to boundaries (as in the first stop in *la bodega*).

Hooper also chooses to distinguish MP rules from what she calls **via rules**, which, again, are said to express relationships between surface forms directly, rather than deriving those surface forms from a common underlying form. Thus, given alternations of the form *divine/divinity*, *derive/derivative* in English, Hooper argues that the speaker stores both alternants (e.g. /dɪvain/ and /dɪvɪn/), but knows that there is a relationship between the two forms, expressible in the following via rule, stored alongside each pair to which it applies:

(2)

[ai] ↔ [ɪ]

It has to be said that it is difficult to judge to what extent this sort of expression constitutes a rule. It looks like a rule in that it contains an arrow-like symbol with symbols on either side. Since it is stored in the lexicon alongside each pair to which it applies, it is not clear that it expresses a *generalisation*. Nor is it clear exactly *what* it expresses: it is vague. Let us consider what is odd about it.

We might interpret the 'rule' as stating that there is some kind of relationship between [ai] and [ɪ], which indeed there is in certain specific cases in English. But just what that relationship might be is left unstated. A standard generative analysis will appeal to a single underlying representation (such as /dɪviːn/) and rules (Trisyllabic Shortening and Vowel Shift) which mediate between this and the surface alternants. Such rules will not relate, for instance, the words *fight* and *fit*. But there is no reason why we should not, in principle, interpret Hooper's very vague (and thus very general) via rule in this way! We can assume that Hooper does not want us to interpret the rule as expressing the relationship between, for instance, the verb *bite* and its past participial form *bit* (the 'rule' itself gives us no indication of whether this is so), but there is nothing in the way the via rule is formulated that prevents us, in principle, from doing so. We may conclude that via rules are barely interpretable as rules, and are so general as to allow a range of undesirable interpretations.

Hooper's position is that pairs like *divine* and *divinity* are simply stored in the lexicon; making that claim commits her to denying that they are related by a rule, and implying that they are no more related than the phonological forms of the morphemes *cat* and *dog*. One the other hand, she feels that speakers perceive some kind of systematic relationship between pairs like these and other pairs like *divide/division*. The 'via rule' notion is therefore an attempt by Hooper to have her cake and eat it, to list the phonological forms in question while simultaneously attempting to state some kind of rule.

Let us move on to the NOC. The argument, again, concerns the question of what sort of knowledge speakers may have. They cannot, Hooper claims, have unconscious knowledge so complex as to be expressed in terms of extrinsically ordered rules. But the NOC will exclude even the simplest and most motivated of derivations with ordered rules. Take our evidence from Tyneside English (see p. 99). We saw that in forms like [hɐ?m̩] and [čɪ?ŋ], we need an account of how the nasal stops and glottal stops are decoded. The simplest analysis, with ordered rules, would look like this:

(3)

	/hɐpən/	/čɪkən/
Schwa Deletion	hɐpn	čɪkn
Nasal Syllabification	hɐpn̩	čɪkn̩
Nasal Assimilation	hɐpm̩	čɪkŋ̩
Reduction	hɐ?m̩	čɪ?ŋ̩
Phonetic Representation	[hɐ?m̩]	[čɪ?ŋ̩]

While it is only by virtue of Schwa Deletion having applied that Nasal Syllabification could apply (their ordering is intrinsic), the ordering relation between Nasal Assimilation and Reduction is extrinsic: Reduction could apply before Nasal Assimilation, but must be ordered to apply after it. It is very difficult to see why we should abandon the highly plausible claim which extrinsic ordering allows us in cases like this. In attributing psychological reality to such analyses, we need not be claiming that each stage in the derivation constitutes a step in the decoding process; rather, we claim that the derivation as a whole expresses the generalisations in question.

We can see a similar argument in favour of extrinsic ordering in the case of the Velar Fronting and Vowel Deletion rules in Lumasaaba. There, the two rules may compete for the same territory: given a representation of the form /ki + ki + a:naga/, either rule could apply. The application of one is not dependent on the other; they are not intrinsically ordered. Thus, the Lumasaaba analysis falls foul of both the TGC and the NOC. And yet it is a highly motivated analysis which captures an important generalisation. It seems that our response must be that the NOC is also too strong a condition to place on phonological analysis. This is true only if the natural generative phonologist accepts that generality is a desired property of phonological analyses. And, of course, NGP does strive for generality, even within its own strictly defined limits. If it did not, there would be no attempt made in NGP to isolate 'true generalisations' from 'spurious' ones: one would simply abandon all attempts at framing generalisations and instead list, for every morpheme, every phonetic shape it can have.

7.2 Theories and Reality

It is quite evident that Hooper's proposals have the effect of wiping out much of what we have taken to count as phonology. Her claims centre on the notion of existence, as Dresher (1981) has pointed out: that which does not exist as a phonetic reality, she is claiming, does not exist in phonological rules or representations. This claim raises several rather fascinating questions as to what may reasonably be said to exist, which, however tantalising they may be, we cannot address in depth here. But let us briefly consider a few example cases.

It is not at all evident that the physical world might be composed, not of solid objects, but of space inhabited by energy and tiny subatomic particles. But that is not to say that a theory which postulates the existence of such a world is in principle on the wrong track. To take another example, it is not clear from our day-to-day existence that the earth rotates, that it is spherical, or that it revolves around the sun. The world *seems* stationary: we can actually see the sun come up, cross the sky and go down, and the surface of the earth does not feel especially curved to us. In many of our theories, we postulate things which may not be evident in our ordinary everyday lives. Such postulated states of affairs are supported by evidence which comes from their *effects*: we cannot see the earth revolving around the sun, but we *can* see the effects of that motion.

So it is with phonology: we cannot get direct access to phonological organisation, because it comes in the form of unconscious knowledge, but we can get access to its *effects*. It is only from those, in interaction with our most general and simple analyses, that we can make a guess as to the nature of phonological organisation. Everyday appearances, made available to us through the senses, and 'common sense', can have no prior claim on our notions of what the world may be like. The idea that we are continually spinning on an axis and orbiting the sun is hardly a commonsensical one. What the world is like is not given; it is for us to guess, through our most general and simple theories, what it is like. We have only evidence and argumentation to go on when it comes to deciding what the world is like: gut reactions based on the 'common sense' notions of everyday life simply have no part to play in the matter. Hooper mistakenly takes phonetic appearances to constitute the entirety of phonological reality; that is rather like taking observations of the sun rising and setting as facts which *directly* tell us how the world is. What we know now is that those observations are the *effects* of the way things really are (as far we can tell from the evidence and argumentation supporting our present theory). One way of putting this (the analogy is Kiparsky's) is to say that identifying the nature of phonological reality is like trying to spot a tiger in long grass: it is only when the tiger moves that we can identify it. If we conceive of alternations in the shape of a morpheme as the movements, and the underlying representation of the morpheme as the tiger, we can take the alternations as the effects, the movements, which allow us to get a glimpse of the object of inquiry.

There is no *a priori* reason why speakers should not be possessed of highly developed abstracting capacities, as Dresher (1981) points out. It is, at the very least, easy to argue that they do possess considerable capacities of that sort, as we can see from cases where *none* of the surface forms of a morpheme corresponds exactly to the underlying form, but where, taken together, the underlying form may be abstracted from them. Take the alternation in the English words *period/periodic/periodicity*. The phonetic forms of the root are, respectively, [pʰiːɹiəd], [pʰiɹiəd] and [pʰiɹiɒd]. With the underlying representation /piːriɒd/, we can derive the surface forms via rules which affect stress placement and vowel weakening. In doing so, we postulate an underlying representation for the morpheme which does not correspond to *any* of its surface forms, but where each vowel in that representation *does* appear in one of those forms. In adopting this analysis and claiming psychological reality for it, we are allowing for a degree of abstracting ability on the part of the speaker, and it is difficult to see this approach as in principle unreasonable.

The question is therefore not whether we have abstracting capabilities, but *how richly developed* they are. At the very least, Hooper has not given evidence to show how limited they may be, but has simply assumed that they are very limited indeed. The consequences of that assumption, we have seen, are undesirable. Hooper further claims that AN analyses are simply untestable. This is an accusation which must be taken seriously; if it were true, it would certainly be a damning indictment of them. Accordingly, we will return to this claim shortly. First, however, we will consider her objections to 'segments which do not appear on the surface'. We postulated, in our analysis of Tamil, a segment /N/, which we took to be a nasal stop unspecified for place of articulation. Clearly, speakers cannot have heard such a sound: it is unpronounceable! But if speakers can decode place of articulation differences and nasal vs oral distinctions, and if we characterise the speaker's knowledge as involving phonological features, then we are allowing that speakers can abstract away particular features from the segments they hear, and thus arrive at representations which are underspecified. A weak point in Hooper's objections therefore is that they are centred on the notion 'segment', rather than 'feature'. There is no *a priori* reason for suggesting that speakers cannot form representations based on phonological properties smaller than that of the unitary segment. The significance of this can be seen in the following well-known example of an AN analysis, given by Hyman (1970), of Nupe (a Kwa language spoken in Central Nigeria). Hyman shows that Nupe has the following vowel system:

(4)

/i/	/u/		/ĩ/	/ũ/
/e/	/o/			
	/a/			/ã/

Palatalised consonants (represented as [Cj]) and labialised consonants ([Cw]) are in complementary distribution: the former occur before the vowels [i] and [e], the latter before [u] and [o]. Before the low vowel [a], consonants are neither palatalised nor labialised. It is clear therefore that both palatalisation and labialisation of consonants in this language are predictable rather than contrastive. Furthermore, the phonetic motivation for this state of affairs seems clear: the consonants are assimilating to the following vowel, where that vowel has a labial or palatal articulation. We may express this regularity informally with a rule of the sort:

(5)

$$/C/ \rightarrow \begin{cases} [Cw] & / \underline{\quad}\{u, o\} \\ [Cj] & / \underline{\quad}\{i, e\} \end{cases}$$

This pattern of complementary distribution breaks down in some cases, all of which involve a following [a]. Thus, while [ega] ('stranger') is unexceptional, [egwa] ('hand') and [egja] ('blood') have unexpected labialisation and palatalisation, respectively. Recall the phonemic principle: it would force us to treat cases like these as minimal pairs, and concede that palatalisation and labialisation on consonants in Nupe are contrastive, rather than allophonic. Hyman responds by taking cases like [egwa] as having an underlying /ɔ/, and cases like [egja] as having an /ɛ/. The rule for the palatalisation and labialisation of consonants is then expanded to include these segments, thus:

(6)

$$/C/ \rightarrow [Cw] \; / \; \_\_\{u,o,ɔ\}$$
$$ [Cj] \; / \; \_\_\{i,e,ɛ\}$$

The feature specifications for these two vowels being, respectively, [+low, +back, +round] and [+low, −back, −round], an AN rule, ordered to apply after the labialisation/palatalisation rule, collapses the underlying distinction between /a/ and /ɛ/ and /ɔ/, as follows:

(7)

$$\begin{bmatrix} +\text{syll} \\ +\text{low} \end{bmatrix} \rightarrow \begin{bmatrix} +\text{back} \\ -\text{round} \end{bmatrix}$$

This analysis is backed up, not only by evidence from rules of stridency assimilation and reduplication in this language, but from the behaviour of loanwords into Nupe, particularly from Yoruba (also a Kwa language), which, unlike Nupe, has surface [ɛ] and [ɔ]. The behaviour of loanwords from Yoruba which contain those vowels is as follows:

(8)

Yoruba	Nupe	
[kɛkɛ]	[kjakja]	'bicycle'
[ɛgbɛ]	[egbja]	a Yoruba town
[tɔrɛ]	[twarja]	'to give a gift'
[kɔbɔ]	[kwabwa]	'penny'

Clearly, Nupe speakers utter the low-mid vowels just as they would if Hyman were right about the phonological representation of [Cwa] and [Cja] in Nupe. Two significant points need to be made here. Firstly, the evidence suggests that speakers can abstract away from the phonetic signal particular phonological properties which may form the basis of phonological rules and representations, and this rather undermines Hooper's objections concerning 'non-existing' segments. Secondly, the evidence which Hyman cites to defend his analysis clearly falsifies Hooper's claim that analyses involving absolute neutralisation may not be tested.

We will therefore take the view that abstract analyses are justified, but that we do need some clear limitation on just how abstract they may be allowed to become. After all, if our model is supposed to character-ise the nature of phonological organisation, then it must not allow in principle for any logically possible analysis. If it did, it would not be making any claims as to what can and what cannot count as a possible human language phonology. It is reasonable to argue that if, in allowing for extrinsic ordering and absolute neutralisation, our model is thus able to allow for *any* conceivable state of affairs, then the model is over-powerful and must be constrained. But we will also argue that this con-straining strategy must preserve significant generalisations. If we can come up with analyses which preserve these generalisations while avoid-ing extrinsic ordering and absolute neutralisation, then we will certainly adopt them.

We might argue, against the GP strategy, that languages are fundamen-tally messy, and that generative grammarians are misleadingly trying to depict messiness as rule-governedness. Now, since we cannot say, *a priori*, whether language is or is not highly rule-governed, there is no way of telling, at first glance, which is the right approach. That is, the claims that language is highly irregular and that language is highly regular are, equally, *a priori* assumptions. What we *can* say about those two opposing assump-tions, though, is this. If we operate on the assumption that language is messy, idiosyncratic and not highly rule-governed, then, faced with a welter of recalcitrant data, we are very likely simply to accept it as being messy in fact. That is, the 'language is messy' approach is self-fulfilling: it is almost bound to turn out to appear true. Compare this with the generative approach: if we assume that language is highly rule-governed, then, faced with an abundance of apparently confused data, we will try to seek order in it. In doing so, we may well make important discoveries. Furthermore, we will only be able to establish that language really is messy if we try our best to show it to be rule-governed and then fail. The irony is that it is only in trying to establish that language is regular that we can establish in a non-trivial way just how messy it is.

7.3 Generality and Abstractness

The preceding remarks have been rather hard on NGP; let us consider a case where Hooper does indeed seem to have point. Saporta (1965), in his analysis of verb alternations in Latin American Spanish, notes the following distinct alternation patterns among verbs which have root-final /s/:

(9)

Infinitive	Gloss	1PS (Indicative)	1PS (Subjunctive)	2PS
[kosɛr]	'to sew'	[koso]	[kosa]	[kose]
[krɛsɛr]	'to grow'	[krɛsko]	[krɛska]	[krɛse]

Saporta wanted to account for the appearance and non-appearance of [k] between the root and the suffix in the first person forms. He did this by postulating underlying representations with a root-final /θ/ for the class of verbs which occur with [k]. Thus, the verb 'to grow' has the phonological representation /kreθ/. He then formulated a rule for insertion of [k], as follows:

(10)

$$\emptyset \rightarrow [k] \; / \; V\theta + \underline{\hphantom{x}} \begin{Bmatrix} a \\ o \end{Bmatrix}$$

In distinctive features, this would be:

(11)

$$\emptyset \rightarrow [k] \; / \; [+syll] \begin{bmatrix} +obs \\ +cont \\ +ant \\ +cor \\ +stri \end{bmatrix} + \underline{\hphantom{x}} \begin{bmatrix} +syll \\ -high \\ +back \end{bmatrix}$$

The rule would need to spell out all of the features for [k], which we have not done here. Saporta then postulated a rule of absolute neutralisation, extrinsically ordered to occur after the [k] Insertion rule, which collapsed the underlying /θ/ into /s/, thus:

(12)

$$/\theta/ \rightarrow [s]$$

In features, this would be:

(13)

$$
\begin{bmatrix}
+\text{obs} \\
+\text{cont} \\
+\text{ant} \\
+\text{cor} \\
-\text{stri}
\end{bmatrix}
\rightarrow [+\text{stri}]
$$

Thus, Latin American Spanish has the four underlying fricatives /f/, /θ/, /s/ and /x/, but only three phonetic fricatives: [f], [s] and [x]; the dental fricative [θ] never appears on the surface. The contrast between the underlying fricatives /s/ and /θ/, distinguished only by their values for the feature [stri], is neutralised in all contexts.

Hooper's conditions will rule out such an analysis: firstly, the extrinsic ordering is excluded; secondly, the postulated underlying contrast between dental and alveolar voiceless fricatives is excluded, since there is no surface contrast of this sort. What should the GP response be to this case? Given our adopted view that abstract analyses are justified, within limits to be defined, the absolute neutralisation rule itself is unexceptional: rules may reasonably change values on features, context-free. But the rule of [k] insertion is entirely without merit: it is not only unmotivated phonetically, but, more seriously, it is completely lacking in generality, and it is the idea of generalisation around which we have built our case for abstractness in phonology. We can therefore reasonably suggest that it should be rejected on the criterion of generality alone. It certainly looks as though the Latin American Spanish case is unlike our abstract analyses of Hungarian and Polish: there, we captured generalisations about a wide range of alternations. Here, no such general coverage is achieved.

By insisting on generality for the rules in cases of absolute neutralisation, we can go some way towards curbing excesses in abstract analyses without throwing the baby out with the bathwater, as Hooper does. Even then, it may be argued, rather strongly, that we must choose in principle whether to allow for absolute neutralisation or not, and that allowing for it in some cases rather than others is rather a weak position to adopt. The problem is that we would welcome a clear principle which will dictate what sorts of limitation we need to impose on abstract analyses, but the TGC and the NOC are not acceptable. Let us briefly consider another such limitation.

7.4 The Alternation Condition

An earlier attempt at dealing with the abstractness problem was formulated by Kiparsky (1968). Kiparsky noted that, although phonological features are said to have intrinsic phonetic content, their function in most

AN cases was merely to act as **diacritics** (special markers) for cases of exceptional rule behaviour. Thus, in our Latin American Spanish case, the feature specification [−stri] on the abstract segment /θ/, which distinguishes it from /s/, merely acts to trigger the [k] insertion rule, and is then switched to [+stri] by an AN rule (it was in fact Kiparsky who coined the term 'absolute neutralisation'). His point was that it is perfectly legitimate to recognise such cases as exceptional and to mark them with an overtly *ad hoc* 'flag' or diacritic, such as [+k insertion]. This is what he referred to as the perfectly legitimate *phonological use of diacritic features*. But to use the phonological feature [+stri] is illegitimate: it amounts to masking an *ad hoc* marking and making it look like part of the internal structure of a segment. This is what Kiparksy referred to as the *diacritic use of phonological features*, which, he suggested, be excluded from phonological analyses. His **Alternation Condition** (AC) stated that underlying segments could not be postulated unless they corresponded to surface phonetic segments. He then dealt with cases like our Hungarian roots with neutral vowels by marking them with a diacritic indicating for which rules they acted as exceptions.

This condition is similar in intent to the TGC, but Kiparsky was not attempting to reduce phonology to a list of the surface forms of morphemes (which is what NGP leans heavily towards). He also allowed for the AC to be given a weaker interpretation, not as an absolute ban on absolute neutralisation analyses, but as a condition expressing the complexity of grammars, such that a grammar was more highly complex, or more *opaque*, than another if it violated the AC.

It should be clear that if we reject the TGC, we will reject the AC, at least in its strong form, on the same grounds. However, we need to seek effective ways of curbing the abstractness of analyses without having the effect of wiping out many of the significant generalisations which lie at the centre of phonological investigation. It is to that conjunction of notions that we turn in the following chapter.

EXERCISES

1. French
We proposed a rule of Nasalisation for French vowels in Chapter 4 (see p. 89); it looked like this:

$$[+syll] \rightarrow [+nas] \: / \: \underline{\quad} \: [+nas] \: \begin{Bmatrix} [+cons] \\ \# \end{Bmatrix}$$

The rule accounted for a wide range of alternations, such as the masculine and feminine forms of the adjective meaning 'good', (*bonne* and *bon*), whose phonetic forms are [bɔn] and [bɔ̃].

(i) Given the NGP distinction between P rules proper, which refer only to phonetic information, and MP rules, which refer to morphological and syntactic information, what will the NGP response to the above rule be?

(ii) Looking back at the derivation on p. 92, involving Nasalisation, Nasal Deletion and Word-Final Schwa Deletion, can you say whether it violates the NOC?

(iii) What about the TGC? What relevance do the following data have for the NGP assessment of our analysis of nasalisation in French vowels?

1.	[bɔnsœʁ] *(bonne soeur)*	'good sister'	2.	[okynsœʁ] *(aucune soeur)*	'any sister'
3.	[bɔntɑ̃t] *(bonne tante)*	'good aunt'	4.	[okynɑ̃t] *(aucune tante)*	'any aunt'
5.	[bɔnvœv] *(bonne veuve)*	'good widow'	6.	[okynvœv] *(aucune veuve)*	'any widow'

2. Uighur

Uighur is a Turkic language (data, modified somewhat, from Anderson 1974; Poppe 1965).

1. (a)	[ɑl]	'take'	(b) [ɑlmɑq]	'taken'
2. (a)	[tur]	'stand'	(b) [turmɑq]	'stood'
3. (a)	[jori]	'decide'	(b) [jorimɑq]	'decided'
4. (a)	[ide]	'eat'	(b) [idemɑq]	'eaten'
5. (a)	[bar]	'give'	(b) [barmɑq]	'given'
6. (a)	[kør]	'see'	(b) [kørmɑq]	'seen'

(i) State informally the generalisation which governs the shape of the [maq]/[mɑq] morpheme.

(ii) There is an umlaut process at work in the language, as the following data show:

7.	[eliʃ]	'the taking'	(*[ɑliʃ])
8.	[elin]	'be taken'	(*[ɑlin])
9.	[beriʃ]	'the giving'	(*[bariʃ])
10.	[berin]	'be given'	(*[barin])

State the umlaut generalisation informally.

(iii) In what sense does the following form appear to violate the harmony rule?

11. [elinmɑq]   'to be taken'   (*[elinmɑq])

(iv) Show that this does not in fact provide counter-evidence to the vowel harmony rule.

(v) Your analysis will violate the NOC and the TGC. In what sense does the vowel harmony rule violate the TGC?

3. Korean (data from Pyun 1987)

Recall (see p. 50) that Korean has contrasts between aspirated, unaspirated and 'glottalised' obstruents (articulated with glottal tension). A rule of Neutralisation (see p. 50) causes stops to be unreleased before another consonant or a word boundary. Another rule, Post-Obstruent Fortition, causes obstruents to become glottalised (marked with a '*') when preceded by unreleased stops (marked with a '˥'), as you can see in the following (data from Pyun 1987):

1.   /kuk + pap/   →   [kuk˥p*ap˥]   'rice and meat soup'
2.   /čip + sin/   →   [čip˥ʃin]   'straw sandal'
3.   /mok+toli/   →   [mok˥t*oɾi]   'scarf'

(The data exhibit two other rules /s/ → [ʃ] / ___i and /l/ → [ɾ] / [+syll]___ [−cons] ; you may ignore these.)

A third rule, Consonant Cluster Simplification, deletes the second of two consonants when they occur word-finally or before another consonant, if that second consonant is coronal; otherwise, it deletes the first, as you can see in the following:

4.   /kaps/   →   [kap˥]   'price'
     /kaps + to/   →   [kap˥ t*o]   'price also'
5.   /saks/   →   [sak˥]   'fee'
     /saks + kwa/   →   [sak˥k*wa]   'fee and'
6.   /talk/   →   [tak˥]   'fowl'
7.   /ilk +ta/   →   [ik˥t*a]   'reads'
     /ilk+ə/   →   [ilgə]   'read!'
8.   /ənč + ta/   →   [ənta]   'places on'

A fourth rule, Epenthesis, operates in compound nouns, inserting a /t/

when the first element in the compound ends with a sonorant and the second element begins with a non-glottalised obstruent.

(i) The underlying representation for the compound meaning 'mountain pass' is /san + kil/, and its phonetic representation is [sank*il]. Give a derivation, showing what order the four rules apply in.
(ii) What ordering relations are contracted? To what extent does the analysis violate the NOC?

4. Maori revisited

In Exercise 2 of Chapter 2, you formulated a phonological analysis of the following active and passive verb forms, and derived gerundives, in Maori:

	Active	Passive	Gerundive	Gloss
1.	[afi]	[afitia]	[afitaŋa]	'embrace'
2.	[hopu]	[hopukia]	[hopukaŋa]	'catch'
3.	[mau]	[mauria]	[mauraŋa]	'carry'
4.	[tohu]	[tohuŋia]	[tohuŋa]	'point out'
5.	[inu]	[inumia]	[inumaŋa]	'drink'
6.	[kimi]	[kimihia]	[kimihaŋa]	'seek'
7.	[patu]	[patua]	[patuŋa]	'kill/strike'
8.	[kite]	[kitea]	[kiteŋa]	'see/find'

(i) The phonological analysis (as opposed to the 'conjugational' analysis) postulates unique underlying representations for the passive and gerundive suffix, and underlying representations for the roots which may end in consonants, along with a rule which deletes word-final consonants. This analysis violates the TGC. In what way?
(ii) Hale (1973: 417) states that Maori speakers use a single form of the passive suffix ([tia]) in loanwords, in nominal stems used as verbs, in certain compounds and in derived causatives (e.g. [fakahopu], 'to cause to catch', is [fakahoputia] in the passive, rather than [fakahopukia]). If Hale's claims are true, what implications do they have for the phonological analysis?
(iii) Do these facts commit us to the conjugation analysis? Discuss.

Notes

There were word-final consonants at some stage in the history of the Polynesian languages, but they were elided. This much is uncontroversial. The question is whether they persist in underlying representation. Hale's claim is that, while the sound change which elided them may at some stage have constituted a synchronic rule of the grammar, later generations of speakers came to reanalyse the verb forms such that the consonants in the passives were taken to be part of the suffix, rather than the stem. Hyman (1975: 184–5), Kenstowicz and Kisseberth (1977: 25) and Lass (1984: 220–2) all agree, on the basis of the evidence Hale cites, that speakers of present day Maori 'choose' the more complex mode of representation whereby there is a single passive suffix beginning with a consonant (-tia in many dialects, -ŋia in others (Julia Tindall, personal communication) and -ʔia in a related Hawaian case) and a large number of exceptions falling into around a dozen conjugational classes. Sanders (1990) disputes this conclusion, arguing firstly that Hale's evidence is, in most respects, factually incorrect, and secondly that, even if it were not, the conclusions he draws from the data are not justified.

Further Reading

Several varieties of 'concrete' or 'natural' phonology emerged in the late seventies, among which is 'natural phonology' as described in Donegan and Stampe (1979). Linell (1979) also presents proposals for a more 'natural' phonology, with a typology of rules somewhat similar to that given by Hooper. For an overview of Linnel's proposals, see Lass (1984a), Chapter 9. The Dresher (1981) paper referred to in Section 7.2 is a robust reply to Hooper's proposals.

It is still worth reading through some of the original papers on the subject in chronological sequence, starting with Kiparsky (1968), followed by Hyman (1970), Kiparsky (1973) and Schane (1974b).

The subsequent development of Kiparsky's thought is picked up in Chapter 8. Alternative conceptions of the abstractness of phonological representations may be found in Section 9.3, on the idea of the CV tier, and in Section 11.3, on non-specification.

An early standard GP analysis of French is given in Schane (1968). Other GP work on French includes Dell (1980), originally published in French in 1973. For concrete analyses of French, and objections to the GP approach, see, amongst others, Tranel (1981) and Love (1981). Morin (1987 and elsewhere) has strongly 'concretist' views on the nature of the French evidence.

8 The Role of the Lexicon

The task facing us at the end of the last chapter was this: we had to find a means of constraining the theory of generative phonology, cutting down on extrinsic ordering and the postulating of abstract segments, without abandoning the significant generalisations which that theory allowed us to express. One restriction on extrinsic rule ordering we have discussed is the Elsewhere Condition. We saw that this general condition on rule application reduced the amount of extrinsic ordering required, since the order of application of some rules will follow from that general principle, rather than having to be stipulated in each grammar. If, in addition to this, certain ordering relations followed as a consequence of the structure of the grammar, that would also constitute an advance. Let us now look at a revision of the organisation of the grammar which has just that consequence.

8.1 Phonology and Morphology Revisited: Lexical Phonology

We have been assuming that the phonological rules of a language apply after words have been built up from morphemes and inserted into syntactic structures. With this idea came the idea of a distinction between morpheme boundaries and word boundaries. We referred briefly (see p. 112) to the idea that the boundary between a clitic and a full word was 'weaker' than that between two full words. We therefore allowed for a hierarchy of boundary types: '+' for morpheme boundary, '#' for clitic boundary and '##' for full word boundary. This distinction between boundary types, we saw, could be used in the standard model to capture certain facts about the way phonological rules applied: they were, in some cases, sensitive to the occurrence of particular sorts of boundary. We saw (see p. 113) that the suffixes of English can be divided into two classes: stress-shifting ('Class 1') and stress-neutral ('Class 2') suffixes; we were able to utilise our boundary types by suggesting that Class 1 affixes are separated from their stems by a '+' boundary, whereas Class 2 affixes are separated from their stems by a '#' boundary. We noted that phonological rules which are sensitive to the class of the affix in a word could be formulated with the appropriate sort of boundary.

Let us adopt a slightly different approach to this distinction between Class 1 and Class 2 affixes in English. Let us assume that the Class 1 affixes are added to roots at a 'first' level of word-structure building. Thus, at this level, we could derive the adjective *personal* from the noun *person* and, in

173

turn, the noun *personality* from the adjective *personal*. Let us also assume that the Class 2 affixes (which include the regular inflectional affixes, such as past tense /ɪd/ and plural /-ɪz/) do not get added until any such first level affixation has taken place. Thus, once the first level has yielded *personality*, the second level may yield *personalities*. But if we insist that the two levels come strictly in this order, then there will be no question of 'returning' to the first level; thus, we would not be able to create *nationalsity* from *nationals*. This approach to word formation is known as the **level-ordered** model of affixation. If we incorporate it into our model of word formation in the lexicon, a fact about English affixes will follow as a consequence: the fact that Level 2 affixes, where they co-occur with Level 1 affixes, always occur 'outside' of them, as shown in *nationalities*. We can depict this new model of word formation like this:

(1)

Lexicon
Lexical entries, e.g. /pɜːsɒn/
Level 1 affixation (*-ity, -al, -eer, -ence, ex-, dis-, in-* and others). Level 1 phonological rules (e.g. Trisyllabic Shortening; see p. 113) e.g.: *person* → *personal* → *personality*
Level 2 affixation (*-ness, -hood, -ship, -like, -less, -er, -ism, -dom, un-* and others; regular inflection (e.g. plural suffix -ɪz, past suffix -ɪd). Level 2 phonological rules (e.g. /ɪd/ Assimilation (see p. 112), /n/ Deletion, as in *damning, columnist*). e.g.: *personality* → *personalities*

This idea of level-ordered morphology has been incorporated into a revised model of generative phonology known as **Lexical Phonology (LP)**, which seeks to carry out our task of constraining analyses without abandoning significant generalisations. Its principal innovation is to assume that, as each level of morphology is added to a root, the phonological rules for that level will apply. For instance, there is a phonological rule of Degemination in English as reported in Kaisse and Shaw (1985), which operates across Level 1 affixes, as in the following examples:

(2)

excite, excell:	[ɛksait],	[ɛksɛl]
	*[ɛkssait],	*[ɛkssɛl]
dissemble, dissent:	[dɪsɛmbl̩],	[dɪsɛnt]
	*[dɪssɛmbl̩],	*[dɪssɛnt]
innumerable, innavigable:	[ɪnjuməɹəbl̩],	[ɪnævɪgəbl̩]
	*[ɪnnjuməɹəbl̩],	*[ɪnnævɪgəbl̩]

But the rule of Degemination does not operate across Level 2 affixes:

(3)

unknown, unnatural:	[ʌnnoʊn],	[ʌnnæčəɹəl]
suddenness, fineness:	[sʌdənnəs],	[fainnəs]
soulless, guileless:	[soʊlləs],	[gailləs]

That is, Degemination is a lexical rule which is restricted to applying at Level 1. Rather than suggesting that the forms in (2) constitute exceptions to Degemination, the LP model simply locates its application at Level 1 in the lexicon. The rule of Trisyllabic Shortening (TSS) in English, which, for instance, shortens the /iː/ in morphemes like /dɪviːn/ (*divine*) when affixes like -*ity* are added, is also restricted to Level 1. It applies in *divinity*, the noun derived from the adjective *divine* by the affixation of the Class 1 suffix -*ity*, but it does not apply in *diviner*, the noun derived from the verb *divine* by affixation of the Class 2 suffix -*er*, even though *diviner* is trisyllabic.

Another important notion in LP is that of **derived environment**. Kiparsky (1982: 152) defines this as follows:

Derived Environment
An environment E is derived with respect to a rule R if E satisfies the structural description of R crucially by virtue of a combination of morphemes or the application of a rule.

We may spell this out as follows. (a) Two segments are said to occur in a derived environment if they are separated by a morpheme boundary. That is, the environment they occur in is derived if it is the result of some affixation or word formation process. (b) A segment is also considered to occur in a derived environment if it is the output of a phonological rule, rather than being present in lexical entries.

In an attempt to impose general constraints on abstractness, Kiparsky (1973) had, prior to the emergence of Lexical Phonology, used the notion 'derived environment' to reformulate the Alternation Condition (see p. 168), as follows:

Revised Alternation Condition
Obligatory neutralisation rules apply only in derived environment.

Thus, TSS, which is an obligatory neutralisation rule (it neutralises, among other contrasts, that between /i: / and /ɪ/) may apply in cases like *divinity*: the number of syllables in *divinity* exceeds two, and thus satisfies the conditions of TSS, and does so by virtue of the affixation of *-ity*. TSS may not, however, apply in a case like *nightingale*: that form does not constitute a derived environment as defined by Kiparsky and must therefore be stored with an underlying /ai/, rather than having an /i:/ which then undergoes TSS. Clearly, the restriction reduces the abstractness of under-lying representations. As far as TSS is concerned, we can now say that it cannot apply in cases like *nightingale* for the reason just stated, and cannot apply in cases like *diviner*, because the rule is a Level 1 rule. That leaves cases like *obesity*, which do satisfy the definition of 'derived environment', but still fail to undergo TSS: *obesity*, unlike *nightingale* and *diviner*, is a true exception to TSS.

With this approach, in which there are phonological rules interleaved with the word formation processes, we need have no recourse to the '+' and '#' brackets in phonological rules. The theory of lexical phonology need only state the level at which a rule applies, and simply impose brackets between morphemes as word formation takes place; thus *persona-lity* is built up from the lexical entry /pɜ:sɒn/, bracketed as [pɜsɒn], from there to the bracketed sequence [[pɜ:sɒn]æl], and then to the noun [[[pɜ:sɒn]æl]ɪti]. Along with the word formation bracket, the lexical pho-nology theory also assumes a principle of **Bracket Erasure**: internal brack-ets are erased at the end of all affixation processes at each level. Thus, once affixation and any relevant phonological rules have applied (such as the one which shifts the stress on the word form, and TSS), the LP model would generate the form [pɜ:sənælɪti]. This would then be available for affixation at Level 2, and any phonological rules which apply there.

The combined notions of Bracket Erasure and level-ordered phonology and morphology express a strong generalisation: that phonological pro-cesses are *modular* in character. As morphological and phonological oper-ations at each level of the lexicon are completed, the entire expression is 'bundled off' to the next level, which has no access to its internal make-up. For example, the suffixation of the plural morpheme functions indepen-dently of whether its stem is morphologically simple or complex: it 'makes no difference' to plural affixation that *nationality* is complex and *city* is not. In both cases, the regular plural suffix is added, and the regular phonologi-cal process which governs the form of that affix applies (the fricative assimilates in voicing to the preceding segment). Thus, regular plural affixation takes place at a later stage of word formation (at Level 2).

We have seen that TSS and Degemination operate at Level 1; it seems clear that stress assignment in English operates at Level 1 too. Consider the following evidence (from Kaisse and Shaw 1985).

(a) Verbs normally have final stress if they end in a consonant cluster: *collápse, resíst* vs *édit*. But the affixation of a Level 2 suffix to create a cluster 'does not count': *édits*, **edíts*. This suggests that stress assignment 'has already taken place', before affixation of the plural suffix, and the idea of level-ordering expresses this idea.

(b) The rightmost stress in English verbs is normally no further back than the penultimate syllable, as in *abólish*, but the affixation of Level 2 suffix syllables does not count: *éditing, édited* have stress before the penultimate syllable, since the generalisation about stress being no further back than the penultimate syllable holds at Level 1, prior to the affixation of the regular Level 2 suffixes *-ing* and *-ed*.

(c) There are Level 2 affixes which depend on the prior assignment of stress at Level 1. The Level 2 suffix *-al*, by which nouns are derived from verbs, can be affixed only if the stress is on the final syllable of the verb, as in *deny, denial, propose, proposal* vs *flatter, flatteral, edit, edital*. Again, stress assignment must have taken place at Level 1 before the affixation of *-al* at Level 2.

The idea here is that many phonological rules which are sensitive to morphological structure can be formulated without reference to boundary types; their restricted mode of application is determined by the structure of the grammar. There is a clear gain to be had in adopting this level-ordered approach: we capture the generalisation that both their ordering and their restricted mode of application follow from the place in which they are located in the grammar. For instance, TSS is both restricted and precedes the Voicing Assimilation of the regular English plural suffix, and these two facts follow from a single fact about the place in the grammar at which those rules apply. This idea that morphological operations are interleaved with certain phonological rules is central to the LP model, and constitutes a major departure from the standard model of generative phonology which we outlined in Chapter 5. There, the phonological rules apply in a block, after morphemes have been inserted into syntactic structure (this was the 'morphology first, phonology later' approach). Here, there are phonological rules which apply in the lexicon, during word formation. In Chapter 5, we said that the lexicon was largely a repository for arbitrary information. While we are not denying this now, we are allowing that certain non-arbitrary, i.e. rule-governed, phenomena take place in the lexicon. We already allowed for this, to some extent, by allowing that regular processes of affixation occurred there, and by allowing that morpheme structure generalisations are stated there. But now, we are allowing for lexical rules such as TSS and Degemination in English, in addition to morpheme structure rules applying during word formation. That is, these rules constitute the phonology of the words of the language. These lexical rules differ in several important respects from **postlexical rules**, which may operate between words. Let us look at an example.

8.2 Lexical and Postlexical Application

The rule of Flapping in American English causes intervocalic /t/ and /d/ to be realised as a voiced alveolar tap ([ɾ]), regardless of whether the segment in question is in a morphologically simple word like *putty*, a morphologically complex word like *witty* or at the end of a word as in *hit it*. In the second of these cases, it is only by virtue of affixation that Flapping applies, whereas in the former case, this is not so. In the last case, it is only by virtue of the word *hit* appearing before another word which begins with a vowel that Flapping applies. Flapping will therefore apply to *any* intervocalic /t/ or /d/, regardless of whether the intervocalic environment is there by virtue of a combination of morphological or syntactic units. That is, it applies *blindly*, regardless of structure.[1] It is thus a rule with a high degree of phonetic motivation: no structural factors will prevent it from applying. It is said to be a typical postlexical rule, since it applies after word formation and after words are entered into syntactic structure. A high degree of phonetic motivation is also said to be one of the primary characteristics of postlexical rules.

This rule is very different in its application from a rule like TSS, which applies purely word-internally, and in restricted morphological environments (with Level 1 affixes only and not to lexical entries). Another feature which allows us to distinguish lexical and postlexical rules is the degree to which they allow exceptions. Lexical rules are more susceptible to exceptions than postlexical rules. Thus, in a grammar which has both Flapping and TSS, there are cases like the word *obesity*, with the phonetic realisation [obi:sɪɾi], which are exceptional with respect to TSS (*obesity* ought to have an [ε] rather than an [i:] in the second syllable) but not with respect to Flapping. Postlexical rules are also said to differ from lexical rules in that they may be implemented in a gradual manner.[2] Thus, the application of the postlexical rule of Aspiration in English yields *degrees* of aspiration: voiceless stops in some positions will be more aspirated than those in others.

A point worth making here is that, by 'lexical rule' and 'postlexical rule', we mean, respectively, 'rule which applies in the lexicon, during word formation' and 'rule which applies after word formation, and after syntactic concatenation (after words have been inserted into syntactic structure)'. That is, the terms do not pick out properties of the rules themselves, but of the place in the grammar where they apply. This lexical/postlexical division has clear implications for rule ordering: if we establish that a rule, Rule A, is postlexical, and that another rule, Rule B, is lexical, then it follows that B precedes A. Thus, the ordering of Flapping and TSS need not be stipulated in the grammar of English: the fact that TSS precedes Flapping follows from a cluster of facts about TSS (it is morpheme-sensitive; it is triggered by Class 1 affixes; it does not apply in non-derived environments; it admits of exceptions) and Flapping (it is insensitive to structure; it has a high level of phonetic motivation; it does not readily admit of exceptions).

8.3 Structure Preservation, Abstractness and Productivity

One of the hypotheses Kiparsky (1985) formulates about the lexical/ postlexical distinction is known as **Structure Preservation**, which may be stated as follows:

Structure Preservation
Lexical rules do not introduce distinctions not present in lexical entries.

The idea is that the underlying phonological distinctions of the language are maintained by the lexical rules, whereas rules introducing distinctions not found at underlying level are introduced by the postlexical rules. The rule of Velar Softening in English, for instance, is clearly lexical. It covers alternations where a stem-final /k/, e.g. in *electric*, is realised as [s], as in *electricity*. Velar Softening is clearly structure preserving: it introduces a distinction which is already present at underlying level: there is a /k/ vs /s/ distinction in English. This is in contrast to the rule of Aspiration, which applies postlexically, wherever its conditions are met. Aspiration, since it introduces the aspirated/non-aspirated distinction, which is not present underlyingly in English, is not structure preserving.

Take the Scottish Vowel Length Rule (SVLR): it is clearly a lexical rule in that it operates strictly within words. Since it creates a long vowel/short vowel distinction, we would expect, if Structure Preservation is correct, to find such a distinction at underlying level. It does seem to be the case that some of the vowels in various Scots dialects are invariably long, and thus need to be represented as such underlyingly. Dialects in which SVLR does not apply to /a/, for instance, seem to have consistently long realisations for this phoneme, as in *bat*, *bad* and *bar*, where the vowel is long regardless of the status of the following consonant with respect to SVLR (the /t/ of *bat* and the /d/ of *bad* do not trigger SVLR, but the /r/ of *bar* does). This justifies representations with /a:/, and forces us to allow for /a:/ as a vowel in the underlying inventory of dialects like these.

It is interesting to reflect on the way in which the division into lexical, structure-preserving rules and postlexical rules reconstructs the distinction between rules which yield allophonically distinct outputs and those which yield phonologically distinct outputs. We discussed this distinction in Chapter 4, where we rejected any attempt to maintain it, on the grounds that, in so doing, loss of generalising power results. But with the LP model, it becomes clear that the output of the lexical phonology (the word-level phonology of the language) will consist of segments which are parallel to the phonemes yielded by the phonemic principle.

This is clear from our SVLR example: we saw in Chapter 4 that the phonemic principle seemed to establish both complementary and parallel distribution, where lengthening occurred before voiced continuants and word-finally, and yet we could cite minimal pairs such as *brood/brewed*, which differ, phonetically, only as to vowel length. The phonemic principle forced us to recognise vowel length as phonemic in these cases, but we argued that such minimal pairs were only 'apparent' or 'surface' minimal pairs: what mattered was the morpheme boundary in cases like *brewed*. Accordingly, we added the morpheme boundary, '+', to the class of environments stated in the rule, and abandoned the purely 'surface-level' phonemic principle. Now, we can allow the 'minimal pair' notion a place in our generative phonological theory: minimal pairs are a word-level phenomenon, holding at the level of the output of the lexical phonology, rather than at the underlying level. Distinctions like this constitute a kind of 'derived contrast' (the term is used by Harris 1990a). Thus, the phoneme notion, as yielded by the phonemic principle, does not, as we previously asserted, hold at underlying level, but at the level of the output of the lexical phonology.

The LP model also allows us to incorporate into the structure of the grammar a depiction of the degree of idiosyncrasy of phonological and morphological processes. The idea is that rules applying at the 'upper levels' in the lexicon are more idiosyncratic than those applying later. Thus, plurals in English like *oxen* are highly idiosyncratic and are depicted as being formed (if they are formed at all, and not simply listed underlyingly) at Level 1, whereas regular plural formation is a Level 2 process. Similarly, the voicing process found in *wife/wives* is restricted to a specific set of morphemes, and is therefore a Level 1 process, whereas the productive rule governing the phonetic realisations of the plural suffix operates at Level 2, alongside regular plural affixation. Irregular past tense formation in English (as in *ride/rode*) is also taken to be a Level 1 process, distinct from regular past tense affixation at Level 2: the historically older past tense formation process has been, as it were, 'deposited' at the highest, least productive, level of the lexicon. We have found a way, in this model, of distinguishing very productive allophonic rules with high phonetic motivation from morphologically sensitive rules, and of depicting the historical transition of a rule from its early existence as an allophonic rule to its later existence as a lexical rule, and its subsequent existence as a 'discarded relic', no longer productive.[3]

In adopting the LP model, we are assuming that the lexicon is more highly structured than we supposed in our standard model. Thus, while we are allowing for a greater role to be played by the lexicon in the grammar, we are doing so in a manner completely distinct from the one adopted in NGP.[4] The extended role of the lexicon there was as a repository of an *even larger range of arbitrary information* than we had first allowed for. The extended role allowed for here is as a part of the grammar where generalisations are stored, *a greater range of generalisations* than we had previously allowed for.

8.4 Redundancy and Underspecification

In our account of the standard model, we encountered one clear case where phonological generalisations were stated in the lexicon, and thus apply prior to the application of the phonological rules of a language: the case of the redundancy rules we called feature co-occurrence restrictions, default rules and morpheme structure rules. These, it will be recalled, stated language-specific and universal generalisations about the phonological form of morphemes in the language. Some were of the sort [+low] → [−high], where it is in the nature of the features themselves that a [+low] segment cannot simultaneously be [+high]. Others were the sort which express the relative 'markedness' of feature values. For instance, sonorants are usually voiced (they are voiced in 'the unmarked case'), and thus may be left unspecified in underlying representation for their values for [voice]; a redundancy rule of the form [−obs] → [+voice] will then fill in the appropriate value. The LP approach to such rules is to say that they are simply lexical rules which happen to fill in, rather than change, values for features.

The question arises as to the extent to which we may reduce the amount of specification of feature values in underlying representations, and this matter has been explored within **underspecification theory (UT)**. We will not dwell on the details of this area of theory here, but we will look at *some* of the proposals that have been made, and then consider its application to a case which induces an ordering paradox in the standard model.

Archangeli (1988) assumes that the grammar of a language is simplest, and thus most highly valued, when the underlying representations contain the minimal amount of specification compatible with maintaining the underlying contrasts of the language. While this claim is itself not especially radical, Achangeli explores its consequences in detail, and in doing so, proposes a further constraint which holds for underlying representations: that no feature is specified underlyingly for *both* values. The values which are not present underlyingly are filled in by two sorts of redundancy rule. Firstly, universal and language-specific redundancy rules of the sort discussed in Chapter 3 (see p. 76) and Chapter 5 (see p. 105) may apply. These rules are referred to by Archangeli as **default rules**. Secondly, **complement rules** may apply to fill in values for features. The idea behind these rules is that, since only one value for a feature may be specified underlyingly, the opposite value may be supplied by a complement rule. Thus, in a system where the feature [ATR] is specified as '−' underlyingly, a complement rule of the form [   ] → [+ATR] may apply. Let us look at a particular case where such a rule is appealed to.

In their analysis of [ATR] vowel harmony in Yoruba, Archangeli and Pulleyblank (1989) (henceforth A&P) suggest that a fully specified matrix for the vowels of the language would look like this:

(4)

	i	e	ɜ	a	ɔ	o	u
high	+	−	−	−	−	−	+
low	−	−	−	+	−	−	−
back	−	−	+	+	+	+	+
ATR	+	+	−	−	−	+	+

The facts of [ATR] agreement in Yoruba are, essentially, that high vowels are always [+ATR], low vowels are always [−ATR] and mid vowels may be '+' or '−', depending on the phonological form of the morpheme they occur in. An interesting claim made by A&P (and, as we will see in Chapters 10 and 11, an increasingly large number of phonologists) is that vowel harmony processes are closely connected with the shape of the vowel systems they operate on. This, A&P claim, is the case with the [ATR] harmony process in Yoruba. For them, the underlying value for [ATR] is '−', as you can see in the underspecified matrix they propose for the Yoruba vowel system, where, in accordance with the theory, each feature is marked for only one value:

(6)

	i	e	ɛ	a	ɔ	o	u
high	−				−	−	
low			+				
back			+	+	+	+	
ATR	−			−			

We do not have the space to comment in detail on the rationale for this matrix, but we will note several points. As we have said, the low vowel /a/ is always [−ATR]. That is, the specification [−ATR] is a redundant property of /a/. For this reason, /a/ is never specified for [−ATR] underlyingly. A default rule of the sort we have just mentioned fills in this value; it takes the form [+low] → [−ATR]. Two further observations can be made about the values for [ATR]. Firstly, [−ATR] is restricted, as noted above, to non-high vowels (i.e. /i/ and /u/ are never [−ATR]): a [−ATR] specification can be linked only to a [−high] vowel (see Chapters 9 and 10 for more on 'linking'). Secondly, mid vowels may be either [+ATR] or [−ATR] when *following* the low vowel /a/, but may only be [−ATR] when *preceding* /a/, thus:

(6)

	a–initial morphemes		a–final morphemes	
/i/	adi	'palm nut oil'	ila	'okra'
/e/	ate	'hat'		_____
/ɛ/	ajɛ	'paddle'	ɛpa	'groundnut'
/a/	ara	'body'	ara	'body'
/ɔ/	asɔ	'cloth'	ɔja	'market'
/o/	awo	'plate'		_____
/u/	atu	type of dress		_____

From this, A&P conclude that [−ATR] spreads in a directional fashion, from right to left. Thus, the [−ATR] which has been assigned to /a/ is transmitted to preceding non-high vowels. Vowels which have still not been assigned a value for [ATR] at the end of a derivation are assigned [+ATR] by a complement rule which, in accordance with the theory, takes the form [ ] → [+ATR]. Take, for instance, the forms [awo] ('plate') and [ɔja] ('market'). We will represent the underlying form of /a/ as /A/ and the underlying form of [o] ~ [ɔ] as /O/. The derivations will be:

(7)

	/AwO/	/OjA/
Default Rule [+low] → [−ATR]	awO	Oja
[−ATR] Spread (R → L)	—	ɔja
Complement Rule [ ] → [+ATR]	awo	—
Phonetic Representation	[awo]	[ɔja]

Thus, there are two ATR redundancy rules, assigning different values: the redundantly [−ATR] vowel /a/ is assigned its specification via a default rule in the lexicon, while redundantly [+ATR] vowels have a default assignment by a complement rule, after vowel harmony (spread of [−ATR]) has taken place. This reflects a hypothesis of UT: that segments are specified for only one value underlyingly, but that this may not always be the unmarked one. This is a more radical hypothesis than the view expressed by what A&P call *contrastive* underspecification: that values are specified only if they are necessary to distinguish at least two segments underlyingly. The Yoruba case is taken by A&P to support the *radical* underspecification thesis: only [−ATR] may be present underlyingly (on the vowels /ɛ/ and /ɔ/) and this is arguably the unmarked value for the feature [ATR].

We have not looked here at the transmission of [−ATR] from vowels other than /a/, since, for A&P, this involves a mechanism we will not introduce until Chapter 10. Nor have we looked at the relative ordering of the redundancy rules. However, we will return to the relationship between vowel harmony processes and vowel systems, and indeed to the nature of the Yoruba vowel harmony process, when we examine the validity of binary-valued features in Chapter 11. Let us now look at a case where underspecification, combined with Structure Preservation, allows us to resolve an ordering paradox.

In Chapter 4, we briefly considered the role that voicing plays in the Russian obstruent system: it is contrastive for the majority of obstruents, but allophonic for a subset of three, which we said then were underlyingly voiceless. A Voicing Assimilation rule, we said, yields the voiced allophones of all underlyingly voiced obstruents. Kiparsky (1985) suggests that we assume, not only that sonorants are universally voiced in the unmarked case, but also that obstruents are universally voiceless in the unmarked case. With this in mind, he formulates a universal default rule which is more general than the [−obs] → [+voice] default rule we gave in Section 3.7. It takes the form:

(8) *Default Voicing*

[α obs] → [α voice]

The idea is that, where a consonant does not already posses a value for the feature [voice] (in underlying representation or via the application of a rule) it will be assigned a default value by Default Voicing (DV). The universality of the rule reflects the claim that, if a language has no voicing contrast for a given obstruent (such as the velar fricative in Russian), it is the voiceless, rather than the voiced, member which will occur. There is certainly something in this idea: there are many languages which lack contrastive voicing among some or all of their obstruents, and they mostly seem to have voiceless rather than voiced series of obstruents:[5] this is clearly true in Russian, and the reader may recall that voicing is not contrastive among Spanish fricatives, which are all voiceless. See too Lass

(1984a: 7.6) for a survey of obstruent systems which tends to bear out the claim.

The Word-Final Devoicing (W-FD) rule (see Section 6.1) is generalised by Kiparsky, to apply not just to obstruents, but to all consonants:

(9) *Word-Final Devoicing*

$[+\text{cons}] \rightarrow [-\text{voice}] / \underline{\quad}]$

While Kiparsky also generalises the Voicing Assimilation (VA) rule (see again Section 6.1) in the same way, we will depart from his treatment by assuming that it affects only obstruents. Kiparsky assumes that Russian sonorants, as in most languages, are unspecified for voicing at the level of lexical representation. A central claim he makes is that all the relevant rules are free to apply lexically and postlexically, constrained only by the principles of the LP model, such as Structure Preservation. Let us see how.

Kiparsky assumes that there is a constraint on the Russian lexicon whereby sonorants may not be marked for voice lexically. Since sonorants lack a value for [voice], they may not acquire one via the operation of lexical rules without violating the constraint. Thus, the universal DV rule may affect only obstruents when it applies lexically in Russian; postlexically, it may apply to sonorants. Furthermore, where the rule applies, it must do so after VA and W-FD. This fact is dictated by the Elsewhere Condition: Default Voicing assigns values for [voice] 'elsewhere', where there is no value present.

W-FD may apply to obstruents only when it applies lexically, because of Structure Preservation: if it applied to sonorants, it would introduce a voicing distinction not present in lexical representations (we will take 'lexical representations' and 'underlying representations' to be synonymous).

Let us return to the problem of '/v/' in Russian. On p. 145, we said that it is odd, since it is like a sonorant in that it does not induce, and is transparent to, VA (we use standard model boundary symbols for ease of exposition):

(10)

#ot#vdov + ɨ# → [odvdovɨ]   'from the widow'

On the other hand, it undergoes W-FD:

(11)

/trezv/ → [trezf]   'sober'

This creates an ordering paradox for the standard model, since W-FD normally precedes (and feeds) VA, as in:

(12)

	# mozg#	('brain')
W-FD	mozk	
VA	mosk	
Phonetic Representation	[mosk]	

but W-FD appears to follow VA in (13):

(13)

	# trezv#	('sober')
VA	——	
W-FD	trezf	
Phonetic Representation	[trezf]	

Kiparksy takes '/v/' to be a sonorant underlyingly, i.e. /w/, which is therefore unmarked for voicing in lexical representations. Following Hayes (1984), he postulates a rule of W Strengthening (WS) which converts the /w/ into an obstruent.[6] This rule may apply only postlexically, since it violates Structure Preservation in introducing a distinction (between a labial sonorant and a labial fricative) which is not present underlyingly.

With the rules formulated and constrained as stated, let us see how they apply to the problematical cases which give rise to the ordering paradox.

(14)

	mozg	trezw (/w/ Lacks a value for [voice])
Lexical Phonology		
WFD	mozk	—— (May not apply to sonorants, lexically)
VA	mosk	——
WS	——	—— ⎫
DV	——	—— ⎬ May not apply lexically
Postlexical Phonology		
WFD	——	trezw̥ (/w/ acquires the value '–' for [voice])
VA	——	——
WS	——	trezf
DV	——	—— (/w/ already has a value)
Phonetic		
Representation	[mosk]	[trezf]

This analysis has consequences, as Kiparsky points out, for the application of VA to Russian obstruents, as discussed in Chapter 4. There, we saw that voicing is distinctive for all obstruents except /t͡s/, /č/ and /x/, which nonetheless have voiced allophones as a result of the application of VA. We rejected the analysis according to the phonemic principle, which insisted on two VA rules: one (a neutralisation rule) which operates on the obstruents which have contrastive voicing, and another which operates on /t͡s/, /č/ and /x/. Our objection was that there is a single voicing assimilation rule in the language, not two. We said that if we *could* distinguish between neutralising and non-neutralising cases without loss of generalisation, we would do so. In the LP model, we may now achieve that aim. Lexical application of VA will yield the neutralising cases, such as [p] ~ [b] and [s] ~ [z]. But the segments /t͡s/ /č/ and /x/ lack a value for [voice] in lexical representations, and get their '−' value via lexical application of Default Voicing. The voiced allophones of those segments get their values via the postlexical application of VA (which cannot apply to those segments in the lexicon without violating SP). We are now able to say that there is a single rule, which when it applies lexically is neutralising and when it applies postlexically is not. Once again, the phonemic representations associated with the phonemic principle are reconstructed in LP as the output of the lexical phonology.

EXERCISES

1. Basque (Ondarroan dialect; data from Hualde 1989)
In this language there is a lexical rule of Vowel Assimilation which raises the vowel /a/ when it is preceded by a high vowel, as you can see from the following absolutive singular and plural nouns and verb forms (data from Hualde 1989). (Basque has, not nominative and accusative cases, as in many European languages, but 'absolutive' and 'ergative'; the distinction is too complex to be explained here.)

	Abs. Sg.			**Abs. Pl.**		
'man'	/giʃon + a/	→	[giʃona]	/giʃon + ak/	→	[giʃonak]
'friend'	/lagun + a/	→	[laɣune]	/lagun + ak/	→	[laɣunak]
'water'	/ur + a/	→	[ure]	/ur + ak/	→	[urak]
'dog'	/čakur + a/	→	[čakure]	/čakur + ak/	→	[čakurak]

/pelota + ka/   [pelotaka]   'throwing a ball'
                      vs
/ari + ka/   [arike]   'throwing stones'
/ka/ = {ADVERBIALISER}

/bat + na/   [bana]   'one by one'
                      vs
/bi + na/   [bine]   'two by two'
/na/ = {DISTRIBUTIVE}

The rule applies strictly at word boundary (']' in LP; we omit these here for ease of exposition), as you can see in the forms above.

(i) The rule also fails to apply in morphologically simple cases:

      /pinta/   →   [piɲča]   'paint'
      /čimista/ →   [čimista]   'lightning'

What reason can be given by the theory of Lexical Phonology for the failure of the rule to apply in these cases?

(ii) This language also has a rule which affects voiced coronal stops in intervocalic position, such that /d/ → [ɾ] / V__V. It applies in the following sorts of case:

      /bide/   [biɾe]   'path'
      /ari + ka + da/ [arikaɾa]   'throwing of a stone'

but not in the following:

      #saspi##domeka#   [saspidomeka]   'seven Sundays'

What would the LP theory say about the location of the rule in the grammar?

(iii) There is also a Word-Final Stop Deletion rule, which applies when a word-final stop is followed by a word beginning with a stop. Thus, when the noun /čakur + a + k/ ('dog', sg, erg) and the verb /dis/ ('it is') are combined in syntactic structure, the result is [čakuratis]. Where in the grammar does this rule apply?

2. *English*

In Section 5.2, we formulated a rule for English which deletes /g/ after the velar nasal, but we restricted its application by means of inclusion of the appropriate boundary, so that it applies in *singer*, but not in *younger*:

	#sıng#ər#	#jʌng + ər#
Nasal Assimilation	#sıŋg#ər#	#jʌŋg + ər#
/g/ Deletion	#sıŋ#ər#	——————
Bracket Erasure	sıŋər	jʌŋgər

(i) Does the rule apply at Level 1 or Level 2 of the English lexicon?
(ii) What claim does this commit us to concerning the level of application of Nasal Assimilation?

3. *German*

In Standard German, the voiceless velar fricative [x] occurs only after back vowels (ignoring a few loanwords from Slavic languages; data from Hall 1989):

1.	[buːx]	'book'	2.	[ʃprʊx]	'saying'
3.	[kɔx]	'cook'	4.	[hoːx]	'high'
5.	[naːx]	'after'	6.	[bɑx]	'brook'

The voiceless palatal fricative [ç] occurs after front vowels:

7.	[ziːç]	'sickly'	8.	[ıç]	'I'
9.	[pɛç]	'bad luck'	10.	[gəʃprɛːç]	'conversation'
11.	[byːçlaen]	'booklet'	12.	[gərʏçtə]	'rumours'

The data in 1–12 suggest that the two are simply in complementary distribution. Note too that the palatal fricative occurs word-initially, and after sonorants:

13.	[çirʊrk]	'surgeon'	14.	[çemiː]	'chemistry'
15.	[zɔlç]	'such a'	16.	[dʊrç]	'through'
17.	[manç]	'many a'			

This has led some to suggest that the underlying form is /ç/, with a lexical rule of Fricative Assimilation which changes /ç/ from [−back] to [+back] after back vowels.

(i) Suggest another analysis with underspecification for [back] in voiceless fricatives, Fricative Assimilation as a feature-filling rule, and a default rule for [back] in voiceless fricatives.

(ii) The ordering of Fricative Assimilation and the default rule need not be stipulated. Why not?

(iii) The following minimal pairs might be taken to suggest that [ç] and [x] are contrastive. Say why these minimal pairs do not establish that the two are contrastive.

Phonetic representation		Phonemic analysis
[ku:xən]	'cake'	/ku:xən/
[ku:çən]	'little cow'	/ku:+ çən/
[taoxən]	'to dive'	/taox + ən/
[taoçən]	'little rope'	/tao + çən/
[pfaoxən]	'to hiss'	/pfaox + ən/
[pfaoçən]	'little peacock'	/pfao + çən/

(iv) In the light of the data in (iii), what restriction must be placed on the domain of application of Fricative Assimilation?

Notes

1. There are in fact restrictions on the application of Flapping, but they concern structures we have yet to examine. We will look at those structures in Chapter 9; nothing we will say there undermines the claim that Flapping applies postlexically.

2. The lexical/postlexical distinction has been extended in an interesting way by Kiparsky (1988) to the study of sound changes in languages. Briefly put, it is said that the 'Neogrammarian' conception of exceptionless sound changes, which may manifest themselves in a phonetically 'gradual' manner, corresponds to postlexical rule application. The 'lexical diffusion' conception of sound changes which are phonetically 'abrupt', or discrete, but spread gradually through the lexicon, is said to correspond to the idea of 'lexical rule application'. See Harris (1989) and McMahon (1991) for case studies.

3. See McMahon (1991) and Carr (1992) for more on the treatment of SVLR from a lexical phonology point of view.

4. McMahon (1990) proposes an interesting and highly constrained (in the sense of 'relatively non-abstract') LP account of English phonology. The crucial issue here is whether such constraints (if they are desirable)

come from within the theory or have to be imposed from outside. If the latter is the case, then the LP theory itself is, for those seeking a non-abstract phonology, in need of revision.

5. There are attested cases of voiced stop series which lack voiceless counterparts; Lass (1984a: 148) reports that these seem to be restricted to Australian languages. We would expect such systems to have developed from systems which once did conform to the unmarked case. For instance, Sudanese Colloquial Arabic (Persson and Persson 1980) has contrastive voicing among stops, except for /b/, which lacks a voiceless counterpart. Since /f/ is unlike most other fricatives in the system in lacking a voiced counterpart, it may be that /f/ has evolved from /p/ (see Section 11.1), or that /b/ has evolved from /v/. The former development is the more likely, for reasons given in Lass (1984a: 7.6).

6. As with '/v/' in Hungarian, this recapitulates the history of the segment; '/v/' in both systems has probably evolved from /w/; what Kiparsky is doing is viewing the historical change as the emergence of the rule of W Strengthening.

Further Reading

For an introduction to Lexical Phonology, see Kaisse and Shaw (1985). For several case studies of rules applying lexically and postlexically, see Kiparsky (1985). A major early paper is Kiparsky (1982); if you have followed the abstractness debate from Kiparsky (1968) to Kiparsky (1973), you can pick up the development of Kiparsky's ideas here, then proceed to Kiparsky (1985) and then later material. Much of the literature on level ordering and the evolution of the notion 'cyclic application' may prove difficult if you are unfamiliar with the issues in morphological theory, but the works cited here should be tractable, if rather dense in places.

Investigations within the LP model, such as Mohanan (1986), have brought out interesting relationships between the notions 'neutralisation', 'derived environment', 'cyclicity', 'underspecification', 'preservation of contrast' and the Elsewhere Condition. It remains to be seen exactly how the relationships between these ideas are best represented. The idea behind the Revised Alternation Condition may be expressed in LP terms as a **Derived Environment Constraint**: lexical rules may apply in derived environments only. It has also frequently been embodied in what is referred to as the **Strict Cyclicity Condition** (SCC): cyclic rules may apply in derived environments only (Kaisse and Shaw 1985: 17). We have not investigated the SCC here because of difficulties in presenting a consensus account of what it is for a segmental rule to be cyclic. Mascaró (1976) defines cyclic rules as non-automatic neutralisation rules, but there is disagreement as to just how much of the lexical phonology of a language must be said to be subject to the SCC. For Halle and Mohanan (1985), the SCC may cease to apply after a given level (in English, after level 1). Booij and Rubach (1987) argue that there is a class of lexical rules which are postcyclic (and thus not constrained by the SCC), which are implicated in certain sorts of cliticisation process (see Section 9.5 for some discussion of cliticisation, albeit of a postlexical sort).

Some phonologists (e.g. Kiparsky 1982) suggest that the SCC need not be stated as an independent principle, since the effects attributed to the SCC follow from the Elsewhere Condition (EC). There is also disagreement as to exactly how strict cyclicity effects may be derived from the EC (see Giegerich 1988 for an alternative account which does not appeal to the notion of a 'lexical identity rule' appealed to by Kiparsky). Other phonologists have denied that the effects of the SCC can be derived from the EC at all. See the sceptical comments made by Anderson (1974: 141) on the applicability of the 'cyclicity' notion to rules other than those which assign word stress, and Hualde (1989) for a claim that there may be cyclic rules which do not obey the derived environment constraint. Some metrical phonologists (see Sections 9.5 and 9.6), such as Liberman and Prince (1977), have sought to show that the notion of the cycle is inapplicable even to word stress assignment. Kiparsky (1979) is a major defence of the cyclic nature of word stress assignment.

Kiparsky (1985) has suggested that Structure Preservation (SP) too may be switched off after a given level. It is clear that, since SP and the SCC are two principal constraining forces in Lexical Phonetics, then any diminution in the number of rules which are subject to those principles will constitute a diminution of the constraints which LP puts on the power of phonological rules.

The idea that there may be 'loops' from one level back to another has also been proposed in the LP literature, and this constitutes a severe compromise on the rationale for the model. Szpyra (1989) denies that the level-ordered approach can be sustained, and thus denies that Lexical Phonology has any intrinsic merit. Halle and Vergnaud (1987) adopt the idea of level-ordered phonology, but not the idea of level-ordered morphology. For them, the morphology forms a separate module in the grammar which precedes the phonology, so that all of the morphology is located in the lexicon prior to the operation of the lexical rules. Otherwise, they accept various parts of the LP approach, such as the lexical/postlexical and cyclic/non-cyclic distinctions. Just how much of the core of Lexical Phonology will survive remains to be seen.

9 Representations Reconsidered (i): Phonological Structure above the Level of the Segment

9.1 Lexical Rules, Phonotactics and the Syllable

There is an aspect of the phonology of word formation which we did not consider in our discussion of Lexical Phonology. It concerns the phonotactics of a language and the way those phonotactics are enforced by the phonological rules which apply in the lexicon. Let us look at an example. The following verb forms from Okpe, an Edo language spoken in Nigeria, exemplify a phenomenon we have encountered before in this book (data from Hoffman 1973: 86–7)

(1)

Root		Infinitive
/ti/	'pull'	[etjo]
/sĩ/	'bury'	[esjõ]
/ru/	'do'	[erwo]
/zũ/	'fan'	[ezwõ]
/dɛ/	'buy'	[ɛdɛ]
/da/	'drink'	[ɛda]

One of the things these data reveal is that when an affix is added to a stem with the result that a high vowel is adjacent to another vowel, the high vowel desyllabifies: it becomes a glide. To characterise this process, which occurs in many languages, we propose a rule of Glide Formation which derives the glide from the high vowel when it immediately precedes another vowel. We have seen that high vowels are especially susceptible to this process, with an underlying /u/ becoming [w], an /i/ becoming [j], and a /y/ becoming a [ɥ], as in the French:

(2)

/nu + er/	→	[nwe]	(*nouer*, 'to knot')	vs	/ʒə#nu/→ [ʒənu] 'I knot'
/ni + er/	→	[nje]	(*nier*, 'to deny')	vs	/ʒə#ni/→ [ʒəni] 'I deny'
/ny + er/	→	[nɥe]	(*nuer*, 'to cloud')	vs	/sa#ny/→ [sany] 'it clouds'

193

The process is very widespread indeed in French; even where alternants are not available, as in *bien* ('well': [bjɛ̃]), *fouet* ('whip': [fwe]) and *puis* ('then': [pɥi]), and many other words in French, we still postulate underlying high vowels: /biɛn/, /fuet/ and /pyis/. This glide formation generalisation[1] in French, incidentally, is another example of why both the Alternation Condition and the True Generalisation Condition impose too strong a constraint on phonological representations: both would class it as a false generalisation in all but the alternating cases. We noted, in Chapter 3, that [w] and [j] are best treated as non-syllabic counterparts of /u/ and /i/. We dealt with such cases by using the feature [syllabic]: /u/ and /w/ differ from one another only with respect to the value for this feature, and the same is true of /i/ and /j/, and /y/ and /ɥ/. Rules like Glide Formation were formulated so as to change this value, thus:

(3) *Glide Formation*

$$\begin{bmatrix} +\text{syll} \\ +\text{high} \end{bmatrix} \rightarrow [-\text{syll}] \ / \ \_\_[+\text{syll}]$$

It is interesting that rules of Glide Formation have much the same format regardless of which language they occur in. While there is some variation in the range of high vowels which may act as input, the triggering environment is constant: adjacency to another vowel. And yet there is nothing in our distinctive feature characterisation which would enforce just the specification [+syll] on the right-hand side of the rule. [+obs] or [−lat] would serve just as well, since they have exactly the same status in distinctive feature theory: they go to make up part of the internal structure of segments. This suggests, rather strongly, that this use of the feature [syllabic] is mistaken. We will, accordingly, supply a means of abandoning it in this chapter.

Another parallelism between French and Okpe is that both languages have rules which delete one of two adjacent vowels. In French, a rule of Elision does this (as in *gréviste*, from /grevə + istə/); in Okpe, a Vowel Deletion rule operates after Glide Formation to delete non-high vowels adjacent to another vowel. There seems to be a generalisation here; the two rules jointly 'conspire', under certain conditions, to 'get rid of' sequences of two vowels within words (and, in some cases, across single word boundaries, as in *l'ami* vs *la vache*). This has the effect of reducing the number of syllables in the word by one. But to express the sense in which Glide Formation and Vowel Deletion are enforcing a ban on a sequence of two vowels within words, we need to appeal to the syllable *per se*, as a linguistic unit over and above individual segments, and to its structure. The syllable as a linguistic unit had no place in the SPE model, but even at the earliest stages of the evolution of generative phonology, Anderson (1969) and Fudge (1969) were insisting that it should; the case was put again in Anderson and Jones (1974), and the circulation of Kahn (1976) (not published until 1980) saw a recognition of the significance of the syllable in stating phonological generalisations. The idea has since gained ground, to the point where syllable structure is considered indispensible for expressing many phonological generalisations. Let us now look at that structure.

A fundamental division within the syllable concerns the unit the **rhyme**. In order to say in what sense two or more words rhyme, we have to appeal to this unit. Thus, in order to say in what sense the English monosyllabic words *height*, *bite*, *trite* and *sprite* rhyme with each other, but not with *hope*, *bean*, *trip* or *spring*, we must pick out the vowel and any segments which follow it: if that sequence is identical in any pair of monosyllabic words, then they rhyme.[2] Using the symbol 'σ' to designate the syllable, we will refer to the segments preceding the rhyme ('R') as the **onset** ('O'), and depict the structure of the syllable thus (using the 'triangle notation' to depict material within a constituent whose structure is not examined):

(4)

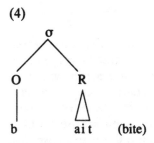

It is clear that onsets in English may consist of a single segment, as in this example, or may be empty, as in the first syllable of *idle*. We will consider the representation of empty onsets shortly. Onsets in English may also be complex, consisting of more than one segment; thus, *sprite* might be represented as:

(5)

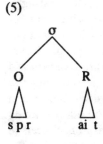

Some languages do not permit complex onsets, and have syllables beginning with a single consonant (C) only. Others do not permit rhymes containing consonants. Such syllables, containing rhymes with only a vowel, are referred to as **open** syllables. The distinction between these and **closed** syllables (whose rhymes are more complex than this, containing one or more consonants) has led many linguists to propose a division, within the rhyme, between the nucleus, which must contain a syllabic element (usually a vowel), and the **coda**, thus:

(6)

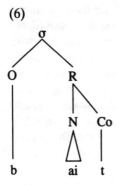

Words in a language permitting neither complex onsets nor closed syllables will, clearly, have the 'simple' syllable structure CV. Other languages may allow a more complex syllable structure than this, as in English, where up to three consonants may fill the onset and coda positions. Such phonotactic restrictions may concern, not just the overall shape of syllables in terms of permitted sequences of Cs and Vs, but restrictions on precisely which classes of consonant may precede and follow each other. In English, for instance, while it is true that onsets may contain two consonants (we will consider cases like *sprite* shortly), as in *prick*, the first consonant in such cases must be an oral stop, and the second a liquid (/r/ or /l/), as in *pram*, *bring*, *please*, *bleat*, *tram*, *dram*, *cram*, *close*, *grow* and *glove*. This restriction rules out sequences of nasal stop followed by another consonant; thus, monosyllabic *mbit* is not a possible phonological representation for an English word. Nor is bisyllabic *mbit*, with a syllabic /m/. Interestingly, when speakers of English pronounce words from languages whose phonotactics allow such syllable structures, they tend to apply the phonotactics of English. Thus names like *Mbabande*, *Ndola* and *Nkomo* tend to be altered so as to conform to the phonotactics of English. For instance, *Nkomo* will tend to be pronounced [ɪŋkomo] or [nɪkomo]; in the former case, the offending syllabic /ŋ/ is uttered so as to occupy coda position in the first syllable, and in the second case, it is transformed into an /n/ (all [ŋ]s being derived from /ng/ sequences, which, we have just said, are disallowed in onsets by the phonotactics of English) and followed by a vowel, so that the /n/ is the sole occupant of the onset position in the first syllable. To the extent that a speaker does this, he is speaking English; to the extent that he does not, he has learned a small aspect of the phonology of the foreign language, and has suppressed his native language phonology.

Syllabic nasals do, of course, occur in English, but never at the level of the initial syllabification of morphemes: *button* may often be uttered as [bʌtn̩], but the phonological form is /bʌtən/, with a vowel in the second syllable. It is the postlexical rules of connected speech which apply to delete the schwa and syllabify the /n/. What we want to say about such cases is that the phonotactic constraint which forbids syllabic nasals holds *within the lexicon*, rather than postlexically. This fact has been stressed in the LP model as evidence for the application of Structure Preservation: while postlexical rules like those which delete the schwa and syllabify the nasal may produce representations which violate the phonotactics of the language, lexical rules may not. Stronger still, we may say that the lexical rules will tend to *enforce* the phonotactics, whereas the postlexical rules may, but need not, do so. Thus, the lexical rules of Glide Formation and Vowel Deletion in French and Okpe enforce a phonotactic which forbids sequences of two adjacent vowels when such sequences arise as a result of affixation.

A further claim made by lexical phonologists is that speakers have some conscious awareness of distinctions introduced by lexical rules (e.g. the stress and vowel quality differences introduced by TSS in English), but they have little ability to perceive distinctions introduced by postlexical rules (such as Aspiration in English). In the case of deviations from the phonotactic constraints of the language, speakers do not readily perceive the distinction between lexical syllabification and surface form. Thus, [bʌtn̩] is perceived as having a vowel in the second syllable. This is what underlies the difficulty many people face in learning to perceive allophonic distinctions in phonetics classes: what one is demanding of students in such classes is the suppression of their native language phonology and the acquisition of a perceptual strategy by which this is bypassed. Cases in which the surface form violates the underlying phonotactics abound. In Japanese, for instance (to simplify somewhat), phonological representations for morphemes must be syllabified with non-complex onsets. The psychological reality of this constraint is evident in at least two ways. Firstly, Japanese speakers, although they will in fact delete vowels in connected speech, yielding forms like [ʃto] from /ʃito/, will simply not accept that the resulting form has only one vowel. Secondly, in uttering loanwords from languages which allow complex onsets, a process of vowel insertion takes place, parallel to the English case described earlier, so that forms like *screw* (/skru:/) are uttered as [sɯkɯrɯ].

9.2 Syllabification and Syllable-based Generalisations

A point often made about syllable structure, which we made in introducing the features [syll] and [cons], is that vowels are the most likely segments to occupy the nucleus of the syllable, and voiceless stops the least likely. This notion of 'degree of eligibility' for the syllabic position in a syllable is essentially to do with the *sonority* of elements, which is closely linked, in articulatory terms, with the degree of blockage of the airstream (what we referred to as degree of constriction or degree of stricture in the phonetics revision chapter). Vowels are the least constricted segments (they are all characterised by a stricture of open approximation). Furthermore, the lower a vowel, the more open the vocal tract, and the less constriction there is. Low vowels are therefore the least constricted, and thus the most sonorous, of all segments. Voicing too plays a role in sonority, since, clearly, voicing is required to produce sonority. Given these two factors, voicing and degree of stricture, we may say that voiced segments are always more sonorous than their voiceless counterparts, and we may postulate a **sonority hierarchy** among segment types, of the following sort where '›' means 'is more sonorous than':

(7)

a › e, o › i, u › r › l › m, n › ð, v, z, ʒ › θ, f, s, ʃ › b, d, g, › p, t, k

Phonologists have used the sonority hierarchy to shed light on the nature of syllable structure; it is claimed that the segments which make up a syllable will tend to increase in sonority as one proceeds from the outermost edge of the syllable towards the nucleus. Thus, in *priest*, the /r/ is more sonorous than the /p/, and the vowel more sonorous than the /r/; as one proceeds from the nucleus to the coda, the /s/ is less sonorous than the vowel, and the /t/ less sonorous than the /s/. There is certainly something in this idea, but it faces problems. Thus, /s/ in English onsets may precede /t/, as in *stop* and *stripe*, and it may follow /t/ in codas, as in *nits*. The latter case can be responded to by pointing out that the [s] here is special in that it is the realisation of a separate morpheme (see later on 'extrasyllabicity'), and there is certainly something exceptional about /s/ in onsets: it is the *only* segment which may precede a sequence of two other segments in an English onset (see Section 9.4 on sC clusters in English as complex segments). There are segment sequences within the syllable in other languages which also seem to violate the constraints imposed by the sonority hierarchy on syllable structure. In Dutch, for instance, onsets of the form /sx/ are perfectly common; but rather than pursue the matter, let us consider the role syllable structure plays in the statement of phonological rules.

It is clear that many phonological generalisations are best stated in terms of syllable structure, or simply cannot be stated at all without reference to it. We will look at two cases in French: Nasalisation, and the distribution of the mid vowels [e] and [ɛ]. Earlier, we formulated a rule of Nasalisation for French according to which a vowel is nasalised if it is immediately followed by a nasal consonant which in turn is followed by a word boundary or consonant:

(8) *Nasalisation*

$$[+syll] \rightarrow [+nas] \; / \; \underline{\hspace{1em}} \; [+nas] \; \begin{Bmatrix} C \\ \# \end{Bmatrix}$$

Nothing in the theory of distinctive features, as we presented it, suggests that # and C form a natural class, and there is thus no reason why they should figure together in the rule. We therefore suspect that there is an unexpressed generalisation lurking behind the rule as formulated. An alternative, syllable-based, generalisation, which involves no appeal to word boundary or to a consonant following the nasal stop, would be to suggest that a vowel nasalises if immediately followed by a nasal consonant in its rhyme. This means that only the following structure (in which we anticipate Section 9.4 somewhat) will result in nasalisation:

(9)

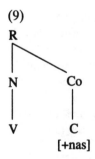

The Nasalisation rule, formulated to operate on such structures, will cover both word-internal cases, as in *banc* and *engagé*, as well as word-final cases like *bon*, in *C'est bon*. The rhyme-based formulation is clearly simpler than the standard one: it states a single context for nasalisation. With this analysis, we assume that the nasal stop occupies the onset position in the following syllable in cases like *bonne* and *bon appétit*, where nasalisation of the vowel does not occur; we will give some justification for this claim shortly.

Let us now look at the relationship between the high-mid and low-mid vowels [e] and [ɛ] in French. There are clear cases in which the two are in parallel distribution:

(10)

1. (a) [ete] (*été*) 'summer' (b) [etɛ] (*étais*)   'was'
2. (a) [te]   (*thé*) 'tea'   (b) [tɛ]   (*tais* (−*toi*)) 2PS *se taire*
                                                                       'to be quiet'
3. (a) [ble] (*blé*) 'wheat' (b) [blɛ] (*blet*)   'overripe'
4. (a) [me] (*mes*) 'my'   (b) [mɛ] (*mais*)   'but'

However, there are many alternations involving these vowels in French, in both derivationally and inflectionally related forms, thus:

(11)

1. [bɛt]   (*bête*)   'stupid'   2. [betiz]   (*bêtise*)   'silliness'
3. [grɛv]   (*grève*)   'strike'   4. [grevist]   (*gréviste*) 'striker'
5. [krɛm]   (*crème*)   'cream'   6. [ekreme] (*écrémé*)   'creamed'
7. [sɛʃ]   (*sèche*)   'dry'   8. [seʃe]   (*sécher*)   'to dry'
9. [ljɛʒ]   (*Liège*)   'Liege'   10. [ljeʒwa] (*liégeois*) 'of/from Liege'
11. [ʒɛspɛr] (*j'espère*) 'I hope'   12. [ɛspere] (*espérer*) 'to hope'
13. [ʒəsɛd] (*je cède*) 'I give in' 14. [sede]   (*céder*)   'to give in'

If we consider syllable structure, a pattern of complementary distribution emerges in such cases, with the low-mid vowel occurring in closed syllables and the high-mid in open syllables. That is, the contrast between the two is neutralised, by a rule of Lowering,[3] in closed syllables, and it is difficult to see how this neutralising context can be stated without appeal to the syllable, and its constituent parts, as units in phonological theory.

In addition to appealing to the constituents 'onset' and 'rhyme' to depict the alternations shown above, we are also appealing to the notion of **resyllabification**. Thus, if *bête* has the structure:

(12)

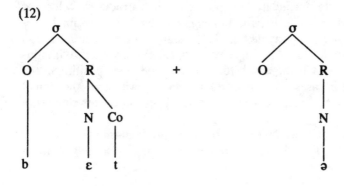

then, after elision of the schwa, it will have the structure:

(13)

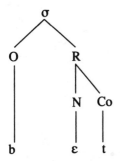

(If the schwa were not elided, the /t/ would occupy the onset position in the second syllable; we will see the justification for this claim later.) Further resyllabification takes place in the case of *bêtise*, whose derivation, simplifying the schwa deletion process somewhat,[4] will be as follows:

(14)

Word formation

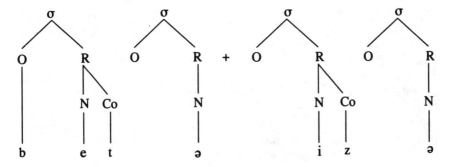

Schwa deletion and resyllabification

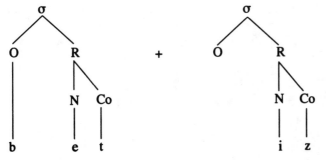

Resyllabification of /t/

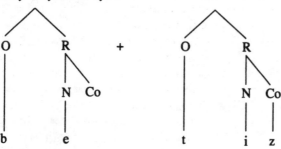

Lowering: conditions not met.

In giving the derivations above, we make several assumptions. We assume that syllable structure is not given in underlying representation, but that there is a level of initial syllabification, and that subsequent resyllabifications may take place. We also assume that the /t/ in *bête* is incorporated into the rhyme at the point of initial syllabification, and that Lowering follows Schwa Deletion and Resyllabification. We do not have the space to examine all of those assumptions, but we will consider the interesting notion that a consonant may be resyllabified into an empty onset slot. Let us approach this idea by briefly looking at a closely related notion: the **Maximal Onset** principle, which is said to hold of languages in general. The principle states that, with a given string of segments in which the consonants may in principle be syllabified in more than one way, syllabification will take place such that consonants which may occupy either rhyme or onset position will occur in the onset rather than in the rhyme. Take the English word *Ettrick*: the /r/ must be syllabified in the onset of the second syllable, since coda sequences /tr/ are disallowed by the phonotactics of the language. But the /t/ may in principle occupy the coda slot in the first syllable or the onset slot, along with the /r/, in the second, without violating the phonotactics of the language. Maximal Onset dictates that the /t/ will occupy the onset position, giving:

(15)

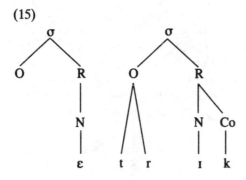

This example concerns initial syllabification, but the tendency to fill empty onsets applies equally where *re*syllabification takes place. Let us return to our French example *bêtise*: we assume that the suffix /izə/ has, at the level of initial syllabification, an empty onset, and that the /t/ in *bête* may 'shift' from the coda position to fill the empty onset position in /izə/. This process is reasonably called resyllabification: it often occurs in cases where word formation may result in changes in the syllabic structure of morphemes; we will look at some cases in English in the exercises at the end of the chapter. Where this resyllabification occurs, the /e/ in /bet/ is not in a closed syllable, whereas in *bête*, resyllabification does not take place, and the /e/ is in a closed syllable. The neutralisation rule which lowers /e/ in closed syllables therefore applies at a level after that of word formation and resyllabification.

The resyllabification notion embodies the following claim: that speakers of French will syllabify sequences of the sort CVCVCV, as in *des amis* ([dezami]), into a sequence of three CV syllables, rather than, say, into one CVC syllable ([dez]) followed by a V syllable ([a]) and a CV syllable ([mi]). This claim is persuasive. If you listen to speakers of French placing emphasis on each syllable of their utterances, and thus imposing pauses where they would not normally occur, the resulting utterance differs in at least one respect from its English counterpart, as far as syllable structure is concerned. An English speaker uttering '*Not a word!*' with primary stress on each word will utter it as [nɒt|æ|wɜːd] (where '|' indicates a pause). A French speaker uttering '*Pas un mot!*' with the same emphasis will, however, say [pa|zɛ̃|mo], with the sequence clearly syllabified into a sequence of three open syllables, i.e. with liaison of the /z/ of /paz/ into the empty onset of the following syllable.

This brings us to the phenomenon of liaison in French and the role syllable structure plays in that phonemenon. There is clearly a difference between the final consonant in words like *bête* (as well as the final consonant in words like *bec*, *mec* and *sec*, which have no schwa word-finally) and the word-final consonant in words like *mes*. The latter participate in the liaison process: they are not realised phonetically before a pause, or if the following word begins with a consonant. The former, on the other hand, are realised phonetically in all environments. This fact has consequences for the Lowering rule, since, among that class of words with a consonant which does participate in liaison, some, like *mes*, have invariable [e], whereas others have invariable [ɛ], as in *mais*. Let us therefore examine the phenomenon of liaison from the point of view of syllable structure, and then look at its consequences for the Lowering rule.

9.3 Extrasyllabicity, the CV Tier and Abstractness

The idea of preference for maximal onsets during the syllabification process leads naturally on, we have seen, to the notion of moving a consonant into an empty onset slot. That notion allows us to characterise liaison in French in a rather simple way. Here are some of the data which exemplify the phenomenon:

(16)

1.	[mebuʃɔ̃]	(*mes bouchons*)	'my corks'
2.	[mezami]	(*mes amis*)	'my friends'
3.	[desepaʒ]	(*des cépages*)	'types of vine'
4.	[dezɔɲɔ̃]	(*des oignons*)	'onions'
5.	[leviɲ]	(*les vignes*)	'the grapes'
6.	[lezø]	(*les oeufs*)	'the eggs'
7.	[nobutej]	(*nos bouteilles*)	'our bottles'
8.	[nozo]	(*nos aulx*)	'our garlics'
9.	[nokav]	(*nos caves*)	'our cellars'
10.	[nozɛtikɛt]	(*nos étiquettes*)	'our labels'
11.	[ptivɛr]	(*petit verre*)	'little glass'
12.	[ptitami]	(*petit ami*)	'boyfriend'

There is a large class of words, including *mes*, *des*, *les*, *nos* and *petit*, with a word-final consonant which appears (subject to certain constraints, to be examined in Section 9.7) when the following word begins with a vowel, but does not if the following word begins with a consonant, or if there is no following word. The standard generative approach to this phenomenon is to formulate a rule of Liaison which converts a VC#V sequence into V#CV and another, usually referred to as Truncation[5] (Dell 1973, 1980), which operates after Liaison and deletes word-final consonants when they precede a word beginning with a consonant (again, subject to the conditions alluded to above), thus:

(17) *Truncation*

$[+\text{cons}] \rightarrow \emptyset / \underline{\hspace{2em}} [+\text{cons}]$

The rule operates to delete the 'latent' consonant in cases of the sort shown in the odd-numbered examples in (16), and fails to have its conditions met in cases of the sort shown in the even-numbered examples. Words with 'fixed', rather than latent, final consonants, like *mec*, *sec*, *bec* and *cap*, all count as exceptions to Truncation under this account.[6] Other phonologists suggest a syllable-based account: the consonant in question is taken over into the empty onset of a vowel-initial word, and is otherwise not realised. We might analyse this latter case in one of two ways. We can say that the consonant begins in coda position, thus:

(18)

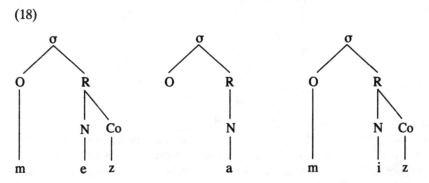

(as in *Il a vu mes amis* ('He saw my friends')) and is then moved into onset position:

(19)

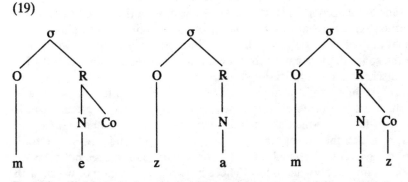

But this syllable-based analysis still requires us to formulate a deletion rule for cases in which the coda consonant does not immediately precede an empty onset. A rather persuasive alternative to this is to appeal to the notion **extrasyllabicity**. This notion is an extension of the notion of 'extrametricality', originally introduced in phonology to account for certain stress assignment phenomena, which we will look at later in this chapter. The idea was extended by Clements and Keyser (1983: 101–14) to cases involving segmental behaviour within syllables. The suggestion in this case is that a word-final 'latent' consonant, unlike, say, the /k/ in *mec* ('guy'), is not initially syllabified into the rhyme: it 'does not count', for the purposes of syllabification. We can represent the resulting syllabification (in a manner which differs somewhat from Clements and Keyser's)[7] as follows:

(20)

Lexical entry: /mez/

Syllabification:

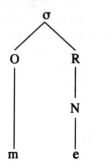

We will assume that the extrasyllabic segment may be 'rescued' by a following empty onset, and would thus be given a place in syllable structure; otherwise, stem-final extrasyllabic consonants in nouns and verbs (but not adjectives) are deleted by a postcyclic lexical rule of Truncation (as in Booij 1983/84); and any extrasyllabic consonants left unsyllabified at the end of the postlexical phonology are not realised phonetically.

It is worth noting that, in the case cited here, the /z/ in *amis*, the plural of *ami*, is also extrasyllabic, and will not be realised unless rescued by a following empty onset. This reflects an application of the notion of segmental extrasyllabicity: that claim is that *affix* consonants, such as plural /z/ in French, may be extrasyllabic. This is an interesting idea, which we do not have the space to pursue here (but see Durand 1990 and Anderson 1991 for some discussion and applications).

To return briefly to our analysis of the Lowering rule for mid vowels in French, there are three different cases involved. Firstly, there are words with word-final consonants which are never deleted, like *crème*, *bête* and *grève*, in which the vowel may alternate with a high-mid vowel. We took these to have /e/ underlyingly, and [ɛ] if resyllabification does not take the consonant into a following onset. There is a second category of words with a word-final consonant which participates in liaison, and an invariable [e] vowel, as in *mes*, *les*, *des*, etc. We also postulate an underlying /e/ in these words, but since we have now characterised the word-final consonants in those words as extrasyllabic, it is clear that they will never close the syllable containing the mid vowel, and thus the low-mid alternant will never emerge. These words contrast with a third category in which the word has an extrasyllabic consonant but an invariable low-mid vowel, as in *mais*. Such words have an underlying /ɛ/, and the possibility of high-mid/low-mid alternations does not therefore arise (since Lowering effects a change in high-mid vowels only).

It is interesting to note, as Clements and Keyser (1983) do, that French 'h-aspiré' words (see p. 143) may be given a simple analysis in terms of syllable structure. Since we postulated an underlying /h/ in cases like *hibou*, which in the plural is [leibu], and not [lezibu], we may now say that this was, in one respect, justified, since the /h/ occupies the onset slot and thus blocks the transition of the /z/ into the onset position. The syllable-based account does not, however, justify the inclusion of the segment /h/ in particular. Rather, it justifies the inclusion of a consonant in onset position, without specification as to which particular consonant. We might represent this, as follows (after Clements and Keyser):

(21)

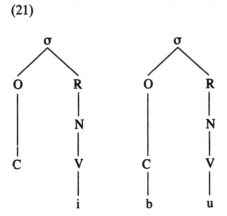

What we are suggesting here is that nodes like O and N dominate, not feature matrices directly, but 'C' and 'V' timing slots (see Section 9.4 for an explanation of 'timing'), which in turn dominate feature specifications. This line of slots is referred to by Clements and Keyser (1983) as the **CV tier**. Many interesting consequences result from the inclusion of a CV tier in phonological representations, and we will examine some of them in Chapter 10. Its use clearly obviates the need for the feature [cons], and the adoption of the 'σ' node just as clearly obviates the need for a feature [syllabic].[8] Thus, the joint work done in setting up major segment classes (consonant, glide, vowel) by the two features [cons] and [syll] is achieved by other means, and the class of phonological features proper specifies just voicing state and place and manner of articulation within consonants, vowels and glides. That is, what phonologists are now suggesting is that notions such as syllabicity and consonantality apply at a level above that of the internal make-up of segments. We have already made implicit appeal to this idea of a CV tier by describing syllable structure in terms of 'C' and 'V' sequences, and by adopting, in our earlier rules, these symbols as 'cover symbols' for sequences of consonants and vowels. For our present purposes, what we achieve in appealing to the CV tier in the 'h-aspiré' cases is the highly plausible claim that, for speakers of French, there is indeed a consonant at the beginning of words like *hibou*, but that this is all the phonological specification there is for that segment.

Resyllabifications of the sort we have just been looking at are sensitive to the occurrence of such slots, rather than to the occurrence of specific feature specifications. Thus, the 'C' on the CV tier blocks resyllabification:

(22)

The extrasyllabic /z/, which we will, following the CV tier idea, represent with a 'C' slot dominating it, fails to be realised since it remains extrasyllabic at the end of the derivation. (We continue to use symbols like 'z', as in the standard model, as an informal means of representing feature specifications.)

Clements and Keyser also show that the syllable-based, extrasyllabic analysis of French liaison has interesting consequences for the abstractness problem faced by our Chapter 6 analysis of 'h-aspiré' words. While we have just given support to the idea that words like *hibou* begin with a consonant, the setting up of an underlying word-initial /h/, as in Chapter 6, forced an absolute neutralisation analysis on us: we had to formulate a rule of /h/ deletion which operated, context-free (h→∅), to neutralise the distinction between /h/ and all the other consonants of French. Worse still, all we required of the abstract consonant at the beginning of such words was that its feature specification be distinct from all those other consonants (so that the deletion rule would delete only this consonant). Thus, /q/ (the voiceless uvular stop) or /ħ/ (the voiceless pharyngeal fricative) or /☉/ (one of the clicks found in the Khoisan languages of Southern Africa) would have sufficed. Any choice among the rather large set of non-French consonants was thus entirely arbitrary; the problem was that our model insisted on a specified segment. What the CV tier allows us is the idea of a consonantal slot which simply does not dominate any feature specification, and thus has no phonetic realisation.

From this analysis, we get a very clear picture of the exact sense in which the consonant is abstract: while it is a consonant, it dominates no feature specification, and is thus unpronounceable. Rather than appealing to a rule of absolute neutralisation, we appeal in this analysis simply to a general convention: that C or V slots which, at the end of the derivation, dominate no feature matrix simply have no phonetic characterisation. The reality of such slots is demonstrated by the Liaison phenomenon. It is also demonstrated by the phenomenon of Elision in French. Let us see how.

Recall that Elision yields vowel-less alternants for some morphemes, such as the articles *le* and *la*, and pronouns like *me*, *te* and *se*, as in *la femme* vs *l'amie*. Earlier (p. 142), we proposed a rule of the form [+syll] → ∅ / ___ ## [+syll] to derive such alternants. Let us now suggest that, like Liaison, Elision operates at the level of the CV tier. That is, rather than referring to the features [syll] and [cons] as part of the internal make-up of segments, it deletes the first of two adjacent Vs across a boundary, independently of what the C and V slots in turn dominate. In the case of *le hibou*, it will be blocked by an intervening C slot:

(23)

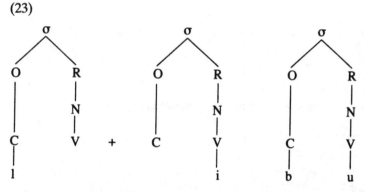

The argument we deployed in support of an underlying consonant in such words was that their 'irregularity' was remarkably regular: they consistently block Elision and, as we put it in Chapter 6, permit Truncation. Analysing elision and liaison as CV tier phenomena allows us to say why this is so without recourse to absolute neutralisation.[9]

9.4 The CV Tier, Segment Length and Complex Segments

We have said that the CV tier is a series of timing slots. We can see what this means by looking at the representation of segment length. Let us represent long consonants and vowels as single feature specifications dominated by two timing slots. Thus, Lowland Scots *bee* ([bi:]) and Italian *ecco* ([ɛk:o]), ignoring, for the sake of convenience, syllable structure, would be:

(24)

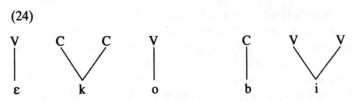

This allows us to overcome a problem which arose in the standard model with the formalisation of rules affecting segment length, like Degemination. We saw in Chapter 6 that the Degemination rule of Lithuanian could be formalised in either of two ways: the rule could delete the first of two identical consonants, or the second, and there was no non-arbitrary way of choosing between these formulations. We saw then that the approach itself was mistaken: degemination is not a matter of deleting one of two segments; rather, it is a matter of shortening a single long segment. We may now represent this as deletion of a timing slot on the CV tier, thus:

(25)

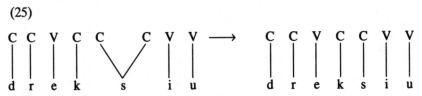

The Degemination rule would thus be formulated as:

(26) *Degemination*

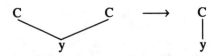

(where *y* is some feature specification).

Just as we have rejected the features [syllabic] and [cons] as features which characterise the internal make-up of segments, so are we now rejecting the use of the feature [long] as a segmental feature: segment length is located at the CV tier level, and may thus be implicated in generalisations about syllable structure. This way of viewing length differences accords well with the distinction between predictable and non-predictable segment length. That distinction is as follows. In some languages, consonants and vowels may both be long, but with the proviso that, within a rhyme, a long consonant and a long vowel may not co-occur. This is the case in Swedish, for instance, where rhymes with long segments may take the form VVC or VCC, but not VVCC (e.g. [wi:t], [wit:], but *[wi:t:]). This kind of case contrasts with that of Limbu (see p. 27) which allows both VCC and VVCC syllables, as in [am:a] and [a:m:a]. What we want to say about this distinction is that there is a restriction on the number of timing slots in the rhyme in Swedish, such that the presence of a long vowel in a rhyme precludes the occurrence of a long consonant, and vice versa.

This way of representing long vowels may be taken to mean that the syllable nucleus may branch, thus:

(27)

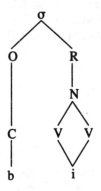

This kind of representation might in turn be taken to suggest that diphthongs too should be represented this way. The English word *bite* might therefore be represented as:

(28)

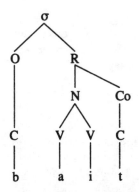

This is consistent with our representation for long vowels, but it fails to show that one element in the diphthong (the /a/) is the more prominent, or salient (it is 'the head'), while the other is less so. We need to be able to represent the distinction between this kind of diphthong (said to be a **'falling'** diphthong, since the perceptual salience of the two vocalic segments decreases from left to right) and others ('**rising**' diphthongs, in which the most salient element is on the right). One solution is to place the appropriate vowel in the onset or the coda; another is to represent, within the nucleus itself, the dependence between the vocalic elements, but we lack the space to investigate these alternative proposals.

Some phonologists (such as Anderson 1976 and Ewen 1982) have suggested that certain segment types, such as pre-nasalised stops, of the sort found in Terena (an Arawakan language spoken in Brazil) and, in certain cases, affricates, are best regarded as complex segments. That is, they 'count' as single segments, as far as the timing slots are concerned, but have more than one set of feature specifications associated with a slot. The Terena words *piho* ('son') and its pre-nasalised form *mbiho* ('my son'), would therefore be represented on the CV tier as:

(29)

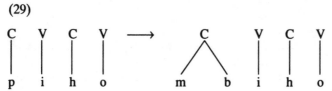

Where affricates count as single segments, the same mode of representation can be employed, as in the English word *chick*:

(30)

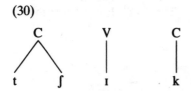

This kind of representation has also been used to deal with violations of the sonority hierarchy in English onsets and codas. Thus, /sC/ clusters in onsets have been taken (e.g. by Selkirk 1982) to be complex segments:

(31)

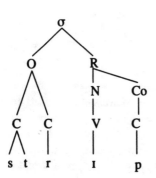

Similar proposals have been made for the problematical /ks/ sequences in English codas, as in *six*. But this account of sonority violations requires us to assess the sonority value of, for instance, the /sC/ sequence, and although it is true that, no matter what this might be, it will still be less sonorous than the /r/ which follows, there is something unsatisfactory about appealing to the sonority hierarchy while not being in possession of a means of assessing the sonority value of a given segment (the same problem occurs with affricates, of course).

In support of the idea that /sC/ onsets are simply 'marked' violations of sonority requirements is the fact that they may be eliminated in the historical development of syllabic structure. Thus, in the historical development of Spanish and French, /sC/ onsets become resyllabified as /es/ syllables followed by a C onset, as in *scola* ('school') → *escola* (with subsequent loss of the /s/ in French).

Another way of approaching /sC/ sequences in English onsets is to say that the /s/ is extrasyllabic. But here we come upon a conception of extrasyllabicity which, as Goldsmith (1990: 108) points out, is distinct from the one we have appealed to, following Clements and Keyser (1983), in discussing liaison in French. There, it was the fact that the extrasyllabic segment has no realisation if not syllabified which gave the idea its appeal; the same approach may be suggested for cases of root-final /n/ following /m/ in English, where the extrasyllabic /n/ will not surface unless rescued by an empty onset, as in *hymn/hymnal*, *damn/damnation*, *solemn/solemnity*, *autumn/autumnal*, *column/columnist*. The 'rescuing' process is restricted to Level 1 of the English lexicon. Under a 'deletion' analysis, deletion is restricted to Level 2. But the conception of extrasyllabicity which is applied to /s/ in English onsets does not appeal to the notion of non-realisation; it is based on the observation that, in many languages, word-initial and word-final positions permit relaxations of phonotactics, or impose even greater restrictions. It is all too easy for recalcitrant segments to be classified, *ad hoc*, as extrasyllabic; we lack the space, however, to investigate the validity of specific cases in which this conception of extrasyllabicity has been deployed.

9.5 Stress Assignment, Rhythm and the Foot

We have now postulated a level of phonological structure, the syllable, which turns out to be crucial for the expression of phonological generalisations. That this is so is hardly surprising: for any level of phonological structure, there are bound to be generalisations which hold at that level; indeed, the postulating of the level can only be given justification if there are such generalisations. Given that this is the case, there is a question which naturally arises in the light of the foregoing discussion: if there are phonological generalisations which hold above the level of the segment, at the level of syllable structure, are there, in turn, generalisations which hold above that level?

Let us consider word stress assignment. In some languages, the location of main stress in polysyllabic words is a fairly straightforward matter, which requires merely a general statement of which syllable position the main stress falls on: in French and Turkish, for instance, it falls on the last syllable in the word, in Polish and Welsh on the penultimate, and in Finnish and Czech, on the initial. But in other languages, the matter is more complex, and in those, syllable structure is often implicated in the assignment of word stress. For instance, one way of describing the stress assignment principle for nouns in English is to say that main stress tends to fall on the penultimate syllable if it contains a long vowel or diphthong, or a short vowel plus two consonants; otherwise, it tends to fall on the antepenultimate (thus *róoster, horízon, veránda, América*). This phenomenon is common in languages: where word stress is sensitive to syllable structure, syllables with a certain sort of structure (VV, VCC or VVC, for instance), usually described as **heavy** syllables, are distinguished from **light** syllables (V or VC, for instance), and attract stress. There is no consensus, unfortunately, on what a universal definition of 'light' and 'heavy' might look like; in some languages, for instance, syllables with a VC rhyme count as heavy, whereas in others they do not (in English, there is a case to be made for the claim that syllables with VC rhymes count as light, as in the generalisation given above). Whatever the problems in attempting to formulate a universal definition of light vs heavy syllables (that is, a universal definition of syllable weight),[10] it appears to be universally true that, where stress assignment is sensitive to syllable structure, it is the rhyme that counts: onsets appear to play no part in the assignment of stress, and this fact gives further support to an onset–rhyme distinction within the syllable. Where stress assignment depends on the structure of the rhyme in this way, we say that it is **quantity-sensitive**: it is sensitive to the phonological weight of the rhyme. The matter is somewhat complicated by the fact that, in some languages, such as English, morphological factors and the lexical category of the word are also implicated in word stress assignment, but we will not examine such cases.

In languages where word stress assignment is quantity-sensitive, it often happens that a particular syllable position in a word 'does not count' for the purpose of stress assignment, or, to put it another way, the statement of the word stress assignment principle for the language is noticeably simplified if such an assumption is made. In such cases, the syllable in question is said to be **extrametrical**. Take the case of the Central Siberian dialect of Yup'ik cited by Goldsmith (1990: 171): there, the main word stress falls on heavy syllables, where those are defined solely as syllables containing rhymes with long vowels (i.e. VC rhymes are not heavy in Yup'ik). But the last syllable in a word is extrametrical: it may not bear stress, even if it is heavy. Extrametrical syllables always occur at the edge of a word: they are the leftmost or rightmost syllable, and cases of extrametrical final syllables are very common (at least one analysis of word stress assignment in English (Hayes 1982) assumes that this is the case with nouns in English). The notion 'extrametrical' has been applied to segments, as well as to rhymes. Thus, in Hayes's (1982) theory, the final consonant in all English words is taken to be extrametrical. To pursue the details of this claim, and indeed the details of word stress assignment in English, would take more space than we have available.[11] However, it should now be clear how the notion 'extrasyllabic', which we appealed to in discussing 'latent' consonants in French, may be seen as a natural application of the extrametricality notion: it also concerned segments at the rightmost edges of words. (The two cases differ, however: the significance of the notion in our French case did not concern stress assignment or syllable weight.)

Sequences of rhymes (and therefore syllables) consisting of a stressed syllable plus one or more unstressed syllables are said to form constituents called **stress feet**. Thus, our word *rooster* may be said to have the following structure (disregarding onsets), where 'F' indicates a foot:

(32)

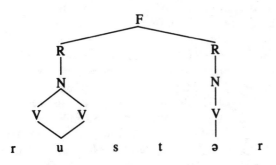

Similarly, the English sentence *Sandra scolded Michael* can be assigned the following structure:

(33)

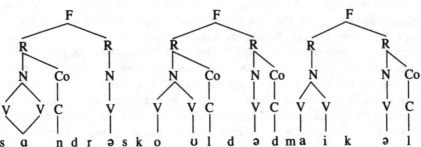

That is, the two rhymes in each word form a stress foot; if you 'tap out' the rhythm of the sentence as you utter it, you should notice that there are regular beats on the first syllable of each word. Since we are dealing with metre (the rhythm of speech) in cases like this, we refer to the structures involved as **metrical** structures, and theories about that structure as metrical theories. Much work has been done in post-SPE phonology on this area of linguistic organisation, within what has come to be known as **metrical phonology**. We will be able to give only the briefest of accounts of some of the central ideas in metrical phonology, but it should nonetheless become apparent that many interesting generalisations, which would otherwise evade us, can be captured by metrical theory.

If stress is assigned at the level of the foot, then the question arises: what are the principles for foot formation in human languages? We have just mentioned one factor: foot formation may be quantity-sensitive, as in English, whereas in other languages (such as French), the weight of the rhyme plays no part in stress assignment. Because of this, we refer to the presence vs absence of quantity-sensitive feet as a **parameter** along which languages may vary. Another parameter in foot formation concerns the position of the main stress within a foot. Many metrical phonologists want to claim that feet in English always have the structure just shown, where the most prominent element (the head) is on the left, followed by one or more less prominent elements to the right. That is, feet in English are **left-headed**, and since other languages have **right-headed** feet, we isolate another parameter along which languages vary with respect to foot formation: feet may be left- or right-headed. Feet in English, we have said, may contain more than one syllable after the head. Thus, in *Michael scolded his teddy*, we have:

(34)

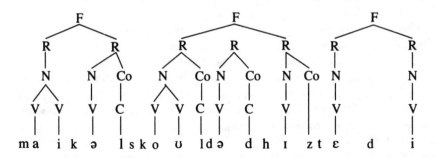

Here, the second foot contains three rhymes: the head, which is the first rhyme in *scolded*, and two unstressed rhymes. Note that if you tap out this sentence when you utter it, the stressed syllables remain at equal intervals, even though there is an extra syllable in the second rhyme, as compared with *Sandra scolded Michael*. This fact about rhythm in English has often been noted: if several syllables intervene between two stressed ones, they are 'bunched up' together, so that the stresses remain equidistant from each other (this is what is meant when it is said that English is 'stress-timed'). Thus, *Sandra flirted with the Frenchman* has three unstressed syllables between the second and third stressed syllables, and *Sandra flirted with the delectable Frenchman* has four. In each case, the timing between the stressed syllables remains the same. This does, of course, put pressure on those unstressed syllables to shorten as much as is possible, or be eliminated; thus, elision of vowels and consonants, and reduction of vowels to schwa, abounds in such cases: the four unstressed vowels referred to in *Sandra flirted with the delectable Frenchman* are all schwas, and the sequence is reduced to [flɜ:tədwəðədə]. The foot structure could be given as:

(35)

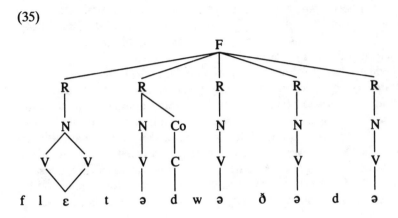

In a case like *The generativist confessed*, where five unstressed syllables may intervene between the stressed syllables, elision of schwa, and thus loss of a syllable, is likely [jɛnɹətɪvɪskən].

This way of representing the stress timing of English suggests that feet in English are **unbounded**; that is, that they may, in principle, contain any number of rhymes (subject only to the constraints imposed by what it is physically possible to utter in the allotted time). That claim is debatable: Selkirk (1984) suggests that feet in English are bounded, being restricted to a maximum of three syllables, but the debate brings out a third parameter along which foot formation in languages may vary: feet may be bounded or unbounded in a given language. With the parameters of English foot formation fixed such that they are (a) quantity-sensitive and (b) left-headed (we leave open the boundedness issue), and with a clear statement of the details of the quantity sensitivity, we can go some way towards constructing foot structures in any given case. But other questions remain. How should the stressed syllable in a foot be represented? Are there general constraints on the overall shape (the geometry) of feet? If there are feet with three rhymes, for instance, what principle dictates that such feet should branch three ways, as above? Might there be a principle that imposes another branching? How should monosyllabic words be represented? What about words containing more than one foot? To answer these questions, i.e. to examine some of the proposals made in metrical phonology concerning the representation of stress levels in feet, and the geometry of those feet, we need briefly to summarise the system of stress assignment adopted in the SPE model, since metrical phonology was developed to remedy perceived inadequacies in the SPE approach.

That model assigns stress in English firstly via a segmental feature [stress] and secondly by means of stress assignment rules which work in conjunction with a set of conventions as follows. The stress rules have access to syntactic information, in the form of labelled and bracketed strings of the sort we briefly considered in Chapter 5, which include boundary symbols. Primary stress, represented by a '1', is assigned to the appropriate vowel in each lexical category by the **English Stress Rule** **(ESR)**, which is sensitive to, among other things, syllable structure, where that structure is defined in terms of sequences of Cs and Vs.

Rules which assign further stresses then apply, such as the **Nuclear Stress Rule (NSR)** which operates on phrases (such as *Mike's teddy* and *dirty dons*), and the **Phrasal Stress Rule (PSR)**, which assigns stress to compounds (such as *pregnancy test* and *driving licence*). A convention of stress demotion, the **Stress Subordination Convention (SSC)**, automatically reduces all other stress levels within the brackets in question by one when primary stress is assigned. Another convention, the **Bracket Erasure Convention (BEC)**, erases the innermost brackets after the application of all the rules, thus creating a new string on which all the rules have a chance to apply. It is this latter process which we described as cyclicity in Chapter 5: the cyclic principle of rule application says that all of the rules have a chance to apply to the material enclosed within the innermost set of brackets, and then, once that has happened, those brackets are erased and a new cycle begins on a string of segments and boundaries which, by definition, contains the old string as a subpart. For *Frenchman*, we have:

(36)

1st Cycle:

ESR	1	1
	[N [A French]A	[N man]N]N
BEC	1	1
	[N French	man]N

2nd Cycle:

PSR	1	
SSC	1	2
	[N French	man]N

The case for representing stress in terms of trees with labelled nodes was put by Liberman and Prince (1977; henceforth, L&P). One of L&P's objections to the SPE system was that it did not properly reflect the fact that stress levels are a matter of *relative prominence*: when we perceive stress differences, we are not assigning *absolute* values such that one syllable has primary stress, another secondary, others tertiary and so on. Rather, we perceive one syllable as more prominent relative to another. L&P claimed that the SPE numerical system (with stress levels ranging infinitely from '1' downwards) expressed the former view, whereas the latter view is directly expressed by trees with nodes labelled 's' and 'w', thus (ignoring syllable structure):

(37)

Frenchman

Some phonologists (e.g. Durand 1990: 224, and Hogg and McCully 1987: 64) find the SPE idea of a potentially infinite number of stress levels absurd. It is claimed that trees with purely local 's/w' relations make no direct claims about degrees of stress between a node in one part of a tree and nodes elsewhere in the tree, and thus obviate this 'absurdity'. And yet, Hogg and McCully (1987: 70) show, following L&P, that a direct translation from metrical trees into SPE numerical stress levels is available, in the form of an algorithm (a procedure for translating from one formal system into another), as follows:

If a terminal node t is labelled 'w', its stress number is equal to the number of nodes that dominate it, plus one. If a terminal node t is labelled 's', its stress number is equal to the number of nodes that dominate the lowest 'w' dominating t, plus one.

(L&P: 259)

Clearly, if such an algorithm exists, then metrical trees do indeed express the idea of an infinite number of stress levels. That idea is not as absurd as it may first appear: while the range of stress levels that human beings can make, and perceive, may be limited, that is no reason to assert that the grammar places a limit on that range. Syntactic parallels are not difficult to find. There is no linguistic limit, for instance, on the number of subordinate clauses a sentence may contain, but there is a limit on the number which a human being can decode (it just might be possible to utter a sentence with 100 such clauses, but that sentence could almost certainly not be decoded by human beings). Nor need we appeal to such extreme cases: with certain types of subordinate clause, the limit is very low indeed. For instance, we can say that the following is a well-formed English sentence: *The rat the cat ate died*. Here, the 'wh' expression 'which' is missing, but its omission causes no decoding problems. However, *The rat the cat the dog chased ate died*, with only two such clauses, is very hard to decode. It appears that the number of such subordinate clauses we can decode with ease is limited to one. But it would be absurd to claim that there is a limit in the grammar of this sort: that would entail denying that the second sentence is well-formed while asserting that the former is, and that is impossible, without contradiction ensuing. Thus, while it is true that stress is a matter of relative prominence, the claim that the SPE numerical system is 'absurd' is somewhat overstated, to say the least. Furthermore, as Durand (1990: 224) acutely observes, the Stress Subordination Convention in SPE *did* express the idea of relative prominence. It is true to say, however, that the SPE notion of assigning primary stress to a primary stressed item was rather odd, and that the notion of relative prominence is much more perspicuously expressed in the metrical phonology notation.

Clearly, this new mode of representing relative prominence requires a reformulation of rules like the NSR and the PSR in terms of metrical trees; those, which we do not have the space to investigate, were claimed, with some justification, to express the generalisations in question more elegantly than their SPE equivalents. Another mode of representing relative prominence in tree structures is directly to encode it in the trees, with the head represented by a vertical line and dependents with non-vertical lines, thus:

(38)

beetle   Frenchman

This is the mode preferred by phonologists working within the theory known as Dependency Phonology (as in Anderson and Durand 1987, and Anderson and Ewen 1987), whose proposals for the representation of segmental structure are discussed in Chapter 11. Without discussing the matter, we will use the labelled node variety.

On the matter of the geometry of feet, some phonologists allow for feet with nodes which have more than two branches, as in (35), while others insist that metrical structure must be **two-way (binary) branching**. A binary branching representation for an English foot with three syllables might look like this:

(39)

flirted   with   elephant

The binary branching theory has consequences not only for cases of the above sort, but also for the representation of monosyllabic words, and for cases like *delinquent*, where we have suggested that a foot boundary occurs within a word.[12] Take the case of monosyllabic words. While some phonologists suggest that these form **degenerate feet**, where the idea of headedness does not apply (since there is no question of stating which of two or more syllables is the more prominent), Giegerich (1985) suggests that all such words do indeed have a binary branching structure, thus:

(40)

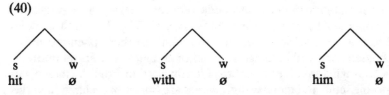

hit   ø   with   ø   him   ø

This, at first sight, looks rather bizarre: the weak node dominates what Giegerich refers to as a **zero syllable**, and one is entitled to ask what possible reality that might have. Giegerich argues that the idea of the zero syllable fits well with two facts about English. Firstly, we referred, in our discussion of liaison in French, to the phenomenon of liaison occurring when the speaker is placing emphasis on each word of the utterance, as in *Pas un mot*! This, we said, differed from the English utterance *Not a word*!, where the pauses come clearly at the end of each word. We said then that the pauses were a consequence of this heavy emphasis. Giegerich brings out the link between the emphasis and the pause by pointing out that the pauses occur in the zero syllable slot. A second fact about English which fits well with the zero syllable notion concerns the behaviour of words of a non-lexical category (such as pronouns, prepositions, conjunctions, articles). Such words are often unstressed because of their non-lexical status, and often act like clitics with respect to words of a lexical category. This cliticisation can be seen in verbs and their object pronouns (*done it*, *got you*, etc), with nouns and prepositions or articles (*cup of*, *lot of*, *[pint of*), and 'wh' expressions and articles (*what a*, as in *what a fuss*). It is noticeable that such expressions often involve weakening of word-final consonants ([gɒčʌ] for /gɒt# juː/ and [lɒɹə] for /lɒt#ɒv/) and are often spelled so as to suggest cliticisation of the second monosyllabic word to form a bisyllabic word: *gimme shelter*, *who dunnit*, *lemme in*, *kinda cute*, *lorra laughs*, *gotcha*, *cuppa*, *pinta*, etc. The cliticisation process is easily represented within Giegerich's approach: the unstressed non-lexical word undergoes 'defooting' and moves into the weak right node of the preceding foot, thus:

(41)

Similar cliticisation processes occur in the widely occurring contraction phenomena of English. Thus, *not* reduces to a syllabic nasal plus /t/ in cases like *shouldn't*, *wouldn't*, *hadn't*, and auxiliary verbs like *will* and *have* reduce to syllabic /l/ and /v/, respectively, in cases like *John'll know* and *the plants've died*. Where the word preceding the auxiliary ends in a vowel, the /l/ or /v/ resyllabifies directly into coda position, leaving a monosyllabic form: *I'll open the bottle* begins with monosyllabic [ail]. This in turn allows cliticisation, as in *He'll've eaten*, with [hilv̩]. All of these phenomena are easily characterised within Giegerich's set of assumptions. Furthermore, if Giegerich is right, that feet are always left-headed in English (they never branch to the left), and monosyllabic words are binary branching, then this explains why, although there are many cliticisation phenomena in English, they all involve cliticisation to an element on the left, never on the right, of the weak syllable. (The former sort is usually referred to as **encliticisation**, as opposed to the latter type, known as **procliticisation**, which is found in many languages.) The representation given in (39) for *flirted with* assumes such a cliticisation of *with* to *flirted*, to form a foot structure parallel to that of *elephant*. The most striking thing about such structures is that the 's–w' relation holds 'all the way up' the metrical tree, and this reflects the claim that relative prominence holds locally, for adjacent nodes, from the lowermost to the uppermost. We can represent such relative prominence patterns in hierarchical structures all the way up to sentence level as follows:[13]

(42)

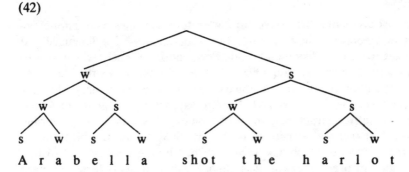

Such a structure presupposes principles whereby feet are assigned relative prominence in words, phrases and clauses. For that purpose, a rule is needed for the location of sentence stress, and the metrical versions of rules like the NSR and PSR need to assign prominence to the correct syllables in polysyllabic words, compounds and phrases. For instance, in the word *Arabella*, we will need to assign the right foot more prominence than the left, as follows (where 'm' designates a phonological word, often referred to in the literature as 'mot'):

(43)

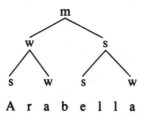

For this purpose, a rule entitled the **Lexical Category Prominence Rule** was proposed by L&P which, subject to certain conditions, assigns prominence to the second foot, so long as it branches, which it does in this case.

The rule is augmented by a set of conditions, which we do not have the space to examine. Nor do we have the space to examine all of the other metrical rules needed to arrive at the correct representations for words, phrases and clauses in English. Let us instead move on to another aspect of rhythm, and a means of representing it. (We will return briefly in Section 9.7 to the matter of what each level of the structure in (42) might be, and how the appeal to such levels might prove fruitful.)

9.6 Symmetry, Clash Avoidance and the Metrical Grid

In our discussion of syllable structure, we referred to the idea of phonological rules imposing, or executing, the phonotactics of a language. As examples, we cited Elision and Glide Formation in French, which may be said to serve to eliminate sequences of vowels disallowed by the phonotactics. If the phonotactics of a language are preferred structures, then the idea can be extended to metrical phenomena; that is, a language may have preferred metrical structures, and those too might be enforced by the rules which affect metrical structure, or by principles or rules which restore preferred structure which has been disturbed by the application of rules. This notion of preference for phonological symmetry is reflected in many languages. In English, for example, it is often claimed that structures with symmetrically spaced feet are preferred. Another, frequently cited, example of preference for symmetry involves the symmetrical sequencing of a high tone followed by a low tone in tone languages.[14] In such languages, phonological rules which delete vowels, operating on the CV tier, will often do so while leaving intact the preferred tonal contours. For instance, if a language has a phonotactic forbidding a sequence of two high tones, and a sequence HLH (where 'H' = 'high' and 'L' = 'low') would be transformed into a sequence HH by a rule which deletes the first of two adjacent vowels, then the HLH sequence is often preserved (say, by formation of a 'contour' tone on the first vowel, representable as HL), thus:

(44)

$$
\begin{array}{ccccccccc}
\text{H} & & \text{L} & & \text{H} & \longrightarrow & \text{H} & & \text{L} & & \text{H} \\
| & & | & & | & & \diagdown & & \diagup & & | \\
\text{C} & \text{V} & + & \text{V} & \text{C} & \text{V} & & \text{C} & \text{V} & + & \text{C} & \text{V}
\end{array}
$$

This latter phenomenon, whereby a preferred sequence is maintained on what we can call the **tonal tier**, independently of the operation of a rule affecting the CV tier, is often accounted for by appeal to the principle known as the **Obligatory Contour Principle (OCP)**.[15] Although this principle started life as a description of a purely tonal phenomenon, the expression 'OCP effect' is now used by phonologists to refer to cases where some preferred, symmetrical, structure is enforced either by phonological rules or by general principles (which may come into operation when the application of other phonological rules result in asymmetrical structures). This enforcement of symmetry usually entails an appeal to the idea of **clash avoidance** (in the case we have just cited, the avoidance of a clash where two H tones end up adjacent to each other).

We may take the same view of the rules of Elision and Glide Formation in French, and indeed of the liaison phenomenon. We could regard a sequence of two vowels, in certain circumstances, as constituting a clash, and take the Elision and Glide Formation rules to serve to repair that clash. Similarly, the liaison process could be viewed as a means of obviating clashes of the sort CC in certain circumstances. In each of these cases, the restriction is on sequences of identical objects, whether Cs, Vs or tones of a particular sort. We might even extend the idea of clash avoidance to cases of segmental dissimilation in sound changes, where, for instance, they function to eliminate sequences of two nasal stops. Thus, in the history of Spanish, *homne* ('man'), from Latin *hominem*, changes to *homre* (and later to *hombre*). The matter is, of course, considerably more complex than we have suggested. (In French, for instance, it is simply untrue to say that any sequence of two Cs or two Vs, even word-internally, is disallowed). But the fundamental idea does concern avoidance of sequences of identical phonological objects, and there is very probably good perceptual motivation for such an avoidance.

Let us now see how the notion 'clash' applies to metrical phenomena. It has often been observed that there are, in English, many cases where a word alternates between two stress patterns. Take the words *antique, thirteen, unknown, Dundee* and *Tennessee*. All have main stress on the final syllable, both when uttered in isolation and when uttered such that they do not premodify a word with primary stress on the first syllable, as in: *Judy swam naked in the Tennessee, His record collection is positively antique, Ron had three glasses of wine, whereas Jackie had thirteen* and *Sandrine's whereabouts in Prague are unknown*. But when they occur in a different syntactic context such that they immediately precede (and usually modify) a word with main stress on the first syllable, a shift of stress takes place: it is striking, and intriguing, that in *antique table, thirteen glasses, unknown artist* and *Tennessee Williams*, the words in question have main stress on their first syllables. The phenomenon is not restricted to words stressed on the final syllable. Thus, *academic* has stress on the third syllable, but stress is shifted to the first in the phrase *academic writer*. The question arises: what is the generalisation underlying such alternations? To answer this question, we will consider a means of representing such aspects of metrical structure, known as the **metrical grid**, originally proposed as an augmentation on metrical trees which would clearly bring out violations of preferred metrical patterns (clashes) in a language. The grid for *unknown* would be given as:

(45)

u n k n o w n
*   *
      *

The principles for grid construction may be given as follows. Working from the bottom-up, and, in larger constituents from the inside out, as in the cyclic approach, place an asterisk below each syllable, and thereafter place a further one below any syllable labelled 's' at any point in the metrical tree. Thus, in *academic*, the tree and grid would be:

(46)

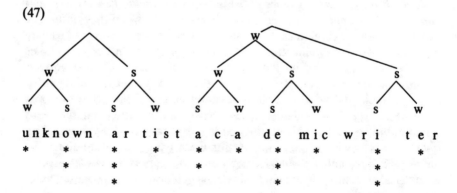

When we combine the word *unknown* with *artist*, and *academic* with *writer*, we arrive at the following representations:

(47)

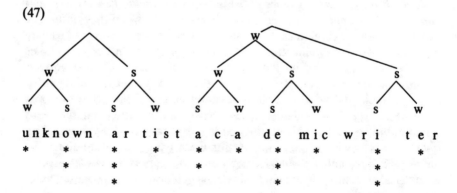

We are now in a position to define a stress clash in such cases. A clash arises when there are two adjacent grid marks at the same level (above the lowermost level). The rule which retracts the stress in such cases, yielding the stress alternations in question, is referred to as **Iambic Reversal**, or the **Rhythm Rule** (it is also sometimes referred to, mnemonically, but rather prosaically, as the 'thirteen men' rule). It may be formulated thus:[16]

(48)

Iambic Reversal is often viewed as an example of a general tendency towards maintaining metrical symmetry, or **eurythmy**, which is reflected in other sorts of 'repair' phenomena, in English and in other languages. An idea which is often appealed to in such cases is that of the 'Perfect Grid'; that is, a grid structure which is entirely symmetrical and is maintained wherever possible.[17] We lack the space to examine these other phenomena, but see Hogg and McCully (1987: 148–54) for some examples and discussion.

The term 'iambic' is a traditional term which identifies right-headed feet (which our trees above allow for in English, but our earlier discussion, following Giegerich 1985, does not), as opposed to 'trochaic' for left-headed feet. Hogg and McCully (1987: 134) suggest that Iambic Reversal is optional, on the grounds that it is possible to say, for instance, *academic writer* such that *academic* has stress on the third syllable, as it would prior to the application of Iambic Reversal (thus: *He's not a pópular writer, he's an académic writer*). We will take the view that Iambic Reversal is obligatory within English sentences, and consider below the fact that other stress contours are possible, as indicated by Hogg and McCully. They also take the reversal phenomenon to suggest that relative prominence is not preserved under embedding, meaning that patterns of relative prominence in a word, phrase or clause are not preserved when that word, phrase or clause is located within a larger domain, as with the adjective *academic* in the expression *academic writer*. But there is no reason not to claim that relative prominence is preserved under embedding *unless* a clash arises, in which case repair operations like reversal come into operation.

Reversal as presented here, while it requires a certain kind of grid configuration to be triggered, is a tree-orientated process, stating that we reverse the 's' and 'w' relation in a tree, and Giegerich suggests that a tree-based formulation of the rule is perfectly adequate. Those who favour grids, however, suggest that this formalism expresses rather clearly the idea of a stress clash, and that Iambic Reversal be defined in terms of grid configurations, or tree-plus-grid configurations. Some phonologists, such as Giegerich (1985), pursue a purely tree-based theory for all metrical phenomena; others (such as Prince 1983 and Selkirk 1984) suggest that the grid is the most appropriate mode of representation for stress and timing phenomena. We lack the space to investigate the debate as to whether metrical theory requires both formalisms, or only one (and if so, which one).[18] We will also be unable to discuss the possible extension of metrical theory to cover the sorts of vowel harmony phenomena we have analysed in earlier chapters; but we will look, in Chapter 10, at their treatment from within what is known as autosegmental theory, which, as we will see, involves crucial reference to the notions 'CV tier' and 'tonal tier' which we have just mentioned.

9.7 Prosodic Domains and the Syntax/Phonology Relationship

It is interesting that many of the proposals made in metrical theory are compatible with the lexical/postlexical distinction made in lexical phonology. We can assume, for instance, that initial syllabification takes place in the lexicon, and that foot formation within the word takes place there too. Thus, the levels syllable, foot and word are all relevant within the lexical phonology. We may also allow for postlexical foot formation, as in our cliticisation processes, and generally wherever feet are formed across word boundaries. Our analysis of liaison in French also assumed that there may be a level of postlexical resyllabification. So we have now allowed for the following domains in which rules may apply: the syllable, the foot and the word. These are referred to as **prosodic domains** (where 'prosodic' means 'applying at a level above that of the segment'); one of the ideas which has been examined in detail in post-SPE phonology is the idea of a hierarchy of such domains, the **prosodic hierarchy**. This generally takes the form syllable › foot › phonological word › phonological phrase › intonational phrase › utterance, or some variation thereon. The postulating of such a hierarchy opens up a range of interesting questions. We may, for example, ask, for any given rule, what level it applies at, and in doing so, we could avoid a fair amount of extrinsic ordering. We may also ask, at a more general level, whether each of these domains is instantiated in all languages. We might also insist that all postlexical rules are defined for the domain within which they apply. These are the sorts of question which work by, for example, Nespor and Vogel (1986) seeks to address. Nespor and Vogel show, for instance, that the Vowel Harmony rule of Hungarian applies at the level of the phonological word. Other rules, like Aspiration in English, apply strictly within the foot. So does the rule which operates on /t/ in accents of

English spoken in the North of England, giving the voiced continuant [ɹ], as in *got a chance* [gɒɹəčɐns], *lot of laughs* [lɒɹələfs] and *hit him* [hɪɹml], but is blocked by a foot boundary, as in *a tie*:[19]

(49)

Nespor and Vogel also claim that Flapping has 'utterance' as its domain of application (we lack the space to investigate this claim). Allowing for a category of postlexical rules not only opens up the possibility of defining their prosodic domains, it also raises the possibility of those rules interacting with the syntax of the language (since such rules operate after words undergo lexical insertion into syntactic structure). For any given postlexical rule which is constrained in some way (and most of them, like Aspiration and Flapping, are constrained in one way or another), we are then faced with the task of deciding whether purely prosodic factors count, or whether syntactic considerations matter, or both. In discussing liaison in French earlier in this chapter, we said that it applied 'in certain circumstances'. It is an intriguing fact that while the /z/ in *amis* is not realised in (50a) below, the /z/ of *ils* is realised in (50b):

(50a)

Mes anciens amis arrivent [mezãsjɛnzamiaʁiv]

(50b)

Ils arrivent [ilzaʁiv]

In both cases, the verb phrase *arrivent* is preceded by a subject, which is a noun phrase in (50a) and a pronoun in (50b). Many phonologists (e.g. Dell 1980 and Selkirk 1984) have suggested that a 'close syntactic link' must exist between the two words in question for the latent consonant to be realised. Thus, the link between the first element (the determiner *mes*) in (50a) and the adjective *anciens* is said to constitute such a case, as are links between adjective and noun, again as in (50a), and indeed between determiner and noun (as in *mes amis*), whereas the link between a subject noun phrase and a following verb phrase, as in (50b), is not. This approach suggests that the syntax may directly influence the phonology, and is thus termed the **Direct Syntax Hypothesis**. In response to this hypothesis, at least as far as our liaison case is concerned, we may argue with some

justification that both (50a) and (50b) constitute identical structures, at the
'topmost' level of the organisation of the sentence, thus:

(51a)   (51b)

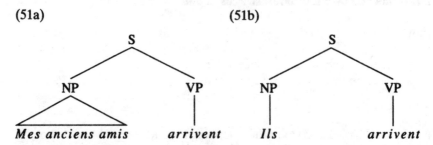

We might suggest therefore that it is the lowermost level of structure (the
bottom line in a syntactic tree) that counts, and that the boundary between
a pronoun and a verb is weaker than that between a full noun phrase and a
verb. That idea is not without its merits; we have already appealed to it in
discussing cliticisation, both in Chapter 5 and in examining Giegerich's
metrical theory. One interesting hypothesis is that liaison occurs only
across the single word boundary of the standard model (see p.113), and not
across the stronger double word boundary. This means allowing, in the
standard model, for 'readjustment rules' (we did not discuss these in
Chapter 5), which would, in this case, weaken the boundary between
determiners and nouns, between adjectives and nouns, and between pronouns and immediately following verbs. This would establish a fairly direct
link between the syntax and the phonology, although it is true that it is
somewhat indirect, since syntactic structure and phonological rules are
mediated by the readjustment rules. A much more direct link between the
two was postulated by Kaisse (1985), but an account of it would require an
appeal to notions in recent syntactic theory (concerning 'c-command'),
which it would be unreasonable to appeal to in a book of this sort. A more
indirect link between syntax and phonology can be postulated if we suggest
that the syntax influences the prosodic structures, which in turn influence
the postlexical rules. This is what we were doing in suggesting that words of
a non-lexical category may cliticise on to a preceding word of a lexical
category, forming a foot with that word. A postlexical rule which is
blocked by a foot boundary would thus be able to apply within the resulting
foot, and syntactic structure would thus indirectly have enabled a phonological rule to apply. We may refer to this theory of the syntax/phonology
relation as the **Indirect Syntax Hypothesis**. Selkirk (1986) and Nespor and
Vogel (1986) allow both direct syntax and indirect syntax rules; the former,
which make direct reference to syntactic information, apply before the
latter, which operate within constitutents on the prosodic hierarchy.
Nespor (1990), following proposals by Hayes (1990), now argues that the
category of direct syntax rules should be eliminated and replaced by a

category of rules which operate within phrases 'precompiled' in the lexicon; we lack the space to investigate this interesting idea, which is said to leave us with a 'syntax-free' phonology. The question of whether syntactic rules are ever influenced by phonological factors lies beyond the scope of this book, but cf Pullum and Zwicky (1988), who argue that, while superficial syntactic information may be implicated in the application of phonological rules, the syntax is 'phonology-free'.

The possibility of syntactic constraints on phonological rules raises an interesting question about the relationship between the prosodic hierarchy and some of the most basic assumptions in generative linguistics. Generativists assume a distinction between **competence** and **performance**, where the former subsumes purely linguistic knowledge, and the latter concerns the exploitation of that knowledge in the context of particular acts of uttering. Thus, factors such as limitations on short -term memory, conversational strategies and non-linguistic knowledge are relevant at the level of performance, but not at the level of competence. The distinction between **sentence** and **utterance** maps on to the competence/performance distinction: sentences are purely linguistic objects, defined by the grammar, whereas utterances are events which occur in particular contexts. A theory of utterances thus requires a full theory of performance (of which the theory of competence is a subpart). When generative linguists engage in syntactic theory, it is the theory of sentences, not utterances, which they are seeking to develop. And when we speak of syntactic constraints on phonological rules, we must therefore be referring to properties of sentences, not utterances. Put another way, since phonological theory is a part of the theory of grammar, it is not clear that it should include reference to utterance phenomena. And yet the domain 'utterance' constitutes the upper point on the prosodic hierarchy, as proposed by Nespor and Vogel (1986), and this suggests that if we proceed from syllable to foot to word to phrase, we then proceed to utterances as the next level. Yet this idea, extended to syntax, is incompatible with the generative linguist's assumptions: we do not claim that there is a syntactic hierarchy, ranging from, say, words, through phrases, and then to utterances. Indeed, such a claim would make no sense: *John*, *To the shops* and *Knew he'd be late* are all linguistic expressions which can be uttered, and when they are, the resulting event is an utterance. Rather, we take sentences to constitute the uppermost point on the syntactic hierarchy, and we allow that any subpart of a sentence may be uttered (and, indeed, ill-formed expressions may be uttered). To be consistent, we need to take the sentence, not the utterance, to constitute the largest domain in the prosodic hierarchy. We may argue that Nespor and Vogel have defined 'utterance' as a purely phonological object, distinct from 'utterance' as understood in general linguistic theory, but it is not clear that this is what they have explicitly and consistently done, nor whether such a terminological manoeuvre is well-advised.

This conception of the prosodic hierarchy has many consequences, and raises many interesting questions. We may show, for instance, that **sentence stress** and **utterance accent** are distinct phenomena. The rule for sentence stress in English is that stress goes on the last lexical item (thus excluding pronouns, prepositions and so on), as in *Arabella shot the harlot* and *Arabella shot him*. We may now reply to Hogg and McCully's point (referred to in Section 9.6) that Iambic Reversal must be optional since it is possible to utter, for example, *academic writer* with stress on the third syllable of *academic*. What is noticeable is that it is possible, given the right context, to utter *any* expression with stress on *any* of its syllables without creating any impression of oddity in one's interlocutor. Consider, for instance, the following:

They repórted him?
No, they depórted him.

It's académic?
No, it's éndemic.

With respect to the sentence stress generalisation we have just given, consider the following:

Arabella shot hím. (Either (a) it was him, and not someone else, she shot
or (b) the speaker is pointing at some male person.)

Arabélla shot him. (It was not someone else who shot him).

Árabella shot him, not Ísabella.

By distinguishing between sentence stress and utterance accent, we maintain our sentence stress generalisation (and indeed all of our other stress placement generalisations for the language), and pave the way for a theory of accent being placed elsewhere in utterances, which, by definition, occur in context. These examples do not show that the sentence stress generalisation is optional in English, nor do they show that the stress contour of *Arabella*, or indeed any other word in English, is optional. And yet, if we follow Hogg and McCully's reasoning, then all of the rules for stress assignment in words, phrases and clauses which have been proposed must be optional, since one can indeed place the emphasis on any syllable in any word, given an appropriate context. The point is a crucial one, and constitutes our reason for denying that Iambic Reversal is optional on the grounds Hogg and McCully cite. This is not the place to pursue the many interesting issues raised by the proposed sentence stress/utterance accent distinction, however.

We have now looked at a range of different levels of phonological structure above the level of the segment, from the syllable up to the sentence.[20] In the next chapter, we begin by moving in the other direction: we will consider the nature of phonological representations as they relate to the internal structure of segments.

EXERCISES

1. London English

We saw, with the French high-mid vowel /e/, that syllable structure may determine allophonic variation: /e/ is lowered in closed syllables. We also showed that word formation may affect syllabification, which may in turn enable the rule to apply or block its application, giving pairs like *bête* and *bêtise*. Bearing this in mind, examine each of the two pairs of vowels from London English given below (data partly from Harris 1990a):

[ɔə]	and		[ou] (< /ɔ:/)	
1. [bɔə]	'bore'	2.	[boud]	'board'
3. [bɔəd]	'bored'	4.	[pʰout]	'port'
5. [pʰɔə]	'pore'	6.	[doun]	'dawn'
7. [pʰɔəd]	'pored'	8.	[loud]	'lord'
9. [dɹɔə]	'draw'	10.	[loun]	'lawn'
11. [dɹɔən]	'drawn'	12.	[pʰoun]	'pawn'

(i) The vowels are contrastive, according to the phonemic principle. Why?

(ii) State a rule referring to syllable structure, which claims that the vowels are in complementary distribution.

(iii) Give derivations, showing application of the rule, and word formation for the words *bored* and *board*. Assume that the /r/ in *bore* and *pore* is extrasyllabic, and not realised unless followed by an empty onset.

[ɒu]		and	[ʌu] (< / ou /)	
1. [ɹɒul]	'roll'	2.	[kʌulə]	'cola'
3. [stɹɒul]	'stroll'	4.	[lʌud]	'load'
5. [ɹɒulə]	'roller'	6.	[ɹʌulənd]	'Roland'

(i) State a generalisation which takes the two vowels to be in complementary distribution and refers to the position of /l/ in syllable structure.

(ii) The words *roller* and *Roland* both have /l/ in the onset of the second syllable. Why doesn't this fact undermine your generalisation?

2. French
The morpheme meaning 'high' in French occurs once in each of 1–4 below. On the basis of this data, suggest a syllabic representation for the masculine adjective *haut*, and then give derivations for *la hauteur* in 3 and *haut edifice* in 4, showing syllable structure.

	Written Form	Gloss	Phonetic Representation
1.	*un haut mur*	'a high wall'	[ɛ̃omyr]
2.	*une haute colline*	'a high hill'	[ynotkolin]
3.	*la hauteur*	'height'	[laotœr]
4.	*un haut edifice*	'a tall building'	[ɛ̃otedifis]

The masculine article *un* has allomorphs [ɛ̃], as above, and [ɛ̃n], as in *un homme*: [ɛ̃nɔm]. Can you suggest, with reference to your proposed syllable structure for *haut*, why *un* takes the form [ɛ̃] in 1 and 4?

3. Tyneside English
A rule of Glottalisation operates in many accents of English, yielding glottalised voiceless stops like [ʔ͡p], [ʔ͡t] and [ʔ͡k]. It is particularly noticeable in Tyneside English, since it applies intervocalically (as well as in other environments) to all three voiceless stops /p/, /t/ and /k/, as in the following:

[hɐʔ͡pi]	'happy'	[hɪʔ͡pɐ]	'hipper'	[kʰlɪʔ͡pɪʔ]	'clip it'
[pʰɹɪʔ͡ti]	'pretty'	[wɪʔ͡ti]	'witty'		
[mɪʔ͡ki]	'Mickey'	[slɪʔ͡kɐ]	'slicker'	[kʰɪʔ͡kɪʔ]	'kick it'

There are cases, however, where it does not apply intervocalically, exemplified in the following:

[əpʰiɐ]	'appear'	[ətʰɐk]	'attack'	[əkʰjuːz]	'accuse'

Can you suggest which prosodic domain the rule operates within?

Notes

1. Durand (1990: 205) notes that Glide Formation is blocked in onsets by a phonotactic which forbids Obs + Liquid + Glide sequences within

that constituent. Thus, although *loue* [lu] → [lwe] in *louer*, the noun *troue* [tʁu] does not have a glide in the corresponding verb *trouer*: [tʁue], * [tʁwe]. This fact is taken to support the claim that cases like *croire* [kʁwaʁ] have a /kr/ onset and a /w/ in the nucleus.

2. This account of what it is for two English words to rhyme is somewhat simplified. It is *stressed* syllables which must rhyme, and even then further riders must be added; thus, *delight* rhymes with *night*, and *writing* with *fighting* and *fighter* but not *heightening*. These details need not detain us; as can be seen from the following section, there is much phonological justification for the rhyme constituent, over and above the matter of giving an account of what it is for two words to rhyme in English.

3. Lowering is otherwise known as /E/ Adjustment or Closed Syllable Adjustment (CSA), as in Casagrande (1984). There, CSA is taken to apply to all three pairs of mid vowels: to [e] and [ɛ], to [ø] and [œ], and to [o] and [ɔ]. However, the latter two pairs contrast in closed syllables, as in *côte* ([kot]) vs *cote* ([kɔt]), and *jeune* ([ʒøn]) vs *jeûne* ([ʒœn]). In the absence of any clear underlying difference between the members of such pairs, we have restricted our closed syllable lowering rule to just the vowel /e/. Durand (1990) points out that the situation is different in Midi French, where high- and low-mid vowels never contrast on the surface. He proposes an underlying contrast, and several formulations of a lowering rule entitled Mid Vowel Lowering (MVLOW) for Midi French, which he takes to be a lexical rule, following Johnson (1987). Johnson's analysis is based on the LP model, and suggests that lowering applies at Level 2, prior to the Level 3 and 4 processes of prefixation and compounding, respectively. Durand agrees, on the grounds that lowering must be a lexical rule, since it is, he says, sensitive to morphological boundaries, not applying in prefixation and compounds. Alternations involving [e], [ɛ] and [ə], as in *céder*, *je cède*, *vous cédez*, respectively, require Lowering to be formulated so as to include schwa in its input. Durand, following Selkirk (1980) and Booij (1983/4), suggests that MVLOW in Midi French might be formulated in terms of the 'foot' constituent (lowering occurs when segments occur between the vowel and a following foot boundary); we look at the foot constituent later in this chapter. Durand also suggests that Lowering in Midi French might be stated in terms of branching rhymes, if 'ambisyllabicity' is assumed; we consider branching rhymes in the following section, but we do not consider ambisyllabicity. See Durand (1990: 217–19) for a brief account, and Anderson and Jones (1974), Anderson (1986), and Anderson and Ewen (1987) for a defence of the notion. For an argument against ambisyllabicity (it appears to be the only known linguistic phenom-

enon to require improper bracketing), and counter-analyses to deal with the data, see Harris and Kaye (1990).

4. We avoid investigation into the matter of possible schwa deletion rules for French, and thus do not address the matter of a possible distinction between word-final and word-internal schwa deletion. There is much literature on the matter of schwa deletion in French. For an introduction, see Casagrande (1984), for discussion, cf Dell (1980). See also Charette (1991) for a Government Phonology account.

5. The terms 'Truncation', 'Liaison' and 'Enchaînement' are used differently by different authors, and therefore require some comment. The term 'Truncation' dates back at least to Schane (1968: 1–7); in this work, and in Schane (1974a), the term covers both elision of vowels and deletion of word-final consonants. We have taken the view here that these are distinct processes. Casagrande (1984: 1–7) distinguishes resyllabification of fixed consonants (which he refers to as 'enchaînement') from resyllabification of 'latent' consonants, for which he reserves the term 'liaison'. Encrevé (1988: 21–30) makes the point that resyllabification is a phenomenon of which 'liaison' of a latent consonant is simply a special case. That is the view we adopt here. It is crucial for Encrevé that resyllabification in general, for which he uses the term 'enchaînement', be distinguished from the matter of whether a consonant is latent or not, and whether, if latent, it is realised phonetically (for him, liaison is defined as phonetic realisation of a latent consonant). Encrevé investigates, among other things, the phenomenon of the phonetic realisation of a latent consonant without resyllabification ('liaison sans enchaînement'). This phenomenon appears to contradict our claim that latent consonants may not appear in non-onset position.

To alleviate the terminological problem, where a rule entitled 'Liaison' is referred to, we use upper case 'L' and where the liaison phenomenon in general is referred to we use lower case:'liaison'.

6. Truncation deletes stem-final latent consonants in verbs and nouns, but not adjectives: *marchand italien* = [maʁɑ̃italjɛ̃], *marchander* = [maʁʃɑ̃de], *marchands italiens* = [maʁʃɑ̃zitaljɛ̃].

7. Clements and Keyser (1983) deny that phonological rules ever refer to onsets or rhymes, and accordingly postulate just two units, the syllable and the nucleus, which occupy different tiers (see Chapter 10 for discussion of multiple tiers). There is much literature supporting at least an onset–rhyme split within the syllable, among which are Anderson (1986) and Fudge (1987). For a theory of syllable structure with an onset–rhyme split, but without the coda constituent, cf Harris and Kaye (1990), and Section 11.5.

8. The phenomenon of liaison in French was cited, by Milner (1967), as providing crucial support for the feature [syll], rather than the earlier [vocalic], which had been used by Schane (1968) in the early generative formulations of the rule of Truncation. The transition was essentially to do with the characterisation of glides, and thus carried over into the abstractness issue, since /h/, as in 'h-aspiré' forms, was taken to be a glide in SPE. This latter claim about [h] (and [ʔ]) was convincingly disputed by Lass (1976a).

9. For more on syllable-based analyses of the data, see Anderson (1982), which has schwa insertion into empty nuclei, and Stemberger (1985), who presents a 'more concrete' synthesis of Anderson (1982) and Clements and Keyser (1983). Klausenberger (1986) raises some objections to Stemberger's account. Booij (1983/4) presents a CV tier analysis couched in LP terms, and examines the interaction of liaison with /e/ Lowering. Charette (1991) presents a Government Phonology (see Section 11.5) account of the schwa-zero alternations which, like Anderson (1982), appeals to the idea of empty nuclei, but does not require insertion or deletion. Charette's treatment of 'h-aspiré' forms is similar to that given by Clements and Keyser (1983), but by appealing to government relations, Charette is able to show why word-final schwa does not delete before 'h-aspire'. She does not give an analysis of /e/ Lowering, or of Nasalisation. For her, zero/[ɛ] alternations (as in *appeler/appelle*) are not connected with the [e]/[ɛ] alternations (as in *espérer/espère*); rather, the [ɛ] in cases like *appelle* is the realisation of any empty nucleus when it is stressed. We have not addressed the matter of whether this tier of timing slots should be *just that*, without Cs and Vs, which encode the notions consonantality and syllabicity; our discussion of syllable structure rather suggests that these two properties are defined by that structure, and are not therefore inherent properties of timing slots. See Chapter 11 for the idea that the tier of timing slots is a *skeleton*, each point of which constitutes a significant intersection of autosegmental planes (where the intersection constitutes a segment, as traditionally understood).

10. It is often suggested that a heavy syllable should be defined as a syllable with a branching rhyme. This is clearly inadequate in languages where VC rhymes count as light. Generally speaking, open syllables with a single V slot almost always count as light, and VV rhymes as heavy, with CV rhymes falling in between these two categories. This, along with evidence from languages which seem to require reference to a three-way weight distinction, has caused some phonologists to set up a theory of phonological weight with three categories. See Hyman (1985) for a theory which states that properties of vowels, rather than the geometry of the rhyme, determine syllable weight.

11. For a clearly laid-out exposition of the development of metrical theory as it relates to English word stress and rhythm, see Hogg and McCully (1987). Since it is a course book. it is best read that way, i.e. from the beginning through to (preferably) the end, or to the end of Chapter 4 (at a pinch, Chapter 3). Chapter 1 of that work gives a clear summary of the SPE system, and Chapters 3 and 4 will serve to introduce the main ideas of metrical phonology, and their development, in more detail than we have been able to provide here. Hogg and McCully are (admirably) not afraid to venture their own views on the various issues; nor should the reader feel obliged to accept all of these views.

12. A theory, such as Giegerich's (1985), which insists on binary branching and, in English, left-headed feet, must deal with words, like *delinquent*, with an odd number of syllables and main stress not on the first syllable. These are represented with two branching, and (of course) left-headed, feet, as in:

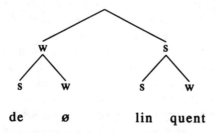

de   ø   lin   quent

The obvious objection to be raised is that the theory imposes more structure than is justifiable; see Giegerich (1985) for a defence.

13. See Section 9.7 on sentence stress vs utterance accent.

14. We have neglected to consider the phenomenon of tone in this book; tone concerns pitch, i.e. rate of vocal cord vibration, which is also implicated in the phenomenon of intonation. While all languages exploit the possibility of variation in pitch, the distinction between intonation and tone is essentially to do with the domain in which the pitch variation occurs; roughly speaking, when pitch variation functions contrastively within morphemes, it may be described as tone, whereas pitch variation across sentences/utterances is described as intonation. Thus, English is not a tone language, but pitch variation nonetheless has a linguistic function at the sentence/utterance level. (We do not pursue the interesting matter of whether intonation functions at both sentence and utterance level, or only one of those.) Tai, on the other hand, is a tone language: in listing Tai morphemes in Chapter 1, we were careful to list morphemes with the same tone (so that the morphemes contrasted only at the segmental level); but tonal contrasts such as nà: (with falling tone, meaning 'face') and ná: (with

rising tone, meaning 'thick') abound. Tone languages also evince intonational contours and the interaction between the two sorts of pitch variation can be complex. See Fromkin (1978) for an introduction to studies in tone.

Tonal contrasts and intonational contours signal very different sorts of 'information', i.e. convey very distinct kinds of meaning. It is a fascinating, and significant, fact that tone and intonation are controlled by different parts of the brain (as revealed by studies of different sorts of aphasia), despite the fact that, at the level of the physiology of the speech organs, they constitute exactly the same thing: variation in the rate of vibration of the vocal cords. On the face of it at least, this seems to pose a problem for those, like Sampson (1989: 206), who claim that 'biological constraints (on language: PC) are limited to matters which are 'trivial' because they *follow from* (emphasis mine: PC) properties of our speech and sense organs which are known to be genetically fixed'.

15. The principle was first proposed by Goldsmith (1979), whose work, based initially on tonal phenomena, laid the foundations of autosegmental phonology (see Chapter 10). It was later investigated, and elaborated on, by, among others, McCarthy (1986). The example given here provides, perforce, only the most rudimentary idea of what the consequences of the principle might be; nonetheless, it is not misleading.

16. Thus stated, the rule is over-general. We need at least to state that the leftmost 'w' node in the input must not be unstressed, since reversal does not apply in cases like *deranged writer*, and even then we face problems with the representations for *deranged* as opposed to *unknown*, since the grid representations given do not distinguish weak syllables with unstressed schwa from those like the first syllable in *unknown*. A further condition concerns the question of possible syntactic constraints on Iambic Reversal. Giegerich (1985: 211), for example, proposes that the right-hand word must not be the head of a syntactic phrase; this would block reversal in cases like *The grapes ripened*. We cannot investigate this interesting question here, but we will look briefly at the idea of syntactic constraints on phonological rules in Section 9.7.

17. Preference for symmetry is reflected in other areas of linguistic organisation. It can be seen at work in the sorts of preferred strategies for syntactic parsing described by Kimball (1973) and further investigated by, among others, Frazier and Fodor (1978). In this case, the preference almost certainly lies outside of the grammar *per se*, and reflects a perceptual (perhaps cognitive) principle. The same may be true of the preference for symmetry in the way we draw inferences; the principle

of conditional perfection, for instance, states that we prefer the symmetrical relation of equivalence to the asymmetrical relation of implication: see Allwood, Anderson and Dahl (1977) for definitions of these terms.

18. For a lucid discussion of metrical phonology from a perspective wider than that of the English specialist, and a critical synthesis of all of the ideas we discuss in Chapters 8–11 (and more), see Goldsmith (1990). The book offers intelligent, non-partisan comment from a scholar with an excellent command of the literature and a finely tuned sense of judgement. It requires careful reading, but is very clear, and will reward any time you spend on it. (It is, incidentally, a very good idea not to skip Goldsmith's footnotes: they contain many useful and perceptive comments.) For a treatment of the material at a level intermediate between the very introductory presentation given here and Goldsmith's discussion, see Chapters 5–8 of Durand (1990), which is well informed and accessible, with the ideas clearly represented, nicely exemplified and well discussed.

19. The matter is more complex than this. Carr (1991) suggests that the 't → r' rule applies only within feet formed postlexically, i.e. feet of the sort yielded by the kind of cliticisation we discussed with reference to the work of Giegerich (1985). Thus, the rule does not apply word-internally, as in *pretty* and *fitter* (except in one or two specific cases).

20. Selkirk (1984) presents a theory which allows for imposition of intonational phrases on syntactic surface structure, followed by grid construction. After the operation of certain rhythmic principles, no reference to 'feet', 'phonological phrases' or 'utterances' is required. We lack space to present the many issues raised by this work.

10 Representations Reconsidered (ii): Autosegmental Phonology

In the discussion of the standard model given in the interlude, we saw (see p. 155) that, where phonological representations are linear sequences of segments, and phonological properties are transmitted from one segment to another, we are unable to capture certain sorts of generalisation, such as the Akan vowel harmony generalisation: that roots are marked as either [+ATR] or [−ATR] and all affixes, whether prefixes or suffixes, agree with (harmonise with) the root in their value for this feature. We will now address this issue of the limitations inherent in a phonological model which allows only for operations on linear sequences of segments, where those segments are represented as unordered bundles of features.

10.1 Nasality, Segmental and Suprasegmental

We will approach this issue by considering a similar case, concerning the spread of nasality, where a linear analysis does not seem to capture the generalisation in question.

In the standard model, nasality was represented invariably as a property of particular segments, as in English, in the word *man*:

(1)

	/m	æ	n/
cons	+	−	+
obs	−	−	−
cont	−	+	−
nas	+	−	+

Similarly, for French, in *bon*, as opposed to *beau*:

(2)

	/b	ɔ	n/		/b	o/
obs	+	−	−	obs	+	−
cont	−	+	−	cont	−	+
nas	−	−	+	nas	−	−

In many accents of French, and in accents of English like New York City, which regularly have nasalisation of vowels preceding nasal stops, we were able to represent nasalisation by means of a rule which operated on these linear sequences of segments (although we now take this to be a syllable-based rule), thus:

(3)

$$[+\text{syll}] \rightarrow [+\text{nas}] \ / \ \underline{\hspace{1cm}} [+\text{nas}] \left\{ \begin{array}{c} \# \\ C \end{array} \right\}$$

In some languages, nasalisation spreads beyond an immediately adjacent vowel, as you can see in the following data from Malay (data from Durand 1987, Onn 1980):[1]

1. /mewah/   → [mẽw̃ãh]   'to be luxurious'
2. /majan/   → [mãj̃ãn]   'stalk'
3. /mən + ajak/   → [mə̃nãj̃ã̃ʔ]   'to sift'
4. /pəŋ + awas + an/ → [pəŋãw̃ãsan]   'supervision'

In cases like these, we could allow our linear rule to apply iteratively, such that nasality spreads from one segment to another, being blocked by obstruents. But consider the following data from Terena, which also exhibit nasal spreading (data from Bendor–Samuel 1960):

1. (a) [emoʔu]   'his word'   (b) [ẽmõʔũ]   'my word'
2. (a) [ajo]   'his brother' (b) [ãj̃õ]   'my brother'
3. (a) [owoku]   'his house'   (b) [õw̃õŋgu]   'my house'
4. (a) [piho]   'he went'   (b) [mbiho]   'I went'
5. (a) [ahjaʔaʃo]   'he desires'   (b) [ãnʒaʔaʃo]   'I desire'

It is clear that the forms in the right-hand column differ from those in the left-hand column in that they express 'first person singular'. The question is: what phonological process signals 'first person singular'? Clearly, it involves nasality. We could express this informally as: nasalise the segments in an (a) form, from left to right, up to the first obstruent, which itself will become nasalised, such that p → mb, t → nd, k → ŋg, s and h → nz, and sj and hj → nʒ. But how can our linear rules and representations express this generalisation? In the case of 1(a) and (b), we might suggest that the representation for [emoʔu], which contains a [+nas] segment, would allow us to spread this value for [nas] to adjacent segments; we would need a rule which looked like this:

(4)

$$[+\text{syll}] \rightarrow [+\text{nas}] \ / \ \left\{ \begin{matrix} [+\text{nas}]\text{———} \\ \text{———}[+\text{nas}] \end{matrix} \right\}$$

The rule would apply iteratively, and would be bounded by obstruents, which are themselves nasalised (strictly speaking, they are pre-nasalised, as indicated in the data). However, even this rule, because it so clearly does not express the generalisation we are after, will fail to apply in all of the other cases in 2–5. This is, of course, because the (a) forms there have no [+nas] segment to spread. What seems to be happening here is that the phonological form of the 'first person singular' morpheme is simply [+nas], and that this is 'overlaid', from left to right, on the (a) morphemes to yield the (b) morphemes. Such a process simply cannot be expressed with the sorts of rule and representation found in the standard model. Consequently, we need a new kind of rule and representation to do so. Let us represent the [+nas] on a separate **tier** from the segmental tier, like this:

(5)

[+ nas]

/ajo/

We can then say that this phonological feature is *superimposed* on the segments in the segmental tier. It is this kind of approach to spreading phenomena which constitutes the essence of the *prosodic phonology* which was practised in the fifties by the London School of Linguistics, and of a development in generative linguistics called **autosegmental phonology**. In this latter model, the features on the 'upper' tier are referred to as **autosegments**, and the superimposition of them onto the lower (segmental) tier is called **association**. We depict the representation after association with broken lines attached to the segmental slots, thus:

(6)

[+ nas]

/a j o/

This process of association is governed by an association convention which states that autosegments are associated with slots on the segmental tier. Additionally, the representations we end up with after association has taken place are subject to a set of **well-formedness conditions (WFCs)**, first given in Goldsmith (1979), as follows:

1. Lines of association must not cross.
2. All appropriate segmental slots must be linked with an autosegment.
3. No autosegment may be left unassociated with an available and appropriate slot.

Note too that, in Terena, it looks as though we must represent nasality both segmentally and suprasegmentally: in /emoʔu/, the bilabial nasal has [+nas] as part of its internal make-up:

(7)

	/e	m	o	?	u/
obs	−	−	−	+	−
cont	+	−	+	−	+
cor	−	−	−	−	−
ant	−	+	−	−	−
nas	−	+	−	−	−
round	−	−	+	−	+
back	−	−	+	−	+
high	−	−	−	−	−
low	−	−	−	−	−
ATR	+		+		+

We can conclude that nasality may function both segmentally and suprasegmentally, and that a model incorporating autosegmental representations could represent both autosegmental spreading, segment-internal nasality and spreading in a strictly local manner, from a nasal segment to an adjacent vowel. This is to allow for the possibility of a phonological property such as nasality being present simultaneously on the segmental and the autosegmental tier, and requires us to allow that a [+nas] autosegment, when overlaid on a morpheme like /emoʔu/, associates vacuously (redundantly) with the segment /m/.[2]

That this autosegmental approach allows us greater generalising power is clear if we consider in more detail another language which is like Terena with respect to the spreading of nasality, the Niger-Kordofanian language Gokana (spoken in Nigeria). Hyman (1982) has shown that we can state the following generalisations about the presence of nasality in the phonological shape of morphemes in Gokana:

(a) If C_1 (the first consonant in the morpheme) is [+nas], then all preceding and following vowels are [+nas]:

[nũ]	'thing'	vs	*[nu]		
[nãã]	'gun'	vs	*[nãa],	*[naa],	
[nɔ̃m]	'animal'	vs	*[nɔm],	*[nɔ̃b],	*[nɔb]
[mɛ̃nɛ̃]	'chief'	vs	*[mɛnɛ],	*[mɛ̃nɛ],	*[mɛlɛ]
[nããnã]	'snake'	vs	*[naana],	*[nããna],	*[nããla], etc.

(b) If C_2 is [+nas], then all preceding and following vowels are [+nas]:

[fĩnĩ]	'monkey'	vs	*[fĩnĩ],	*[fĩni]
[kũũnĩ]	'cooking stove'	vs	*[kuũnĩ],	*[kuunĩ], *[kũũni]

(c) Where a $\tilde{V}$ occurs, all following segments are [+nas]:

[dɛ̃m]	'tongue'	vs	*[dɛ̃b]

(d) If C_1 is [v], [l] or [z], all following segments are [−nas]:

[va]	'wife'	*[vã]	
[li]	'root'	*[lĩ]	
[zɔ]	'pain'	*[zɔ̃]	
[zib]	'thief'	*[zĩm]	*[zim]

Hyman further shows that there are suffix alternations involving nasality, such that, for instance, [ɔ] alternates with [ɔ̃] and [a] alternates with [ã]:

(8)

[ækʲɔ]	'he spoiled it'	vs	[æɡʲɔ̃]	'he hid it'
[ækʲɔa]	'it spoiled'	vs	[æɡʲɔ̃ã]	'he hid himself'

It is clear from these data that suffixes agree in nasality with their stems. It also appears that, while [m] in C_2 position is derived from /b/, in C_1, [b] contrasts with [m]:

(9)

[bã]	'pot'	vs	[mã]	'breast'

Thus, we seem justified in setting up a /b/ vs /m/ distinction.

Hyman shows that if we consider a standard model analysis of Nasal Spreading, we could account for the data by means of two rules:

(10a)

[+voice] → [+nas] / [+nas]___

(10b)

$$\begin{bmatrix} +\text{voice} \\ +\text{cont} \end{bmatrix} \rightarrow [+\text{nas}] \ / \ \#\_\_\_ \begin{bmatrix} -\text{cons} \\ +\text{nas} \end{bmatrix}$$

This analysis assumes that nasality spreads rightwards from underlying nasalised vowels in V_1 position via rule (10a) and leftwards via rule (10b), thus yielding all of the generalisations stated in (a)–(d) above. Rule (10b) nasalises /l/, /v/ and /z/ in C_1 position when they are followed by a nasalised vowel (giving [n], [ɱ] and [ɲ], respectively). However, as in our linear analysis of Akan vowel harony, we seem to be missing a single generalisation here: that root morphemes are either [+nas] or not, and that nasality spreads through the root and from the root on to the affixes.

We would express this in an autosegmental analysis by taking [+nas] (which we will now write as [+N]) to be a property of *morphemes*, rather than particular segments, in Gokana. If we assume that each morpheme has at most one [+N] autosegment, we will get the following sorts of representation:

(11a)

[+N]   [+N]
          /\
/lu/ →   /lu/   (=[nũ]) 'thing'

(11b)

/li/ →   [li] 'root'

(11c)

[+N]   [+N]
          ¦
/ba/ → [ba]   (= [bã]) 'pot'

(11d)

/ba/ →   [ba] 'arm'

Unlike the morphemes in (11a) and (11c), the morphemes in (11b) and (11d) simply lack a nasal autosegment in underlying representation. The autosegments are then associated with segments, according to the WFCs. The spread of nasality is bounded by # #or #C. Nasal autosegments are not associated with voiceless segments in any position or with voiced stops in C_1 position.

Hyman further suggests that we also take [m] in C_1 position to be autosegmentally derived. To do this, he introduces the idea of a **lexically bound autosegment** (shown with a solid line of association). Lexically bound autosegments are not attached to their segments by means of the association convention, but are represented in the lexicon as permanently bound (rather than being initially unassociated, as with the **free autosegments** shown above), thus:

(12)

[+N]
|
/b/

Hyman treats the syllabic nasals of Gokana this way too, thus:

(13a)

```
[+N]   [+N]              [+N]   [+N]
 |                        |    ⁄⁄↗
 |                        |   ⁄⁄⁄ |
/ b  l  ɔ  b /  ⟶   / b  l  ɔ  b /   (= [nnɔ̃m])
     'bird'                              |
```

(13b)

```
[+N]                     [+N]
 |                        |
/ b  g  a /  ⟶     / b  g  a /   (= [ŋga])
   'needle'                           |
```

This treatment might be objected to on the grounds that it undermines Hyman's claim that a morpheme may have at most one [+N] autosegment. It also raises the problem of preventing the lexically bound autosegment from associating with the /g/ and the /a/ in (13b). Hyman responds to this latter problem by reformulating the mapping scheme such that it skips a syllabic nasal (we will consider an alternative solution later, in which we stipulate that lexically bound autosegments may not associate).

We might object to this notion of lexically bound nasal autosegments in this case: we could suggest that, as in Terena, nasality in Gokana may function segmentally *and* autosegmentally. Both syllabic nasals and the [m] in C_1 position would then be taken to be represented just as in English /m/. But the idea of lexically bound autosegments seems clearly justified in other cases, specifically in the autosegmental treatment of vowel harmony, which we now turn to.

10.2 Vowel Harmony

Let us begin by summarising the linear treatment of vowel harmony; it possesses the following properties:

1. Harmonic features are contained within root segments.
2. The underlying form of affixes may be underspecified for harmonic features.
3. To deal with neutral vowels, rules are formulated such that these vowels do not trigger harmony (i.e. the triggering environment in the structural description is stated such that it excludes them).
4. Rule application is such that rules may fill in or change values for harmonic features by operating linearly from left to right or right to left.
5. Segments such as consonants and neutral vowels, which are unaffected, must be included in the structural description of the rule, in parentheses.

Let us now look at the autosegmental approach. In Gokana, we saw that, with this approach, a simple generalisation could be expressed concerning nasality: morphemes either do or do not possess a free [+N] autosegment in their underlying representation. The same strategy can profitably be adopted for cases of vowel harmony. We wanted to say that, in Akan, roots were either [+ATR] (henceforth, [+A]) or not. We will therefore say that [+A] autosegments are either present or absent in the underlying representations of Akan roots:

(14)

>   [+A]
>
> / f I t I/ 'to puncture'   vs   / č I r E / 'to show'

Where there are no affixes, association gives:

(15)

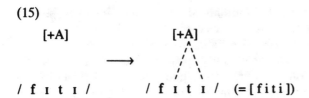

/ f ɪ t ɪ /   / f ɪ t ɪ /   (= [f i t i])

In the case of root morphemes like / č I r E /, we are assuming that, rather than marking these as containing a [−A] autosegment (as in (16a) below), we represent them as simply lacking a [+A] autosegment, as in (16b):

[−A]

(16a)   (16b)

/ č I r E /   / č I r E /

Representation (16b) entails an assumption about the default value for [ATR] in representations like /I/: we are assuming that, with no specification for [ATR], a segment like /I/ is a high front, unrounded vowel which lacks ATR and is to be interpreted phonetically as [ɪ]. Similarly, /O/ and /E/ are interpreted, respectively, as [ɔ] and [ɛ] when not associated with a [+A] autosegment.

We might ask, at this juncture, what the difference is between an underlying representation for a non-ATR morpheme like / č I r E / with a [−A] autosegment, and one which simply lacks a [+A] autosegment. That is, what is the difference between [−X] and 'lacking the feature [X]'? This is an interesting question, which requires us to spell out exactly what the '−' in [−X] means. To answer this, we need briefly to return to the idea of *contrast* which we appealed to in our phonemic analyses. Take a phonemic analysis which distinguishes, say, between the following phonemes in a language: /p/, /b/, /t/, /d/, /k/, /g/. In such cases, we said that both voicing and place of articulation are *contrastive*. One way of expressing this was to say that /p/ and /b/ are *in opposition* to one another: /p/ vs /b/ constitutes an **opposition**. So too does /p/ vs /t/ vs /k/. It was observed by phonologists working within what was known as the **Prague School of Linguistics**, particularly in the work of N. S. Trubetzkoy (as in Trubetzkoy 1969, Chapter III), that oppositions like /p/ vs /b/ seem distinct from oppositions like /p/ vs /t/ vs /k/. In the former case, we may view the relationship between the members as involving simple presence vs absence of a phonological property (in this case, voicing): /b/ is /p/ with voicing overlaid on it. This kind of contrast was referred to as a **privative** opposition. The place of articulation cases were taken to be distinct from these: they seem to involve more than just the overlaying of one phonological property on top of a given articulation;

such cases were referred to as **multilateral** oppositions, involving several phonological properties (such as, in this case, labial, coronal, velar).

The '+' and '−' values used in the distinctive feature approach seem well equipped to express these latter sorts of opposition. But when we consider our case of ATR harmony, or our nasal vs non-nasal contrasts in Gokana and Terena, we have appealed to the idea of 'overlaying' a phonological property on a given articulation: [õ] is [o] with overlaid nasality, and [i] is [ɪ] with overlaid ATR. Our autosegmental representations are thus expressing a view of nasality and ATR as entering into privative oppositions in these cases. Given that this is the case, if we wish to bring out the conceptual content of the privative opposition idea, namely presence vs absence of a phonological property, we ought to represent absence of nasality or ATR by simply omitting an ATR or nasal autosegment in the representation, as in (16b) on p. 249.

Having done so, we must now ask whether there is any force in the value '+' in our autosegmental representations: if we wish to claim that oppositions involving nasality in Gokana and ATR in Akan are truly privative, then, to be consistent, we ought to represent 'nasal' or 'ATR' simply as [N] or [A], without a '+' value. We will, henceforth, adopt this notation. It is important to note that this is not a 'merely notational' matter: the difference in notation expresses a difference in how we conceive of the nature of the phonological contrast. The [±X] notation expresses the notion 'multilateral opposition', whereas the [X] notation expresses the 'privative opposition' notion.[3]

To return to our Akan case, where harmonically alternating affixes occur, we may say that these lack harmonic properties in underlying representations, and are assigned these by association where an autosegment is present (as in (17a) below), or otherwise are non-ATR by default (as in (17b)):

(17a)

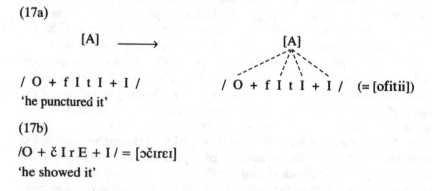

/ O + f I t I + I /
'he punctured it'

/ O + f I t I + I /   (= [ofitii])

(17b)

/O + č I r E + I / = [ɔčɪrɛɪ]
'he showed it'

Thus far, with the autosegmental treatment, we are able to capture the fact that ATR in this language is, like (most cases of) nasality in Gokana, a property of morphemes, and will spread from the autosegment specified for a morpheme to any affixes which are added to it. A further complication arises, however, in the shape of what are known as **opaque vowels**. These are a type of neutral vowel which may block the spread of the harmonising property. In Akan, [ɑ] is opaque to ATR harmony; that is, it blocks the spread of ATR through the word. For example, the root morpheme [bisɑ] ('to ask') is an ATR root which also has an opaque vowel underlyingly. We refer to such roots as **disharmonic roots**. Where a prefix is added, the [A] of the root is associated with it, but where a suffix is added, the opaque vowel blocks the association of [A]. Thus, where [bisɑ] has a prefix added, it harmonises, but where a suffix is added, it does not, as in the form [obisɑ] ('he asked for it'). The autosegmental treatment of opaque vowels we will adopt here involves lexically assigning a [~A] autosegment to the opaque vowel, in a manner reminiscent of Hyman's lexically bound nasal autosegments:

(18)

$$
\begin{array}{ccc}
\text{[A] [~A]} & \longrightarrow & \text{[A] [~A]} \\
\end{array}
$$

/ O + b I s A + I /   / O + b I s A + I /   (= [obisaɪ])

'he asked for it'

As before, we have represented vowels minus harmonising autosegments with upper case symbols, such that /O/ and /I/, where they remain unassociated with an [A] autosegment, lack ATR, and have the phonetic values [ɔ] and [ɪ].

There are also disharmonic roots in which the order of the free autosegment and the lexically bound one is reversed:

(19)

$$
\begin{array}{ccc}
\text{[~A] [A]} & \longrightarrow & \text{[~A] [A]} \\
\end{array}
$$

/ O + k A r I + I /   / O + k A r I + I /   (= [ɔkɑrii])

'he weighed it'

Spreading of [A] in Akan is **bidirectional**: it spreads both from right to left (from root to prefix) and from left to right (from root to suffix), unless it is blocked. As we will see, some spreading processes are directional. We will therefore assume that the grammar of a given language contains stipulations as to which autosegments spread, which segment types they are associated with, whether spreading is bidirectional or directional, and if directional, whether it is left to right or right to left. The WFCs will ensure in each of the Akan cases just given that the free autosegment, which spreads bidirectionally, does not end up being associated beyond the lexically bound one.

Note that in Gokana all voiced segments were susceptible to nasalisation, whereas in Akan only *vowels* may be associated with harmonic autosegments. This fact will be given in the stipulation as to which categories of segments may undergo association. In some cases of vowel harmony, we must specify a particular subset of the vowels, as in the case of Turkish roundedness harmony, to which we now turn. The Turkish vowel system is given in (20) and some alternations are given in (21):

(20) *Turkish vowel system*

	Front		Back	
High	y	i	u	ɨ
Low	ø	e	o	ɑ

(21) *Turkish possessives and plurals*

	Gloss	Nom.	Poss. (3PS)	Plural
1.	'footprint'	[is]	[izi]	[izler]
2.	'reason'	[sebep]	[sebebi]	[sebebler]
3.	'rose'	[gyl]	[gyly]	[gyller]
4.	'desert'	[čøl]	[čøly]	[čøller]
5.	'anchor'	[demir]	[demiri]	[demirler]
6.	'rump'	[kɨč]	[kɨči]	[kɨčlɑr]
7.	'head'	[baʃ]	[baʃɨ]	[baʃlɑr]
8.	'worm'	[kurt]	[kurdu]	[kurdlɑr]
9.	'arm'	[kol]	[kolu]	[kollɑr]
10.	'loaf'	[somun]	[somunu]	[somunlɑr]

In Turkish, a vowel after the initial syllable in a word is round if it is a high vowel and is preceded by a round vowel. Vowels in first syllables are freely round or non-round. As you can see, the possessive suffix is a high vowel and therefore undergoes roundedness harmony, whereas the plural suffix has a non-high vowel and does not. We can express the roundedness harmony rule in a linear analysis as follows:

(22) *Turkish Roundedness Harmony Rule*

$$\begin{bmatrix} +\text{syll} \\ +\text{high} \end{bmatrix} \rightarrow [+\text{round}] \ / \ \begin{bmatrix} +\text{syll} \\ +\text{round} \end{bmatrix} C_0 \ (+) \ C_0 \underline{\quad}$$

The rule will operate iteratively, as in [somunu]. In an autosegmental treatment, we could deny that roundedness is spread iteratively from one vowel to another, and allow for free [round] (henceforth [R]) auto-segments, just as we did with our [ATR] harmony case. These would take care of standard cases of the sort given above, and would be restricted, in non-initial syllables, to associating, left to right, only with high vowels, thus:

(23)

[R] $\longrightarrow$ [R]

/ s A m I n + I + m I /   / s A m I n + I + m I /   (= [somunumu])
'loaf'   'his'   'is it?'
'is it his loaf?'

As in our Akan case, we are assuming default values for /I/ and /A/. /I/ is high, non-front and non-rounded by default: [ɨ], whereas /A/ is non-high, non-front, non-rounded [a]. The phonological form of the possessive suffix is therefore simply /I/, with allomorphs [i], [y], [u] and [ɨ], depending on whether roundedness and/or frontness harmony have applied. The plural morpheme has the representation /lAr/, with allomorphs [ler] and [lar], depending on whether frontness harmony has taken place.

Morphemes like this, with the low vowel /A/, are opaque to rounded-ness harmony in Turkish. That is, not only do they have a non-high vowel, and therefore do not undergo roundedness harmony, but they block the spread of roundedness on to any following high vowels. Thus, when we add the suffix /InIz/ to the plural form /somunlAr/, the resulting form is [somunlarɨnɨz], without rounding on the last two vowels. We may treat these as we treated opaque /a/ in Akan, with a lexically bound [~R] autosegment:

(24)

[R] [~R]   [R] [~R]
 | | $\longrightarrow$ /\ | ,
/sAmIn + IAr + InIz /   /sAmIn + IAr + InIz /   (= [somunlarɨnɨz])
'your (plural) loaves'

This contrasts with:

(25)

[R]   [R]

/sAmIn + InIz /   ⟶   /sAmIn + InIz /   (= [somununuz])
'your (singular) loaf'

In the latter case, where /lAr/ is not present to block the association of [R], the /InIz/ suffix has rounded vowels.

Anderson (1980), in his perceptive discussion of vowel harmony in Turkish, points out that there are roots which have a low vowel followed by a high rounded vowel, such as /hɑvruz/ ('pot'), /hɑmul/ ('patient') and /mɑjmum/ ('monkey').[4] These take rounded affixes. We may represent them with a free [R] autosegment which may spread left to right, and a bound [~R] on the low vowel, as follows:

(26)

[~R][R]   [~R][R]

/hAvrIz + InIz /   ⟶   /hAvrIz + InIz /   (= [hɑvruzunuz])
'your pot'

We have now seen how ATR and roundednness harmony would be treated by the autosegmental theory, but what of back/front harmony, which also occurs in Turkish? In Hungarian, we saw that, with the standard model, there were three possible analyses: affix vowels are underlyingly unspecified for the feature [back], and the rule fills in the values, or they are underlyingly [−back] and are fronted by the VH rule, or, finally, they are underlyingly front and the VH rule changes their values for [back] from '−' to '+'.

If front/back harmony in Turkish is frontness harmony (we will assume that it is), our distinctive feature approach would suggest a [−back] autosegment. But we could extend our privative approach to these cases, and suggest that frontness is overlaid on a back vowel articulation to create a fronted sound. Thus, we could derive all four surface high vowels from an underlying representation /I/, which is back by default, as well as unrounded by default. We have said that /I/, if it does not undergo either roundedness harmony or frontness harmony, is to be interpreted as the non-front, non-round high vowel [ɨ]. With roundedness harmony alone, this would then be [u], with frontness harmony alone, [i], and with both frontness and roundedness, [y]. Similarly, /A/, where it undergoes frontness harmony, will emerge as the non-high, front, unrounded vowel [e], and where it does not, will surface as [ɑ]. In initial syllables, /A/ may be round, and may therefore be realised as the non-high, non-front, rounded vowel [o], or, under frontness harmony, the front equivalent [ø].

Let us adopt an [F] autosegment which will characterise standard cases of frontness harmony as follows (locating the [F] on a separate tier from [R]):[5]

(27)

/ s A b A b /   / s A b A b /   (= [sebep])

    [F]   ⟶   [F]

    'reason'

(28)

/ d A m I r /   / d A m I r /   (= [demir])

    [F]   ⟶   [F]

    'anchor'

What about cases where both frontness *and* roundedness harmony occur? We will continue to represent these with the [R] and the [F] on different tiers, as follows:

(29)

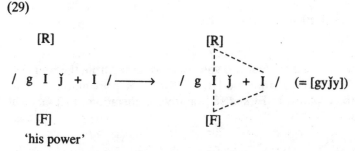

    'his power'

The theory assumes that the two autosegmental tiers function independently of each other,[6] and that only two sorts of autosegment are required: free [X] and lexically bound [~X]. Let us see how it fares with an opaque morpheme in Turkish. The progressive affix /IjAr/ is opaque in that it blocks the spread of frontness. It has the allomorphs [ijor], [yjor], [ɨjor] and [ujor]. That is, the first vowel of the suffix undergoes both roundedness and frontness harmony, but the second vowel is invariable. We will treat it as an opaque vowel, and represent it with a lexically bound [~F] autosegment. With a front root like [gel] ('come'), the phonetic form of /gAl + IjAr + Im/ ('I am coming') is [gelijorum], where the final affix is not front, but *is* rounded. It looks as though we are obliged to amend our theory and account for roundedness harmony in the final affix by means of an [R] autosegment bound to the second vowel of /Ijor/, thus:

(30)

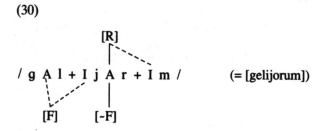

$(= \text{[gelijorum]})$

The [R] does not associate with any of the vowels preceding the /A/ to which it is linked, since roundedness harmony is directional in this language, spreading left to right. Representations, for roots with [R] but not [F], will look, after association, like this:[7]

(31)

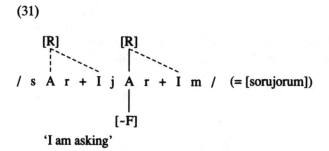

$(= \text{[sorujorum]})$

'I am asking'

In this case, we see that the first two vowels are rounded from the root [R], whereas /Im/ is rounded from the [R] on /IjAr/. Representations, after association, for roots with [F] and [R], and with affixation of /IjAr/, will look like this:

(32)

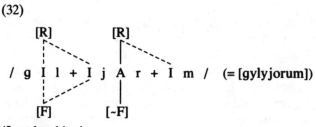

$(= \text{[gylyjorum]})$

'I am laughing'

Finally, representations for roots with neither [R] nor [F], and /IjAr/ affixed, will look, after association, like this:

(33)

$$
\begin{array}{c}
[R] \\
\text{/ I s I n + I j A r + I m /} \quad (= [\text{isinijorum}]) \\
[\sim F]
\end{array}
$$

'I am warming'

Although we have been representing autosegmental tiers as being linked to segments, we really ought to conceive of them as being linked to timing slots on the CV tier, as described in Chapter 9. The representations we have given in this chapter should therefore be interpreted as a kind of shorthand for more elaborate structures with many tiers linking up to slots on the CV (or skeletal) tier. We have not pursued here the question of whether autosegmental tiers function independently of each other in all cases; we will see in Chapter 11 that there are many cases showing dependence of one tier on another. Work in the field known as **feature geometry** assumes that *all* segmental features are located on tiers, and investigates the way those tiers are organised. We will consider this work in Section 11.2.

In Hungarian, frontness harmony can be treated autosegmentally too. The data we presented in Chapters 5 and 6 looked like this:

1. (a) [hɑːz] 'house' (b) [hɑːstoːl]
2. (a) [moːkuʃ] 'squirrel' (b) [moːkuʃtoːl]
3. (a) [vɑːroʃ] 'city' (b) [vɑːroʃtoːl]
4. (a) [ørøm] 'joy' (b) [ørømtøːl]
5. (a) [byːn] 'crime' (b) [byːntøːl]
6. (a) [rɑdiːr] 'eraser' (b) [rɑdiːrtoːl]
7. (a) [taɲeːr] 'plate' (b) [taɲeːrtoːl]
8. (a) [beːkɑ] 'frog' (b) [beːkɑtoːl]

Roots like [ørøm], which take front affixes like [tøːl], have [F] auto-segments, whereas roots like [mokuʃ], which take affixes like [toːl], lack such an autosegment:

(34)

    [F]   [F]

$\longrightarrow$

/ O r O m + t O O l /   / O r O m + t O O l /   (= [ørømtø:l])

(35)

/ m O k U ʃ + t O O l / = [mokuʃto:l]

What about our 'mixed' roots, containing back vowels and neutral vowels, like [rɑdi:r]? These take back affixes, and can therefore be represented as lacking an [F] autosegment:

/ r A d i: r + t O O l / = [rɑdi:rto: l]

With this kind of approach, we would need to allow that the /i:/ in this root is specified as front segmentally.

Roots which are disharmonic with respect to frontness harmony can also be treated like our disharmonic Akan cases:

(36)

   [-F]   [F] $\longrightarrow$ [-F] [F]

/ ʃ O ff O r + t O O l /   / ʃ O ff O r + t O O l /   (= [ʃofførtø:l])

However, we encounter problems with our two classes of all-neutral roots; they might be treated as follows:

(37)

/ h i: d + t O O l / = [hidto:l]

(38)

    [F]   [F]

$\longrightarrow$

/ ʃ II n + t O O l /   / ʃ II n + t O O l /   (= [ʃi:ntø:l])

At this point, our notion of default values for vowels begins to run into difficulty. Roots like [hi:d] must lack an [F] autosegment, and roots like [ʃi:n] must possess one. If this is so we can say that the vowel in [ʃi:n] is underlyingly high and unrounded, but underspecified for [F]; it becomes front by association with the autosegment, as above. Roots like [hi:d], however, have vowels which are phonetically front. We might suggest that they have frontness as part of their segmental make-up (as above), or, alternatively, that they are underspecified for frontness and are assigned this property by a default rule which operates after the vowel harmony process.[8]

We can sum up our description of the autosegmental treatment of vowel harmony as follows:

1. Harmonic properties are represented as autosegments; they are often properties, not of specific segments, but of larger domains such as the morpheme. We have allowed for free autosegments on both root and affix morphemes. Many cases of what we want to call vowel harmony (VH) are bounded only by the occurrence of blocking segments; VH can be said not to be restricted to a given number of syllables, and in this sense it is unbounded (it is not best described as a local phenomenon).
2. The association convention and the well-formedness conditions, in conjunction with the autosegmental form of representation, enable us to state both left-to-right and right-to-left harmonising, as well as bidirectional harmony (this appears rather difficult for a linear phonology to do).
3. We may represent opacity by means of a lexically bound '[~X]' autosegment, and some cases of neutral vowels with segmentally specified values for harmonic features, but we noted problems with this latter idea.

We have seen how the autosegmental account deals with regular harmony and with disharmonic roots and opaque vowels. Let us now look at another vowel harmony phenomenon and see how the theory can be used there.

10.3 Dominant/Recessive Harmony

In the data we have looked at so far, root morphemes have been specified as being marked for a harmonic property which spreads across the word form (omitting neutral vowels) unless blocked by an opaque vowel. These data allowed us to maintain our definition of vowel harmony as a dependency of affix vowels on properties of roots.

There are systems, however, where, given two sets of vowels, say an ATR set and a non-ATR set, the ATR set counts as 'dominant', such that, given the presence of a vowel from the dominant set anywhere in the word form, whether in the root or in an affix, its harmonic property will spread (subject to blocking). A dominant vowel in an affix can therefore dictate the harmonic value of root vowels. Akan, Nez Perce (a Sahaptian language of North America) and Kalenjin (an East African language) provide good examples; we will look at the case of Kalenjin.

The Kalenjin system (data from Halle and Vergnaud 1981) looks like this:

(39)

Dominant: marked for [A]   **Recessive**: not marked for [A]

i	u		ɪ	ʊ
e	o		ɛ	ɔ
a				ɑ

The morphemes 'shut' and 'saw' are, respectively, non-ATR and ATR morphemes (for ease of exposition, phonetic representations are given with morpheme boundaries included):

(40)

[kɪ + ɑ +   gɛr]   'I shut it'
1PS   PAST 'shut'

(41)

[ki + a +   ge:r + in]   'I saw you (singular)'
1PS   PAST 'see'   2PS

The underlying representations for these two morphemes are therefore:

(42)

$$\qquad\qquad [A]$$
/ gEr /   vs   / gE:r /
'shut'   'see'

Affixes harmonise for ATR: the lPS prefix has alternants [ki] and [kɪ], and the PAST affix has variants [a] and [ɑ], as you can see in (40) and (41). The 2PS alternants are [in] and [ɪn], as you can see if you contrast (41) with (43):

(43)

[kɪ + ɑ + bɑr + ɪn]   'I killed you (singular)'

We will assume that [A] spreading in Kalenjin is bidirectional, as in Akan:

given a root morpheme with an [A] autosegment, the [A] will spread to harmonising affixes, whether they are prefixes or suffixes.

The progressive suffix in this language has only one phonetic shape: [e]. Furthermore, when it is added to a non-ATR root, it spreads ATR to all other vowels in the word (so long as they are not the vowels of opaque morphemes: see below). Recall that we represented the root morpheme /fɪtɪ/ in Akan with a free [A] autosegment which may spread to adjacent vowels. We will adopt the same strategy here: we will represent the PROG morpheme in Kalenjin as /E/ with a free [A] autosegment:

(44)

[A]

/E/   (= [e])

When this morpheme is added to a word with a non-ATR root, the entire word becomes associated with this [A], including the root:

(45)

$$[A] \longrightarrow \qquad\qquad [A]$$

/ k I + A + g E r + E /   / k I + A + g E r + E /   (= [ki + a + ger + e])
'I was shutting it'

There are three **opaque morphemes** in Kalenjin. They are: the negative prefix [ma], the perfective morpheme [ka] (alternant: [ga]) and the reflexive suffix [kɛ:] (alternant: [gɛ:]). Parallel to our treatment of the opaque vowel [a] in Akan, we will represent these in the lexicon with a lexically bound [~A]:

(46)

[~A]   [~A]   [~A]
| | |
/mA/   /kA/   /kE:/

The effect of these morphemes on Kalenjin words can be seen in the following:

1.   [ki + a + un + gɛ:]   'I washed myself'
2.   [ma + ti + un + gɛ:]   'don't wash yourself'

3.   [kɪ + mɑ + a + geːr + ak]   'I didn't see you' (plural)
4.   [kɪ + mɑ + gɑ + go + geːr + a]   'and he hadn't seen me'

Although /Un/ ('wash') and /gEːr/ ('see') are both ATR verbs, the three opaque morphemes in question remain non-ATR. Furthermore, in (3) and (4), the opaque morphemes /mA/ and /gA/ block the spread of [A] to the prefix /kI/, as follows:

(47)

(48)

Thus, we can capture the nature of dominant/recessive harmony without recourse to any new devices.[9] We allow lexical association of a negatively specified autosegment on opaque morphemes, and free autosegments on affixes such as, in this case, the PROG morpheme. This analysis embodies the claim that there are two sorts of lexical morpheme in this language with respect to ATR vowel harmony: those with free [A] autosegments and those without. What distinguishes dominant/recessive harmony systems from others is the fact that, in dominant recessive systems, free autosegments may appear in *affix* morphemes.

The autosegmental model arose from Goldsmith's (1979) work on tone languages; it soon came to be extended to phenomena like nasal spreading and vowel harmony. One question which we would want to raise is just how many phonological phenomena can be treated in this way. It is also interesting that, in appealing only to the WFCs and certain stipulations about association, we are committed to denying that languages (or at least those we have looked at) have vowel harmony or nasal spreading *rules*. Since principles of association are universal (defined independently of any particular language), all we need state, for each language, is the form of its representations; these general principles will then operate to yield the surface phonetic regularities. This is quite a step away from the rule-based phonology of the standard model, and we will consider, in the final chapter, a hypothesis which will take us even further away from the assumptions of the standard model: that human language phonologies are simply *not* rule-based. As for phonological representations, we have argued that there are phonological phenomena which are best character- ised in terms of privative oppositions. We will also entertain, in our final chapter, the interestingly radical hypothesis that *all* phonological oppo- sitions are privative.

EXERCISES

1. Khalkha Mongolian
Khalkha, spoken in the Mongolian Peoples' Republic, is a major dialect of Eastern Mongolian. (Data from Halle and Vergnaud 1981, and Goldsmith 1985.) The Mongolian languages, along with the Turkic and Tungusitic languages, constitute the Altaic language family.

The surface phonetic vowel system of Khalkha (ignoring vowel length, which is contrastive, and diphthongs) is:

	Front		Back	
High	i	y	u	
Low	e	ø	ɑ	o

You will have noticed that, unlike Turkish, Khalkha lacks a high back unrounded vowel.

The language has root-internal frontness and roundness harmony:

1. (a) [xɑrɑ]   'look'   (b) [dolo:ŋ]   'seven'
2. (a) [teme:n]   'camel'   (b) [gørøs]   'antelope'

(i) Give underlying representations for these roots, showing, where appropriate, [F] and [R] autosegments (on separate tiers).

Khalkha has root-to-affix frontness and roundness harmony, as shown in the following:

3. (a) [org + ox]   'to raise'   (b) [ot + ox]   'to keep watch on'
   (c) [ɑvr + ɑx]   'to save'   (d) [hem + ex] 'to add'
   (e) [oril + ox]   'to weep'   (f) [øgø + øx] 'to give'
4. (a) [jɑbɑ + jɑ:] 'let me go'   (b) [ne: + je:] 'let me open'
   (c) [øgø + jø:]   'let me give'   (d) [ny + je:] 'let me move'
   (e) [oro + jo:]   'let me enter'   (f) [su: + jɑ:] 'let me sit down'

5. (a) [dy:]   'younger   (b) [dy:ge:s]   'from the younger
                     brother'   brother'
   (c) [morin]   'horse'   (d) [morino:s]   'from the horse'
6. (a) [dɑg]   'to follow'   (b) [dɑgu:l]   'to cause to follow'
   (c) [med]   'to know'   (d) [medu:l]   'to cause to know'
7. (a) [xorin + o:d] 'by twenties'   (b) [døči + ø:d] 'by forties'

(ii) The high front unrounded vowel /i/ is neutral with respect to frontness
     and roundedness harmony. What do the following data reveal about
     the status of /u/ with respect to roundedness harmony?

   [xojor + dugɑ:r]   'second'

   [jøs + dyge:r]   'ninth'

   [bodg + u:l + ɑx]   'to hinder'

(iii) Suggest an appropriate autosegmental representation for /u/.
(iv) Give a representation for the suffix (first person voluntative) whose
     alternants are [je:], [jø:], [jo:] and [jɑ:]. Say what the default form of
     the suffix is.
(v) Give phonological representations, with autosegments where necess-
     ary, for the roots 'go', 'give', 'open' and 'enter'. Show association of
     the [F] and [R] autosegments where appropriate, with the first person
     voluntative suffix, in 4(a), 4(b), 4(c) and 4(e).
(vi) Bearing in mind your response to (iii), give autosegmental represen-
     tations for the 'sit' and 'move' roots. Show how association works for
     4(d).
(vii) The following roots seem to invalidate our claim that Khalkha has
     root-internal roundedness harmony. Say why these data do not consti-
     tute counter-evidence to our claim, and give underlying represen-
     tations for them, with appropriate autosegments, where necessary.

8. (a) [ulɑ:ŋ]   'red'   (b) [gɑlu:]   'goose'
9. (a) [yne:]   'cow'   (b) [eny:n]   'this'

2. Kirghiz
This language has the same vowel system (in phonemic terms) as Turkish:

	Front		Back	
High	y	i	u	ɨ
Low	ø	e	o	ɑ

Also like Turkish, it has both roundedness harmony and frontness harmony (data from Johnson 1980):

	Root	**Gloss**	**Past definite**	**Past participle**	**Verbal noun**
1.	bil	'know'	bildi	bilgen	bily:
2.	ber	'give'	berdi	bergen	bery:
3.	kyl	'laugh'	kyldy	kylgøn	kyly:
4.	kør	'see'	kørdy	kørgøn	køry:
5.	kɨl	'do'	kɨldɨ	kɨlgan	kɨlu:
6.	al	'take'	aldɨ	algan	alu:
7.	tut	'hold'	tuttu	tutkan	tutu:
8.	bol	'be'	boldu	bolgon	bolu:

(i) Give underlying representations, of the sort we have used in Chapter 10, for the three suffixes, showing autosegments where appropriate, and say what the default values for the vowels in those suffixes are.

(ii) Assuming that frontness harmony and roundedness harmony function on independent tiers, and ignoring the past participle of 'hold', give representations for all the roots, and show how [F] and [R] spreading operate from root to affix.

(iii) What problem is posed by the past participle of 'hold'? What condition has to be imposed on the spreading of roundedness harmony from root to affix?

Notes

1. Durand does not place a nasalisation diacritic above any of the segments {j, w, ʔ, h}, but his paper indicates that the velum remains lowered throughout their production in such cases; I take the diacritic to indicate that the velum is lowered. I have adopted the same convention with /j/ and /w/ in Terena.

2. Many versions of autosegmental theory explicitly prohibit the occurrence of a feature on more than one tier. Cf, for example, Goldsmith (1990: 9).

3. An alternative conception of the notion 'privative opposition' occurs in Goldmsith (1990); for Goldsmith, an opposition is privative if it involves only one *value* for a feature, either '+' or '−'. Thus, a privative opposition may be founded on a phonological property [−X]. This is a somewhat weaker version of the notion 'privative' than the one adopted here.

4. There appears to be something disturbing about such roots. It is claimed by Anderson (1980) and others that they reflect a minor generalisation (referred to as Labial Attraction) about the shape of morphemes in Turkish: where a root has a low vowel /ɑ/, followed by a labial consonant, followed by a high vowel, the high vowel is round. We have suggested, in our representations, that in such morphemes the roundedness of the second vowel is an arbitrary property of the morpheme. If Labial Attraction is a valid generalisation, then that is not the case. This has consequences for our treatment of roundedness harmony in Turkish, since it suggests that, once roundedness is specified on the last vowel in a root, it is then transmitted from that vowel to suffix vowels. This may then be taken as evidence that roundedness harmony in this language is not suprasegmental after all, but is transmitted iteratively from one vowel to another, which is Anderson's view. At the very least, such evidence presents a challenge for the autosegmental account. Clements and Sezer (1982), arguing that Labial Attraction is a spurious generalisation about Turkish roots, present a set of 24 roots which have /ɑ/, followed by a labial consonant, followed by /i/, which, when added to Lees's (1966) list of 13 such cases, makes 37 examples of roots which violate Labial Attraction as against a list of 61 which constitute the evidence in favour of the generalisation and a set of 61 which have ɑCu, where the C is not labial. Zimmer (1969) offers psycholinguistic evidence against the psychological reality of Labial Attraction. It appears that the status of Labial Attraction is undecided.

The debate between suprasegmental and segmental approaches to vowel harmony in Turkish certainly pre-dates the emergence of generative phonology. Poppe (1965) and Trubetzkoy (1958) offer assimilatory, segmental analyses. Waterson (1956) presents a prosodic (London School) analysis for Turkish which strongly resembles the later autosegmental analyses; the issues raised by the formalism of autosegmental phonology are, however, not raised in the prosodic analysis treatment. Thus, autosegmental phonology is more than a revamping, or 'mere formalisation', of earlier prosodic analysis; issues such as the nature of opaque and neutral vowels and the relationship between vowel systems, harmony processes, neutrality and opacity have arisen precisely because of the nature of the representations given in autosegmental and related theories (cf Chapter 11 for further discussion of these issues). Harris (1951: 125–49) suggests a morpheme marking approach, which expresses the claim made by autosegmental theory that harmonic features are properties of domains above that of the segment. In early generative work, Lightner (1965) argues in favour of the morpheme marking approach for Turkish. Zimmer (1967) argues against the morpheme marking approach for Turkish, while accepting that it is appropriate for some systems, such as vowel harmony in Igbo.

5. Our theory runs into problems with loanwords from English, Persian and Arabic, like /harf/ ('letter'), /saat/ ('hour'), /kalp/ ('heart') and /gol/ ('goal') which take front affixes, as in [saatler]. In these cases, there is no [F] autosegment in the root.

6. This hypothesis that tiers always operate independently of one another is, of course, an empirical one, and is almost certainly untenable; it is, however, adequate for the purpose of setting out the core of the autosegmental approach. For some hypotheses on the interaction of tiers, cf van der Hulst (1989), and in particular the idea of 'parasitic' harmony, where a harmonic property on one tier is dependent on a property on another. See also Rennison (1987) for 'stacking' of tiers.

7. We have now tested, and had to modify, the theory that there are only two sorts of autosegment: free '[X]' and lexically bound '[~X]', where the [~X] indicates opacity, and may not undergo association. Turkish roundedness harmony forces us to allow for lexically bound [X], which may associate, as in [sorujorum], where the roundedness on the last vowel comes from a lexically bound [R] autosegment on the second vowel of /I j A r/. For the position whereby only free autosegments may associate, cf Halle and Vergnaud (1981). For a theory whereby bound autosegments may associate, and the principle that free autosegments take precedence in association over bound ones, cf Goldsmith's (1979) Precedence Convention I. For discussion, cf van der Hulst and Smith (1982). On spreading of [+X] and [−X], cf van der Hulst and Smith (1982), and Clements and Sezer (1982) on Turkish. Against spreading of [−X], cf van der Hulst (1988, 1989).

8. See Clements (1976) for an autosegmental treatment of Hungarian neutral vowels. For an overview of segmental and autosegmental approaches to vowel harmony in Hungarian, see van der Hulst (1984).

9. The Halle and Vergnaud (1981) paper makes a claim not made here: that dominant/recessive spreading is bidirectional and achieved via autosegmental association, while directional harmony is effected via metrical mechanisms. It also treats front/back harmony in Khalkha Mongolian as backness harmony. For an alternative to Halle and Vergnaud's position on dominant vs directional harmony, couched in the lexical phonology framework and using underspecification, cf Kiparsky (1985).

11 Representations and the Role of Rules

We begin by examining, in Sections 11.1 and 11.2, the claim that segments are better characterised as having more internal structure than that allowed for in standard GP representations. In Section 11.2, we will see how autosegmental representations can be extended to express this idea, and how they can be tied into the idea of a tier consisting of a set of timing slots (as in the CV tier). In Sections 11.3–11.5, we look at three theories which claim that all phonological oppositions are privative.[1] The theory presented in Section 11.4 combines this notion with the idea of government between phonological units and the idea of tier structure introduced in Section 11.2. The final section, Section 11.5, presents a privative theory which incorporates the bold claim that rules are dispensable in phonology.

11.1 The Internal Structure of Segments

Consider the following data from Japanese (from Hinds 1986)

(1)

1.	[çito]	'person'
2.	[hebi]	'snake'
3.	[ɸɯne]	'ship'
4.	[ho:riʦɯ]	'law'
5.	[hap:jo:]	'publish'

There is a case here for analysing [ç], [h] and [ɸ] as realisations of the same phoneme. Historically, they probably all derive from a segment /p/, whose history (unlike that of long /p:/) is something like:[2]

(2)

[p] → [ɸ], then
[ɸ] → [h] before vowels other than [ɯ], followed by
[h] → [ç] / ___ i

That is, a voiceless stop changes to a voiceless fricative, which then changes to a glottal fricative, which may then emerge as palatal [ç] before the palatal articulation /i/ (as in the pronunciation of words like *huge* in English

269

as [çuːj̆]), thus depositing [ç], [ɸ] and [h] as allophones in present-day Japanese. A similar phenomenon can be seen in some alternations in Lumasaaba, where /p/ is realised as [p] after nasal prefixes, and elsewhere as [j] before the vowels /i/ and /e/, [w] before the vowels /u/ and /o/, and [h] before /a/, as illustrated in the following:

(3) *Lenition of /p/ in Lumasaaba* (data from Brown 1972)

1.	/i + N + paja/	→	[iːpaja]	'a male goat'
2.	/ka + paja/	→	[kahaja]	'a small male goat'
3.	/i + N + piso/	→	[iːpiso]	'a needle'
4.	/ka + piso/	→	[kajiso]	'a small needle'
5.	/i + N + pusu/	→	[iːpusu]	'a cat'
6.	/ka + pusu/	→	[kawusu]	'a small cat'

Again, there has been a historical development of /p/ to [h], possibly with [ɸ] or [f] at an intermediate stage. We will return to the lenition process which results in [j] and [w] in Section 11.3 and in the exercises. Such histories, in which voiceless stops become voiceless fricatives, and then become [h], are very common.[3] Spanish *hijo* ('son'), for instance, once had /f/ as the initial segment (from Latin *filium*), which then weakened to [h], which has now *elided* such that *hijo* is [ixo]. In a paper concerning this kind of lenition, Lass (1976c) proposed that we need to view this phenomenon as loss of articulatory activity: there is less blockage of airflow in a fricative than in a stop, and there is loss of articulation in the oral cavity when voiceless fricatives reduce to the glottal fricative [h]. Finally, at the stage at which [h] is elided, there is complete loss of articulation.

Lass suggests we can express the way in which this process works by recognising two distinct **gestures** within a segment: the laryngeal (in the glottis) and the supralaryngeal (in the vocal tract above the glottis). The idea is that there are two independent parameters present when we articulate a segment: what is going on in the glottis is independent of articulation in the oral tract. The transition from voiceless oral fricative to glottal fricative can then be viewed as loss of supralaryngeal gesture: [h] simply lacks vocal tract articulation. If we represent these gestures as submatrices within a feature matrix, then we can view weakening of this sort as transfer of some feature specifications from the supralaryngeal to the laryngeal matrix, followed by, or simultaneous with, deletion of the matrix representing the supralaryngeal gesture, as follows (for /s/→[h]):

(4)

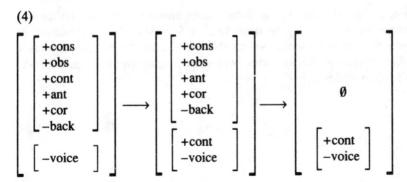

Elision of [h] is then viewed as deletion of the remaining laryngeal matrix, as follows:

(5)

$$\begin{bmatrix} \emptyset \\ \begin{bmatrix} +cont \\ -voice \end{bmatrix} \end{bmatrix} \longrightarrow \begin{bmatrix} \emptyset \\ \emptyset \end{bmatrix}$$

For Lass, glottal fricatives (and also glottal stops) represent obstruents which are not fully specified for both gestures: one of them is empty. This approach can be extended to the treatment of reduction in vowels (e.g. reduction to schwa in English) and underspecification of place of articulation in nasals adjacent to obstruents, as Lass suggests in his paper. Details of, and problems with, the formalism are not fully spelled out in Lass's paper; for instance, it is not clear what the form of phonological rules would have to be to operate on just one submatrix, and neither is it clear whether Lass is forced to represent the transition from voiceless fricative to [h] via a two-stage process involving the transfer of feature specifications from one submatrix to another. Nonetheless, the paper contains an important proposal:[4] with this kind of approach, we begin to build into our representations a greater amount of internal structure for segments than was previously recognised in our standard model, with its unordered bundle of features. Let us see how this idea can be expressed using the autosegmental mode of representation and the timing tier introduced in Section 9.4.

11.2 Feature Geometry

The idea that features may be grouped together into gestures may be married to the idea of the CV timing tier which we introduced in Chapter

9, to the idea of autosegmental tiers introduced in Chapter 10, and to underspecification theory as described in Section 8.4. We assumed, in Chapter 9, that the Cs and Vs on the CV tier dominate sets of feature specifications, as in the following representation for the first consonant in the English word *bit*:

(6)

	C V C
obs	+
cont	−
back	−
high	−
voice	+
nas	−
stri	−
cor	−
ant	+

Clements (1985) suggests greater internal structure within segments, and groups features into gestures, which may in turn subsume other subgestures, as follows (for similar proposals, see Sagey 1986):

(7)

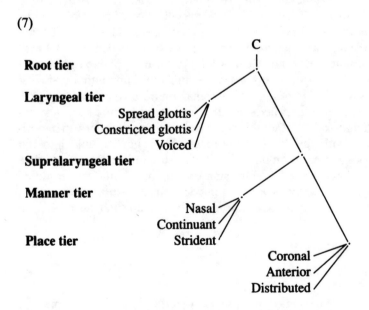

Root tier

Laryngeal tier
        Spread glottis
      Constricted glottis
          Voiced

Supralaryngeal tier

Manner tier
         Nasal
      Continuant

Place tier   Strident

              Coronal
              Anterior
           Distributed

The root tier is the 'anchor' to which the other tiers are tied: we may represent it as in turn linked to a 'C' or 'V' on the CV tier, or to a simple 'timing slot' (represented 'x') on the timing tier, if the CV tier is to be represented as a timing tier without indication of consonantality/vocalicness.[5] The structure in (7) shows that, like Lass, Clements allows for distinct laryngeal and supralaryngeal gestures, but views them as tiers within the segment. Under the laryngeal node, the feature specification [+spread glottis] characterises /h/, and [+constricted glottis] characterises /ʔ/. Purely glottal segments like /ʔ/ and /h/ are specified only on the laryngeal tier, and may pick up supralaryngeal features from neighbouring segments by assimilation. This is what we observed in the case of Japanese [h], which becomes [ç] before the vowel /i/. Similarly, in Korean, /h/ picks up labiality from a following /y/, /ø/ or /u/, and becomes [ɸ].

Clements further subdivides the supralaryngeal tier into separate place and manner tiers. Let us consider each of these. Recall from Chapter 5 that we used Greek Letter Variable notation to express assimilation (in place of articulation) of nasal stops to following obstruents. However, we required different sets of features for the Nasal Assimilation rule in different languages, depending on how many place of articulation distinctions were made among the obstruents of the language. Lass (1976c) had observed that the notion 'gesture' could be extended to such cases, where a nasal agrees in its values for all relevant place features, whatever they may be in the language in question. The illegitimate use of expressions like [αplace] in the standard model (incoherent, since there was never any such feature as '[place]') was an attempt to express the idea that agreement in such cases is for every relevant place feature. In feature geometry, the nasal will simply agree on the place tier with a following obstruent, quite independently of what the relevant features and values are for the language in question. Clements also suggests that the place node may be subdivided into the 'primary' features given in (7), and secondary features, namely the vowel features [high], [low], [back] and [round].

Sagey (1986) argues that the Place node dominates three distinct articulator nodes: labial (subsuming [round]), coronal (subsuming [ant] and [distributed]) and dorsal (involving the body of the tongue, and subsuming [high], [low] and [back]), as follows:

(8)

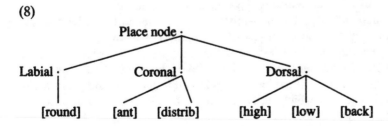

Let us see how this conception of segment structure may be connected with Underspecification Theory (UT). One of the hypotheses of UT is that, where a language has an epenthetic vowel (a vowel inserted into appropriate slots, such as /ɯ/ in Japanese pronunciations of loan onsets like /skr/ in English), it will be the one which is the least specified. That is, epenthesis is a matter of inserting a vowel, without reference to its feature make-up; the least specified vowel will be selected by default, and no language-specific stipulation as to the nature of the epenthetic vowel need be made. A similar idea was already present in Hooper (1976), where it is 'the weakest' vowel which acts as the epenthetic vowel. The matter of which vowel is the least specified depends on the nature of the system: in Section 8.4, we saw that Archangeli and Pulleyblank (1989) take /i/ to be the least specified vowel in the Yoruba system. In Section 11.3, we will see that in Nez Perce, it is, according to Anderson and Durand (1988), the vowel /e/.

Epenthetic consonants do not seem to vary across systems in the same way: it is extremely common for coronals to act as epenthetic consonants (as is the case in Korean: see Chapter 7, p. 170). This has led phonologists, such as Paradis and Prunet (1989), to assume a principle of **coronal underspecification**: coronal is the 'default' place of articulation, and coronals may therefore be represented as lacking a place node. The hypothesis is backed up by evidence suggesting that coronality plays a similar default role in first language acquisition.[6] This means that the upper part of the diagram in (8) may be represented as:

(9)

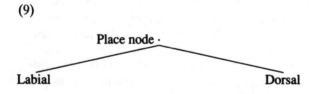

That is, in the absence of a place node specification, a consonant will be coronal.

It is less clear that agreement as to *manner* of articulation need be expressed in terms of 'block' agreement on the manner tier in the same way: while place features do often function in a block, this does not seem to be true of manner features; [nas] and [cont], for instance, seem to operate independently of one another (but see Clements 1985 for arguments that they do, and Iverson 1989 for reanalysis of the data). Iverson (1989) argues that, while a laryngeal tier is required, the supralaryngeal tier, subsuming place and manner tiers, should be abandoned. The place tier, Iverson suggests, should be directly linked to the root node, as should the manner features, which function independently and are not grouped into a manner tier, as follows:

(10)

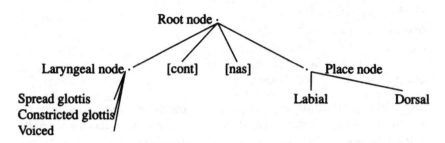

Iverson's treatment of /h/ and /ʔ/ suggests that they be specified, not only as [+spread glottis] and [+constricted glottis], respectively, on the laryngeal tier, but also [+con] and [−cont], respectively, on the neighbouring [cont] manner node, as follows:

(11a)   (11b)

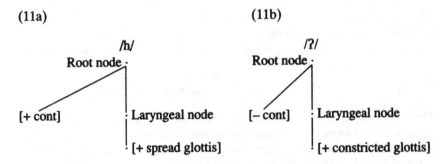

These representations incorporate into feature geometry Lass's idea that glottal fricative is a 'reduction' version of voiceless fricatives, and glottal stop a reduction version of voiceless stops. In analysing the obstruent system of Korean, Iverson combines them with the idea of underspecification, as follows. The glottal fricative is specified as [+cont] in underlying representations in Korean, and the glottal stop, in accordance with the principles of UT, gets its [−cont] specification via a complement rule ([ ]→[−cont]) which fills in the opposite value from the underlying one. This means that /ʔ/ may be completely unspecified in languages where glottal constriction is not contrastive; that is, [ʔ] is the default, minimally specified, obstruent. Let us see what relevance this has for the analysis of the Korean obstruent system.

   As shown on p. 32, Korean has a three-way distinction among obstruents whereby they may be unaspirated, aspirated or glottalised (by 'glottalised', we mean, in this case, characterised by glottal tension; the unaspirated/aspirated distinction does not apply to the fricatives in the system):[7]

(12) *Korean obstruents*

Labial:	/p/	/pʰ/	/p*/
Coronal:	/t/	/tʰ/	/t*/
	/č/	/čʰ/	/č*/
	/s/		/s*/
Velar:	/k/	/kʰ/	/k*/

Using underspecification and assuming that the labials and velars get their place of articulation features from the labial and dorsal nodes subsumed by the place node, Iverson characterises the coronals (which, of course, lack place features) as follows:

(13)

/t/	/tʰ/	/t*/
[ ]	[+spread glottis]	[+constricted glottis]

/č/	/čʰ/	/č*/
[−cont/+cont]	[−cont/+cont, +spread glottis]	[−cont/+cont, +constricted glottis]

/s/		/s*/
[+cont]		[+cont, +constricted glottis]

The expression '[−cont/+cont]' indicates that the segment is an affricate. The representations are accompanied by the following default rules [   ]↦[−spread glottis]; [   ]↦[−constricted glottis] and [   ]↦[−cont], as dictated by UT.

We referred, in Chapter 7 (see p. 170) to a rule of Neutralisation of obstruents which causes syllable-final obstruents to be unreleased (although this is not how we expressed it). An interesting fact about this rule is that it operates on segments according to major place features, such that the labials /pʰ, p, p*/ are all reduced to [p⌐], the coronals /tʰ*, t, t*, čʰ, č, č*/ are all reduced to [t⌐], and the velars /kʰ, k, k*/ are reduced to [k⌐]:

(14)

/jəpʰ/	→	[jəp⌐]	'side'
/pap/	→	[pap⌐]	'cooked rice'
/patʰ/	→	[pat⌐]	'field'
/tat + ta/	→	[tat⌐t*a]	'closes'
/pičʰ/	→	[pit⌐]	'light'
/čəč + ta/	→	[čət⌐t*a]	'is wet'
/puəkʰ/	→	[puək⌐]	'kitchen'
/čʰɛk/	→	[čʰɛk⌐]	'book'
/k*ək* + ta/	→	[k*ək⌐t*a]	'breaks off'

The process is elegantly characterised by Iverson as delinking of the terminal features of syllable-final obstruents, as exemplified in the following for /p/, /čʰ/ and /k*/ (where '//' indicates delinking).

(15a)

$$/p/ \rightarrow [p^{\urcorner}] \qquad /č^h/ \rightarrow [t^{\urcorner}] \qquad /k*/ \rightarrow [k^{\urcorner}]$$

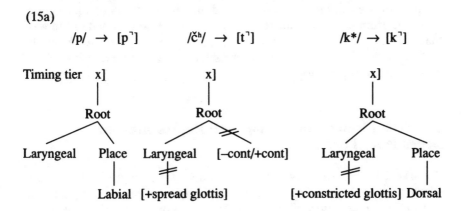

It is interesting that /s/ and /s*/ also neutralise to [t˥]; and, intriguingly, so does /h/:

(16)

/cas/	→	[cat˥]	'pine nuts'
/cas + i/	→	[caʃi]	'pine nuts (subjective)'
/iss + ta/	→	[it˥t*a]	'exists' (the second /s/ is deleted via Consonant Cluster Simplification: see Chapter 7, p. 170)
/kɨləh + so/	→	[kɨrəss*o]	'Yes it is!' (‹kɨrət˥s*o)

The coronal fricatives are unproblematical for Iverson, and, interestingly, so is /h/: its terminal features [+cont] and [+spread glottis] in (11a) are delinked. Thereafter, like the other obstruents, it picks up the default values for [constricted glottis], [spread glottis] and [cont], all of which are '−'. The coronals and /h/ are coronal by default, and the delinking process leaves intact the labial and dorsal place features of the labial and velar series. Thus, Iverson's model sheds considerable light on the question of why /tʰ, t, t*, čʰ, č, č*, s, s*, h/ should act as natural class and result in [t˥].

In 'factoring out' the features nasality, roundedness, frontness and ATR in Chapter 10, we were already anticipating some of the ideas of feature geometry, and the work done in this field is clearly an extension of the autosegmental, tier-based, approach to segment structure; it also links up easily with the 'CV tier' approach to syllable structure. Much work remains to be done on the content of tiers, and the way they interact; Mester (1989) covers a wide range of data bearing on the matter of tier interaction. As we will see in Section 11.4, these issues remain relevant even in frameworks which abandon the binary-valued feature. Work in feature geometry is also integrated with work in UT (it is assumed that the geometry of a segment is derivabie from its feature make-up, which may be determined in the way that UT suggests). UT in turn is, as we have seen in Chapter 8, easily embedded within the LP model. Let us look now at an extension of the notion 'underspecification'.

11.3 The Elements of Phonological Representation: Dependency Phonology

We asked, in the last chapter, what the values for X might be in a theory which allowed, in harmony processes, for simple presence or absence of a feature [X] on an autosegmental tier. We will now consider the answer to this question, with respect to vowel harmony, given by **Dependency Phonology (DP)**, one of our cluster of theories which maintain that all oppositions are privative.

Vowel systems may vary considerably in complexity. The most simple which is often encountered is the 'three vowel triangular system' reported in Lass (1984b: 140), as follows:

(17)

/i/   /u/

     /a/

That is, a system with a high front unrounded vowel, a high back rounded one and a low one. In DP, these three vowel qualities are taken to reflect three basic components of vowel articulations: palatality, gravity and sonority. Those components are identified in DP as the **elements** of vowel representation,[8] and are represented, respectively, as {i}, {u} and {a} . The meaning of the term 'palatality' should be clear enough. The term 'gravity' is an acoustic one, whose details we will not spell out here. The articulatory gestures which induce gravity are velar constriction and roundedness, and in distinctive feature notations which are based on acoustic properties, the feature [+grave] picks out velar and labial articulations as a natural class, to the exclusion of coronal articulations. The elements {i} and {u} are taken to be vowel 'colours' which are overlaid on a vocalic articulation (we will pursue the distinction between these two elements and {a} in Section 11.4). With this means of representing vowels, we may think of lenition of Lumasaaba /p/ to [w] before /u/ and /o/, to [j] before /i/ and /e/, and to [h] before /a/ as delinking of the place node, as in Iverson (1989), and then relinking to the palatality of /i/ and /e/, the gravity of /u/ and /o/, and no linking at all with /a/, which lacks both palatality and gravity.

We may conceive of more elaborate vowel systems as elaborations on the basic one such that it is characterised in terms of the three vocalic elements from which vowel systems are constructed. Thus, a five vowel system with a mid vowel set, as in:

(18a)

/i/ /u/
/e/ /o/
  /a/

can be represented as in:

(18b)

{i}   {u}
{i, a}   {u, a}
    {a}

The ',' here indicates simple combination of elements. In addition to allowing for different combinations of the three basic vocalic elements, DP allows for governing relations between those elements. For example, a seven vowel system with high- and low-mid vowels, as in:

(19a)

/i/ /u/
/e/ /o/
/ɛ/ /ɔ/
  /a/

will be represented as in:

(19b)

{i}   {u}
{i; a}   {u; a}
{a; i}   {a; u}
    {a}

Representations like {i; a} and {u; a} reflect a combination of two elements in which the first is dominant, or governs, such that palatality (or gravity) governs sonority, whereas, in representations like {a; i} and {a; u}, it is the sonority element which governs. One can think of this in perceptual terms: {i; a} is perceived as more palatal than {a; i}; palatality is perceptually more salient in this case than openness, whereas in {a; i}, openness, or sonority, is more salient than palatality.[9]

Let us see what implications this privative theory of vowel representations has for the treatment of vowel harmony. With our binary-valued features for vowels, the range of possible harmony processes is high; such processes can be founded on any of the following harmonic properties: (a) [+back], (b) [−back] (we considered both of these possibilities for Hungarian), (c) [+round], (d) [−round], (e) [+high], (f) [−high], (g) [+low], (h) [−low], (i) [+ATR], (j) [−ATR] (as in the analysis of vowel harmony in Yoruba given by Archangeli and Pulleyblank (1989), which takes it to be best characterised as spreading of [−ATR]; see p. 183). Thus, with just these features, the distinctive feature theory will allow for ten different harmonic properties.

This contrasts markedly with the account of vowel harmony given by privative theories, which have available to them just the three elements {i}, {u} and {a}, plus perhaps an ATR element (let's call it 'A'), and thus allow for at most four harmonic properties.[10] That is, such an approach would allow for {i} harmony, i.e. palatal harmony (corresponding to the [F] harmony we allowed for in Chapter 10), {u} harmony, i.e. labial harmony (corresponding to our [R] harmony), {a} harmony, or lowness harmony, which we have not yet considered, and ATR harmony. These theories therefore provide an answer to the question we posed in Chapter 10: what may the values of 'X' be in a system that allows only for harmony on features entering into privative oppositions? The answers are: palatality, gravity and sonority, the three building blocks of vowel systems (plus, possibly, ATR).[11]

One of the most attractive aspects of the privative theories is that they claim a fundamental, non-arbitrary, connection between the nature of vowel systems and the nature of vowel harmony processes in those systems: {i}, {u} and {a} are the elements out of which vowel systems are built, and are also the properties which feature in harmony processes. This kind of connection is achieved in DP via the notion 'non-specification', which we might regard as an extension of the notion 'underspecification'.

We considered 'dominant/recessive' harmony in Chapter 10, and decided that it was not a qualitatively distinct kind of harmony from other sorts of harmony process: it required no new autosegmental devices beyond those adopted in that chapter, and was characterised simply in terms of free autosegments on affixes. The harmony process we looked at there was that of Kalenjin. A similar situation, but with an added complexity, occurs in the Sahaptian language Nez Perce (Sahaptian is one of the North

American Indian language families). The surface vowel system is [i æ a o u]; [u] is variably rounded, but we will ignore this fact for the sake of simplicity of exposition. Anderson and Durand (1988; henceforth, A&D) take the front low vowel [æ] to correspond to /e/, with a late, low level rule which yields [æ] as the phonetic realisation of the /e/. Again, for the sake of expository convenience, we will ignore this detail and transcribe [æ] as [e].

Like Kalenjin, Nez Perce has two vowel sets, one dominant and one recessive, but unlike Kalenjin, the two sets appear to overlap. They are, dominant /i, a, o/ and recessive /i, e, u/. Some examples are given in the following (data from Anderson and Durand 1988):

(20)

Dominant root morphemes
toot	'father'
?aat	'go out'
wat	'wade'

Dominant affixes
lajkin	'near'
aja	'for'
qa	'recent past'

Recessive root morphemes
meq	'paternal uncle'
tiseq	'skunk'
weejik	'go across'

Alternating affixes
[se] ~ [sa]	'distant past'
[se] ~ [sa]	Progressive
[ne] ~ [na]	'long ago'
[e?] ~ [a?]	Vocative
[tulee] ~ [tolaa]	'with the foot'

Thus:

| [?aatsa] | 'I am going out' | vs | [weejikse] | 'I am going across' |
| [?aatsana] | 'I went out long ago' | vs | [weejiksene] | 'I went across long ago' |

Rather than suggesting that the underlying system is simply /i, e, a, o, u/, A&D propose two specified vowels underlyingly: /i/ and /u/, represented as {i} and {u}, and a non-specified vowel { }, i.e. a vowel which is not specified at all for vocalic elements. This unspecified vowel corresponds to the /e/ just mentioned; the value {i, a} for this unspecified vowel is determined by one of a set of universal principles for selecting non-specified vowels. The principle in question, A&D's 'system-geometric principle 2' is stated as follows:

Where the system geometry is {X}, {X, a}, {Y}, the unspecified vowel has the form {X, a}

The default rule which follows from this state of affairs is therefore { }→{X, a}.

In principles of this sort, X and Y have values ranging over {i} and {u}. The reason why the {X, a} vowel (in this case, {i, a}) is selected is that it, unlike the other two vowels, involves combination; it is therefore the 'odd man out'. That is, the principles for the selection of underspecified vowels have the function of increasing the symmetry of the underlying system. The point is that general (universal) principles of system geometry allow us to pick out the unspecified vowel, and the nature of the default rule for the language (in this case, { }→{i, a}) follows from this selection. A&D also allow for a 'prosodic component', the third element of vocalic represen-tation, {a}. We may think of this prosodic component as an autosegment in the shape of a DP element. This autosegment, when present in represen-tations, will associate with vowel slots (with the exception of transparent vowels, which we will discuss later). Just as we characterised dominant morphemes in Kalenjin with a free autosegment and recessive morphemes as lacking such an autosegment, so A&D take dominant morphemes in Nez Perce as possessing an {a} prosody in lexical representation. When a dominant morpheme, such as 'go out' (informally, /ʔaat/), has affixes attached, the {a} prosody associates with the affix vowels, as in the following (where representations for consonants are simplified):

(21)

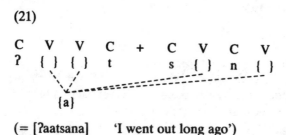

(= [ʔaatsana]   'I went out long ago')

Just as in Kalenjin, a dominant affix morpheme, such as /qa/ ('recent past'), when added to a recessive root morpheme, such as /weːjik/ ('go across'), induces harmony in the root vowels plus any other affix vowels, as in the following:

(22)

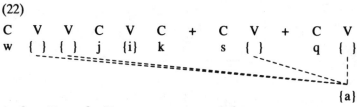

(= [waajiksaqa] 'I went across recently')

That 'go across' (represented, again ignoring the details of the consonants, as /w { } { } j {i} k/) is a recessive morpheme can be seen in the fact that it takes recessive forms of alternating affixes, as in [weejik + se + ne] ('I went across long ago'), in which, unlike [ʔaat + sa + na] ('I went out long ago'), the suffixes are in the recessive forms [se] and [ne] rather than [sa] and [na].

Association of the harmonic property {a} with the unspecified vowel { } will yield {a}, as [waajiksaqa]. Where there is no prosodic {a} present, the default rule will operate on the unspecified vowel slots to give {i, a}, as in the following:

(23)   w {   } {   } j {i} k + s {   } + n {   }

Default rule ({   }→{i, a})   w {i, a} {i, a} j {i} k s {i, a} n {i, a}
                          (= [weejiksene])

Association of {a} with {u} will yield {u, a}, as in the following:

(24)   C   V   V   C
                     t {u}   {u} t

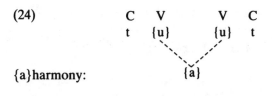

{a}harmony: {a}

(= [toot] 'father')

The vowel {i}, however, is transparent with respect to {a} harmony, so that in ([waajiksaqa]), the {i} does not become {i, a} (that is, [e]). That this is so can be seen in dominant morphemes which contain only {i} vowels, but which nonetheless induce {a} spreading, as in /cik'il/ ('destroy'), which, with affixes added, is [tolaack'ilksa], where the prefix has the dominant form [tolaa] and the suffix has the dominant form [sa]. This contrasts with the morpheme /qitti/ ('place firmly') which, with affixes added, is [tuleeqittise], where the affixes are in the recessive forms [tulee] and [se]. We may represent these as in the following:

(25)

t {u} l {   } {   } + q {i} t t {i} + s {   }

{a}harmony: _____

Default rule: t {u} l {i, a} {i, a} q {i} tt {i} s {i, a}

                      (= [tuleeqittise])

(26)

t {u} l {   } {   } + c {i} k' {i} l + s {   } {a}

{a}harmony: t {u,a} l {a} {a} c {i} k' {i} l s {a}

Default rule: _____

                      (= [tolaack'ilsa])

A&D's approach makes the assumption that harmony processes apply before default rules do, which seems perfectly reasonable; the 'default value' notion (here and in underspecification theory: see Section 8.4) is essentially the idea of a value which is assigned after all other value assigment processes have applied. And if it is a general principle that default rules, by their very nature, apply after regular harmony processes, then the accusation of extrinsic ordering cannot be levelled at their analysis. As A&D point out, the interaction between, and possible ranking of, the principles for selecting the unspecified vowel in a system remain to be worked out. But their proposals are certainly suggestive.

11.4 Elements, Government and Tiers

The theory of vocalic representations proposed by van der Hulst (1988, 1989, henceforth vdH) allows, as in DP, for the three elements {i}, {u} and {a}, but not for an additional element of centrality; nor does it allow for an ATR element. It is thus, as far as the elements of phonological representation are concerned, the most tightly constrained of the privative theories. We mentioned on p. 278 that {i} and {u} can be seen as the 'colours' which are overlaid on top of a vocalic articulation to produce a range of different vowel qualities. This distinction between the elements {i} and {u}, on the one hand, and {a} on the other hand, is of considerable significance for vdH. In Ewen and van der Hulst (1988), the following representation of the relationship between the three elements is envisaged:

(27)

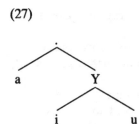

The elements {i} and {u} are subsumed under a node Y which is interpreted as tongue body constriction, which, as Ewen and Hulst show, is
implicated in many harmony processes. The idea is developed in vdH
(1989), where it is claimed that the following representation properly
expresses the relationship between the elements:

(28)

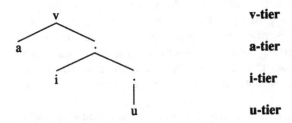

Recall that, in Chapter 10, we treated two different sorts of harmony in
Turkish: frontness and roundedness harmony. We represented these on
tiers which functioned independently of one another, but noted that tiers
are often dependent on one another, and that there is much to be investigated about interaction between tiers. Much of that work has been carried
out, using binary-valued features, within feature geometry, as mentioned
on p. 278 (cf, for instance, Mester 1989 and Sagey 1986). What vdH is
seeking to do is to spell out the relationship between tiers in vowel systems
using only elements, rather than binary-valued features. Let us take the
topmost tier in vdH's diagram, as given in (28), to correspond to a 'V' on
the CV tier.[12] What vdH wants to achieve is a statement of the way the
different vocalic tiers, which feed into this vocalic tier, relate to each other
(in terms of government relations) and how they are interpreted, phonetically; as we will see, these questions are closely linked. Let us begin by
looking at vdH's proposals for the phonetic interpretation of each of his
elements.

For vdH, the elements have component parts (thus rendering the term
'atom' of phonological representation' somewhat inappropriate). The pho-

netic interpretation of the elements is stated in terms of government relations between those component parts, as follows.

For the element {a}, vdH proposes the two components, pharyngeal constriction and openness. He notes that these are intimately connected, and assumes that the former governs the latter.

VdH's theory makes interesting claims about the element {i}. This, vdH claims, contains the components palatal constriction and advanced tongue root, with the former governing the latter. That ATR and palatal constriction are intimately connected is evident; vdH points out (a) that advancement of the tongue root induces palatal constriction, (b) that palatal harmony and ATR harmony never seem to coexist in a language, and (c) that there are cases where the former sort of harmony develops into the latter historically. As we will see, vdH takes ATR harmony to be characterised by dependent {i} in representations.

As for the element {u}, we have already seen that {u}, which, in acoustic terms, corresponds to gravity, subsumes two distinct articulatory properties: velar constriction and lip rounding. The question therefore arises whether these two components of {u}, these sources for the acoustic effect we refer to as gravity, may govern one another, and if so, whether the direction of government may vary. VdH responds to this question by supplying a phonetic interpretation for {u} where velar constriction governs rounding; he points out that the phonetic justification for this is that lip rounding enhances the acoustic effect of velar constriction (vdH 1988: 79).

To return to vdH's diagram, vdH proposes that, to associate with the 'v-tier', a vocalic element on a given tier must 'pass through' any others situated above it. Components passing through a tier pick up certain 'extrinsic' properties, namely:

a   tongue body constriction;
i   velar constriction;
u   none (no component can pass through the u–tier).

As we have said, in passing through a tier, a component activates the extrinsic value for the tier in question. For instance, in a 'primitive' three vowel system (/i/, /u/, /a/), the vowel /u/ will have the following representation:

(29)

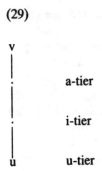

a-tier

i-tier

u-tier

That is, the i-tier contributes velar constriction to the roundedness on the u-tier, and the a-tier contributes tongue body constriction.

This approach to governing relations between elements allows vdH to characterise an interesting phenomenon concerning co-occurrence restrictions (i.e. harmony) between vowels within words in a variety of languages, which vdH refers to as **parasitic harmony**. These cases all involve agreement between vowels for some feature on the condition that they agree with respect to some other feature. This phenomenon can be seen in the case of Ngbaka, a Congo-Kordofanian language spoken in East Africa. The vowel system of Ngbaka is as follows:

(30) *Ngbaka*

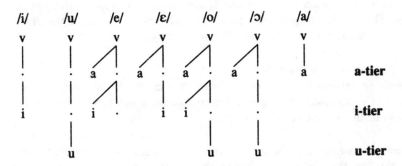

Representations such as those for the mid vowels, with the element {a} shown to the left on the a-tier, indicate dependent {a}, as opposed to governing {a} in /a/.

In this language, ATR harmony yields alternations between the high-mid and low-mid vowels (thus, the representations for the ATR vowels /e/ and /o/ contain dependent {i}), but neither the high vowels nor /a/ admit of ATR alternations. Additionally, there are interesting co-occurrence restrictions in disyllabic words. These may be stated as follows:

1. If a disyllabic word contains /i/, it does not contain /u/, and vice versa.
2. If it contains /e/,   it does not contain /ɛ/, /ɔ/ or /o/.
3. If it contains /ɛ/,   it does not contain /e/, /ɔ/ or /o/.
4. If it contains /o/,   it does not contain /e/, /ɛ/ or /ɔ/.
5. If it contains /ɔ/,   it does not contain /e/, /ɛ/ or /o/.

The restrictions can be seen in the following examples (data from van der Hulst 1989):

[liki]	'to heat'	[tulu]	'mushroom'
*[liku], *[luki]			
[bɔnɔ]	'brains'	[bɛnɛ]	'to cement'
[ʔele]	'to forget'	[zoko]	'beautiful'
*[zokɔ], *[zɔko],		*[zekɛ], *[zɛke]	
[pɛpu]	'wind'	[ninɛ]	'amusement'
[sɛti]	'luck'	[kɔpu]	'cup'

Mester (1989) sums up the overall pattern by noting (a) that the low vowel /a/ occurs freely with other vowels, including itself, (b) that a bisyllabic word can contain two identical mid vowels or high vowels, but not two different high or mid vowels, and (c) that high and mid vowels may co-occur.

Faced with (a) the pattern of permitted vowel combinations and (b) the restriction on ATR harmony to mid vowels, vdH is able to demonstrate that these two phenomena are closely linked to (c) the shape of the vowel system. The co-occurrence restrictions are statable in terms of the representation of the vowel system in (30), as follows:

Ngbaka co-occurrence restriction
Complete agreement is obligatory between vowels which are identical on the a-tier (i.e. the mid vowels and the high vowels, which form two distinct classes in terms of a-tier configuration).

It is clear from (30) that the mid vowels are characterised by dependent {a}; vdH can therefore characterise the restriction on ATR harmony (characterised by dependent {i}) as being conditioned by the occurrence of dependent {a}. That is, the occurrence of dependent {i} (ATR) is dependent on, or parasitic on, the existence of dependent {a}. We can refer to this as parasitic dependency. Both this dependency and the co-occurrence restrictions are a matter of parasitic harmony of lower tiers on higher tiers; vdH points out that the reverse situation holds for parasitic harmony in Ainu, where identity on the lower tiers implies identity on the a-tier.

Let us see how the vdH theory deals with vowel harmony in Yoruba which we looked at in Section 8.4. In that section, we saw that Archangeli and Pulleyblank (1989), using binary-valued features, treated the harmony process as involving spreading of [−ATR]. One of the attractive features or the privative theories, we have said, is that they allow for a more constrained range of hypotheses. Any hypothesis involving spreading of [−X], for instance, is not available. Consider the following characterisation of the Yoruba system (after vdH):

(31)

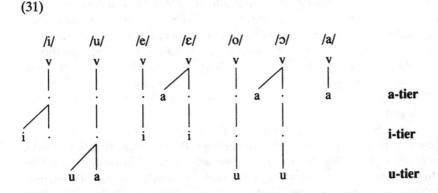

VdH (1988) takes vowel harmony in Yoruba to be spreading of {a}, that is, lowness harmony, as in the DP analysis of Nez Perce. The vowels which induce this spreading are /ɛ/, /ɔ/ and /a/: precisely those vowels in the system which have {a} in their representations. The vdH approach to phonological government yields interesting results when applied to vowel systems and processes, and may be extended to consonantal phenomena, to which we now turn.

11.5 Phonology without Rules: Government Phonology

We have considered several attempts at dealing with the problems which arise in a rule-based phonology. Those problems include the abstractness problem, which follows as a possible consequence of extrinsic ordering, and the problem of ordering paradoxes. The solutions we have considered attempted to reduce the amount of extrinsic ordering and to impose general principles governing the way rules apply. The last of the privative theories we will consider, Government Phonology,[13] retains the idea of phonological derivations, but dispenses with the notion of phonological rules altogether. The rationale for this approach to phonology stems from work in syntax, where early generative work allowed for extrinsically ordered syntactic rules, and resulted in a model of syntactic structure which was said to be over-powerful; that is, capable of defining rules which are known to fall outside the class of possible human language rules. In response to this problem, much work in syntactic theory now focusses, not on the formulation of rules, but on defining certain parameters along which the syntax of human languages may vary; it is claimed that, once these parameters are fixed, the syntactic structures of the language emerge, constrained by a set of universal principles which govern the well-formedness of syntactic representations.[14]

We have already been edging towards a similar conception of phonological organisation: work on vowel harmony in autosegmental phonology, for instance, appeals to a set of universal well-formedness conditions which define the well-formed phonological structures of the language, once certain other parameters in the language are fixed (such as directionality of association). The work of van der Hulst, particularly vdH (1989), also seeks to isolate universal parameters for the determination of vowel systems, and thus the nature of the harmony processes which operate within those systems.

Government Phonology (we will shorten this to 'GvP', to avoid confusion with 'GP', for generative phonology) thus seeks to isolate universal principles governing the form of phonological representations; it claims that phonological representations are built up from a fixed set of elements, in accordance with these principles. The elements of vocalic representation are similar to those of DP, Rennison and van der Hulst; we will consider some proposed elements of consonant representation, and the principles that are said to govern their occurrence and combination.

Many of the principles of GvP concern the place of segments in syllabic and metrical structure. This follows from the syntactic slant on phonology adopted in the theory: just as constraints on governing relations in syntactic structures determine the well-formedness of those structures, so do constraints on governing relations in metrical and syllablic structures determine the well-formedness of those structures. The theory recognises governing relations at three levels: between syllabic constituents (**constituent government**), between contiguous syllables (**interconstituent government**), and between syllabic nuclei which are heads of metrical structures of the sort we have referred to as feet (**nuclear projection government**). Let us consider each of these.

The theory recognises three syllabic constituents:[15] onset, rhyme and nucleus, but not coda. Segments in the 'coda' position are described simply as rhymal complements[16] (the positions in a rhyme governed by the head of the rhyme, i.e. the nucleus). Constituent government occurs in each of the following cases:[17]

(32) *Constituent Government*

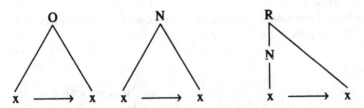

The arrow indicates the direction of government: all constituent government operates from left to right. Thus, within branching onsets and nuclei, the leftmost skeletal position governs the rightmost, and within branching rhymes, the rhymal complement is governed by the skeletal slot which is governed by the nucleus.

The relation between an onset and a preceding rhymal consonant constitutes interconstituent government, as follows:

(33) *Interconstituent Government*

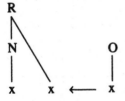

The directionality of government in constituent and interconstituent government is said to be fixed universally. Directionality of government at the level of nuclear projection is not thus fixed, but is a parameter along which languages vary (we have already encountered this in our discussion of left- vs right-headedness of feet in Section 9.5).

Nuclear Projection Government can be depicted as follows:

(34) *Nuclear Projection Government*

N   O   N   N   O   N

x   (x)   x   x   (x)   x

A central claim of GvP is that all phonological positions, except the head position, must be licensed, where this means 'permitted by the principles of government'. We do not have the space to investigate all of the proposed principles of licensing (and thus government), but we can briefly mention three: the Projection Principle, the principle of Coda Licensing and the Complexity Condition.

The **Projection Principle** is formulated by Kaye, Lowenstamm and Vergnaud (1990) as follows:

Projection Principle
Governing relations are defined at the level of lexical representation and remain constant throughout a phonological derivation.

This principle further constrains the theory, as it rules out the possibility of the sorts of resyllabification of segments which we allowed for in Chapter 9.

The **Complexity Condition** states that a segment occupying a governed position cannot be more complex than its governor; we will examine this in more detail later.

The **Coda Licensing Condition** states that a post-nuclear position in a syllable must be licensed by a following onset. This means that monosyllabic words have 'codas' which are onsets followed by empty nuclei, as follows, for *bit*:

(35)

What justification is there for these empty nuclei? We noted in Section 9.1 that some languages permit open syllables while others do not, and we further noted in our discussion of extrametricality in Section 9.5 that word-edge positions are 'special' in either lifting restrictions on syllable structure or imposing greater such restrictions. This variation is exemplified (but without reference to word-initial position) in the following (from Kaye 1990):

(36)

	Hawaiian	Gur languages	Japanese	English
CV syllables only?	yes	yes	no	no
C# permitted?	no	yes	no	yes

Kaye (1990) suggests that if the licensing of empty nuclei and branching rhymes are parameters along which languages vary, then the observed variation may be elegantly characterised: languages which permit closed syllables license branching rhymes, and languages which permit C# license empty nuclei – no reference to extrametricality is required. English, according to this theory, is a language which licenses both branching rhymes and empty nuclei. We will see some further proposed justification for empty nuclei in English shortly, in discussing lenition of /t/. An objection that might be raised to this theory, however, is this: while GvP's derivation of the pattern of variation from a set of two parameters is impressive, it makes no reference to the word-initial position, and thus splits off word-final extrametricality phenomena from word-initial.

A strong claim made by GvP is that there are no such phonological processes as insertion and deletion. This claim follows from the aim of the theory, which seeks to reduce the power of grammars by reducing the range of operations (such as insertion and deletion) which can be carried out by them. The refusal to accept insertion or deletion analyses leaves GvP with only two possible phonological operations: composition (the building up of structures from elements) and decomposition (the loss of elements). The existence of phenomena which seem to demand insertion and deletion analyses (epenthesis and elision, lenition and fortition) therefore constitutes an interesting challenge for the theory. Charette (1991) seeks to show how the principles and parameters of GvP allow an explanatory account of a phenomenon (schwa-zero alternations in French) which is normally analysed as involving insertion and/or deletion. When we considered Lass's (1976) analysis of consonantal lenition (weakening) to [h] and then elision to 0, we appealed to the idea of deletion as reflecting loss of articulatory information. Lenition phenomena thus constitute a case where GvP must provide convincing alternative analyses. Let us see how GvP characterises the phenomenon of lenition in consonants.

The vocalic elements {i} and {u} (represented as I and U) are extended by Kaye, Lowenstamm and Vergnaud (1990) to the characterisation of consonants, such that the former defines palatality and the latter labiality in consonants.[18] An element {v} which we lack the space to investigate, defines velarity, an element {N} nasality, {R} coronality, {ʔ} occlusion and {h} continuancy. Harris (1990b) redefines {h} such that it is interpreted as a 'noise' component, found in fricatives and in the release phase of stops.[19] The voiceless stops /p/ /t/ and /k/ are therefore represented thus (where each element occupies its own autosegmental tier):

(37)

```
p           t           k
x           x           x
|           |           |
?           ?           ?
|           |           |
U           |           |
|           R           |
|           |           v
|           |           |
h           h           h
```

Their lenition to the voiceless fricatives f, s and x is a matter of loss of occlusion, as foilows:

(38)

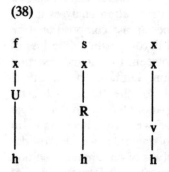

```
f           s           x
x           x           x
|           |           |
U           |           |
|           R           |
|           |           v
|           |           |
h           h           h
```

Further lenition of voiceless fricatives to [h] involves, as we saw in our discussion of Lass's (1976) proposals, loss of articulation in the oral cavity:

(39)

```
x
|
h
```

Finally, complete elision would involve loss of the remaining element, thus leaving a timing slot dominating no segmental material. For Harris, calculating the strength (or complexity) of a segment is a matter of simply counting the number of elements it contains: lenition is loss of elements (decomposition) and fortition is thus addition of elements (composition).

For the t → r lenition phenomenon implicated in Flapping in American English, the following loss of elements occurs:

(40)

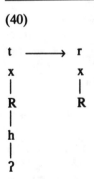

This lenition process is sensitive to metrical structure (i.e. structure at the level of nuclear projection). This sensitivity is expressed by Harris (1990) by appealing to the idea that such segments act as 'potential barriers to government' at the level of nuclear projection. Let us see how.

In many dialects of English, /t/ is weakened to either [ɾ]or [ʔ] intervocalically where the first vowel is stressed, as in *city*, and, in some dialects, also word-finally as in *bite*. Harris shows that the idea of Nuclear Projection Government allows us to express these two apparently distinct environments as one:

(41a)   (41b)

$$
\begin{array}{ccc}
 & \longrightarrow & \\
N & O & N \\
| & | & | \\
\text{s ı} & t & i
\end{array}
\qquad
\begin{array}{ccc}
 & \longrightarrow & \\
N & O & N \\
\wedge & | & | \\
\text{b ai} & t & \emptyset
\end{array}
$$

Harris's point is that, while the /t/ in such cases is not governed at the nuclear projection level, it nonetheless intervenes between the elements in a governing domain, and thus constitutes a potential barrier to government. It is thus under pressure to reduce in complexity. Harris goes on to show how variation in lenition of /t/ across dialects can be characterised rather elegantly in terms of licensing of empty nuclei.

But there is something odd about the inclusion of onsets at the level of nuclear projection: it is not clear that they should be visible at that level, if the level is indeed that of projection or nuclei (and not onsets). One of the phenomena that is said to hold at this level is that of stress assignment, and this, no doubt, is correct: we have seen that stress assignment holds at the level of the foot, where feet are projections from rhymes. But stress assignment phenomena show that onsets play no part in stress assignment, and this is to be expected if the 'foot' level is indeed a level projected from rhymes. It is true that the non-nuclear content of rhymes appears to play a part in (quantity-sensitive) stress assignment, which forces us to consider

more than just nucleic material at the level of nuclear projection, but if
Hyman (1985) is correct, and quantity-sensitivity concerns, not the structure of the rhyme, but the nature of the nucleus, then a level of nuclear
projection which is truly that would be possible. At any rate, the inclusion
of onsets at the level of nuclear projection looks undesirable.

Let us apply the GvP theory of lenition and fortition to a case of fortition
in Lumasaaba. We know that approximants strengthen (become stops)
following nasals in Lumasaaba (see Sections 2.1 and 2.2). Thus, the forms
/zi + N + ß ua/ ('dogs'), /zi + N + li/ ('roots') and /zi + N + jo: jo/ ('buds')
are realised as [zimbua], [zindi] and [ziɲɟo:jo], respectively. As we saw in
(33), at the level of interconstituent government, an onset is said to govern
a preceding rhymal complement. The GvP theory would therefore assign
the following representations to those forms (we will consider the segment-
internal representations shortly):

(42a)

(42b)

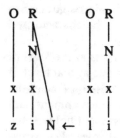

(42c)

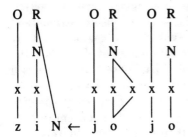

In each case, the onset slot in the root governs the preceding rhymal complement slot, which is a nasal stop without place of articulation features; it may be characterised as containing an N element and a ʔ element. Segmental representations for the three forms would be (ignoring voicing, which is constant throughout the derivations):

(43a)   (43b)   (43c)

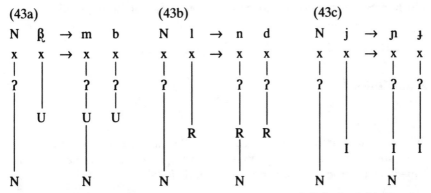

The governing approximant contains, in the case of /ß/, the labiality element {U}, in the case of /l/, the coronality element {R}, and in the case of /j/, the palatality element {I}. Since the Complexity Condition requires that a governor is not less complex than its governee, there is pressure on the governor to strengthen. This strengthening to [b], [d] and [ɟ], respectively, is reflected in the addition of the element {ʔ}.

But the place elements {U}, {R} and {I} are also transmitted from the onset segment to the preceding nasal; bidirectional assimilation occurs, with the nasal contributing its {ʔ} element to the onset segment, and the onset contributing its place element to the nasal. The resulting stops all have two elements, and the nasals three, which is hardly the desired result: the nasals remain stronger, according to Harris's analysis, than the stops.[20] The problem is, of course, that acquisition of place elements in such cases hardly counts as fortition. It appears that a calculation of complexity, for the characterisation of lenition and fortition, cannot proceed on the basis of a simple counting of elements, since place of articulation assimilation will often increase the number of elements in a segment, without apparently strengthening it. Other examples include the palatalisation (and velarisation) of consonants by adjacent vowels, as characterised by Charette (1989). Such assimilations increase the number of elements in the affected consonant, but it is not clear that a palatalised consonant is a strengthened version of a non-palatalised one. Similarly, vowels undergoing I-umlaut, as also described by Charette (1989), become more complex in Harris's terms, but the resulting umlauted vowels do not seem reasonably described as strengthened versions of their non-umlauted forms.

In examining Lass's (1976c) and Iverson's (1989) proposals, we saw that there is indeed something in the idea that lenition is to be equated with loss of elements (and, thus, fortition as addition of elements). Harris's GvP account is certainly more elegant than Lass's, but the theory requires further development: in the case we have just looked at, it is elements relating to sonority that count (although addition of place elements in the transition of /h/ to an oral fricative does count as fortition). A GvP account which incorporates structuring of tiers would seem to be required.

EXERCISES

1. *Djingili*

Djingili is an Australian language. The following forms of the masculine noun meaning 'branch' exemplify a widespread harmony process in Djingili (data from van der Hulst and Smith 1985):

	Number	Stative (phonemic representation)	Stative (phonetic representation)	Root (phonetic representation)
(a)	singular	/galal + ji/	[gililji]	[galal]
(b)	dual	/galal + ji + il + a/	[gililjiila]	
(c)	plural	/galal + ji + wala/	[gililjiwala]	

(i) Djingili has, in phonemic terms, a basic {i, u, a} vowel system. Suggest a DP analysis of the vowel system and the harmony process. Your analysis should take one of the vowels in the system to be the non-specified vowel, it should include a default rule for that vowel, autosegments on certain affixes, an indication of which element spreads, and in what direction.

(ii) Give a derivation for the stative plural of 'branch'.

(iii) The spreading process does not occur root-internally. Thus, the phonetic representation for the masculine noun 'rib' is [galimad]. How would the Lexical Phonology model accommodate this fact?

(iv) Is the spreading process structure-preserving?

(v) When a suffix containing /i/ is added to roots like /galimad/, which contains, in phonemic terms, both /i/ and /a/, only the last vowel of the root changes: /galimad + ji/ → [galimidji]. The same thing happens with roots like /laŋura/ ('lizard'), which have /a/ and /u/: /laŋura + ala + ŋa + ji/ → [laŋuriilinji].

What does this tell us about /i/ and /u/ with respect to palatal harmony in Djingili? Bearing in mind our treatment of such cases in Chapter 10, give appropriate representations for /galimad + ji/ and /laŋgura + ala + ŋa + ji/ and show how their surface forms are derived.

2. Turkish
The Turkish vowel system as given by van der Hulst (1988) is:

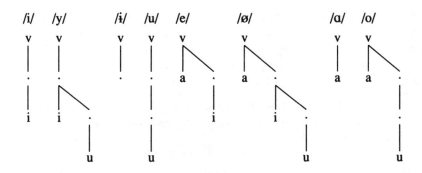

(i) Looking back at our analysis of Turkish roundedness and palatal harmony (see pp. 252–7), can you say how van der Hulst characterises the set of vowels which undergo roundedness harmony?

(ii) How is roundedness harmony characterised?

(iii) How is palatal harmony characterised?

(iv) How do the van der Hulst representations characterise the default value for the alternants [i], [y], [u] and [ɨ]?

(v) Try giving DP representations for the Turkish vowel system using simple combination (not government). Recalling Anderson and Durand's analysis of Nez Perce, can you say how DP might represent the default vowel in the [i] ~ [y] ~ [u] ~ [ɨ] alternations?

3. Lenition processes

The following data exhibit different lenition effects on bilabials:

(a) Lumasaaba /p/   →   [h], [j], [w] (data: Brown 1972)

/i + N + paja/   →   [i: paja]   'a male goat'
/ka + paja/   →   [kahaja]   'a small male goat'
/i + N + piso/   →   [i: piso]   'a needle'
/ka + piso/   →   [kajiso]   'a small needle'
/i + N + pusu/   →   [i: pusu]   'a cat'
/ka + pusu/   →   [kawusu]   'a small cat'

(b) Korean /pʰ/   →   [p˺] (data: Iverson 1989)

/apʰ/   →   [ap˺]   'front'
/apʰ + to/   →   [ap˺.t*o]   'front also'
/apʰ + i/   →   [a.pʰi]   'front' (subjective)

('.' indicates syllable boundary.)

(c) Korean /p/   →   [w] (data: Harris 1990b, modified)

Stem	Gloss	Indicative	Stative
/čʰup/	'to be cold'	[čʰup˺.t*a]	[čʰu.wə]
/ki:p/	'to sew'	[ki:p˺.t*a]	[ki.wə]
/ətup/	'to be dark'	[ətup˺.t*a]	[ətu.wə]
/tə:p/	'to be hot'	[tə:p˺.t*a]	[tə.wə]
/ku:p/	'to bake'	[ku:p˺,t*a]	[ku.wə]

(Recall that /p/ is unaspirated and contrastive with /pʰ/ in Korean; '˺' denotes an unreleased stop and '*' a stop with glottal tension.)

(d) Japanese /ɸ/   →   [h] (data: Hinds 1986)

/ɸɯne/   →   [ɸɯne]   'ship'
/ɸara/   →   [hara]   'field'
/ɸebi/   →   [hebi]   'snake'
/ɸo:rit/   →   [ho:ritsɯ]   'law'
/ɸito/   →   [çito]   'person'

(i) Adopting Harris's GvP analysis of lenition, give representations for the transition from the bilabial stop to its lenited form in each of the cases in (a)–(c). What problems arise?

(ii) What government factors might be at work to induce lenition in (a) and (b) and (c)?

(iii) What problem is raised for Harris's analysis by the neutralisation of /p/ and /pʰ/ (not to mention /p*/) to [p˺] in Korean, as evidenced in (b) and (c)?

(iv) Give GvP representations showing the transition of /ɸ/ to [h] in (d). Discuss any problems raised in determining government factors which induce this weakening. If the (d) forms have an underlying /h/, rather than /ɸ/, how would Harris represent the /h/ → [ç] transition? Given that Japanese /ɯ/ has a very weak labial constriction, what problems arise in characterising the /h/ → [ɸ] transition? Discuss any problems in determining what government factors might induce these fortitions.

(v) How would Iverson's model of feature geometry characterise the lenition of /ɸ/ → [h] in the (d) forms? If these cases have an underlying /h/, rather than /ɸ/, how would he characterise the /h/ → [ç] / ___i and /h/ → [ɸ] / ___ɯ fortitions?

(vi) Now try Iverson's model with the Lumasaaba cases, taking the vowels {/i/, /e/} to be dorsal, and {/u/, /o/} labial.

Notes

1. Another privative theory, **particle phonology**, is presented in Schane (1984). Rennison (1987, 1991) has developed an interesting privative theory which, regrettably, we lack the space to present. Its principal feature is that it uses elements, but not government, opting instead for 'visibility' relations between stacked tiers.

2. The story is much more complex than this. The segment is reconstructed as a fricative as early as the seventh century. But evidence that this in turn evolved from /p/ comes from sporadic alternations involving [h], [p] and [b]. It may also be that /h/ → [ɸ] / ___ɯ. Nonetheless, the general point being made here about lenition is valid.

3. Notice that the lenition involves a transition across the sonority hierarchy, from 'most consonantal' (voiceless stops) to 'less consonantal' (voiceless fricatives), to minimally consonantal ([h]), to elision. Fortition is the reverse phenomenon; see Lass (1984a: 8.3) for more details on both.

4. That proposal is expanded in Dependency Phonology (see Section 11.3) to three gestures. The first of these, the categorial gesture, defines the degree of sonority of classes of segment. The elements here are |V| and |C|, which represent the properties 'consonantality' and 'vocalicness'. These enter into combination and government relations (again, see Section 11.3), allowing a characterisation of the sonority hierarchy in terms of the elements |V| and |C|. The second is the initiatory gesture. This characterises glottal stricture and airstream mechanism types, where 'O' represents glottal opening. The glottal fricative [h] is represented as 'V' in the categorial gesture dependent on 'O' in the initiatory gesture. Lenition of the voiceless fricative to /h/, and then elision of /h/, may be represented as:

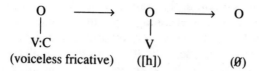

O	$\longrightarrow$	O	$\longrightarrow$	O

V:C V

(voiceless fricative) ([h]) (∅)

The third is the articulatory gesture, subsuming place of articulation properties. We lack the space to examine the details, but see Section 11.5 for a parallel privative theory.

5. Piggott (1988) also recognises a distinction between the laryngeal and supralaryngeal nodes, but argues convincingly, both there and in Piggott (1987), that the feature [nasal] is not subsumed under the 'manner' node. Since work in this area is still in its early stages, a consensus view of the feature geometry hierarchy has yet to emerge. See Sagey (1988) for a hierarchy which differs somewhat from that adopted by Piggott (1988).

6. See Lass (1984a: 7.6) for a survey of obstruent systems which lends some weight to the claim, particularly with respect to the coronal fricative /s/. Historical change does, however, skew the occurrence of 'unmarked' segments. See again Lass (1975) on the matter of markedness.

7. What is interesting about Korean is that it has a three-way 'state of the glottis' distinction which does not include the feature [voice]. Contrastive voicing has been eliminated in the history of Korean, which used to have (until, roughly, the mid-fifteenth century) the voiced fricatives /z/ and /β/.

8. Lass (1984b) gives an interesting survey of contrastive vowel distinctions and suggests a five height classification system with three vertical axes. Even then, it is interesting that there are many gaps (non-attested distinctions) among the low vowels, which tends to lend support to the 'triangular' view of vowel systems, as shown in (17), adopted by Rennison (1987) and DP.

9. The notions 'government' and 'dependency' (the one entails the other) are of considerable significance in the work of J. M. Anderson, since, for him, the dependency relation is central to the organisation of linguistic knowledge. A principle of *structural analogy* suggested by Anderson (1986) maintains that the relation is pervasive throughout the grammar: in the syntax, the morphology, segment-internally, and in domains above that of the segment – the syllable, the foot, the phonological phrase.

10. DP also allows for a centrality element {ə} which is used in the characterisation of, not only centralised vowels, but also back, unrounded vowels. The principal problem with this element, with

regard to our claim that harmonic properties are simply the elements of vocalic organisation, is that there does not seem to be any clear sense in which centrality harmony may be said to exist.

11. Government Phonology (see Section 11.5) allows for an ATR element. Rennison's (1991) theory allows for {i}, {u}, {a}, ATR and L (labiality, distinct from velarity). This theory faces the problem that only the first three seem to be implicated in the most basic vowel systems; the last two must somehow be given an auxiliary status. Van der Hulst (see Section 11.4) attempts to accommodate all known harmony processes with just {i}, {u} and {a}.

12. Or, alternatively, to the categorial gesture as in DP: see note 4 above.

13. The theory is outlined in Kaye, Lowerstamm and Vergnaud (1985) and further developed in Charette (1989, 1991), Harris (1990b), Harris and Kaye (1990), Kaye (1990), and Kaye, Lowenstamm and Vergnaud (1990).

14. For arguments against the idea that the same sorts of principle operate in both syntax and phonology, see Bromberger and Halle (1989).

15. It may well strike the reader as odd that GvP recognises O, R and N as 'syllabic constituents', but does not recognise the syllable itself as a constituent; this raises the question: what are O, R and N constituents of, if not the syllable? The motivation for this peculiar stance is that, with a definition of 'government' (essentially, the notion 'c-command') which, derives from the 'minimality condition' in syntactic theory, the 'σ' node in a syllable tree is defined as governing the 'R' node, as well as the 'N' node, and this proves problematical. GvP prefers to abandon the syllable node rather than the syntactic definition of government. It remains to be seen whether this view will receive widespread support.

16. The term 'complement' is taken from syntactic theory, where it describes constituents which are governed by a head and whose presence is obligatory. Thus, with the verb 'shoot', as in '*Harlequin shot Pierrot*', the verb requires a noun phrase complement, which it governs. Since 'rhymal complements' are in no sense obligatory with nuclei in the same way, the parallelism with syntax is at best only partial.

17. Charette (1989) allows for a fourth type of government within the syllable: a nucleus may govern an onset. While this allows her to account for palatalisation of onset consonants by palatal nuclei, it seems to violate the Complexity Condition (a governed segment may not be more complex than its governor): if nuclei may govern onsets, then we would expect /t/'s (and indeed obstruents in general) in onset position to undergo the sorts of lenition process Harris (1990) describes, but they often do not.

18. GvP differs from the other privative theories in that it does actually use binary-valued features in representing the internal make-up of the elements (thus the term 'element' ceases to mean 'atomic unit' in any absolute sense). These are crucial for the GvP approach to 'fusion' of elements, such as monophthongisation (e.g. of /au/ to /o/) and vowel harmony: in such cases, it is the 'hot' element of the governee which is contributed to the resulting fused segment. GvP also incorporates a theory of 'charm', whereby elements have positive, negative or neutral charm, corresponding, roughly speaking, to sonority: nuclear governors (vowels) are said to have positive charm, non-nuclear governors (stops) negative charm, and governees neutral charm. The charm value of an element is said to determine its combinability with other elements.

19. The treatment does not distinguish between [ɹ] and [r]. Broadbent (1991) analyses 'intrusive/linking r' in English as Glide Formation, such that [ɹ] is a glide formed from the low vowel element A. This analysis has the merit of establishing a link between 'intrusive r' and the set of vowels it follows (almost all of which contain A as the governing element).

20. The problem is less acute, but still unresolved, if we follow Kaye, Lowenstamm and Vergnaud (1990) in taking 'h' to represent continuancy and thus include it in the representations of the approximants. The /n/ here may be syllabic, but that does not resolve the problem either.

Feature Specifications for Consonants

Obstruents

	p	t	c	k	q	b	d	ɟ	g	G	t͡s	d͡z	č	ǰ	ɸ	f	θ	s	ʃ	š	ç	x	χ	β	v	ð	z	ʒ	ž	j	ɣ	ʁ
cons	+	+	+	+	+	+	+	+	+	+	+	+	+	+	+	+	+	+	+	+	+	+	+	+	+	+	+	+	+	+	+	+
syll	−	−	−	−	−	−	−	−	−	−	−	−	−	−	−	−	−	−	−	−	−	−	−	−	−	−	−	−	−	−	−	−
voice	−	−	−	−	−	+	+	+	+	+	−	+	−	+	−	−	−	−	−	−	−	−	−	+	+	+	+	+	+	+	+	+
obs	+	+	+	+	+	+	+	+	+	+	+	+	+	+	+	+	+	+	+	+	+	+	+	+	+	+	+	+	+	+	+	+
cont	−	−	−	−	−	−	−	−	−	−	−	−	−	−	+	+	+	+	+	+	+	+	+	+	+	+	+	+	+	+	+	+
del rel	−	−	−	−	−	−	−	−	−	−	+	+	+	+	−	−	−	−	−	−	−	−	−	−	−	−	−	−	−	−	−	−
asp	−	−	−	−	−	−	−	−	−	−	−	−	−	−	−	−	−	−	−	−	−	−	−	−	−	−	−	−	−	−	−	−
lat	−	−	−	−	−	−	−	−	−	−	−	−	−	−	−	−	−	−	−	−	−	−	−	−	−	−	−	−	−	−	−	−
nas	−	−	−	−	−	−	−	−	−	−	−	−	−	−	−	−	−	−	−	−	−	−	−	−	−	−	−	−	−	−	−	−
ant	+	+	−	−	−	+	+	−	−	−	+	+	−	−	+	+	+	+	−	−	−	−	−	+	+	+	+	−	−	−	−	−
cor	−	+	−	−	−	−	+	−	−	−	+	+	+	+	−	−	+	+	+	+	−	−	−	−	−	+	+	+	+	−	−	−
high	−	−	+	+	−	−	−	+	+	−	−	−	+	+	−	−	−	−	+	+	+	+	−	−	−	−	−	+	+	+	+	−
low	−	−	−	−	−	−	−	−	−	−	−	−	−	−	−	−	−	−	−	−	−	−	−	−	−	−	−	−	−	−	−	−
back	−	−	−	+	+	−	−	−	+	+	−	−	−	−	−	−	−	−	−	−	−	+	+	−	−	−	−	−	−	−	+	+
round	−	−	−	−	−	−	−	−	−	−	−	−	−	−	−	−	−	−	−	−	−	−	−	−	−	−	−	−	−	−	−	−
stri	−	−	−	−	−	−	−	−	−	−	+	+	+	+	−	+	−	+	+	+	−	−	+	−	+	−	+	+	+	−	−	+

Sonorants

	m	n	ɳ	ŋ	N	ß	w	ʋ	ð	ɹ	j	ɣ	ʁ	l	ɭ	ʎ	r	R	ɽ	ɾ
cons	+	+	+	+	+	−	−	−	−	−	−	−	−	+	+	+	+	+	+	+
syll	−	−	−	−	−	−	−	−	−	−	−	−	−	−	−	−	−	−	−	−
voice	+	+	+	+	+	+	+	+	+	+	+	+	+	+	+	+	+	+	+	+
obs	−	−	−	−	−	−	−	−	−	−	−	−	−	−	−	−	−	−	−	−
cont	−	−	−	−	−	+	+	+	+	+	+	+	+	+	+	+	+	+	−	−
del rel	−	−	−	−	−	−	−	−	−	−	−	−	−	−	−	−	−	−	−	−
asp	−	−	−	−	−	−	−	−	−	−	−	−	−	−	−	−	−	−	−	−
lat	−	−	−	−	−	−	−	−	−	−	−	−	−	+	+	+	−	−	−	−
nas	+	+	+	+	+	−	−	−	−	−	−	−	−	−	−	−	−	−	−	−
ant	+	+	−	−	−	+	−	+	+	+	−	−	−	+	−	−	+	−	−	+
cor	−	+	+	−	−	−	−	−	+	+	−	−	−	+	+	−	+	−	+	+
high	−	−	−	+	−	−	+	−	−	−	+	+	−	−	−	+	−	−	−	−
low	−	−	−	−	−	−	−	−	−	−	−	−	−	−	−	−	−	−	−	−
back	−	−	−	+	+	−	+	−	−	−	−	+	+	−	−	−	−	+	−	−
round	−	−	−	−	−	−	+	−	−	−	−	−	−	−	−	−	−	−	−	−

Sample Answers to Exercises

Chapter 1

C. Polish
The devoiced allophone occurs between voiceless sounds, and between a voiceless sound and a word boundary.

G. Tamil

(a) #__; m__; V__V.

(b) /p/ → $\begin{Bmatrix} [b] \ / \ m\_\_ \\ [\beta] \ / \ V\_\_V \end{Bmatrix}$

(c) /ʈ/ → $\begin{Bmatrix} [ɖ] \ / \ ɳ\_\_ \\ [ð] \ / \ V\_\_V \end{Bmatrix}$ /k/ → $\begin{Bmatrix} [g] \ / \ ŋ\_\_ \\ [ɣ] \ / \ V\_\_V \end{Bmatrix}$

(d) Yes: #__; ɳ__

(e) [ʈ]; voiced retroflex fricative: [ʐ].

(f) Yes. [s] is the intervocalic allophone of /ʧ/.

3. Tamil
The [ɯ] allophone occurs word-finally when the preceding vowel is unrounded.

Chapter 2

C. English

/r/ → $\begin{Bmatrix} \emptyset \quad \underline{\quad} \ \begin{Bmatrix} C \\ \# \end{Bmatrix} \\ [ɹ] \ / \ \text{voiceless segment} \ \underline{\quad} \end{Bmatrix}$

E. Japanese Verbs

(a) [eba]; [ta] and [da].
(b) [maʦ] and [mat]; /mat/.
(c) [ʦɯkɯɾ] and [ʦɯkɯt]; /tɯkɯɾ/ and /tɯkɯt/.

For /tɯkɯt/: /t/ → [ɾ] / V__V

For /tɯkɯɾ/: /r/ → [t] /__t (or: a voiceless segment)

Both involve assimilation: intervocalic voicing and devoicing before a voiceless segment.

The stem and the provisional form of 'wait' show that /t/ does not become [ɾ] between vowels.

(d) 'read': [jom] and [jon]; 'call': [job] and [jon].

For 'read' as /jom/: /m/ → [n] /___d (or t; or both t and d: more data needed)
For 'read' as /jon/: /n/ → [m] / V___V

For 'call' as /job/: /b/ → [n] /___d
For 'call' as /jon/: /n/ → (b) / V___V

The 'read' morpheme is /jom/ and the 'call' morpheme is /job/. The rule /n/ → [b] / V___V is phonetically unmotivated and falsified by the data (e.g. the stem of 'die'); this rules out /jon/ for 'call'. The rule /n/ → [m] / V___V suffers the same fate and this rules out /jon/ for 'read'. The analysis appealing to these rules is also incoherent: it asserts both that /n/ becomes [m] between vowels *and* that it becomes [b] between vowels.

In the unfalsified analysis the rule /m/ → [n] / ___d is well-motivated phonetically. The rule /b/ → [n] / ___d is phonetically motivated in that it involves assimilation of place of articulation but is unmotivated as far as nasality is concerned.

Chapter 4

2. Standard English

(i) /æŋgər/

(ii) *Singer* is /sɪŋ + ər/; it is morphologically complex, i.e. has a morpheme boundary, which *anger* does not.

(iii) It will delete the /g/ where it is preceded by an ŋ.

(iv) It will apply, as in *sing* and *singer*, when there is a morpheme or word boundary following the /g/, thus:

$$/g/ \rightarrow \emptyset \,/\, \eta \underline{\quad} \left\{ \begin{matrix} + \\ \# \end{matrix} \right\}$$

(v) Nasal Assimilation applies first.

(vi) The non-occurrence of [ŋ] word-initially follows from the restriction on #NC sequences; in this case, #ng: all occurrences of [ŋ] come from /ng/ sequences.

(vii) They are comparative forms of adjectives; that is, the *-er* in these cases is a different morpheme (the comparative morpheme) from the *-er* in *singer*, which is a nominalising morpheme, used to derive nouns from verbs.

(viii) It means that the morpheme boundary in *singer* differs from that in *stronger*. (See Section 5.2 on the '+', '#' and '##' boundaries: the *-er* in *singer* is a 'Class 2' affix, whereas the *-er* in *stronger* is a 'Class 1' affix.)

(ix) The accents with the [g] simply lack the Voiced Velar Stop Deletion rule.

(x) It lends support to it: it is the postulated /n/ in /sprɪŋ/ which is transposed from the position following the stressed vowel in *Springtime* to the position following the stressed vowel in *Hitler*, leaving behind the postulated underlying /g/.

(xi) These cases are exceptions to the rule: the words must have an underlying /ng/, since, according to our analysis, all [ŋ]s derive from underlying /ng/ sequences. But the /g/ Deletion rule should not operate on morphologically simple forms; *hangar* and *dinghy* should behave like *anger*. They are, however, loanwords.

Those speakers who delete the /g/ have nativised the words; those who do not
have not done so. See Chapter 8 on exceptions to 'Level 1' rules in Lexical
Phonology.

It might be argued that the small number of adjectives (three) which fail to
undergo /g/ Deletion in the comparative form constitute scant justification for
making the rule sensitive to a particular sort of morpheme boundary. We may
reply (a) that many rules in English are sensitive to such distinctions (see again
Chapter 8) and (b) that it is mere coincidence that there happen to be only
three adjectives ending in [ŋ] which take the comparative suffix: the three
morphemes constitute a natural class in English which just happens to be
small. To this reply, the critic might respond that it would be interesting to try
to elicit the comparative form *wronger* from native speakers and see whether it
had the predicted non-application of /g/ Deletion.

Chapter 5

2. Akan vowel harmony

(i)

	i	ɪ	e	ɛ	u	ʊ	o	ɔ	ɑ
high	+	+	−		+	+	−	−	−
low	−	−	−	−	−	−	−	−	+
ATR	+	−	+	−	+	−	+	−	−
back	−	−	−	−	+	+	+	+	+
round	−	−	−	−	+	+	+	+	−

(ii) Prefixes: [o] ~ [ɔ]: [e] ~ [ɛ].
   Suffixes: [i] ~ [ɪ]; [o] ~ [ɔ].

(iii)

	/O/
high	−
low	−
ATR	
back	+
round	+

(iv) $[+ \text{syll}] \longrightarrow [\alpha \text{ATR}] \; / \; \underline{\quad\quad} \; (+) \; C \begin{bmatrix} + \text{syll} \\ \alpha \text{ATR} \end{bmatrix}$

(v) $[+ \text{syll}] \longrightarrow [\alpha \text{ATR}] \; / \; \left\{ \begin{array}{l} \underline{\quad\quad} \; (+) \; C \begin{bmatrix} + \text{syll} \\ \alpha \text{ATR} \end{bmatrix} \\ \begin{bmatrix} + \text{syll} \\ \alpha \text{ATR} \end{bmatrix} C \; \underline{\quad\quad} \end{array} \right\}$

(vi) The rule says that prefix vowels agree with the first vowel of the root, and suffix
   vowels with the last. But there seems to be only one generalisation, not two:
   since roots themselves must contain all [+ATR] or all [−ATR] vowels, it is

not a *particular* vowel in the root which induces the harmony; rather, the root itself is either a [+ATR] or a [−ATR] root, and harmony affects any affixes, irrespective of whether they be prefixes or suffixes (it operates from left to right and from right to left simultaneously). We will return to this matter in the interlude and in Chapter 10.

Chapter 6

2. French
(i)   They have an initial consonant (possibly /h/; crucially a consonant which does not otherwise occur in the French consonant system). This induces Truncation and blocks Elision.
(ii) A context-free rule which deletes the /h/: /h/ → ∅
(iii) It must be ordered after those rules.
(iv) It contracts a counter-bleeding relation with Truncation: if the AN rule applied before Truncation, it would bleed it. It contracts a counter-feeding relation with Elision: if ordered before Elision, it would feed it.
(v)   The explanation does not work: the presence of a written ‹h› does not induce speakers to assume that the word begins with an /h/. It would also be interesting to find out whether French children acquire the appropriate rules and representations before learning to read: if so, it is difficult to see what relevance written forms could have. The 'influence of writing' explanation also predicts that illiterates pronounce words such as 'hibou' and 'hache' with Elision of the vowel in the definite article and non-truncation of the /z/ in *les mes*, etc. It would be interesting to learn whether this is the case. If it is not, the critic might fall back on arguments about the influence of literate on illiterate speakers.

Chapter 8

1. Ondarroan Basque
(i)   The rule applies in derived environment only. Because of this, these cases cannot undergo the rule, even where they have an /a/ at a word formation bracket, preceded by a high vowel, e.g. [pinta] and [čimista] (where ']' = word formation bracket).
(ii) The rule is a lexical rule and thus does not apply in cases like 'seven Sundays'.
(iii) It applies postlexically.

Chapter 9

1. London English
(i)   bored/board.
(ii) /ɔ:/ is [ɔə] in open syllable, and [ou] elsewhere.

(iii) *Initial syllabification*:

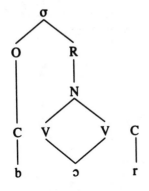 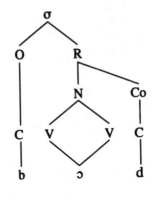

Rule: b ɔə (r) b o u d

Word formation
[[bɔə]d]

Final syllabification:

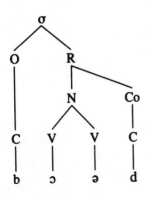 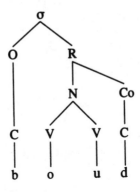

References

Allwood, J., Anderson, L.-G. and Dahl, O. (1977). *Logic in Linguistics*. Cambridge: Cambridge University Press.

Anderson, J. M. (1969), 'Syllabic or non-syllabic phonology?'. *Journal of Linguistics* 5: 136–42.

Anderson, J. M. (1986). 'Structural analogy in case grammar'. *Lingua* 70: 79–129.

Anderson, J. M. (1991). 'Contrastivity and non-specification in dependency phonology'. *Studia Anglica Posnaniensia* **XXIV**.

Anderson, J. M. and Durand, J. (eds) (1987). *Explorations in Dependency Phonology*. Dordrecht: Foris.

Anderson, J. M. and Durand, J. (1988). 'Vowel harmony and non-specification in Nez Perce'. In van der Hulst and Smith (eds), Part II: 1–17.

Anderson, J. M. and Ewen, C. J. (1987). *Principles of Dependency Phonology*. Cambridge: Cambridge University Press.

Anderson, J. M. and Jones, C. (1974) 'Three theses concerning phonological representations'. *Journal of Linguistics* 10: 1–26.

Anderson, S. R. (1974). *The Organisation of Phonology*. New York: Academic Press.

Anderson, S. R. (1976). 'Nasal consonants and the internal structure of segments'. *Language* 52: 326–44.

Anderson, S. R. (1980). 'Problems and perspectives in the description of vowel harmony'. In Vago (ed.): 1–48.

Anderson, S. R. (1981). 'Why phonology isn't natural'. *Linguistic Inquiry* 12: 493–553.

Anderson, S. R. (1982). 'The analysis of French schwa: or how to get something for nothing'. *Language* 58: 534–73.

Anderson, S. R. (1985). *Phonology in the Twentieth Century*. Chicago: Chicago University Press.

Archangeli, D. (1988). *Underspecification in Yawelmani Phonology and Morphology*. New York: Garland.

Archangeli, D. and Pulleyblank, D. (1989). 'Yoruba vowel harmony'. *Linguistic Inquiry* 20: 173–217.

Asher, R. E. (1982). *Tamil*. London: Croom Helm.

Baetens-Beardsmore, H. (1971). *Le Français Régional de Bruxelles*. Brussels: Presses Universitaires de Bruxelles.

Bendor-Samuel, J. T. (1960) 'Some problems of segmentation in the phonological analysis of Terena'. *Word* 16 (3): 348–55. Reprinted in Palmer (1970): 214–21.

Booij, G. (1983/84). 'French C/Ø alternations, extrasyllabicity and lexical phonology'. *The Linguistic Review* 3: 181–207.

Booij, G. and Rubach, J. (1987). 'Postcyclic vs postlexical rules in lexical phonology'. *Linguistic Inquiry* 18: 1–44.

Boyce, W. B. (1834). *A Grammar of the Kafir Language*. Graham's Town: Wesleyan Mission Press.

Broadbent, J. (1991). 'Linking and intrusive r in English'. *University College*

London Working Papers in Linguistics **3**: 281–302.

Bromberger, S. and Halle, M. (1989). 'Why phonology is different'. *Linguistic Inquiry* **20**: 51–70.

Brown, G. (1972). *Phonological Rules and Dialect Variation: A Study of the Phonology of Lumasaaba*. Cambridge: Cambridge University Press.

Bruck, A., LaGaly, B. and Fox, G. (eds) (1974). *Papers from the Parasession on Natural Phonology*. Chicago: Chicago Linguistics Society.

Carr, P. (1990). *Linguistic Realities*. Cambridge: Cambridge University Press.

Carr, P. (1991). 'Lexical properties of postlexical rules: postlexical derived environment and the Elsewhere Condition'. *Lingua* **85**: 255–68.

Carr, P. (1992). 'Strict cyclicity, structure preservation and the Scottish Vowel Length Rule'. *Journal of Linguistics* **28**: 91–11.

Casagrande, J. (1984). *The Sound System of French*. Georgetown: Georgetown University Press.

Charette, M. (1989). 'The minimality condition in phonology'. *Journal of Linguistics* **25**: 159–87.

Charette, M. (1991). *Conditions on Phonological Government*. Cambridge: Cambridge University Press.

Chomsky, N. and Halle, M. (1968). *The Sound Pattern of English*. New York: Harper & Row.

Chomsky, N., Halle, M. and Lukoff, F. (1956). 'On accent and juncture in English'. In: Halle *et al*. (eds) *For Roman Jakobson*: 65–80. The Hague: Mouton.

Clements G. N. (1981). 'Akan vowel harmony: a non-linear account'. *Harvard Studies in Phonology* **2**: 108–77.

Clements, G. N. (1976). 'Neutral vowels in Hungarian vowel harmony: an autosegmental interpretation'. In Kagl, J., Nash, D. and Zaenen, A. (eds) *Proceedings of the 7th Annual Meeting of NELS*. Cambridge, Mass.: Linguistics Department, MIT.

Clements, G. N. (1985). 'The geometry of phonological features'. *Phonology Yearbook* **2**: 225–53.

Clements, G. N. and Keyser, J. (1983). *CV Phonology: A Generative Theory of the Syllable*. Cambridge, MA: MIT Press.

Clements, G. N. and Sezer, (1982). 'Vowel and consonant disharmony in Turkish'. In van der Hulst and Smith (eds), vol. 2: 213–56.

Dell, F. (1973) 'Two cases of exceptional rule ordering'. In F. Keifer and N. Ruwet (eds), *Generative Grammar in Europe*: 141–53. Dordrecht: Reidel.

Dell, F. (1980). *Generative Phonology and French Phonology*. Cambridge: Cambridge University Press. (Translation of *Les Regles et les Sons: Introduction a la Phonologie Generative*. 1973. Paris: Hermann.)

Derwing, B. (1973). *Transformational Grammar as a Theory of Language Acquisition*. Cambridge: Cambridge University Press.

Donegan, P. J. and Stampe, D. (1979). 'The study of natural phonology'. In Dinnsen, P. (ed.), *Current Approaches to Phonological Theory*: 126–73. Bloomington: Indiana University Press.

Dresher, B. E. (1981). 'Abstractness and explanation in phonology'. In Hornstein, N. and Lightfoot, D. (eds), *Explanation in Linguistics*: 76–115. London: Longmans.

Durand, J. (1987) 'On the phonological status of glides: evidence from Malay'. In Anderson and Durand (eds): 79–107.

Durand, J. (1990). *Generative and Non-linear Phonology*. London: Longmans.

Encrevé, P. (1988). *La Liaison avec et sans Enchaînement. Phonologie Tridimensionnelle et Usages du Francais*. Paris: Seuil.

Ewen, C. J. (1982). 'The internal structure of complex segments'. In van der Hulst and Smith (eds), vol. 2: 27–67.

Ewen, C. J. and van der Hulst, H. (1988). '[high], [low] and [back] or [I], [A] and [U]?' In Coopmans, P. and Hulk, A. (eds), *Linguistics in the Netherlands 1988*: 49–58. Dordrecht: Foris.

Foley, J. (1977). *Foundations of Theoretical Phonology*. Cambridge: Cambridge University Press.

Frazier, L. and Fodor, J. D. (1978). 'The sausage machine: a new two-stage parsing model'. *Cognition* 6: 291–325.

Fromkin, V. (1971) 'The non-anomalous nature of anomalous utterances'. *Language* 47: 27–52.

Fromkin, V. (1978). *Tone: A Linguistic Survey*. New York: Academic Press.

Fudge, E. (1969). 'Syllables'. *Journal of Linguistics* 5: 253–86.

Fudge, E. (1987) 'Bracketing structure within the syllable'. *Journal of Linguistics* 23: 359–77.

Gazdar, G., Klein, E. Pullum, G. and Sag, I. (1985). *Generalised Phrase Structure Grammar*. Oxford: Blackwell.

Giegerich, H. (1985). *Metrical Phonology and Phonological Structure*. Cambridge: Cambridge University Press.

Giegerich, H. (1988). 'Strict cyclicity and elsewhere'. *Lingua* 75: 125–34.

Goldsmith, J. (1979). *Autosegmental Phonology*. New York: Garland Press.

Goldsmith, J. A. (1985). 'Vowel harmony in Khalkha Mongolian, Yaka, Finnish and Hungarian'. *Phonology Yearbook* 2: 251–75.

Goldsmith, J. A. (1990). *Autosegmental and Metrical Phonology*. Oxford: Blackwell.

Goyvaerts, D. L. (1978). *Aspects of Post-SPE Phonology*. Ghent: Story-Scientia.

Gussman, E. (1980). *Studies in Abstract Phonology*. Linguistic Inquiry Monograph 4. Cambridge, MA: MIT Press.

Hale, K. (1973). 'Deep-surface canonical disparities in relation to analysis and change: an Australian example'. In Sebeok, T. A. (ed.), *Current Trends in Linguistics*, vol. 11: 401–58. The Hague: Mouton.

Hall, T. A. (1989). 'Lexical phonology and the distribution of German [ç] and [x]'. *Phonology* 6: 1–17.

Halle, M. (1959). *The Sound Pattern of Russian*. The Hague: Mouton.

Halle, M. and Clements, N. (1983). *Problem Book in Phonology*. Cambridge, MA: MIT Press.

Halle, M. and Mohanan, K. P. (1985). 'Segmental phonology of Modern English'. *Linguistic Inquiry* 16: 57–116.

Halle, M. and Vergnaud, J. R. (1981). 'Harmony processes'. In Klein, W. and Levelt, W. (eds), *Crossing the Boundaries in Linguistics*. Dordrecht: Reidel.

Halle, M. and Vergnaud, J. R. (1987). *An Essay on Stress*. Cambridge, MA: MIT Press.

Harris, J. (1989) 'Towards a lexical analysis of sound change in progress'. *Journal of Linguistics* 25: 35–56.

Harris, J. (1990a). 'Derived phonological contrasts'. In Ramsaran, S. (ed.), *Studies in the Pronunciation of English*: 87–105. London: Routledge.

Harris, J. (1990b) 'Segmental complexity and phonological government'. *Phonology* 7: 255–300.

Harris, J. and Kaye, J. (1990). 'A tale of two cities: London glottaling and New York City tapping'. *The Linguistic Review* 7: 251–74.

Harris, J. G. (1975). 'A comparative word list of three Tai Nua dialects'. In Harris and Chamberlin (eds), *Studies in Tai Linguistics*: 202–30.

Harris, J. G. and Noss, R. (eds) (1972). *Tai Phonetics and Phonology*. Bangkok: Central Institute of English Language.

Harris, Z. (1951). *Methods in Structural Linguistics*. Chicago: University of Chicago Press.

Hayes, B. (1982). 'Extrametricality and English stress'. *Linguistic Inquiry* 13: 227–76.

Hayes, B. (1984). 'The phonetics and phonology of Russian voicing assimilation'. In Aronoff and Oerhle (eds), *Language Sound Structure*: 318–28. Cambridge, MA: MIT Press.

Hayes, B. (1990). 'Precompiled phrasal phonology'. In Inkelas, S. and Zec, D. (eds), *The Phonology–Syntax Connection*: 85–108. Chicago: University of Chicago Press.

Hinds, J. (1986). *Japanese*. London: Croom Helm.

Hoffman, C. (1973). 'The vowel harmony system of the Okpe monosyllabic verb'. Ibadan: Research Notes from the Department of Linguistics and Nigerian Languages.

Hogg, R. and McCully, C. (1987). *Metrical Phonology: A Coursebook*. Cambridge: Cambridge University Press.

Hooper, J. B. (1976). *An Introduction to Natural Generative Phonology*. New York: Academic Press.

Hualde, I. (1989). 'The strict cycle condition and noncyclic rules.' *Linguistic Inquiry* 20: 675–80.

Hulst, H. van der (1984). 'Vowel harmony in Hungarian: a comparison of segmental and autosegmental analyses'. In van der Hulst and Smith: 267–303.

Hulst, H. van der (1988). 'The geometry of vocalic features'. In van der Hulst and Smith (eds): 77–125.

Hulst, H. van der (1989). 'Atoms of segmental structure: components, gestures and dependency'. *Phonology* 6: 253–84.

Hulst, H. van der and Smith, N. (eds) (1982). *The Structure of Phonological Representations* (2 vols). Dordrecht: Foris.

Hulst, H. van der and Smith, N. (eds) (1984). *Advances in Nonlinear Phonology*. Dordrecht: Foris.

Hulst, H. van der and Smith, N. (1985). 'Vowel features and umlaut in Djingili, Nyangumarda and Warlpiri'. *Phonology Yearbook* 2: 277–303.

Hulst, H. van der and Smith, N. (eds) (1988). *Features, Segmental Structure and Harmony Processes* (2 vols). Dordrecht: Foris.

Hyman, L. (1970). 'How concrete is phonology?' *Language* 46: 58–76.

Hyman, L. (1975), *Phonology: Theory and Analysis*. New York: Holt, Rinehart & Winston.

Hyman, L. (1982) 'The representation of nasality in Gokana'. In van der Hulst and Smith (eds), Part I: 111–30.

Hyman, L. (1985). *A Theory of Phonological Weight*. Dordrecht: Foris.

Iverson, G. (1989). 'On the category supralaryngeal'. *Phonology* 6: 285–303.

Johnson, D. C. (1980). 'Regular disharmony in Kirghiz'. In Vago (ed.): 201–36.

Johnson, W. (1987). 'Lexical levels in French phonology'. *Linguistics* 25 (5): 889–913.

Joos, M. B. (ed.) (1958). *Readings in Linguistics*. Chicago: University of Chicago Press.

Kahn, D. (1980). *Syllable-based Generalisations in English Phonology*. New York: Garland.

Kaisse, E. (1985). *Connected Speech: the Interaction of Syntax and Phonology*. Orlando: Academic Press.

Kaisse, E. and Shaw, P. (1985). 'On the theory of lexical phonology'. *Phonology Yearbook* 2: 1–30.

Kaye, J. (1981). 'Recoverability, abstractness and phonotactic constraints'. In Goyvaerts, D. L. (ed.), *Phonology in the 1980s*: 469–81. Ghent: Story Scientia.

Kaye, J. (1990). '"Coda" licensing'. *Phonology* 7: 301–30.

Kaye, J., and Lowenstamm, J. and Vergnaud, J. R. (1985). 'The internal structure of phonological elements: a theory of charm and government'. *Phonology Yearbook* 2: 305–28.

Kaye, J., Lowenstamm, J. and Vergnaud, J. R. (1990). 'Constituent structure and government in phonology'. *Phonology* 7: 193–231.

Kenstowicz, M. and Kisseberth, C. (1973). 'Unmarked bleeding orders'. In Kisseberth (ed.), *Studies in Generative Phonology*: 1–12. Champaign, IL: Linguistic Research Inc.

Kenstowicz, M. and Kisseberth, C. (1977). *Topics in Phonological Theory*. New York: Academic Press.

Kenstowicz, M. and Kisseberth, C. (1979). *Generative Phonology*. New York: Academic Press.

Kenstowicz, M. and Rubach, J. (1987). 'The phonology of syllabic nuclei in Slovak'. *Language* 63: 463–97.

Kimball, J. (1973). 'Seven principles of surface structure parsing in natural language'. *Cognition* 2: 15–47.

Kiparsky, P. (1968). 'How abstract is phonology?' Reprinted in Fujimura (ed.) (1974). *Three Dimensions of Linguistic Theory*. Tokyo: TEC Co. Ltd.

Kiparsky, P. (1973). '"Elsewhere" in phonology'. In Anderson and Kiparsky (eds), *A Festschrift for Morris Halle*: 91–106. New York: Holt, Rinehart & Winston.

Kiparsky, P. (1979). 'Metrical structure assignment is cyclic'. *Linguistic Inquiry* 10: 421–42.

Kiparsky, P. (1982). 'From cyclic to lexical phonology'. In van der Hulst and Smith (eds): 131–75.

Kiparsky, P. (1985). 'Some consequences of lexical phonology'. *Phonology Yearbook* 2: 85–138.

Kiparsky, P. (1988). 'Phonological change'. In Newmeyer, F. (ed.), *Linguistics: The Cambridge Survey*, vol. 1: 363–415. Cambridge: Cambridge University Press.

Klausenberger, J. (1986). 'How concrete is extrasyllabicity?'. *Journal of Linguistics* 22: 439–41.

Ladefoged, P. (1982). *A Course in Phonetics* (2nd edn). New York: Harcourt, Brace, Jovanovich.

Lass, R. (1975). 'How intrinsic is content? Markedness, sound change and "family universals"'. In Goyvaerts and Pullum (eds), *Essays on the Sound Pattern of English*. Ghent: Story-Scientia.

Lass, R. (1976a). *English Phonology and Phonological Theory*. Cambridge: Cambridge University Press.

Lass, R. (1976b). 'On defining pseudo-features: some characteristic arguments for "tenseness".' In Lass (1976a): 39–50.

Lass, R. (1976c). 'On the phonological characterization of [ʔ] and [h].' In Lass (1976a): 145–67.

Lass, R. (1984a). *Phonology: An Introduction to Basic Concepts*. Cambridge: Cambridge University Press.

Lass, R. (1984b) 'Vowel system universals and typology'. *Phonology Yearbook* 1: 75–111.

Lees, R. B. (1966). 'On the interpretation of a Turkish vowel alternation'. *Anthropological Linguistics* 89: 32–9.

Liberman. M. and Prince, A. (1977). 'On stress and linguistic rhythm'. *Linguistic Inquiry* 8: 249–336.

Lightner, T. M. (1965). 'On the description of vowel and consonant harmony'. *Word* 19: 376–87

Linell, P. (1979). *Psychological Reality in Phonology*. Cambridge: Cambridge University Press.

Love, N. (1981). *Generative Phonology: A Case Study from French*. Amsterdam: Benjamins.

McCarthy, J. (1986). 'OCP effects: gemination and antigemination'. *Linguistic Inquiry* 17: 207–63.

McMahon, A. M. S. (1990). 'Vowel shift, free rides and strict cyclicity'. *Lingua* 80: 197–225.

McMahon, A. M. S. (1991). 'Lexical phonology and sound change: the case of the Scottish vowel length rule'. *Journal of Linguistics* 27: 29–53.

Majewicz, A. F. (1986). *A Contrastive Analysis of Japanese and Polish Phonemic and Phonetic Systems*. Poznan: Wydawnictwo Naukowe Uniwersytetu Im. Adama Mickiewicza.

Mascaró, J. (1976). *Catalan Phonology and the Phonological Cycle*. Ph.D. dissertation, MIT, distributed by Indiana University Lingustics Club.

Mester, R. A. (1989). *Studies in Tier Structure*. New York: Garland.

Milner, J. C. (1967). 'The French truncation rule'. *Quarterly Progress Report* 86: 273–83. Cambridge, MA: MIT Press.

Mohanan, K. P. (1986). *The Theory of Lexical Phonology*. Dordrecht: Reidel.

Morin, Y. C. (1987). 'French data and phonological theory'. In *Linguistics* 25: 815–43.

Nespor, M. (1990). 'Vowel deletion in Italian: the organisation of the phonological component'. *The Linguistic Review* 7: 375–98.

Nespor, M. and Vogel, I. (1986). *Prosodic Phonology*. Dordrecht: Foris.

O'Connor, J. D. (1973). *Phonetics*. Harmondsworth: Penguin.

Onn, F. M. (1980). *Aspects of Malay Phonology and Morphology*. Kuala Lumpur: Universiti Kebangsaan Malaysia.

Ohala, J. J. (1974). 'Phonetic explanation in phonology'. In Bruck *et al*. (eds).

Palmer, F. K. (ed.) (1970). *Prosodic Analysis*. Oxford: Oxford University Press.

Paradis, C. and Prunet, J. F. (1989) 'On coronal transparency'. *Phonology* 6:

317–48.

Persson, A. and Persson, J. (1980). *Sudanese Colloquial Arabic for Beginners*. Horsely's Green, High Wycombe, Bucks: Summer Institute of Linguistics.

Piggott, G. (1987). 'On the autonomy of the feature [nasal]'. In Bosch *et al.* (eds), *CLS 23*: *Proceedings of the Parasession on Autosegmental and Metrical Phonology*: 223–37. Chicago: Chicago Linguistics Soctety.

Piggott, G. (1988). 'A parametric approach to nasal harmony'. In van der Hulst and Smith (eds): 131–67.

Pike, K. (1947). *Phonemics*. Ann Arbor: University of Michigan Press.

Poppe, N. (1965). *Introduction to Altaic Linguistics*. Wiesbaden: Otto Harrasowitz.

Prince, A. (1983). 'Relating to the grid'. *Linguistic Inquiry* **14**: 19–100.

Pullum, G. and Zwicky, A. (1988). 'The syntax–phonology interface'. In Newmeyer, F. (ed.), *Linguistics: The Cambridge Survey*, vol. 1: 255–80. Cambridge: Cambridge University Press.

Pyun, K. S. (1987). *Korean–Swedish Interlanguage Phonology*. Stockholm: University of Stockholm Institute of Oriental Languages, Koreanological Studies 2.

Rennison, J. R. (1987). 'Vowel harmony and tridirectional features'. *Folia Linguistica* **XXI/2–4**: 337–54.

Rennison, J. R. (1991). 'On the elements of phonological representations: the evidence from vowel systems and vowel processes'. *Folia Linguistica* **XXIV**: 175–244.

Rubach, J. (1984). *Cyclic and Lexical Phonology: The Structure of Polish*. Dordrecht: Foris.

Sagey, E. (1986). *The Representation of Features and Relations in Non-Linear Phonology*. MIT Ph.D. thesis.

Sagey, E. (1988). 'Degree of closure in complex segments'. In van der Hulst and Smith (eds): 169–208.

Sanders, G. (1990). 'On the analysis and implications of Maori verb alternations'. *Lingua* **80**: 149–96.

Sampson, G. (1989). 'Language acquisition: growth or learning?'. *Philosophical Papers* 18.3: 203–40.

Saporta, S. (1965). 'Ordered rules, dialect differences and historical change'. *Language* **41**: 218–24.

Schane, S. (1968). *French Phonology and Morphology*. Cambridge, MA: MIT Press.

Schane, S. (1973). *Generative Phonology*. Englewood Cliffs, NJ: Prentice Hall.

Schane, S. (1974a). 'There is no French Truncation rule'. In Campbell, Goldin and Wang (eds) *Linguistic Studies in Romance Languages*: 89–99. Washington: Georgetown University Press.

Schane, S. (1974b). 'How abstract is abstract?'. In Bruck *et al.* (eds): 297–318.

Schane, S. (1984). 'The fundamentals of particle phonology'. *Phonology Yearbook* **1**: 129–55.

Selkirk, E. O. (1980). 'The role of prosodic categories in English word stress'. *Linguistic Inquiry* **11**: 563–605.

Selkirk, E. O. (1982). 'The syllable'. In van der Hulst and Smith (eds), Vol. 2: 335–83.

Selkirk, E. O. (1984). *Phonology and Syntax: The Relation between Sound and*

Structure. Cambridge, MA: MIT Press.

Selkirk, E. O. (1986). 'On derived domains in sentence phonology'. *Phonology Yearbook* **3**: 371–405.

Smith, N. V. and Wilson, D. (1979). *Modern Linguistics: The Results of Chomsky's Revolution*. Harmondsworth: Penguin.

Stemberger, J. (1985). 'CV phonology and French consonants: a concrete approach'. *Journal of Linguistics* **21**: 453–57.

Swadesh, M. (1944). 'South Greenlandic (Eskimo)'. In Hoijer, H. *et al.* (eds), *Linguistic Structures of Native America*. Reprinted 1971, Johnson Reprint Co., New York.

Szpyra, J. (1989). *The Phonology–Morphology Interface*. London: Routledge.

Tranel, B. (1981). *Concreteness in Generative Phonology*. Berkeley: University of California Press.

Trubetzkoy, N. (1958). *Grundzuge der Phonologie*. Gottingen: Vandenhoeck & Ruprecht. (Trans. Baltaxe, C. A. M. (1969): *Principles of Phonology*. Los Angeles: University of California Press.)

Vago, R. (1980a). *The Sound Pattern of Hungarian*. Washington, DC: Georgetown University Press.

Vago R. (ed.) (1980b). *Issues in Vowel Harmony*. Amsterdam: Benjamins.

Waterson, N. (1956). 'Some aspects of the phonology of the nominal forms of the Turkish word'. *Bulletin of the School of Oriental and African Studies* **18**: 578–91. Reprinted in Palmer (1970): 174–87.

Weidert, A. and Subba, B. (1985). *Concise Limbu Grammar and Dictionary*. Amsterdam: Lobster.

Windfuhr, G. L. (1979). *Persian Grammar*. The Hague: Mouton.

Wood, S. (1975). 'Tense and lax vowels: degree of constriction or pharyngeal volume?'. Working Papers in Linguistics, Lund University: 109–34.

Zimmer, K. E. (1967). 'A note on vowel harmony'. *IJAL* **3**: 166–71.

Zimmer, K. E. (1969). 'Psychological correlates of some Turkish morpheme structure conditions'. *Language* **45**: 309–21.

Subject Index

(Page references for definitions are set in bold)

321

Language Index